Textcerpts

Mastering College Textbook Reading

SECOND EDITION

Gene Wintner

Northern Essex Community College

PEARSON
Longman

New York   San Francisco   Boston
London   Toronto   Sydney   Tokyo   Singapore   Madrid
Mexico City   Munich   Paris   Cape Town   Hong Kong   Montreal

Acquisitions Editor: Melanie Craig
Associate Editor: Frederick Speers
Marketing Manager: Tom DeMarco
Senior Supplements Editor: Donna Campion
Media Supplements Editor: Jenna Egan
Project Coordination, Text Design, and Electronic Page Makeup: Pre-Press Company, Inc.
Cover Design Manager: Wendy Ann Fredericks
Cover Designer: Base Art Company
Cover Illustration/Photo: Julian Opie, *Incident in the Library II,* 1983. Courtesy Lisson Gallery, London Limited.
Manufacturing Buyer: Lucy Hebard
Printer and Binder: Courier Corporation
Cover Printer: Phoenix Color Corporation

Library of Congress Cataloging-in-Publication Data

Wintner, Gene.
    Textcerpts: mastering college textbook reading / Gene Wintner.--2nd ed. p. cm.
    ISBN 0-321-36470-8
    1. Reading (Higher education) 2. Reading comprehension. I. Title.
LB2395.3.W575 2007
428.4071'1--dc22   2006041554

Please visit us at www.ablongman.com

Credits: Part I: p. 6: from Lester A. Lefton, *Psychology,* 7th Ed. Published by Allyn and Bacon, Boston, MA. Copyright © 2000 by Pearson Education. Reprinted by permission of the publisher; pp. 7–8: from W. J. Seiler & M.L. Beall, *Communication: Making Connections* 4th ed. Published by Allyn and Bacon, Boston, MA. Copyright © 1999 by Pearson Education. Reprinted by permission of the publisher. **Part II:** pp. 21–22, 24–25 from W. J. Seiler & M.L. Beall, *Communication: Making Connections* 4th ed. Published by Allyn and Bacon, Boston, MA. Copyright © 1999 by Pearson Education. Reprinted by permission of the publisher; pp. 26–27: from *The Media of Mass Communication,* 7th Ed., 2006 Update, by John Vivian. New York: Pearson Education, 2006; pp. 30–31: excerpt pp. 540–541from *The American People: Creating a Nation and a Society,* 5th Ed., by Nash, Jeffrey, Howe, Frederick, Davis and Winkler. Copyright © 2001 by Longman. Reprinted by permission; pp. 34–35: from *The Art of Being Human,* 8th Ed., by Richard Janaro and Thelma Altshuler. Copyright © 2006 by Richard Janaro and Thelma Altshuler. Reprinted by permission of Pearson Education, Inc; pp. 38–39: excerpt p. 879 from *Civilization Past and Present,* 9th Ed., by Brummett et al. Copyright © 2000 by Pearson/Longman. Reprinted by permission; pp. 43–44, 46–47: from Lester A. Lefton, *Psychology,* 7th Ed. Published by Allyn and Bacon, Boston, MA. Copyright © 2000 Pearson Education. Reprinted by permission of the publisher; pp. 48–49: from Henslin, James M. *Sociology: A Down to Earth Approach,* 7th Ed. Published by Allyn and Bacon, Boston, MA. Copyright © 2005 by Pearson Education. Reprinted by permission of the publisher; pp. 52–53: from Barbara D. Miller, *Cultural Anthropology,* 3rd Ed. Published by Allyn and Bacon, Boston, MA. Copyright © 2005 by Pearson Education. Reprinted by permission of the publisher; pp. 56–57: excerpt p. 278 from *American Government: Continuity and Change,* 2006 Edition by Karen O'Connor and Larry J. Sabato. Copyright © 2006 by Pearson Education, Inc. Reprinted by permission; pp. 60–61: excerpt pp. 179-180 from *Essentials of Economics,* 4th Ed., by Paul R. Gregory. Copyright @1999 by Addison Wesley Longman. Reprinted by permission; pp. 65–66, 69–70: Daub, G. William; Seese, William S., *Basic Chemistry,* 7th Ed., © 1995, pp. 52–54. Reprinted by permission of Pearson Education, Inc., Upper Saddle River, NJ; pp. 71–72: excerpt p. 11 from *Life,* 5th Ed., by Ricki Lewis, et al. New York: McGraw-Hill, 2004. Reprinted by permission of the publisher; pp. 75–76: excerpt pp. 76–77 from *Principles of Environmental Science: Inquiry and Applications,* 2nd Ed., by William P. Cunningham and Mary Ann Cunningham. New York: McGraw-Hill, 2004. Reprinted by permission of the publisher; pp. 79–80 Permission to reproduce *New Perspectives on Computer Concepts,* 7th Ed., Introductory 7th edition, by PARSONS/OJA, copyright (c) 2004 Course Technology, a division of Thomson Learning, has been granted to Pearson Education / Longman Publishers for class use. All rights reserved. Aside from this specific exception, no part of this book may be reproduced, stored in a retrieval system, or transcribed in any form by any means – electronic, mechanical, photocopying, recording or otherwise – without permission in writing from the Thomson Learning Global Rights Group: www.thomsonrights.com. Fax 800-730-2215; pp. 83–84: Sullivan, Jim, *Prealgebra: Journey into a Mathematical World,* 1st Ed. © 2002, pp. 626–627. Reprinted by permission of Person Education, Inc. Upper Saddle River, NJ; pp. 88–89, 91–92: excerpt p. 175 from *Health: The Basics,* 6th Ed. by Rebecca J. Donatelle. Copyright © 2005 by Pearson Education, Inc. Reprinted by permission; pp. 93–94: reprinted from *Fundamentals of Nursing,* 5th Ed., pp. 104–105, by Patricia Potter and Anne Griffin Perry, 2001, with permission from Elsevier; pp. 97–98 excerpt pp. 168–170 from *Criminal Justice,* 3rd Ed., by Jay S. Albanese. New York: Pearson Education, 2005. Reprinted by permission; pp. 101–102: Rachman/Mescon/Bovee/Thiss, *Business Today,* 8th Ed., © 1997, pp. 340–341. Reprinted by permission of Pearson Education, Inc., Upper Saddle River, NJ; pp. 105–106 Bovee, Courtland L.; Thill, John V., *Business Communication Today,* 5th Ed., © 1998, pp. 56, 58. Adapted by permission of Pearson Education, Inc., Upper Saddle River, NJ. **Part III:** pp. 110–134 from Henslin, James M. *Sociology: A Down to Earth Approach,* 7th Ed. Published by Allyn and Bacon, Boston, MA. Copyright © 2005 by Pearson Education. Reprinted by permission of the publisher; pp. 138–172 from *The Art of Being Human,* 8th Ed., by Richard Janaro and Thelma Altshuler. Copyright © 2006 by Richard Janaro and Thelma Altshuler. Reprinted by permission of Pearson Education, Inc.; pp. 176–196 from Albanese, Jay S., *Criminal Justice,* 3rd Ed. Published by Allyn and Bacon, Boston, MA. Copyright © 1999 by Pearson Education. Reprinted by permission of the publisher; pp. 200–211 Daub, G. William; Seese, William S., *Basic Chemistry,* 7th Ed., © 1995, pp. 1–11. Reprinted by permission of Pearson Education, Inc., Upper Saddle River, NJ; pp. 215–246 excerpt from *The World of Psychology,* 5th Ed., by Samuel Wood, Ellen Green Wood, and Denise Boyd. New York: Pearson Education, 2005; pp. 250–275 from John Vivian, *The Media Of Mass Communication,* 7th Ed. Published by Allyn and Bacon, Boston, MA. Copyright © 2005 by Pearson Education. Reprinted by permission of the publisher; pp. 280–332 from *Health: The Basics,* 6th Ed. by Rebecca J. Donatelle. Copyright © 2005 by Pearson Education, Inc. Reprinted by permission; pp. 336–374 Excerpt pp. 197–235 from *America Government: Continuity and Change,* 2006 Edition by Karen O'Connor and Larry J. Sabato. Copyright © 2006 by Pearson Education, Inc. Reprinted by permission.

ISBN 978-0-321-36470-8
ISBN 0-321-36470-8
5 6 7 8 9 10—CRK—09

Contents

MATH AND SCIENCE

CAREER-RELATED DISCIPLINES

PART III.   *Chapter Practice*   109

Preface

Textcerpts: Mastering College Textbook Reading introduces students to the challenges of college textbook reading. It provides extensive practice with samples and full chapters from a variety of college textbooks. Drawing from over twenty subjects, *Textcerpts* exposes students to the fundamental vocabulary and introductory concepts of many of the traditional college disciplines.

Textcerpts is intended for use as a supplementary text. It is a practice book. Traditional developmental texts teach students the how-to's of textbook reading, but do not contain extensive amounts of real textbook content. *Textcerpts* provides developmental reading instructors with material that models the applications of key skills and strategies they are teaching, and provides students with routine, repeated opportunities to apply the skills and strategies they are learning.

Rationale

Based on conversations with colleagues and students, as well as informal surveys at my own institution, I am convinced that many of today's college freshmen do not view reading as a primary learning tool and, thus, they are beginning their college education with a major deficit. Because they do not view reading as a primary learning tool, they are unlikely to engage meaningfully with the textbook reading assigned to them. A vicious cycle is created. The less effort students put into reading their assignments, the less they get out of them. The less they get out of them, the more they reinforce their beliefs that reading does not serve them as an important learning tool.

To break this cycle, students need instruction, direction, and extended practice with college textbook reading. Developmental reading courses provide the instruction and direction. *Textcerpts* is intended to provide a semester's worth of practice material. Completion of the *Textcerpts* exercises will enable a student to develop confidence in his or her ability to learn from textbooks.

Content and Organization

The organization of *Textcerpts* is simple. The book has three parts. Part I reviews textbook reading strategies and introduces students to several of the traditional college disciplines. Part II provides practice with twenty short samples. Part III provides extensive practice with eight full-length textbook chapters.

Part I of the text begins with a discussion of the special features of textbooks and the need for special textbook reading strategies. It continues with an introduction of vocabulary and comprehension strategies for textbook reading, including surveying, concept acquisition, SQ4R, and textbook marking. An application exercise accompanies the description of each strategy. Part I concludes with a brief overview of traditional college disciplines.

Part II of *Textcerpts* contains 20 short samples from 18 college disciplines. Each of the excerpts is followed by 10 comprehension questions, a pattern of organization question, five vocabulary questions, and three critical response questions. The comprehension questions include written response, multiple-choice, and true/false/can't tell items. Each sample is prefaced by a preamble that introduces students to the discipline from which the sample was obtained.

Part III of *Textcerpts* contains eight complete chapters, each representing a major college discipline. Each chapter is interrupted periodically by comprehension checks and vocabulary questions. "Section Review" questions pertain only to the section just read, whereas "Cumulative Review" questions pertain to previous sections as well. Each section review instructs the students annotate and summarize the section completed. The exercises for each chapter conclude with seven critical response questions. Each chapter begins with instructions that remind the students to apply the strategies discussed in Part I.

Features

- Eight full-length textbook chapters: *Textcerpts* contains the complete text of eight college textbook chapters. The eight chapters represent the following disciplines: sociology, humanities, criminal justice, chemistry, psychology, media, health, and political science.

- Twenty short samples: *Textcerpts* contains 20 short excerpts representing a wide range of college disciplines. In addition to the disciplines listed previously, these include American and world history, communications, economics, anthropology, biology, mathematics, music, literature, environmental science, computer science, nursing, and business.

- Comprehension exercises: Each of the 20 short excerpts is followed by 10 comprehension questions. Each of the eight full-length chapters is interrupted with section review and cumulative review comprehension questions. Comprehension questions include written response, multiple-choice, true/false/can't tell questions, and a "patterns of organization" question.

- Vocabulary exercises: Each of the 20 short excerpts is accompanied by a vocabulary exercise consisting of five multiple-choice questions. The vocabulary is selected from the context of the excerpt. Each of the Cumulative Review sections in Part III includes a vocabulary exercise consisting of 10 multiple-choice questions for vocabulary selected from the chapter.

- Critical reading: Each of the 20 short excerpts is accompanied by three critical response questions. Each of the eight chapters is accompanied by seven critical response questions. The critical response questions can be used for classroom discussion and/or written assignments.

- Writing practice: *Textcerpts* provides students with extensive opportunities for writing practice. Each excerpt and chapter is accompanied by questions requiring written response and a series of critical response questions that can be used for writing assignments. In addition, Part III asks students to write notes summarizing key points in the chapters. Instructors may also want to direct students to other forms of summary writing.

- Application of skills and strategies: Part I introduces students to basic skills and strategies for textbook reading, including vocabulary strategies, textbook surveying, SQ4R, and textbook marking. Exercises in Part I ask the students to apply these skills and strategies to textbooks from their current courses. Part III asks students to apply them to the eight chapters within this book.

- Readability: The readability scores for each of the eight chapters in Part III are provided in the instructor's manual.

- Chapter tests: Tests for the eight chapters in Part III are provided in the *Instructor's Manual*.

- Answer key: A separate answer key is available.

Changes to the Second Edition

Several important changes make the second edition of *Textcerpts* an even better resource than the first edition.

New and Updated Content

- Four of the original chapters in Part III have been replaced with entirely new chapters from current textbooks in humanities, criminal justice, media, and psychology.

- Three chapters from Part III have been updated to correspond to the current edition of the source textbook.

- All eight chapters in Part III represent the most recent editions of their source texts at the time of this printing. Most are 2005 and 2006 editions.

- In Part II, nine excerpts have been replaced with new material, and three have been updated to correspond to current editions.

Interest

The new Part III chapters have been selected with student interest and relevance in mind. These chapters present the subjects of love, crime victims and perpetrators, stress and health, and the Web. Topics for the new selections in Part II include youth gangs, animal communication, population growth, family, nursing skills, the Harlem Renaissance, e-mail, and probability.

Organization by Discipline

The short selections in Part II have been grouped into four broad discipline categories: humanities, social sciences, science and math, and career-related disciplines.

Patterns of Organization

An introduction to five common patterns of organization has been added to Part I, and a pattern recognition question has been added to each exercise in Part II. In Part III, the directions ask students to identify patterns of organization as they work through each section of each chapter.

Sample Annotations

In addition to the annotated sample passage in Part I, an annotated sample of the first selection in each section is included in Part II of the text.

The Longman Basic Skills Package

A complete **Instructor's Manual/Test Bank** is available to accompany *Textcerpts*. This print supplement includes a complete answer key for the text, as well as preformatted quizzes for each chapter. Ask your Longman sales representative for ISBN 0-321-38996-4.

A separate **Answer Key** is also available. Please ask your Longman sales representative for ISBN 0-321-38736-8.

In addition, a series of other valuable ancillaries is available.

Support Materials For Reading and Study Skills Instructors

Printed Test Bank for Developmental Reading (Instructor / 0-321-08596-5) Offers more than 3,000 questions in all areas of reading, including vocabulary, main idea, supporting details, patterns of organization, critical thinking, analytical reasoning, inference, point of view, visual aids, and textbook reading. (Electronic version also available; see CDs)

Electronic Test Bank for Developmental Reading (Instructor / CD 0-321-08179-X) Offers more than 3,000 questions in all areas of reading, including vocabulary, main idea, supporting details, patterns of organization, critical thinking, analytical reasoning, inference, point of view, visual aids, and textbook reading. Instructors simply choose questions, then print out the completed test for distribution or offer the test online.

The Longman Guide to Classroom Management (Instructor / 0-321-09246-5) This guide is designed as a helpful resource for instructors who have classroom management problems. It includes helpful strategies for dealing with disruptive students in the classroom and the "do's and don'ts" of discipline.

The Longman Guide to Community Service–Learning in the English Classroom and Beyond (Instructor / 0-321-12749-8) Written by Elizabeth Rodriguez Kessler of California State University—Northridge, this monograph provides a definition and history of service–learning, as well as an overview of how service–learning can be integrated effectively into the college classroom.

The Longman Instructor's Planner (Instructor / 0-321-09247-3) This planner includes weekly and monthly calendars, student attendance and grading rosters, space for contact information, Web references, an almanac, and blank pages for notes.

For Students

Vocabulary Skills Study Cards (Student/ 0-321-31802-1) Colorful, affordable, and packed with useful information, Longman's *Vocabulary Study Card* is a concise 8-page reference guide to developing key vocabulary skills such as learning to recognize context clues, reading a dictionary entry, and recognizing key root words, suffixes, and prefixes. Laminated for durability, students can keep this Study Card for years to come and pull it out whenever they need a quick review.

Reading Skills Study Card (Student / 0-321-33833-2) Colorful, affordable, and packed with useful information, Longman's *Reading Skills Study Card* is a concise 8-page reference guide to help students develop basic reading skills such as concept skills, structural skills, language skills, and reasoning skills. Laminated for durability, students can keep this Study Card for years to come and pull it out whenever they need a quick review.

The Longman Textbook Reader, Revised Edition (with answers—Student / 0-321-11895-2; without answers—Student / 0-321-12223-2) Offers five complete chapters from our textbooks: computer science, biology, psychology, communications, and business. Each chapter includes additional comprehension quizzes, critical thinking questions, and group activities.

The Longman Reader's Portfolio and Student Planner (Student / 0-321-29610-9) This unique supplement provides students with a space to plan, think about, and present their work. The portfolio includes a diagnostic area (including a learning style questionnaire), a working area (including calendars, vocabulary logs, reading response sheets, book club tips, and other valuable materials), and a display area including a progress chart, a final table of contents, and a final assessment as well as a daily planner for students that includes daily, weekly, and monthly calendars.

The Longman Reader's Journal, by Kathleen McWhorter (Student / 0-321-08843-3) The first journal just for student readers, The *Longman Reader's Journal* offers a place for students to record their reactions to and questions about any reading.

The Longman Planner (Student / 0-321-04573-4) Ideal for organizing a busy college life! Included are hour-by-hour schedules, monthly and weekly calendars, an address book, and an almanac of tips and useful information.

10 Practices of Highly Effective Students (Student / 0-205-30769-8) This study skills supplement includes topics such as time management, test taking, reading critically, stress, and motivation.

***Newsweek* Discount Subscription Coupon (12 weeks) (Student / 0-321-08895-6)** *Newsweek* gets students reading, writing, and thinking about what's going on in the world around them. The price of the subscription is added to the cost of the book. Instructors receive weekly lesson plans, quizzes, and curriculum guides as well as a complimentary *Newsweek* subscription. The price of the subscription is 59 cents per issue (a total of $7.08 for the subscription). *Package item only.*

Interactive Guide to *Newsweek* (Student / 0-321-05528-4) Available with the 12-week subscription to *Newsweek,* this guide serves as a workbook for students who are using the magazine.

Research Navigator Guide for English, H. Eric Branscomb and Doug Gotthoffer (Student / 0-321-20277-5) Designed to teach students how to conduct high-quality online research and to document it properly, Research Navigator guides provide discipline-specific academic resources in addition to helpful tips on the writing process, online research, and finding and citing valid sources. Research Navigator guides include an access code to Research Navigator™, which provides access to thousands of academic journals and periodicals, the *New York Times* Search by Subject Archive, Link Library, Library Guides, and more.

Penguin Discount Novel Program In cooperation with Penguin Putnam, Inc., Longman is proud to offer a variety of Penguin paperbacks at a significant discount when packaged with any Longman title. Excellent additions to any developmental reading course, Penguin titles give students the opportunity to explore contemporary and classical fiction and drama. The available titles include works by authors as diverse as Toni Morrison, Julia Alvarez, Mary Shelley, and Shakespeare. To review the complete list of titles available, visit the Longman–Penguin–Putnam website: http://www.awl.com/penguin.

Oxford American College Dictionary (Student / 0399144153) Drawing on Oxford's unparalleled language resources, including a 200-million-word database, this college dictionary contains more than 175,000 entries and more than 1000 illustrations, including line drawings, photographs and maps. *Available at a significant discount when packaged with a Longman textbook—only $15.*

The New American Webster Handy College Dictionary (Student / 0-451-18166-2) A paperback reference text with more than 100,000 entries.

Multimedia Offerings

Interested in incorporating online materials into your course? Longman is happy to help. Our regional technology specialists provide training on all of our multimedia offerings.

MyReadingLab (www.myreadinglab.com) This exciting new Web site houses all the media tools any developmental English student needs to improve their reading and study skills, in one easy-to use place. Resources for reading and study skills include:

■ **Reading Road Trip 5.0 Web Site.** The best selling reading software available, Reading Road Trip takes students on a tour of 16 cities and landmarks throughout the United States, with each of the 16 modules corresponding to a reading or study skill. The topics include main idea, vocabulary, understanding patterns of organization, thinking critically, reading rate, note-taking and highlighting, and graphics and visual aids. Students can begin their trip by taking a brand-new diagnostic test that provides immediate feedback, guiding them to specific modules for additional help with reading skills. New version 5.0 includes a brand new design, a new Pioneer Level (4th–6th grade level), and new readings.

■ **Longman Vocabulary Web Site.** This component of MySkillsLab features hundreds of exercises in 10 topic areas to strengthen vocabulary skills. Students will also benefit from "100 Words That All High School Graduates Should Know," a useful resource that provides definitions for each of the words on this list, vocabulary flashcards, and audio clips to facilitate pronunciation skills.

■ **Longman Study Skills Web Site.** This site offers hundreds of review strategies for college success, time and stress management skills, study strategies, and more. Students can take a variety of assessment tests to learn about their organizational skills and learning styles, with follow-up quizzes to reinforce the strategies they have learned.

■ **Research Navigator.** In addition to providing valuable help to any college student on how to conduct high-quality online research and to document it properly, Research Navigator provides access to thousands of academic journals and periodicals (including the *New York Times* Archive), allowing reading students to practice with authentic readings from college-level primary sources.

State-Specific Supplements

For Florida Adopters

Thinking Through the Test: A Study Guide for the Florida College Basic Skills Exit Test, by D.J. Henry *For Florida adopter only.* This workbook helps students strengthen their reading skills in preparation for the Florida College Basic Skills Exit Test. It features both diagnostic tests to help assess areas that may need improvement and exit tests to help test skill mastery. Detailed explanatory answers have been provided for almost all of the questions. *Package item only—not available for sale.*

Available Versions:

Thinking Through the Test A Study Guide for the Florida College Basic Skills Exit Tests: Reading and Writing, with Answer Key, 3/e 0-321-38739-2

Thinking Through the Test A Study Guide for the Florida College Basic Skills Exit Tests: Reading and Writing (without Answer Key), 3/e 0-321-38740-6

Thinking Through the Test A Study Guide for the Florida College Basic Skills Exit Tests: Reading, with Answer Key, 3/e 0-321-38737-6

Thinking Through the Test A Study Guide for the Florida College Basic Skills Exit Tests: Reading (without Answer Key), 3/e 0-321-38738-4

Reading Skills Summary for the Florida State Exit Exam, by D. J. Henry (Student / 0-321-08478-0) *For Florida adopter only.* An excellent study tool for students preparing to take Florida College Basic Skills Exit Test for Reading, this laminated reading grid summarizes all the skills tested on the Exit Exam. *Package item only—not available for sale.*

CLAST Test Package, 4/e (Instructor/Print ISBN 0-321-01950-4) These two, 40-item objective tests evaluate students' readiness for the Florida CLAST exams. Strategies for teaching CLAST preparedness are included.

For Texas Adopters

The Longman THEA Study Guide, by Jeannette Harris (Student / 0-321-27240-0) Created specifically for students in Texas, this study guide includes straightforward explanations and numerous practice exercises to help students prepare for the reading and writing sections of the THEA Test. *Package item only—not available for sale.*

TASP Test Package, 3/e (Instructor / Print ISBN 0-321-01959-8) These 12 practice pre-tests and post-tests assess the same reading and writing skills covered in the Texas TASP examination.

For New York/CUNY Adopters

Preparing for the CUNY-ACT Reading and Writing Test, edited by Patricia Licklider (Student / 0-321-19608-2) This booklet, prepared by reading and writing faculty from across the CUNY system, is designed to help students prepare for the CUNY-ACT exit test. It includes test-taking tips, reading passages, typical exam questions, and sample writing prompts to help students become familiar with each portion of the test.

Acknowledgments

I would like to express my sincerest gratitude to Frederick Speers, who guided me with insight, wisdom, and humor throughout this project. I would also like to thank Joe Opiela and Steve Rigolosi for their significant contributions to the first edition of this textbook. I am grateful to all of the unsung heroes at Pearson Longman, without whose skill and hard work this project could not have reached fruition.

In addition, I would like to thank the reviewers whose candid feedback provided the impetus for many of the changes in this edition:

Jennifer Robey, Century College
Beth Wilson, Green River Community College
Patricia Grega, University of Alaska—Anchorage
Catherine Packard, Southern Illinois College
Janet Gilligan, Broome Community College
Lisa Albers, Pierce College

Gene Wintner
Newburyport, Massachusetts

PART I

How to Read a College Textbook

Why Read Textbooks?

There is an old joke (not a very good joke) about an unusual relationship that goes something like this:

Question: Why did the elephant and mouse get married?
Answer: Because they had to.

Unfortunately, if you asked most college freshmen why they read their textbooks, you would probably receive a similar response: "Because I have to."

Textbook reading has long been a traditional and important part of college study. College textbooks are assigned because they collect, within a single volume, an extensive amount of carefully selected material on a given subject and organize that material into a logical learning sequence. In other words, textbooks are user friendly. Their authors have surveyed the vast body of information that has been accumulated in their respective fields, determined which information and ideas are most important for newcomers to the subject, and organized the material to facilitate its learning.

Characteristics of College Textbooks

Before we review the primary characteristics of college textbooks, please complete the following exercise.

Exercise 1	**CHARACTERISTICS OF COLLEGE TEXTBOOKS**

Directions. Use the following space to list five ways in which reading a textbook is different from reading other materials (newspapers, magazines, novels, etc.):

1. _____

2. _____

3. _____

4. _____

5. _____

As you have just discovered from your list, reading a textbook differs in several ways from reading other types of materials. Of course, one critical difference is the reader's purpose. You approach textbook reading with a set of specific learning goals, which direct your understanding and retention of new ideas and information.

Textbooks differ significantly from other reading materials in the following respects:

1. *Most freshman textbooks emphasize breadth over depth.* Because they survey an extensive amount of material, most freshman textbooks will not provide a lot of information about any one specific topic. While a trade book on dreams may devote 200 or 300 pages to the detailed examination of various dream theories, a psychology textbook will probably allocate no more than a few pages to the study of dreams. In those few pages, the authors will briefly summarize some of the most important concepts and research relating to psychologists' study of dreams.

2. *Textbooks are carefully organized.* Textbook authors are selective in deciding what information to include in their texts, and they are also very careful about organizing the information in a logical manner to facilitate student learning. Textbook authors make the organization apparent through the use of special organizational features (for example, a table of contents, chapter outlines, and various levels of headings).

3. *Textbooks include a variety of special features to facilitate their use.* Charts, tables, graphs, and visual aids are included to help the reader absorb information and understand concepts. Definitions for key terms are highlighted within the text and/or placed in the margins. Chapter summaries and review exercises help the reader consolidate her understanding and reinforce her memory of the chapter material.

4. *Textbooks are intended to be used as reference tools as well as learning tools.* No one expects to remember everything he reads in a textbook. However, you can return to your textbook at any time to locate information. Understanding the organizational features of the textbook will help you make effective use of your textbook as a reference aid.

5. *Textbooks are terminology dense.* Textbooks are loaded with terms that will be new to most college readers. An important goal in reading any textbook chapter is the mastery of the new terms contained within it.

6. *Textbooks are information dense.* Textbooks provide a tremendous amount of information in a limited space. Information is seldom repeated, and textbook authors confine themselves to a few carefully chosen details to develop their main ideas. In other words, there is more information to learn and remember on a page of college text than on a page of a typical trade book, newspaper, or magazine.

7. *Textbooks are objective.* While any given textbook will reflect the author's approach to her subject, textbook authors and publishers make every attempt to free their texts of bias. When opinions are included, they are identified as such, and contrasting opinions will almost certainly be provided. You may be asked from time to time to think critically about a controversial topic, but your primary focus in reading texts will remain on the understanding and remembering of important information and ideas.

See Box 1 for strategies for effective textbook reading.

Box 1	1. Read at a regular time and place.
	2. Survey before reading.
10 Best Strategies for Effective Textbook Reading	3. Identify and clarify your learning goals.
	4. Use the special features and aids provided by the author(s).
	5. Use a study reading formula to develop a methodical approach to textbook reading.
	6. Anticipate and question as you move from section to section.
	7. Monitor and clarify your understanding, rereading as necessary.
	8. After reading a paragraph or section, underline/mark key points and make marginal notes.
	9. Connect the material to class lecture and discussion and to real-life situations.
	10. Review and self-test at the end of each session.

Surveying a Textbook

Given the special features of a textbook, surveying your new textbooks soon after you have purchased them is a very useful habit. To survey a textbook, take ten to fifteen minutes to look it over and familiarize yourself with its content, organization, and special features. Surveying your textbooks will enable you to use them with more confidence, efficiency, and enjoyment.

To survey a textbook, follow these steps:

1. *Note the title, author, and date of publication.*
   * See if the title provides clues to the authors' approach to their subject.
   * Read about the authors' backgrounds and credentials.
   * Note the date of publication, or copyright date, to determine how current the text's information is.

2. *Read or skim the preface.* The preface provides basic information about the contents and organization of the text.

3. *Review the table of contents.* Some texts contain a brief version of the table of contents along with a complete table of contents. For your initial survey, just review the brief version.

4. *Note what the text includes in addition to the main chapters, such as the following:*
   * Appendixes (note the purpose of each),
   * Indexes (information may be indexed by name and/or subject),
   * A glossary, and
   * Practice tests and answer keys.

5. *Quickly skim one chapter to become familiar with the chapter layout and special features:*
   * Does the chapter begin with a set of learning objectives?
   * Are definitions of key terms located in the margin?
   * Which types of visual aids are used? Are there textual inserts as well?
   * Are review exercises inserted throughout the chapter?
   * What study aids can be found at the end of the chapter (review quizzes, discussion questions, or lists of terms)?

Familiarizing yourself with your textbooks in this manner will enable you to use them more successfully.

| Exercise 2 | **TEXTBOOK SURVEY** |

Directions. Select any textbook you are using in another class. Following the five steps previously described, take ten to fifteen minutes to survey the book, and then answer the following questions:

1. What is the title of the textbook?

   _____

2. Who wrote the textbook? What information is provided about the author(s)?

   _____

3. When was the book published?

   _____

4. How many major units or parts does the textbook contain? What major topics or issues will the textbook address?

   _____

5. How many chapters does the textbook contain?

   _____

6. What additional material is included at the end of the textbook, after the last chapter (for example, index or glossary)?

   _____

7. What special features does each chapter contain to help the reader learn and understand the material?

   _____

8. What do you hope to learn from this textbook?

   _____

9. What difficulties do you anticipate in working with this textbook?

   _____

10. What strategies will help you read the text most effectively?

   _____

Learning the Vocabulary

One of the biggest obstacles to textbook comprehension is the advanced level of vocabulary used by textbook authors. You will encounter two types of vocabulary that you must master to be a successful college reader: (1) general vocabulary words and (2) subject vocabulary terms.

General vocabulary words are those that are likely to appear in any reading material; they are not specific to a subject. Subject vocabulary terms, on the other hand, are the words and phrases that belong to a particular discipline, and have a special meaning within that discipline.

Read the following paragraph, selected from a psychology textbook:

> Psychologists use the term *conditioning* in a general sense, to mean learning. But **conditioning** is actually a systematic procedure through which associations and responses to specific stimuli are learned. It is one of the simplest forms of learning. For example, consider what generally happens when you hear the theme from *The X-Files*. You expect that something supernatural or otherworldly will appear on your TV screen, because the theme music introduces a program that usually includes aliens or weird events—and if you're a fan of the show, you probably feel a pleasant sense of anticipation. You have been *conditioned* to feel that way. In the terminology used by psychologists, *The X-Files* theme music is the *stimulus,* and your excitement and anticipation is the *response.*
>
> —From *Psychology*, 7th ed., by Lester A. Lefton. Boston: Allyn & Bacon, 2000.

In this paragraph, the author introduces the term *conditioning.* What does the author do within the paragraph to help the reader understand the concept of conditioning? What other psychology terms are introduced at the end of the paragraph? Were there any general vocabulary words within the paragraph that were unfamiliar to you?

Now read the next paragraph from the same section of the text:

> When psychologists first studied conditioning, they found relationships between specific stimuli and responses. They observed that each time a certain stimulus occurs, the same reflexive response, or behavior, follows. For example, the presence of food in the mouth leads to salivation; a tap on the knee results in a knee jerk; a bright light in the eye produces contraction of the pupil and an eye blink. A **reflex** is an automatic behavior that occurs involuntarily in response to a stimulus and without prior learning and usually shows little variability from instance to instance. Conditioned behaviors, in contrast, are learned. Dental anxiety—fear of dentists, dental procedures, and even the dentist's chair—is a widespread conditioned behavior (Jongh et al., 1995). Many people have learned to respond with fear to the stimulus of sitting in a dentist's chair, since they associate the chair with pain. A chair by itself (a neutral stimulus) does not elicit fear, but a chair associated with pain becomes a stimulus that can elicit fear. This is an example of *conditioning.*

The author begins this paragraph with a little information about the study of conditioning and an example. In the middle of the paragraph, the author introduces and defines the term *reflex,* and contrasts reflex with conditioning. What does the author do in the last few sentences to reinforce the reader's understanding of the concept of conditioning?

Reread the second paragraph. Were there any general vocabulary words within the paragraph that were unfamiliar to you? What does *elicit* mean?

You usually learn general vocabulary words from context clues and consultation with the dictionary. Subject vocabulary terms, however, are normally defined in the textbook, and you should learn the definitions that the text provides. The definitions are often boldfaced within the text or shown in the margin. They may also be contained in the book's glossary.

Learning subject vocabulary terms often involves learning new concepts. A concept is an abstract idea. Learning new concepts usually requires repeated exposure to the concept and continued effort (thought!). Often we need to examine several examples before a new concept becomes clear to us. It is probably more accurate to say that our minds build concepts rather than absorb them, and that a concept is always a work in progress.

Several strategies are especially useful for learning subject vocabulary terms:

1. Survey the section you are about to read to identify key terms and concepts.
2. Paraphrase each definition after studying it.
3. Note the examples given in the text, and think of one or two examples of your own.
4. Apply the concept to real-life situations.
5. Compare and contrast related concepts.

Exercise 3 — TEXTBOOK VOCABULARY

Directions. The following passage on perception and selection was taken from a communications textbook. Underline unfamiliar words while reading the passage. Then answer the questions that follow the passage.

The Perception Process

Many people imagine the brain to be similar in operation to a camera or tape recorder; information enters through the eyes or ears and is stored in the brain. Actually, far too much information exists for the brain to absorb at once, so the brain ignores much of it. It accepts a certain amount of information and organizes it into meaningful patterns. It discards a tremendous amount of information. Much of what we know about the way we perceive events, objects, and people seems to involve how we select, organize, and interpret information. All of these connections happen in milliseconds.

Selection

Since it is impossible to attend to, sense, perceive, retain, and give meaning to every stimulus we encounter, we narrow our focus. A **stimulus** incites or quickens action, feeling, or thought. Although we are exposed to millions of bits of stimuli, or data, at one time, the mind can process only a small fraction of them. On both the unconscious level of the nervous system and the conscious level of directing attention, **selection** occurs as the brain sorts one stimulus from another, based on criteria formed by our previous experiences. There are three kinds of selection: selective exposure, selective attention, and selective retention.

SELECTIVE EXPOSURE. The deliberate choices we make to experience or to avoid experiencing particular stimuli are referred to as **selective exposure.** For example, you may dislike violent and sexist lyrics in the music you listen to, so you avoid purchasing tapes by certain individuals or groups known for such lyrics. When we choose to communicate with certain individuals instead of others, we are also using selective exposure.

SELECTIVE ATTENTION. Focusing on specific stimuli while ignoring or downplaying other stimuli is called **selective attention.** That is, you concentrate on the data you wish to attend to, in order to eliminate or reduce the effects of all extraneous stimuli. This task is often easier said than done. Paying attention to something usually requires decisive effort, but even the best attempts to concentrate may be interrupted by distractions. For example, a book dropped in a quiet classroom, a loud sneeze, background talking, a siren, a baby's cry, a call for help, an odor, or a movement can avert [sic] our attention from the task we are involved in. Continuing to attend to the original task may require extra effort. Similarly, when we converse with someone in a crowded lounge with loud music playing in the background, we focus on each other's words more attentively and ignore the other sounds. This blocking out of all extraneous stimuli to concentrate on the other person is an instance of selective attention. To make sense out of the multitude of stimuli that surrounds us, we learn to focus our senses on a few stimuli at a time.

SELECTIVE RETENTION. Because we cannot possibly remember all the stimuli we encounter, we also select the information we will retain. **Selective retention** occurs when we process, store, and retrieve information that we have already selected, organized, and interpreted. We are more likely to remember information that agrees with our views and to selectively forget information that does not. Also, after perceiving and selecting certain stimuli, we may retain only a portion of them. For example, how many times have you listened to someone tell you how to do something, and later, after thinking that you had completed the task, found that you had done only a portion of it? Chances are that you had retained the pleasant parts of the task and had forgotten the not-so-pleasant parts. Selection plays an important role in what, why, and how we communicate.

—From *Communication: Making Connections*, 4th ed., by William J. Seiler and Melissa L. Beall.
Boston: Allyn & Bacon, 1999.

1. a. List and define the five key subject vocabulary terms that the passage introduces.

   _____

   _____

   _____

   _____

   _____

   b. What did the authors do to help you learn these concepts?

   _____

   _____

2. Define each of the following general vocabulary words, as used in the context of the passage. Consult your dictionary when necessary.

    a. discards _____

    b. milliseconds _____

    c. incites _____

    d. extraneous _____

    e. avert _____

Using a Study Reading Formula

In the 1940s, a man named Francis Robinson developed the SQ3R study reading formula for textbook reading. (SQ3R stands for Survey, Question, Read, Recite, Review.) Since then, many variations of SQ3R have been developed, all emphasizing a similar, methodical approach to the reading of college texts. Research has confirmed that students who make effective use of SQ3R, or a similar approach, understand and remember more from their textbook reading assignments than students who "just read" the material.

Textcerpts introduces you to a variation of SQ3R called SQ4R. The steps of SQ4R are Survey, Question, Read, Recite, Rite (misspelling deliberate!), Review. Apply them as follows:

1. *Survey.* Survey the chapter by reading the title, introduction, headings and subheadings, summary, and end-of-chapter material. Also, glance at visual aids, such as charts, diagrams, tables, and pictures.

2. *Question.* Return to the first heading and invert the heading into a question. This question will help you know what to look for as you read the section. For example, the heading "Causes of the Civil War" would be inverted into the question, "What were the causes of the Civil War?" Write your question in the margin of the textbook, or on the left side of a separate sheet of paper to be used for SQ4R notes.

3. *Read.* Read a small amount of material (a paragraph or a short section), looking for the answer to your question and any other important points of information.

4. *Recite.* Mentally review and clarify what you have just read. Explain the main points to yourself in your own words. Note whether you have found an answer to the question you have raised.

5. *Rite.* On the right side of your note sheet, write down the main points of what you have just read. You may wish to first underline key sentences in the passage. Do not copy verbatim from the text. Force yourself to paraphrase, that is, to restate the ideas using your own wording.

Repeat steps 2–5 for each new section of the chapter.

6. *Review.* When you have finished the chapter, review the entire chapter. Do this by rereading your questions and seeing if you remember the answers. If you don't remember, reread your notes.

Using SQ4R will help you to read textbooks actively. In addition, use of SQ4R will help you distinguish main ideas from details as you read from paragraph to paragraph.

See Table 1 for an example of SQ4R notes.

TABLE 1 ■ *Sample SQ4R*

Courts

In criminal courts, legal responsibility is determined through interpretation of the law in relation to the circumstances of individual cases. More than 17,000 courts and related agencies operate in the United States, mostly at the state and local levels. These courts can be grouped into the federal court system (courts that interpret federal law) and state court systems (courts that interpret state and local laws). Both the state and the federal court systems have three basic types of jurisdiction. Courts of **limited jurisdiction** have narrow legal authority and may arbitrate only in certain types of disputes; these include family courts, municipal courts, and special courts such as tax courts. Courts of **general jurisdiction,** on the other hand, usually are referred to as trial courts. These are the courts in which felonies and civil cases go to trial. General jurisdiction courts across the country may be called county courts, circuit courts, and even supreme courts in some jurisdictions. The highest level of jurisdiction is **appellate jurisdiction.** Appellate courts review specific legal issues raised by cases in courts with general jurisdiction. An appellate court may uphold or reverse a conviction in a criminal case tried in a trial court. The sequence in which a case moves from a trial court to an appellate court occurs in every state and in the federal court system, although the names of the courts vary.

Notes

How are courts in the U.S. grouped?	*There are two court systems, federal and state.*
	Most courts work at state and local levels.
	State and federal courts both have three kinds of jurisdiction.
What are the three types of jurisdiction?	*Courts of limited jurisdiction only have authority over specific types of cases (example: tax courts).*
	Courts of general jurisdiction are the courts where most trials take place.
	Appellate courts handle appeals from general courts dealing with specific issues of the law.
	Appellate courts have the authority to overturn (or uphold) criminal convictions.

Exercise 4   SQ4R

Directions. On a separate sheet of paper, make a set of SQ4R notes for a three- to five-page section from a textbook you are using in another class. Divide your paper into two columns, with the right column approximately twice as wide as the left column. Use the left column for questions, and the right column for answers/main points (see Table 1 above).

Recognizing Patterns of Organization

Recognizing the relationships among the ideas in your text is critical to your comprehension and retention of the material. Text material is usually organized by logical relationships we can call patterns of organization. While there are many possible patterns of organization employed by textbook authors, there are five common patterns that are especially useful for college readers. They are:

- definition
- chronological order
- listing or enumeration
- comparison–contrast
- cause–effect

Definition Pattern

The definition pattern is common in college textbooks that introduce students to the terminology of a new subject. When the definition pattern is used, the definition is usually followed by explanation and/or examples to clarify the meaning. The challenge for the student is, first, to understand the definition, and then, of course, to remember the new term and its meaning.

Example

Hypnosis may be formally defined as a procedure through which one person, the hypnotist, uses the power of suggestion to induce change in thoughts, feelings, sensations, perceptions, or behavior in another person, the subject. Under hypnosis, people suspend their usual rational and logical ways of thinking and perceiving and allow themselves to experience distortions in perceptions, memories, and thinking. They may experience positive hallucinations, in which they see, hear, touch, smell, or taste things that are not present in the environment. Or they may have negative hallucinations, in which they fail to perceive things that are actually present.

—From *The World of Psychology*, 5th ed., by Samuel E. Wood, Ellen Green Wood, and Denise Boyd. New York: Pearson Education, 2005.

The preceding paragraph provides the reader with a definition of hypnosis. The authors clarify the definition with a brief explanation of the hypnotic state and some examples of hypnotic experience.

Chronological Order

Chronological order means time order. When chronological order is used, the material is presented in a time sequence. Events are described in the order in which they actually occurred. Chronological order is common in history textbooks, which usually trace sequences of events through time. Chronological order is also used for directions or steps in a process when the steps must be followed in a particular order.

Example

In October 1780, Washington sent Nathanael Greene south to lead the continental forces. It was a fortunate choice, for Greene knew the region and the kind of war that had to be fought. Determined, like Washington, to avoid large-scale encounters, Greene divided his army into small, mobile bands. Employing what today would be called guerrilla tactics, he harassed the British and their Loyalist allies at every opportunity, striking by surprise and then disappearing into the interior. . . .

In time, the tide began to turn. At Cowpens, South Carolina, in January 1781, American troops under General Daniel Morgan won a decisive victory, suffering fewer than 75 casualties to 329 British deaths, and taking 600 men prisoner. In March, at Guilford Court House in North Carolina, Cornwallis won, but at a cost that forced his retreat to Wilmington, near the sea.

In April 1781, convinced that British authority could not be restored in the Carolinas while the rebels continued to use Virginia as a supply and staging area, Cornwallis moved north. With a force of 7,500, he raided deep into Virginia, sending Governor Jefferson and the Virginia legislature fleeing from Charlottesville into the mountains. But again Cornwallis found the costs of victory high, and again he turned toward the coast for protection and resupply. On August 1, he reached Yorktown.

—From *The American People: Creating a Nation and a Society*, 5th ed., by Gary Nash and Julie Roy Jeffrey. Boston: Addison-Wesley, 2001.

The preceding paragraph provides a chronology of important military events during a ten-month period of the American Revolution. Note the sequence of dates, which allows the reader to follow the story's time order.

Listing or Enumeration

Listing and its variant, enumeration, are simple and commonly used patterns that you will find in virtually every college textbook. In the listing pattern, the author lists related points of information. The reader must ask himself, "What is the purpose of the listing, and which items on the list are important to remember?" When the listed information is numbered, the pattern is called enumeration.

Example

During the past decade, research has suggested three main reasons for the widespread neglect of the signs of heart disease in women:

1. Physicians may be gender-biased in their delivery of health care and tend to concentrate on women's reproductive organs rather than on the whole woman.
2. Physicians tend to view male heart disease as a more severe problem because medical training has traditionally focused on it as a "male" problem.
3. Women decline major procedures more often than men do.

Other explanations for diagnostic and therapeutic difficulties encountered by women with heart disease include the following:

- Delay in diagnosing a possible heart attack
- The complexity involved in interpreting chest pain in women
- Typically less aggressive treatment of women who are heart attack victims

- Their older age, on average, and greater frequency of other health problems
- The fact that women's coronary arteries are often smaller than men's, which makes surgical or diagnostic procedures more difficult technically
- Their increased incidence of postinfarction angina and heart failure

—From *Health: The Basics,* 6th ed., by Rebecca J. Donatelle. San Francisco: Benjamin Cummings, 2005.

The preceding paragraph begins with an enumeration of three main reasons for neglect of women's heart disease. The enumeration is followed by a bulleted listing of other possible explanations for this neglect.

Comparison–Contrast

In comparison–contrast, another commonly used pattern, the author shows the similarities and differences between two or more people, places, groups, theories, or other items. The comparison–contrast pattern is often used in social science textbooks, but can be found in texts from almost any discipline. The reader must understand and remember the key points of comparison (similarity and difference) or contrast (difference).

Example

Some of the writing you'll do on the job requires very little planning. For a memo to your staff regarding the company picnic or a letter requesting information from a supplier, you can often collect a few facts and get right down to writing. In other cases, however, you won't be able to start writing until you've done extensive research. This research often covers both the audience you'll be writing to and the subject matter you'll be writing about. Technology can help you with planning tasks, with research tasks, and with outlining your thoughts once you've done your research.

—From *Business Communication Today,* 5th ed., by Courtland Bovee and John Thill. Upper Saddle River, NJ: Prentice Hall, 1998.

This paragraph contrasts two types of writing: writing that doesn't require much planning and writing that requires a significant amount of planning and research.

Cause–Effect

The cause–effect pattern is used to show how one factor is the reason for another, or how one factor results from another. Cause–effect patterns are common in social science and science textbooks. The reader must understand the cause-and-effect relationship that is described in the passage and determine which causes and effects are important to remember.

Example

Starting in the early seventeenth century, colonists came to the New World for a variety of reasons. Often it was to escape religious persecution. Others came seeking a new start on a continent where land was plentiful. The independence and diversity of the settlers in the New World made the question of how best to rule the new colonies a tricky one. More than merely an ocean separated England from the colonies; the colonists were independent people, and it soon became clear that the

Crown could not govern the colonies with the same close rein used at home. King James I thus allowed some local participation in decision making through arrangements such as the first elected colonial assembly, the Virginia House of Burgesses, and the elected General Court that governed the Massachusetts Bay Company and that colony after 1629. Almost all the colonists agreed that the king ruled by divine right; but English monarchs allowed the colonists significant liberties in terms of self-government, religious practices, and economic organization. For 140 years, this system worked fairly well.

—From *The Essentials of American Government*, 3rd ed., by Karen O'Connor and Larry Sabato. Boston: Allyn & Bacon, 1998.

The preceding paragraph starts by stating some of the reasons (causes) why the colonists came to the New World. The paragraph also discusses some of the results (effects) of the independence and diversity of the colonists, and tells why the king allowed them some degree of self-rule.

Exercise 5   PATTERNS OF ORGANIZATION

Directions. Using textbooks from your other classes, find: (1) a paragraph or short passage that uses the definition pattern; (2) a paragraph or short passage that uses chronological order; (3) a paragraph or short passage that uses listing or enumeration; (4) a paragraph or short passage that uses comparison–contrast; and (5) a paragraph or short passage that uses cause–effect. Photocopy your passages and tape them on to paper, naming the corresponding pattern beside each one. Briefly explain how each pattern is used in its selection.

Marking the Textbook

Effective textbook underlining is a skill that is developed through thought and practice. Effective underlining serves two important purposes for the college reader: (1) It helps you attend, while reading, to the distinction between main ideas and details; and (2) it enables you to identify important ideas for later review.

TABLE 2 ■ *Useful Symbols and Abbreviations for Annotating Textbooks*

*	Use asterisks for key concepts.
( ) [ ]	Use parentheses or brackets to distinguish main ideas and other important information.
(1), (2), . . .	Use numbers to show a listing or sequence of ideas.
?	Use question marks to identify unclear sections or statements.
→	Use arrows to connect related ideas.
Ex.	Use *Ex.* to label examples.
Def.	Use *Def.* to label important definitions.

Suggestions for Effective Underlining

1. *Read and recite before underlining.* Read a whole paragraph or short section and mentally review the key points before attempting to underline. This will enable you to distinguish important points from details.

2. *Limit your underlining.* If you mark too much of the text, it will do you little good when you return to the book later for further review and study. A good rule of thumb is to limit yourself to underlining no more than 25 percent of the material you have read.

3. *Underline complete thoughts.* Read over what you have marked to ensure that what you have selected will be clear on later rereading.

4. *Avoid repetition.* Authors often repeat important ideas. When underlining, it is not necessary to underline the same idea more than once.

5. *Enhance your underlining with annotation.* Annotation means additional marking and writing in the textbook (use the margins for this purpose). Develop your own set of annotation symbols, and add brief explanatory comments when needed. Examples of annotation symbols include asterisks and brackets for important ideas, and abbreviations (such as *Ex.* to mean *example*). See Table 2 for a list of commonly used annotation symbols.

See Box 2 for an example of effective textbook marking.

Box 2

Marked Text

Two levels of courts, state & federal

Three types of jurisdictions ①

EX.

②

③

Courts

In criminal courts, legal responsibility is determined through interpretation of the law in relation to the circumstances of individual cases. More than 17,000 courts and related agencies operate in the United States, mostly at the state and local levels. These courts can be grouped into the federal court system (courts that interpret federal law) and state court systems (courts that interpret state and local laws). Both the state and the federal court systems have three basic types of jurisdiction. Courts of [**limited jurisdiction**] have narrow legal authority and may arbitrate only in certain types of disputes; these include family courts, municipal courts, and special courts such as tax courts. Courts of [**general jurisdiction,**] on the other hand, usually are referred to as trial courts. These are the courts in which felonies and civil cases go to trial. General jurisdiction courts across the country may be called county courts, circuit courts, and even supreme courts in some jurisdictions. The highest level of jurisdiction is [**appellate jurisdiction.**] Appellate courts review specific legal issues raised by cases in courts with general jurisdiction. An appellate court may uphold or reverse a conviction in a criminal case tried in a trial court. The sequence in which a case moves from a trial court to an appellate court occurs in every state and in the federal court system, although the names of the courts vary.

From *Criminal Justice*, 3rd ed., by Jay S. Albanese. New York: Pearson Education, 2005.

Exercise 6   MARKING THE TEXT

Directions. Select a one- to two-page section from a textbook you are using for another class. Mark the text, using the guidelines from the previous pages. When you are finished, be sure to reread what you have marked to judge how useful your markings would be for later study.

College Disciplines

College subjects are often referred to as *disciplines*. You are probably more familiar with the word *discipline* when it is used to mean control of behavior, as in self-discipline or discipline imposed by an authority figure. Actually, the word *discipline* derives from a Latin word meaning teaching or instruction.

In short, a college discipline is a branch of learning or a field of study. Psychology is a discipline. History is a discipline. Computer science is a discipline. (See Box 3.)

Characteristics of a College Discipline

Each college discipline is unique in certain ways. Each has its own history and evolution, as well as its own pioneers and leaders. Each has developed its own approaches and *methodologies,* or procedures of study. Each has its own set of terminology and its own particular set of questions to be addressed.

Some of the college disciplines will seem familiar to you, because you studied the same or similar subjects in high school. Nevertheless, the approach to that field of study may be different in college from what it was in high school. For example, you may have found that in your high school history classes, the emphasis was on learning and remembering historical facts, whereas in college, the emphasis may be more on understanding why events occurred or analyzing historical trends.

Many college disciplines will be new to you. The learning task for a college student approaching a new subject is a challenging one: not only to learn to think about the discipline, but also to learn to think *within* the discipline (for example, to learn to think like a psychologist). This includes learning how the subject is researched and familiarizing yourself with the terminology—the vocabulary—of the discipline.

The Disciplines

A look at any college catalog will reveal a long list of subjects for study and possible majors or minors. Although most colleges follow a similar approach to organizing their disciplines and departments, substantial variation can occur from school to school. Large universities tend to divide their academic areas into large units, which are often referred to as schools or colleges (for example, the School of Engineering or the College of Liberal Arts).

For practice purposes, in *Textcerpts* we will focus on four major discipline areas: social sciences, humanities, natural and technical sciences, and

Box 3

Major College Disciplines

Social sciences, the disciplines concerned with what people do and why they do it.

Political science, the study of government and the principles of government.

Economics, the study of the production, distribution, and use of wealth and resources.

Behavioral sciences, the social sciences concerned with human and animal behavior and interactions, including psychology, sociology, and anthropology.

Psychology, the study of behavior and mental processes. Psychology studies people as individuals, seeking to understand and predict human behavior.

Sociology, the study of society and group behavior. Sociology studies people in large and small groups. Sociologists are especially interested in group dynamics, social organizations, and intragroup interactions.

Anthropology, the study of human culture. Anthropologists compare human cultures, looking for similarities and differences. Anthropologists also study group behavior in the animal kingdom.

Humanities, the disciplines concerned with human thought, relations, and culture.

History, the record and study of human events.

Literature, the study of literary works, including poetry, drama, novels, short stories, and essays.

Philosophy, the study of the principles underlying human thought and conduct, and the nature of existence.

Arts, the disciplines concerned with the study, practice, and theory of visual and performing arts, such as dance, music, painting, and sculpture.

Communications, the study of the theory and forms of human communication.

Natural sciences, the disciplines that study the natural, physical universe.

Biology, the study of living organisms and life processes.

Chemistry, the study of the composition and properties of substances, and the interactions of substances.

Physics, the study of the interrelationship of matter and energy.

Geology, the study of the physical composition and history of the earth.

Astronomy, the study of the universe, including stars and other heavenly bodies.

Technical sciences, the disciplines that study the concepts and development of technological processes.

Computer science, the study of the functions and applications of computers.

Electronics, the study of electricity and electrons, and their technical applications.

Career-oriented disciplines, the disciplines that study the theories and practices associated with specific careers.

Business, the application of economic principles to human commerce.

Nursing, the study of the ethics and medical practices of the nursing profession.

Criminal justice, the study of the causes, treatment, and prevention of crime.

career-oriented disciplines. Developing your skills through practice readings with these disciplines should enable you to read successfully in almost any undergraduate discipline.

| Exercise 7 | **RECOGNIZING COLLEGE DISCIPLINES** |

Directions. Identify the subject, or discipline, in which you would probably encounter each of the following items. Refer to Box 3 (page 17) as necessary.

Example:
A procedure to calculate the distance between stars.   *Astronomy*

1. An experiment that has been designed to determine the type of reinforcement most likely to motivate rats to run faster.

   _____

2. A series of recommendations for giving a speech in front of a small audience.

   _____

3. An analysis of the effects of a war on a nation's economy.

   _____

4. A description of the human digestive organs and their functions.

   _____

5. A theory explaining how some groups come to exercise more power within a society than other groups.

   _____

6. Instructions on how to test the effectiveness of various materials to be used as semi-conductors within an appliance.

   _____

Box 4	
Useful Qualities for College Textbook Readers	*patience* **curiosity** **persistence** open-mindedness

PART

II

Practice Readings in the Disciplines

Part II provides practice with 20 excerpts from a variety of college disciplines. Each excerpt is followed by questions that will help you check your understanding of the passage and ask you to think critically about what you have read.

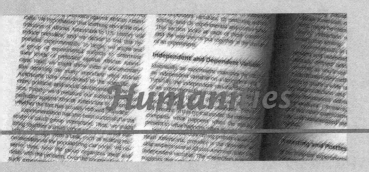

Humanities

Communications

THE IMPORTANCE OF LANGUAGE

Communications has become a popular college major in recent years. Although communications is not a traditional humanities discipline, communications courses deal with many of the same themes as the longer-established humanities courses.

Language is central to the human experience. Complete Exercise 1 to learn about the importance of language to human communications, relationships, and behavior.

THE IMPORTANCE OF LANGUAGE

Language is a structured system of signs, sounds, gestures, or marks that is used and understood to express ideas and feelings among people within a community, nation, geographic area, or cultural tradition. . . . Without language, there would be little or no human communication as we now know it.

5　Language allows us to encounter our world in a meaningful way because it allows us to share meaning with others. Can you imagine what it would be like to be unable to tell someone what you know or think or feel? Language is a powerful tool! But it is only as effective and efficient as the person or persons using it. Despite the fact that we often believe that language is neutral, in actu-

10　ality, it communicates much about what we are and what we think and thus must be carefully used.

Language Is Powerful

We depend not only on our own experiences to gain information, but also we rely on communicating with people we know and do not know. Because we use language and are able to communicate, we are not limited to experiencing

15　the world only through our own personal experiences and knowledge. We can learn by talking with others, taking courses, watching television, and reading newspapers, magazines, books, and information posted on the Internet.

Using language allows us to change, to cooperate, to create, and to resolve conflicts. It can prevent wars or start them, create friends or enemies, and

20　change our behavior or the behavior of others. Yet most of us take language for granted and ignore its potential effects. We regard language as a "mere matter of words," forgetting that words have the power to affect our minds, feelings, thoughts, will, actions, and being. Successful communicators respect language and have learned how to use it effectively.

Language Affects Thought

25   The misuse of language involves more than the misuse of words. Misused language also affects our ability to think. Thought and language are inseparable. But which comes first? As with the chicken and the egg, the answer is debatable, but most scholars agree that words help us to form thoughts. For example, at times we may think we know what we want to say, but find that we
30   don't know how to say it. However, if we really knew what we wanted to say, we would probably have no trouble expressing it. At other times we speak and later realize that we did not say what we meant. This usually occurs either because we did not carefully think about what we were saying or we did not carefully choose the words to express our thoughts.

35   It is also important to consider word choice carefully *before* speaking. Erasing the effect of something already said is extremely difficult. You can correct or retract a statement, and you can even apologize for saying it, but you cannot eliminate the fact that you said it.

From *Communication: Making Connections*, 4th ed., by William J. Seiler and Melissa L. Beall. Boston: Allyn & Bacon, 1999.

Comprehension Questions

1. Why is language powerful?

_____

2. According to the passage, how can we use language more effectively?

_____

_____ 3. Which of the following statements best paraphrases the authors' *definition* of language? Language is
   a. a system of symbols that communicate ideas and feelings.
   b. a group of words whose meaning is determined by the community that uses them.
   c. the structured use of sound to record and communicate important information.
   d. the most effective means for human beings to express their feelings and emotions.

_____ 4. The authors imply that
   a. the misuse of words is unlikely to affect our thoughts.
   b. the misuse of language invariably detracts from our thinking.
   c. thought and language are best understood as separate processes.
   d. we can think effectively even if we can't use language effectively.

_____ 5. The authors suggest that successful communicators
   a. recognize that language is neutral.
   b. appreciate the power of language.
   c. distrust information from others.
   d. know that language is merely a matter of words.

Directions. Mark each of the following statements True (T), False (F), or Can't Tell (CT). Mark the statement Can't Tell if it is neither supported nor contradicted by the passage.

_____ 6. Human beings cannot communicate without words.

_____ 7. The authors believe that language enables us to learn from the experiences of others.

_____ 8. Language may not precede thought, but it is clear that language plays a major role in the formation of our thoughts.

_____ 9. Language is more likely to influence a person's behavior positively rather than negatively.

_____10. It is easier to correct false impressions than to create them.

Recognizing Organizational Patterns

What is the primary pattern of organization used in this passage? Explain your answer.

_____

_____

Vocabulary Questions

Directions. Choose the meaning for the underlined word that best fits the context. You may consult the dictionary as needed.

_____ 1. Language is a structured system of signs, sounds, gestures.... [Line 1]
   a. words
   b. movements
   c. concepts
   d. expressions

_____ 2. ... within a community, nation, geographic area, or cultural tradition. [Lines 2–3]
   a. customary
   b. learned
   c. pertaining to a nation
   d. relating to the collected practices of a group

_____ 3. Despite the fact that we often believe that language is neutral.... [Line 9]
   a. neither male nor female
   b. having no importance
   c. not committed
   d. neither positive nor negative

_____ 4. Thought and language are inseparable. [Line 26]
   a. cannot be separated
   b. of great importance
   c. hard to understand
   d. separate but equal

_____ 5. You can correct or <u>retract</u> a statement. . . .
        [Lines 36–37]
        a. amend
        b. repeat
        c. take back
        d. deny

Critical Response Questions

1. Provide an example of someone you know personally, or a famous person, whom you consider to be a good communicator. What makes him or her an effective communicator?

   _____

   _____

   _____

2. Why is written language critical to the functioning of society?

   _____

   _____

   _____

3. Do you believe that language precedes thought? Explain your opinion.

   _____

   _____

   _____

Sample Annotations for Exercise 1

THE IMPORTANCE OF LANGUAGE

Def.   * **Language** is a structured system of signs, sounds, gestures, or marks that is used and understood to express ideas and feelings among people within a community, nation, geographic area, or cultural tradition. . . .   Without language, there would be little or no human communication as we now know it.

power of 5 <u>Language allows us to encounter our world in a meaningful way because it</u>
language   <u>allows us to share meaning with others.</u> Can you imagine what it would be like

to be unable to tell someone what you know or think or feel? Language is a powerful tool! But it is only as effective and efficient as the person or persons using it. Despite the fact that we often believe that language is neutral, in actu-
10 ality, it communicates much about what we are and what we think and thus must be carefully used.

Language Is Powerful

We depend not only on our own experiences to gain information, but also we rely on communicating with people we know and do not know. Because we use language and are able to communicate, we are not limited to experiencing
15 the world only through our own personal experiences and knowledge. We can *ex.* learn by talking with others, taking courses, watching television, and reading newspapers, magazines, books, and information posted on the Internet.

Using language allows us to change, to cooperate, to create, and to resolve conflicts. It can prevent wars or start them, create friends or enemies, and
20 change our behavior or the behavior of others. Yet most of us take language for granted and ignore its potential effects. We regard language as a "mere matter of words," forgetting that words have the power to affect our minds, feelings, thoughts, will, actions, and being. Successful communicators respect language and have learned how to use it effectively.

Language Affects Thought

thought & 25 The misuse of language involves more than the misuse of words. Misused lan-
language guage also affects our ability to think. Thought and language are inseparable. But which comes first? As with the chicken and the egg, the answer is debatable, but most scholars agree that words help us to form thoughts. For example, at times we may think we know what we want to say, but find that we
30 don't know how to say it. However, if we really knew what we wanted to say, we would probably have no trouble expressing it. At other times we speak and later realize that we did not say what we meant. This usually occurs either because we did not carefully think about what we were saying or we did not carefully choose the words to express our thoughts.

choose words 35 It is also important to consider word choice carefully *before* speaking. Eras-
carefully ing the effect of something already said is extremely difficult. You can correct or retract a statement, and you can even apologize for saying it, but you cannot eliminate the fact that you said it.

From *Communication: Making Connections*, 4th ed., by William J. Seiler and Melissa L. Beall. Boston: Allyn & Bacon, 1999.

Music

EARLY ROCK 'N' ROLL

Humanities subjects include literature, art, music, and philosophy. The humanities emphasize those aspects of life that make us distinct as human beings—human thought, relationships, language, and culture.

Humanities authors, then, view their discipline as an exploration of the depth and richness of human experience. Humanities readings may therefore be more subjective than science readings, and will often reflect the value system of the particular author. Insight is as important in the humanities as the establishment of fact.

Exercise 2 provides a brief account of the origins of rock 'n' roll. As you complete the exercise, notice how the author gives shape to a series of events to tell the story of rock 'n' roll's beginnings.

EARLY ROCK 'N' ROLL

Music aficionados quibble about who invented the term *rock 'n' roll*. There is no doubt, though, that Memphis disc jockey **Sam Philips** was a key figure. From his job at WREC, Phillips found an extra $75 a month to rent a 20-foot-by-35-foot storefront, the paint peeling from the ceiling, to go into business

5   recording, as he put it, "anything, anywhere, anytime." His first jobs, in 1949, were weddings and bar mitzvahs, but in 1951 Philips put out his first record, "Gotta Let you Go" by blues singer Joe Hill Louis, who played his own guitar, harmonica and drums for accompaniment. In 1951 Phillips recorded B. B. King and then Jackie Breston's "Rocket 88," which many musicologists call the first

10 rock 'n' roll record. Phillips sold his early recordings, all by black musicians, mostly in the blues tradition, to other labels.

In 1952 Phillips began his own Sun Records label and a quest to broaden the appeal of the black music he loved to a wide audience. "If I could find a white man who had the Negro sound and the Negro feel, I could make a billion dol-

15 lars," he said. In a group he recorded in 1954, the Starlight Wranglers, Sam Phillips found Elvis Presley.

Elvis' first Sun recording, "That's All Right," with Scotty Moore and Bill Black, found only moderate success on country radio stations, but Sam Phillips knew that he was onto something. It wasn't quite country or quite blues, but it was a

20 sound that could move both white country fans and black blues fans. Elvis moved on to RCA, a major label. By 1956 he had two of the nation's best-

selling records, the flip-side hits "Don't Be Cruel" and "Hound Dog," plus three others among the year's top 16. Meanwhile, Sam Phillips was recording Carl Perkins, Roy Orbison, Johnny Cash and Jerry Lee Lewis, adding to the distinctively
25   American country-blues hybrid: wild, thrashing, sometimes reckless rock 'n' roll.

The new music found a following on radio stations that picked up on the music mix that Cleveland disc jockey Alan Freed had pioneered a early as 1951—occasional rhythm 'n' blues amid the mainstream Frank Sinatra and Peggy Lee. By 1955 Freed was in New York and clearly on a roll. Freed helped
30   propel Bill Haley and the Comets' "Rock Around the Clock" to number one. Rock's future was cemented when "Rock Around the Clock" was the musical bed under the credits for the 1955 movie *Blackboard Jungle.* Young people flocked to the movie not only for its theme of teen disenchantment and rebellion but also for the music.

From *The Media of Mass Communication,* 7th ed., by John Vivian. Boston: Pearson Eduction, 2006.

Comprehension Questions

1. What was Alan Freed's contribution to the development of rock 'n' roll?

_____

2. What were some of the qualities of Elvis Presley's music that contributed to his popularity?

_____

_____ **3.** Regarding the origin of the term *rock 'n' roll,* the reader can conclude that
  a. Sam Phillips invented the term.
  b. Sam Phillips did not invent the term.
  c. many rock 'n' roll artists claimed credit for the invention of the term.
  d. we are not sure who invented the term.

_____ **4.** Phillips was especially interested in Elvis Presley because Presley
  a. was exceptionally good-looking.
  b. could appeal to both black and white audiences.
  c. had an exceptionally good voice.
  d. recorded a best-seller.

_____ **5.** Alan Freed was a disc jockey who
  a. was the first to play live rock 'n' roll.
  b. preferred mainstream music to rhythm 'n' blues.
  c. contributed to the success of early rock 'n' roll.
  d. placed "Rock Around the Clock" into the score of the movie *Blackboard Jungle.*

Directions.   Mark each of the following statements True (T), False (F), or Can't Tell (CT). Mark the statement Can't Tell if it is neither supported nor contradicted by the passage.

_____ 6. Phillips was interested in Elvis Presley because of Presley's appeal to black audiences.

_____ 7. Phillips wanted to make black music more accessible to white audiences.

_____ 8. Phillips lost confidence in Presley after his first recording was unsuccessful.

_____ 9. "Rock Around the Clock" was the best-selling single in 1955.

_____10. *Blackboard Jungle* was popular with adolescents because it dealt with themes of concern to them.

Recognizing Organizational Patterns

What is the primary pattern of organization used in this passage? Explain your answer.

_____

_____

Vocabulary Questions

Directions.   Choose the meaning for the underlined word that best fits the context. You may consult the dictionary as needed.

_____ 1. Music <u>aficionados</u> quibble. . . . [Line 1]
  a. fishermen
  b. composers
  c. fans
  d. critics

_____ 2. Music aficionados <u>quibble</u>. . . . [Line 1]
  a. research
  b. argue
  c. question
  d. invent

_____ 3. . . . Phillips began . . . a <u>quest</u> to broaden the appeal of the black music he loved. . . .
  [Lines 12–13]
  a. advertising campaign
  b. request
  c. effort
  d. study

_____ 4. . . . the distinctively American country-blues <u>hybrid</u>. . . . [Lines 24–25]
  a. mix
  b. success
  c. invention
  d. rhythm

_____ 5. . . . its theme of teen <u>disenchantment</u> and rebellion. . . . [Lines 33–34]
  a. excitement
  b. alienation
  c. rebellion
  d. process of maturing or growing up

Critical Response Questions

1. Why does the author consider Sam Phillips a key figure in the origins of rock 'n' roll?

_____

_____

_____

2. How was rock 'n' roll different from previous forms of popular music?

_____

_____

_____

3. Does the author provide an objective or subjective account of the roots of rock 'n' roll? Explain your answer.

_____

_____

_____

American History

THE SECOND GREAT REMOVAL

History textbooks tell the story of human experience. Historians are concerned with reconstructing events: accurately reporting what occurred and attempting to explain why it occurred. They seek to recognize important historical trends and to establish cause-and-effect relationships between events.

Complete Exercise 3 to understand how historians view the treatment of Native Americans in the nineteenth century.

THE SECOND GREAT REMOVAL

Black Elk, an Oglala Sioux, listened to a story his father had heard from his father.

> A long time ago . . . there was once a Lakota [Sioux] holy man, called Drinks Water, who dreamed what was to be; and this was long before the coming of the Wasichus [white men]. He dreamed . . . that a strange race had woven
> 5 a spider's web all around the Lakotas. And he said: "When this happens, you shall live in square gray houses, in a barren land, and beside those square gray houses you shall starve."

So great was the wise man's sorrow that he died soon after his strange dream. But Black Elk lived to see it come true.

10 As farmers settled the western frontier and became entangled in a national economy, they clashed with the Indian tribes who lived on the land. In California, disease and violence killed 90 percent of the Native American population in the 30 years following the gold rush. Elsewhere, the struggle among Native Americans, white settlers, the U.S. Army, and government officials and reform-
15 ers was prolonged and bitter. Although some tribes moved onto government reservations with little protest, most tribes, including the Nez Percé in the Northwest, the Apache in the Southwest, and the Plains Indians, resisted the attempts to curb their way of life and to transform their culture.

Background to Hostilities

The lives of most Plains Indians revolved around the buffalo. Increased emigra-
20 tion to California and Oregon in the 1840s and 1850s disrupted tribal pursuits and animal migration patterns. Initially, the federal government tried, without much success, to persuade the Plains tribes to stay away from white wagon trains and white settlers. As Lone Horn, a Miniconjou chief, explained when

American commissioners at the 1851 Fort Laramie Council asked him if he
would be satisfied to live on the Missouri River, "When the buffalo comes close
to the river, we come close to it. When the buffaloes go off, we go off after
them."

During the Civil War, the eastern tribes that were forced to relocate in Oklahoma divided, some, especially the slaveholders, supporting the Confederacy
and others the Union. After the war, however, all were branded as "traitors."
The federal government callously nullified earlier pledges and treaties, leaving
Indians defenseless against further incursions on their lands. As settlers pushed
into Kansas, the tribes living in Kansas were shunted into Oklahoma.

The White Perspective

When the Civil War ended, red and white men on the Plains were already at
war. In 1864, the Colorado militia had massacred a band of friendly Cheyenne
at Sand Creek, Colorado, despite the fact that Chief Black Kettle waved both a
white flag of truce and an American flag. Militia leader John Chivington urged
his men on. "Kill and scalp all, big and little." Before long, Cheyenne, Sioux, and
Arapaho were responding in kind. The Plains wars had begun.

From *The American People: Creating a Nation and a Society,* 5th ed., by Gary B. Nash, Julie Roy Jeffrey,
et al. Boston: Addison-Wesley Educational Publishers, 2001.

Comprehension Questions

1. Briefly summarize the events discussed in the passage.

_____

2. How did the Native Americans feel about being moved? How did they respond?

_____

_____ 3. Black Elk was a Sioux Indian who
   a. dreamed that the white man would conquer his tribe.
   b. witnessed the white man conquering his tribe.
   c. led the Plains Indians in their fight against white settlers.
   d. believed his father's vision, which predicted the destruction of his people.

_____ 4. The Plains wars were triggered by
   a. the end of the Civil War.
   b. the California Gold Rush.
   c. Indian participation in the Civil War.
   d. a massacre of Cheyenne Indians.

_____ 5. Which of the following *cannot* be inferred from the passage?
   a. Some tribes fought for the South during the Civil War.
   b. The Indians who fought for the Union during the Civil War were better treated than those who fought for the South.
   c. Some Indian tribes were slaveholders.
   d. Some Indian tribes were forced to move from Kansas to Oklahoma.

Directions. Mark each of the following statements True (T), False (F), or Can't Tell (CT). Mark the statement Can't Tell if it is neither supported nor contradicted by the passage.

_____ 6. Most Apaches were unwilling to move onto reservations.

_____ 7. The westward migration of white Americans had little significant impact on the migration patterns of the American buffalo.

_____ 8. During the American Civil War, most Native Americans fought for the Union.

_____ 9. The Plains wars began a few years after the Civil War ended.

_____10. Additional migration of Native Americans was forced by the failure of the U.S. government to honor its treaties.

Recognizing Organizational Patterns

Identify two patterns of organization that are used in this passage. Explain your answer.

_____

_____

Vocabulary Questions

Directions. Choose the meaning for the underlined word that best fits the context. You may consult the dictionary as needed.

_____ 1. . . . this was long before the coming of the Wasichus. . . . [Lines 3–4]
   a. a Lakota term meaning *white man*
   b. a Lakota term meaning *people*
   c. a Lakota term meaning *enemy*
   d. a European term meaning *white man*

_____ 2. Increased emigration . . . disrupted tribal pursuits. . . . [Lines 19–20]
   a. destroyed
   b. broke up
   c. distracted
   d. eliminated

_____ 3. The federal government callously nullified earlier pledges and treaties. . . . [Line 31]
   a. suspiciously
   b. carefully
   c. cruelly
   d. wickedly

_____ 4. The federal government callously nullified earlier pledges and treaties. . . . [Line 31]
   a. multiplied
   b. canceled
   c. subtracted
   d. violated

_____ 5. ... leaving Indians defenseless against further
incursions on their lands. [Lines 31–32]
    a. invasions
    b. treaties
    c. reductions
    d. claims to ownership

Critical Response Questions

1. Why was the buffalo important to Native American culture?

_____

_____

_____

2. Why weren't white Americans fair to the Native Americans?

_____

_____

_____

3. Does the author provide an objective account of the events of this period? Explain
your answer.

_____

_____

_____

Literature

THE HARLEM RENAISSANCE

The study of literature allows us to gain insights into ourselves and our fellow human beings. Literature texts typically include the literature itself (stories, poems, essays, etc.), and analysis and discussion of the literature.

Exercise 4 is excerpted from a humanities textbook chapter on literature. Complete Exercise 4 to learn about an important American literary movement of the early twentieth century.

THE HARLEM RENAISSANCE

From time to time there emerge conscious literary movements, the brainchildren of people drawn together by the common aim of bringing their creative efforts to the attention of a wider audience. One such movement was the Irish Renaissance of the early twentieth century. Another was the Harlem Renais-

5 sance, which, from the mid-1920s to the mid-1930s, launched the careers of dozens of African American artists, including a number of poets.

Before this time, African American poets, for the most part, had been writing in traditional forms in order to gain recognition, using rhythm and often rhyme. Similarly, the poets who ushered in the Harlem Renaissance also

10 wrote in traditional forms, but the content of the poems was anything but traditional.

On the night of March 21, 1924, Charles S. Johnson, editor of the literary magazine *Opportunity,* invited a number of distinguished white literary figures, including playwright Eugene O'Neill, to attend a celebration of African Ameri-

15 can literature. Also present to read some of their work were about a dozen relatively unknown poets. Word spread rapidly, and soon Manhattan was buzzing about the astonishing array of talent that had been assembled. Through newspaper articles and radio interviews, many hitherto obscure personalities began to make their presence felt.

20 Georgia Douglas Johnson (1886–1966) was one such presence. Now considered the first major female African American poet of the twentieth century, she adapted the traditional style of the lyric poem while communicating anything but lyrical images of the painful hardships endured by a neglected but crucial sector of America. Her poem illustrates how a modern poet can make a

25 reader see life with a different set of eyes.

Black Woman

Don't knock at my door, little child,
*   I cannot let you in,*
You know not what a world this is
*   Of cruelty and sin.*
30 *Wait in the still eternity*
*   Until I come to you,*
The world is cruel, cruel, child,
*   I cannot let you in!*
Don't knock at my heart, little one,
35 *   I cannot bear the pain*
Of turning deaf-ear to your call
*   Time and time again!*
You do not know the monster men
*   Inhabiting the earth,*
40 *Be still, be still, my precious child,*
*   I must not give you birth!*

A modern poem is rarely over until the final line. Although Johnson gives away her theme early in the piece, the poem is not really complete until the shock of the ending. This structure almost defines modern poetry, which is intended to move, 45 startle, give sudden insight, and it has done so with ever-increasing complexity. Aware of their competition with other media, particularly visual media requiring little thought, a good many modern poets go their own way, knowing they will reach a small, understanding audience, one accustomed to seeing with new eyes and willing to work, if need be, to grasp what can be the mystery of the last line.

From *The Art of Being Human: Humanities for the 21st Century*, 8th ed., by Richard Paul Janaro and Thelma C. Altshuler. New York: Pearson Education, 2006.

Comprehension Questions

1. What was the Harlem Renaissance?

_____

2. What is a "conscious literary movement"?

_____

_____ 3. Before the Harlem Renaissance, most African American poets
    a. imitated the poetry of successful European poets.
    b. used traditional forms for their poetry.
    c. imitated the poetry of other African American poets.
    d. experimented with new forms in order to gain recognition.

____ 4. The celebration of African American literature on March 21, 1924, was important because
  a. it was the first public reading of African American poetry.
  b. it was the first time that white Americans heard or read poetry written by African American poets.
  c. until that time, the media had refused to publish African American poetry.
  d. it gave recognition to previously unknown, talented African American poets.

____ 5. The author suggests that modern poets
  a. have abandoned the use of rhyme and rhythm.
  b. have emphasized the need for new uses of rhyme and rhythm.
  c. prefer to leave their poems unfinished.
  d. expect their audience to work at interpreting the meaning of their poems.

Directions. Mark each of the following statements True (T), False (F), or Can't Tell (CT). Mark the statement Can't Tell if it is neither supported nor contradicted by the passage.

____ 6. The authors believe that the reader can recognize the theme of "Black Woman" early in the poem.

____ 7. African American poets use rhyme and rhythm more than white poets.

____ 8. Those who attended the celebration on March 21 were at first unimpressed with the poems they heard that night.

____ 9. Georgia Douglas Johnson used her poetry to communicate the joy and excitement in the lives of African American women.

____10. The narrator of "Black Woman" is warning her young daughter to beware of evil men.

Recognizing Organizational Patterns

What is the primary pattern of organization used in this passage? Explain your answer.

_____

_____

Vocabulary Questions

Directions. Choose the meaning for the underlined word that best fits the context. You may consult the dictionary as needed.

____ 1. . . . the poets who ushered in the Harlem Renaissance . . . [Line 9]
  a. understood
  b. organized; managed
  c. brought; guided
  d. created

____ 2. . . . soon Manhattan was buzzing about the astonishing array of talent that had been assembled. [Lines 16–17]
  a. lack
  b. collection
  c. skill; achievements
  d. amount

_____ 3. Through newspaper articles and radio interviews many <u>hitherto</u> obscure personalities began to make their presence felt. [Lines 17–19]

    a. famous

    b. about to become

    c. currently

    d. up to now

_____ 4. Through newspaper articles and radio interviews many hitherto <u>obscure</u> personalities began to make their presence felt. [Lines 17–19]

    a. popular

    b. unknown

    c. interesting

    d. important

_____ 5. . . . she adapted the traditional style of the lyric poem while communicating anything but <u>lyrical</u> images . . . [Lines 22–23]

    a. expressing lofty emotions

    b. popular

    c. pretty in an artificial way

    d. powerful

Critical Response Questions

1. What is the value of poetry in today's fast-paced, multimedia world?

_____

_____

_____

2. To whom is the poet of "Black Woman" speaking? What is the message of the poem?

_____

_____

_____

3. What special contributions might minority authors make to their mainstream culture?

_____

_____

_____

World History

GANDHI AND CIVIL DISOBEDIENCE

The *who* in history sometimes refers to groups of people, as it does to the Native Americans in Exercise 3. Often, however, history texts focus on the actions of individuals who have contributed significantly to the shaping of human events.

Complete Exercise 5 to learn about Mahatma Gandhi's practice of nonviolent resistance and his efforts to liberate his homeland from British authority.

GANDHI AND CIVIL DISOBEDIENCE

The foremost nationalist leader in India was Mohandas Gandhi (1869–1948). Born of middle-class parents, Gandhi went to London to study law; later he went to South Africa to defend Indians there against the abuses of the planters. Gandhi's encounter with South African discrimination against "nonwhites"

5 transformed him. In South Africa, Indians were subject to numerous legal restrictions that hampered their freedom of movement, prevented them from buying property, and imposed added taxes on them. Gandhi worked aggressively for the legal and political rights of the oppressed. He repudiated wealth, practiced ascetic self-denial, condemned violence, and advocated service to

10 others. He launched a community (*ashram*) that served as a model for living out those principles. With Gandhi as their leader, the Indians in South Africa adopted the tactic of "civil disobedience"—they carried out various protests, refused to work, held mass demonstrations, and marched into areas where their presence was forbidden by law. Through "passive resistance" and nonco-

15 operation, Gandhi forced the government to remove some restrictions, thereby attracting worldwide attention.

When he returned to his native land shortly after the outbreak of World War I, Gandhi was welcomed as a hero. Initially, he supported the British in the war effort, but soon he went on the offensive. A crucial factor in his decision

20 was a journey he took in 1917 to Champaran, in Bihar in northeastern India, at the invitation of an impoverished peasant. The peasant had dogged Gandhi's steps until he persuaded him to come and see the terrible conditions of the indigo sharecroppers in his district. Gandhi already had a reputation; his visit alarmed the authorities, who threatened to jail him. But the intrepid lawyer

25 mobilized support and launched a nonviolent campaign for reform and justice

for the peasants. Gandhi viewed this episode as seminal. "What I did," he explained, "was a very ordinary thing. I declared that the British could not order me around in my own country."

30   In India Gandhi founded another ashram based on service, living simply, and self-reliance. He lived there off and on for the rest of his life, but his attention was increasingly turned to agitating for British withdrawal. In response to the Rowlett Act Gandhi launched a campaign of civil disobedience. A mass strike was declared in which all work was to cease and the population was to pray and fast. Gandhi argued that moral force would triumph over physical force.

From *Civilization: Past and Present*, 9th ed., by Palmira Brummett et al. Boston: Addison-Wesley Educational Publishers, 2000.

Comprehension Questions

1. What is civil disobedience?

_____

2. What motivated Gandhi to become involved in South Africa?

_____

_____ **3.** Gandhi's ashrams were primarily
   a. model communities that demonstrated the principles in which Gandhi believed.
   b. places where Gandhi could study and develop political strategy without fear of being spied on.
   c. sanctuaries where revolutionaries were safe from the authorities.
   d. sanctuaries where Gandhi could retain personal privacy and hide from the authorities.

_____ **4.** The British attitude toward Gandhi could best be described as
   a. admiring of his heroism.
   b. encouraging and supportive of his goals.
   c. alarmed and threatened by his initiatives.
   d. contemptuous of his philosophy and political strategies.

_____ **5.** Gandhi helped his people by doing *all* of the following *except*
   a. providing an example of successful peaceful resistance.
   b. confronting British authority with acts of civil disobedience.
   c. negotiating political compromises with the British government.
   d. fighting against unfair social and economic conditions.

Directions. Mark each of the following statements True (T), False (F), or Can't Tell (CT). Mark the statement Can't Tell if it is neither supported nor contradicted by the passage.

_____ 6. Gandhi did not seek personal wealth or power.

_____ 7. The South African protests and demonstrations resulted in full equality under the law for the Indians of South Africa.

_____ 8. After Gandhi left South Africa, the government retracted most of the rights that had been granted.

_____ 9. Gandhi's primary goal in India was to use nonviolence to force British withdrawal from his country.

_____10. Gandhi's philosophy can best be summarized as "the ends justify the means."

Recognizing Organizational Patterns

What is the primary pattern of organization used in this passage? Explain your answer.

_____

_____

Vocabulary Questions

Directions. Choose the meaning for the underlined word that best fits the context. You may consult the dictionary as needed.

_____ 1. He repudiated wealth.... [Line 8]
   a. rejected
   b. admired
   c. condemned
   d. accumulated

_____ 2. ...practiced ascetic self-denial....
   [Line 9]
   a. pertaining to art and beauty
   b. painful
   c. religious
   d. limited to bare necessities

_____ 3. ...the terrible conditions of the indigo sharecroppers.... [Lines 22–23]
   a. landowners
   b. people who farm someone else's land
   c. poor people
   d. individuals suffering from a rare disease

_____ 4. ...the intrepid lawyer mobilized support....
   [Lines 24–25]
   a. clever
   b. skillful
   c. brave
   d. dishonest

_____ 5. Gandhi viewed this episode as seminal.
   [Line 26]
   a. primary; influential
   b. final
   c. unfortunate
   d. resulting in victory

Critical Response Questions

1. Why is an understanding of Gandhi's personality and philosophy important to an understanding of his achievements?

_____

_____

_____

2. Compare Martin Luther King, Jr.'s leadership of the American civil rights movement with Gandhi's efforts in India.

_____

_____

_____

3. Why is civil disobedience an effective means of achieving change?

_____

_____

_____

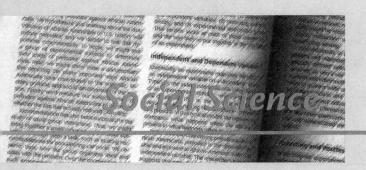

Social Science

Psychology

THREE PRINCIPLES OF SCIENTIFIC ENDEAVOR

While most people think of science as the study of subjects such as biology and chemistry, the word *science* also has a broader meaning. The word *science* is derived from a Latin root meaning knowledge. Many academic professionals consider themselves scientists, even though they are not studying the traditional "hard" or "natural" sciences.

Complete Exercise 6 to learn more about why psychologists consider themselves to be scientists.

THREE PRINCIPLES OF SCIENTIFIC ENDEAVOR

As a science, psychology is committed to objectivity, accuracy, and healthy skepticism about the study of behavior and mental processes. These three basic principles are at the very core of psychology—they are part of what makes it a science. They can also help you be a critical thinker in your day-to-day life.

Objectivity

5   For psychologists, objectivity means evaluating research and theory on their merits, without preconceived ideas. For example, when scientists challenged the validity and usefulness of lie detector tests to select truthful employees, both believers and skeptics stepped up offering case studies, as well as anecdotal experiences, that supported their own assessments of the usefulness of

10   these tests. Psychologists attempt to bring scientific objectivity to the research arena; they know that anecdotal reports are seldom objective and that though they can explain events after they have happened, they are too limited to support predictions about future behavior or mental processes. Remember, scientists want to both describe *and* predict. Common sense relies heavily on look-

15   ing backward—using hindsight—but is not very objective or reliable when it comes to making predictions about behavior.

Accuracy

Psychologists are concerned with gathering data from the laboratory and the real world in precise ways—that is, with accuracy. For instance, to conclude

20   from a small number of eyewitness accounts that whole communities have
been abducted by aliens falls considerably short of scientific accuracy. Might
there be another plausible explanation for astonishingly similar accounts of
small, ghostly figures levitating people into flying-saucer laboratories? Might
those reporting such incidents suffer from similar psychological disorders?
Rather than relying on limited samples and immediate impressions, psycholo-
25   gists base their thinking on precise, detailed, and thorough study.

Healthy Skepticism

One needn't be a scientific researcher to realize that although life *is* full of incredible events, people's reports of strange phenomena must be taken with a
grain of salt. Most people think twice when they hear stories like that of the
woman who reported that she was saved from falling off an alpine precipice by
30   an angelic rescuer who suddenly appeared and then disappeared. Intriguing as
accounts of alien abductions or angelic rescues may be, psychologists maintain
a healthy skepticism—a cautious view of data, hypotheses, and theory until results are repeated, verified, and established over time.

From *Psychology*, 7th ed., by Lester A. Lefton. Boston: Allyn & Bacon, 2000.

Comprehension Questions

1. Using your own words, briefly explain the three principles of scientific endeavor.

_____

_____

2. How do psychologists ensure the accuracy of their data?

_____

_____

____ 3. One important drawback of anecdotal reports is that
   a. they tend to be inaccurate and dishonest.
   b. they sometimes contradict each other.
   c. they are not reliable for formulating predictions.
   d. they provide insights into events that have already occurred.

____ 4. For scientific data to be considered accurate, it must be
   a. consistent with common sense.
   b. limited to immediate impressions.
   c. derived from precise, repeatable laboratory experiments.
   d. thorough and exact.

_____ 5. Scientific skepticism is best understood as
    a. an unwillingness to accept unfamiliar ideas.
    b. an unwillingness to accept information unless it can be tested and repeated.
    c. the tendency to disbelieve whatever one hears.
    d. the ability to examine ideas without bias or prejudice.

Directions. Mark each of the following statements True (T), False (F), or Can't Tell (CT). Mark the statement Can't Tell if it is neither supported nor contradicted by the passage.

_____ 6. Psychology is concerned with the study of behavior and mental processes.

_____ 7. Anecdotal reports play an essential role in bringing scientific objectivity to psychological research.

_____ 8. Most people do not believe that anyone has ever been rescued by an angel.

_____ 9. Psychologists do not rely on common sense to make predictions about human behavior.

_____10. Eyewitness accounts are useful to psychologists in that they provide the most accurate and reliable data from which predictions about behavior can be made.

Recognizing Organizational Patterns

How does the author use the definition pattern to organize this passage?

_____

_____

Vocabulary Questions

Directions. Choose the meaning for the underlined word that best fits the context. You may consult the dictionary as needed.

_____ 1. . . . psychology is committed to objectivity, accuracy, and healthy skepticism. . . .
[Lines 1–2]
    a. accuracy
    b. doubt
    c. credibility
    d. verifiable data

_____ 2. . . . as well as anecdotal experiences, that supported their own assessments. . . .
[Lines 8–9]
    a. individual accounts
    b. experiments
    c. clinical observations
    d. theories

_____ 3. Might there be another plausible explanation. . . . [Lines 20–21]
    a. scientific
    b. logically acceptable
    c. supported by verifiable evidence
    d. equivalent

_____ 4. . . . people's reports of strange phenomena must be taken with a grain of salt.
[Lines 27–28]
    a. aliens
    b. unusual talent
    c. belief in the supernatural
    d. events

_____ 5. Intriguing as accounts of alien <u>abductions</u> or
          angelic rescues may be. . . . [Lines 30–31]
          a. rescues
          b. kidnappings
          c. travels
          d. examinations

Critical Response Questions

1. Based on what you have read, do you consider psychology a science? Why or why not?

   _____

   _____

   _____

2. Are the three principles equal in importance? How are they related?

   _____

   _____

   _____

3. How can the three principles help you to be a critical thinker in your day-to-day life?

   _____

   _____

   _____

Sample Annotations for Exercise 6

THREE PRINCIPLES
OF SCIENTIFIC ENDEAVOR

[As a science, psychology is committed to objectivity, accuracy, and healthy skepticism about the study of behavior and mental processes. These three basic principles are at the very core of psychology—they are part of what makes it a science. They can also help you be a critical thinker in your day-to-day life.

Objectivity

① 5 [For psychologists, objectivity means evaluating research and theory on their merits, without preconceived ideas.] For example, when scientists challenged *ex.* the validity and usefulness of lie detector tests to select truthful employees, both believers and skeptics stepped up offering case studies, as well as anecdotal experiences, that supported their own assessments of the usefulness of these tests. Psychologists attempt to bring scientific objectivity to the research

10 arena; they know that anecdotal reports are seldom objective and that though *importance of* they can explain events after they have happened, they are too limited to sup-*predicting* port predictions about future behavior or mental processes. Remember, scientists want to both describe *and* predict. Common sense relies heavily on looking backward—using hindsight—but is not very objective or reliable when

15 it comes to making predictions about behavior.

Accuracy

② [Psychologists are concerned with gathering data from the laboratory and the real world in precise ways—that is, with accuracy.] For instance, to conclude from a small number of eyewitness accounts that whole communities have *ex.* been abducted by aliens falls considerably short of scientific accuracy. Might

20 there be another plausible explanation for astonishingly similar accounts of small, ghostly figures levitating people into flying-saucer laboratories? Might those reporting such incidents suffer from similar psychological disorders? Rather than relying on limited samples and immediate impressions, psychologists base their thinking on precise, detailed, and thorough study.

Healthy Skepticism

don't believe 25 One needn't be a scientific researcher to realize that although life *is* full of in-*easily* credible events, people's reports of strange phenomena must be taken with a grain of salt. Most people think twice when they hear stories like that of the *ex.* woman who reported that she was saved from falling off an alpine precipice by an angelic rescuer who suddenly appeared and then disappeared. Intriguing as *Require proof* 30 accounts of alien abductions or angelic rescues may be, psychologists maintain a healthy skepticism—a cautious view of data, hypotheses, and theory until results are repeated, verified, and established over time.

From *Psychology*, 7th ed., by Lester A. Lefton. Boston: Allyn & Bacon, 2000.

Sociology

WHAT IS A FAMILY?

Sociologists are interested in group interaction and in social organization. The family has been much studied, therefore, by sociologists (as well as anthropologists, who study human culture).

Complete Exercise 7 to learn how sociologists have wrestled with defining the all-important but elusive concept of family.

WHAT IS A FAMILY?

"What is a family, anyway?" asked William Sayres at the beginning of an article on this topic. By this question, he meant that although the family is so significant to humanity that it is universal—every human group in the world organizes its members in families—the world's cultures display so much variety that

5 the term *family* is difficult to define. For example, although the Western world regards a family as a husband, wife, and children, other groups have family forms in which men have more than one wife (**polygyny**) or women more than one husband (**polyandry**). How about the obvious? Can we define the family as the approved group into which children are born? This would overlook the

10 Banaro of New Guinea. In this group, a young woman must give birth before she can marry—and she *cannot* marry the father of her child.

And so it goes. For just about every element you might regard as essential to marriage or family, some group has a different custom. Consider the sex of the bride and groom. Although in almost every instance the bride and groom

15 are female and male, there are exceptions. In some Native American tribes, a man or woman who wanted to be a member of the opposite sex went through a ceremony (*berdache*) and was *declared* a member of the opposite sex. From then on, not only did the "new" man or woman do the tasks associated with his or her new sex, but also the individual was allowed to marry. In this in-

20 stance, the husband and wife were of the same biological sex. In the 1980s, several European countries legalized same-sex marriages. In 2003, so did the province of Ontario, Canada.

What if we were to say that the family is the unit in which children are disciplined and that parents are responsible for their material needs? This, too, is

25 not universal. Among the Trobriand Islanders, the wife's eldest brother is responsible for making certain that his sister's children have food and for disci-

plining them when they get out of line. Finally, even sexual relationships don't universally characterize a husband and wife. The Nayar of Malabar never allow a bride and groom to have sex. After a three-day celebration of marriage, they
30 send the groom packing—and never allow him to see his bride again. (In case you're wondering, the groom comes from another tribe. Nayar women are allowed to have sex, but only with approved lovers—who can never be the husband. This system keeps family property intact—along matrilineal lines.)

Such remarkable variety means that we have to settle for a broad definition.
35 A **family** consists of people who consider themselves related by blood, marriage, or adoption. A **household,** in contrast, consists of people who occupy the same housing unit—a house, apartment, or other living quarters.

We can classify families as **nuclear** (husband, wife, and children) and **extended** (including people such as grandparents, aunts, uncles, and cousins
40 in addition to the nuclear unit). Sociologists also refer to the **family of orientation** (the family in which an individual grow up) and the **family of procreation** (the family formed when a couple have their first child). Finally, regardless of its form, **marriage** can be viewed as a group's approved mating arrangements—usually marked by a ritual of some sort (the wedding) to indi-
45 cate the couple's new public status.

From *Sociology: A Down-to-Earth Approach*, 7th ed., by James Henslin. New York: Pearson Education, 2005.

Comprehension Questions

1. Why is *family* difficult to define?

_____

_____

2. What is the difference between a family and a household?

_____

_____

_____ 3. The author mentions the Banaro of New Guinea to show that
    a. polygamy is common in many cultures.
    b. a family cannot necessarily be considered the group into which children are born.
    c. same-sex marriages are accepted in some cultures.
    d. the need for family is universal.

_____ 4. The author states that sexual relationships
    a. are not always a part of marriage.
    b. are always part of a marriage.
    c. are viewed as the cornerstone of family existence in most cultures.
    d. are generally forbidden outside of marriage in most cultures.

_____ 5. We can conclude that
   a. most cultures favor nuclear families.
   b. a person's extended family is usually more important than her nuclear family.
   c. a person's nuclear family cannot also be his family of orientation.
   d. a person's family of orientation may not be the same as her family of procreation.

Directions. Mark each of the following statements True (T), False (F), or Can't Tell (CT). Mark the statement Can't Tell if it is neither supported nor contradicted by the passage.

_____ 6. Families exist in all human cultures.

_____ 7. Some New Guinea tribes practice polygyny.

_____ 8. Bride and groom are always male and female in all cultures.

_____ 9. The Trobriand Islanders do not allow sex between bride and groom.

_____10. Marriage usually involves a ritual that makes public the couple's new status.

Recognizing Organizational Patterns

What is the primary pattern of organization used in this passage? Explain your answer.

_____

_____

Vocabulary Questions

Directions. Choose the meaning for the underlined word that best fits the context. You may consult the dictionary as needed.

_____ 1. ... the family is so significant to humanity that it is <u>universal</u> ... [Lines 2–3]
   a. necessary
   b. popular
   c. appealing
   d. present everywhere

_____ 2. This system keeps family property <u>intact</u>— along matrilineal lines. [Line 33]
   a. complete
   b. incomplete
   c. valuable
   d. lacking ownership

_____ 3. This system keeps family property intact— along <u>matrilineal</u> lines. [Line 33]
   a. through the mother
   b. through the father
   c. through the family
   d. through a system of derived merit

_____ 4. ... usually marked by a <u>ritual</u> of some sort (the wedding) to indicate the couple's new public status. [Lines 44–45]
   a. party or large-scale celebration
   b. announcement
   c. written statement
   d. ceremony; formal observance

_____ 5. . . . usually marked by a ritual of some sort
(the wedding) to indicate the couple's new
public status. [Lines 44–45]
   a. observation
   b. marriage
   c. position
   d. pride in achievement

Critical Response Questions

1. Why is there so much variation from culture to culture as to what constitutes a family?

   _____

   _____

   _____

2. Why do sociologists distinguish between family of orientation and family of procreation? Why is this distinction important?

   _____

   _____

   _____

3. Why is marriage an important cultural institution?

   _____

   _____

   _____

EXERCISE

Anthropology

YOUTH GANGS

Anthropologists compare human cultures, studying similarities and differences from culture to culture. Like sociologists, they are interested in social organization. All cultures have social groups.

Youth gangs are a kind of social group found in many cultures. Complete Exercise 8 to learn how a cultural anthropologist approaches the study of youth gangs.

YOUTH GANGS

The term *gang* can refer to a variety of groups, such as one's friends, as in "I think I'll invite the gang over for pizza." The more specific term **youth gang** refers to a group of young people, found mainly in urban areas, who are often considered a social problem by adults and law enforcement officials.

5　　Youth gangs vary in terms of how formally they are organized. Gangs—like clubs and fraternities—often have a recognized leader, formalized rituals of initiation for new members, and symbolic markers of identity such as tattoos or special clothing. An example of an informal youth gang with no formal leadership hierarchy or initiation rituals is that of the "Masta Liu" in Honiara, the capi-

10　　tal city of the Solomon Islands, the South Pacific. The primary unifying feature of the male youth who become Masta Liu is the fact that they are unemployed. Most have migrated to the city from the countryside to escape what they consider an undesirable lifestyle there: working in the fields under control of their elders. Some *liu* live with extended kin in the city, others organize liu-only

15　　households. They spend their time wandering around town (*wakabaot*) in groups of up to ten: "They stop at every shop on their way, eager to look at the merchandise but afraid to be kicked out by the security guards; they check out all the cinemas only to dream in front of the preview posters . . . not even having the $2 bill that will allow them to get in; they gaze for hours on end, and with-

20　　out moving, at the electronic equipment displayed in the Chinese shops, without saying a word: one can read in their gaze the silent dreams they create."

"Street gangs" are a more formal variety of youth gang. They generally have leaders and a hierarchy of membership roles and responsibilities. They are named, and their members mark their identity with tattoos or "colors." Much

25　　popular thinking associates street gangs with violence, but not all are involved

30

in violence. An anthropologist who did research among nearly forty street gangs in New York, Los Angeles, and Boston learned much about why individuals join gangs, providing insights that also contradict popular thinking. One common perception is that young boys join gangs because they are from homes with no male authority figure with whom they could identify. In the gangs studied, just as many gang members were from intact nuclear households. Another common perception is that the gang replaces a missing feeling of family. This study showed that the same number of gang members reported having close family ties as those who didn't.

35

40

What, then, might be the reasons behind joining a male urban gang? A particular personality type characterized many gang members, a type that could be called a "defiant individualist." The defiant individualist type has five traits: intense competitiveness, mistrust or wariness, self-reliance, social isolation, and a strong survival instinct. A structurist view* suggests that poverty, especially urban poverty, leads to the development of this kind of personality structure. Within the context of urban poverty, such a personality structure becomes a reasonable response to the prevailing economic obstacles and uncertainty.

*structurist view: the view that an individual's choices are shaped by larger social, economic, and political forces.

From *Cultural Anthropology*, 3rd ed., by Barbara D. Miller. New York: Pearson Education, 2005.

Comprehension Questions

1. What is a youth gang?

_____

2. Why do some youth in Honiara become Masta Liu?

_____

_____ **3.** Which is *not* mentioned as a feature of gang organization?
   a. private or secret language
   b. leadership and hierarchy
   c. initiation rituals
   d. identity markers

_____ **4.** Regarding violence, the author states that
   a. gang members who come from nuclear homes are less likely to be violent.
   b. violence among gangs is increasing.
   c. violence among gangs is decreasing.
   d. not all gangs participate in violent activity.

_____ 5. The author suggests that the defiant individualist type personality results from
     a. unfavorable economic conditions.
     b. lack of family.
     c. exposure to physical and emotional abuse.
     d. genetic (inherited) tendencies.

Directions. Mark each of the following statements True (T), False (F), or Can't Tell (CT). Mark the statement Can't Tell if it is neither supported nor contradicted by the passage.

_____ 6. The Masta Liu in Honiara are poor youth who wander about the town looking for opportunities to steal merchandise or sneak into theaters.

_____ 7. All gangs have recognized leaders and initiation rituals.

_____ 8. A special tattoo or special clothing may be used to mark gang identity.

_____ 9. Gang members are almost always young people from broken homes.

_____ 10. Many people believe that gang members are almost always young people from broken homes.

Recognizing Organizational Patterns

Definition, comparison–contrast, and cause–effect are all used in this passage. Which pattern of organization most helped you to understand the main ideas of this passage? Explain your answer.

_____

_____

Vocabulary Questions

Directions. Choose the meaning for the underlined word that best fits the context. You may consult the dictionary as needed.

_____ 1. Youth gangs . . . often have . . . formalized rituals of underline{initiation} for new members . . .
[Lines 5–7]
     a. difficulty
     b. testing
     c. secrecy
     d. admission

_____ 2. An example of an informal youth gang with no formal leadership underline{hierarchy} . . .
[Lines 8–9]
     a. recognized leadership
     a. ranking order
     c. skills
     d. process by which leaders are selected

_____ 3. ...a type that could be called a "<u>defiant</u> individualist." [Lines 36–37]
   a. rebellious
   b. angry
   c. wanting to be on one's own; solitary
   d. possessing leadership qualities

_____ 4. The defiant individualist type has five traits: intense competitiveness, mistrust or <u>wariness</u> ... [Lines 37–38]
   a. competitiveness
   b. cautiousness
   c. sociability
   d. cleverness

_____ 5. Within the context of urban poverty, such a personality structure becomes a reasonable response to the <u>prevailing</u> economic obstacles and uncertainty. [Lines 41–42]
   a. complete
   b. unpredictable
   c. unfavorable
   d. widespread

Critical Response Questions

1. In your opinion, why do young people join gangs?

_____

_____

_____

2. Why might gangs use initiation rituals?

_____

_____

_____

3. How do gangs harm society? How do gangs help society?

_____

_____

_____

Political Science

THE U.S. PRESIDENCY

Political scientists study government and politics. The following excerpt was taken from an American government textbook. Complete Exercise 9 to learn more about the powers and responsibilities of the American presidency.

THE U.S. PRESIDENCY

The authority granted to the president by the U.S. Constitution and through subsequent congressional legislation makes it a position with awesome responsibility. Not only did the Framers not envision such a powerful role for the president, but they could not have foreseen the skepticism with which many presi-

5   dential actions are now greeted in the press, on talk radio, and on the Internet. Presidents have gone into policy arenas never dreamed of by the Framers. Imagine, for example, what the Framers might have thought about President Bush's 2004 State of the Union message, which advocated colonizing Mars and addressed steroid use.

10   The modern media, used by successful presidents to help advance their agendas, have brought us closer to our presidents and made them seem more human, a mixed blessing for those trying to lead. Only two photographs exist of Franklin D. Roosevelt in a wheelchair—his paralysis was a closely guarded secret. Five decades later, Bill Clinton was asked on national TV what kind of un-

15   derwear he preferred (briefs). Later, revelations about his conduct with Monica Lewinsky made this exchange seem tame. This demystifying of the president and the increased mistrust of government make governing a difficult job.

    A president relies on more than the formal powers of office to lead the nation: public opinion and public confidence are key components of his ability

20   to get his programs adopted and his vision of the nation implemented. As political scientist Richard E. Neustadt has noted, the president's power often rests on his power to persuade. To persuade, he not only must be able to forge links with members of Congress, but he also must have the support of the American people and the respect of foreign leaders.

25   The abilities to persuade and to marshal the informal powers of the presidency have become more important over time. In fact, the presidency of George W. Bush and the circumstances that surround it are dramatically different from the presidency of his father George Bush (1989–1993). America is

30   changing dramatically and so are the responsibilities of the president and people's expectations of the person who holds that office. Presidents in the last
century battled the Great Depression, fascism, communism, and several wars
involving American soldiers. With the Cold War over, until the war in Iraq,
there were few chances for modern presidents to demonstrate their leadership
in a time of crisis or threat.

From *American Government: Continuity and Change,* 2006 ed., by Karen O'Connor and Larry Sabato.
New York: Pearson Education, 2006.

Comprehension Questions

1. Who are the Framers referred to in this passage?

_____

2. According to the passage, how have the media influenced public perception of the
presidency?

_____

_____ 3. The authors suggest that issues facing modern presidents
   a. are inconsistent with the Constitution.
   b. were anticipated by the Constitution's Framers.
   c. could not have been anticipated by the Constitution's Framers.
   d. are essentially the same as those faced by earlier presidents.

_____ 4. Which of the following is not mentioned in the passage as a source of presidential
power?
   a. Supreme Court rulings
   b. public opinion
   c. legislation
   d. the Constitution

_____ 5. We can conclude from the passage that future presidents
   a. will avoid media exposure.
   b. will face different issues and expectations.
   c. will face more serious crises.
   d. will not face more serious crises.

Directions. Mark each of the following statements True (T), False (F), or Can't Tell
(CT). Mark the statement Can't Tell if it is neither supported nor contradicted by the
passage.

_____ 6. Many Americans did not realize that Franklin Roosevelt was paralyzed.

_____ 7. The more effective a president's persuasive skills, the more likely he is to succeed with his agenda.

_____ 8. There has been little change in the challenges facing American presidents since World War II.

_____ 9. President Clinton was embarrassed when asked about his underwear preferences.

_____ 10. Much of the authority of the president is derived from the Constitution.

Recognizing Organizational Patterns

Identify two cause–effect relationships discussed in the passage.

_____

_____

Vocabulary Questions

Directions. Choose the meaning for the underlined word that best fits the context. You may consult the dictionary as needed.

_____ 1. The authority granted to the president . . . through subsequent congressional legislation . . . [Lines 1–2]
   a. new
   b. important
   c. repeated
   d. following

_____ 2. . . . they could not have foreseen the skepticism with which many presidential actions are now greeted . . . [Lines 4–5]
   a. surprise
   b. doubt
   c. appreciation
   d. ridicule

_____ 3. . . . President Bush's . . . message, which advocated colonizing Mars . . . [Lines 7–8]
   a. supported
   b. addressed
   c. mentioned
   d. criticized

_____ 4. This demystifying of the president and the increased mistrust of government make governing a difficult job. [Lines 16–17]
   a. trusting without question
   b. criticizing without reason
   c. making more mysterious
   d. making less mysterious

_____ 5. The abilities to persuade and to marshal the informal powers of the presidency have become more important over time. [Lines 25–26]
   a. a law enforcement officer
   b. assemble
   c. arrest
   d. convince

Critical Response Questions

1. How does public opinion affect the decisions and actions of the president? Give one or two examples.

_____

_____

_____

2. Has the job of the president become harder or easier? Explain your answer.

_____

_____

_____

3. In your opinion, what are the most important qualities for a good president?

_____

_____

_____

Economics

WHAT IS MONEY?

Economics is the social science that studies the use and distribution of resources. Macroeconomics studies large-scale economic issues (such as inflation). Microeconomics studies the parts of the economic system on a smaller scale (such as how a company sets the prices for its products).

Money is central to modern economies. Complete Exercise 10 to gain a better understanding of money as an economic concept and its importance in a modern economic system.

WHAT IS MONEY?

Throughout history, a number of things—gold or silver coins, paper money, cattle, and even beads, stones, and red parrot feathers—have served as money. Money is the medium of exchange used in transactions that transfer ownership of goods and services and assets from one person to another.

The Three Functions of Money

5   **Money** is used to buy things, to measure values, and as a mode for savings. Thus, money carries out the three functions discussed below.

Money Serves as a Medium of Exchange

For money to serve its most important function as a medium of exchange, it must be generally accepted as a means of paying for things and settling debts. Money serves as a common object acceptable to all parties in a transaction

10   and eliminates the necessity of barter. If there were no generally acceptable medium of exchange, the shoemaker who wanted to buy a bushel of wheat would have to find a wheat farmer who wanted to buy shoes and the two would have to strike an agreement on the terms of exchange. It is difficult to conceive of a modern economy functioning efficiently on this double coin-

15   cidence of wants. With money as a medium of exchange, the shoemaker who wants to buy wheat can buy from any seller of wheat, not just one who wants shoes; the buyer of shoes can buy from any seller of shoes, not just one who wants to buy wheat.

Money Is a Unit of Value

The value of a good is what it can be exchanged for in the economy. In a barter
20 economy, a pair of shoes might be worth, for example, two cotton shirts, 1 percent of a milk cow, or ten loaves of bread. It is, obviously, inconvenient to keep
track of the value of a particular commodity by remembering its terms of exchange with every other commodity, and it becomes very complicated when
fractions of commodities—such as 1 percent of a cow—are involved. Money
25 prices serve as the common denominator in which the values of all goods and
services are expressed. Relative prices are determined by dividing one money
price by another. If a pair of shoes costs $40, a loaf of bread $1, and a cow $1000,
the price of shoes relative to all these commodities is immediately evident.

Money Is a Store of Value

People accumulate wealth by not spending all their disposable income. They
30 accumulate assets—stocks, bonds, gold, works of art—which can be held over
a period of time and can be converted eventually into money. But wealth can
also be stored in the form of money. The medium of exchange can act as a
store of value. Inflation reduces the usefulness of money as a store of value because the amount of goods and services that each "stored" dollar can purchase
35 falls as prices rise.

From *Essentials of Economics*, 4th ed., by Paul R. Gregory. Boston: Addison-Wesley Educational
Publishers, 1999.

Comprehension Questions

1. What is money?

_____

2. What is a relative price?

_____

____ 3. One reason money is superior to barter is that
   a. money makes goods less expensive.
   b. services cannot be exchanged through barter.
   c. money provides a common medium of exchange.
   d. the value of money does not change.

_____ 4. Money's function as a *unit of value* refers to its
   a. tendency to increase in value when stored.
   b. convenience in expressing the value of goods.
   c. ability to convert wealth into various forms.
   d. convenience as a means of exchange.

_____ 5. One effect of inflation is that
   a. the stored value of money is reduced.
   b. people tend to store more money.
   c. money is no longer accepted as a medium of exchange.
   d. the value of a service can no longer be expressed in dollars.

Directions. Mark each of the following statements True (T), False (F), or Can't Tell (CT). Mark the statement Can't Tell if it is neither supported nor contradicted by the passage.

_____ 6. Parrot feathers are still used in some parts of the world as money.

_____ 7. The three functions of money are of equal importance.

_____ 8. The author implies that a modern economy could not function effectively without money.

_____ 9. In a barter system, all goods are of approximately equal value.

_____ 10. Wealth cannot be accumulated without money.

Recognizing Organizational Patterns

What is the primary pattern of organization used in this passage? Explain your answer.

_____

_____

Vocabulary Questions

Directions. Choose the meaning for the underlined word that best fits the context. You may consult the dictionary as needed.

_____ 1. Money is the medium of exchange used in transactions. . . . [Line 3]
   a. average
   b. in between
   c. best form
   d. means

_____ 2. . . . that transfer ownership of goods and services and assets from one person to another. [Lines 3–4]
   a. forms of money
   b. things of value
   c. goods or services
   d. modes of exchange

_____ 3. In a barter economy, a pair of shoes might be worth . . . two cotton shirts. . . . [Lines 19–20]
   a. trade
   b. money
   c. value-based
   d. commodity

_____ 4. It is, obviously, inconvenient to keep track of the value of a particular commodity. . . . [Lines 21–22]
   a. service
   b. precious material
   c. product that has economic value
   d. a useful object that is sold at a high price

_____ 5. People accumulate wealth by not spending all their disposable income. [Line 29]
   a. cash
   b. spendable
   c. more than is needed for life's necessities
   d. accumulated

Critical Response Questions

1. Which function of money is considered most important? Why?

_____

_____

_____

2. What are some possible advantages of a barter system over a money system?

_____

_____

_____

3. If inflation were high, how might wealth be stored to protect its value? (That is, what are some alternatives to money?)

_____

_____

_____

Math and Science

EXERCISE

Chemistry

COMPOSITION AND PROPERTIES OF MATTER

The natural sciences include subjects such as biology, physics, chemistry, earth science, geology, astronomy, and meteorology. These are the sciences that study the physical world.

The natural sciences rely almost exclusively on objective research: careful collection of verifiable evidence, formulation of verifiable hypotheses, and accurate measurement.

Reading in the natural sciences, then, involves several key differences from reading in other disciplines:

- Knowledge is cumulative; that is, knowledge is based on, or derived from, previous knowledge.
- Concepts are more precisely defined and must, therefore, be more precisely understood.
- Scientific reading material tends to be *dense,* meaning that it contains more information with fewer examples and less discussion.
- Often the reader's task is to follow the steps of a process or understand how a concept is applied. In other words, abstract scientific concepts apply to observable, real-world phenomena.

In this excerpt from a chemistry textbook, the authors discuss two types of matter. Complete Exercise 11 to learn the differences between heterogeneous and homogeneous matter.

COMPOSITION AND PROPERTIES OF MATTER

Regardless of its physical state, all matter is either homogeneous or heterogeneous.

Heterogeneous and Homogeneous Matter

Homogeneous and heterogeneous matter differ from one another in very clear ways. **Homogeneous matter** is *uniform* in composition and properties. It is the same throughout. **Heterogeneous matter** is *not uniform* in composition and properties. It consists of two or more physically distinct *portions* or *phases*

5

unevenly distributed. A class consisting of all women would be analogous to homogeneous matter, while a class of both men and women would be analogous to heterogeneous matter.

10   Heterogeneous matter is also commonly called a *mixture*. This type of **mixture** is composed of two or more pure substances, each of which retains its identity and specific properties. The properties of the mixture depend on what part of the mixture is being observed. In many mixtures, substances can be readily identified by visual observation. For example, in a mixture of salt and

15   sand, the human eye or a hand lens can be used to distinguish between the white salt crystals and the tan sand crystals. Similarly, in a mixture of iron and sulfur, visual observation can identify the yellow sulfur and the black iron. Mixtures can usually be separated by a simple operation that does not change the composition of the several pure substances comprising the mixture. For exam-

20   ple, a mixture of salt and sand can be separated by using water. The salt dissolves in water, but the sand does not. If, after removing the sand, we evaporate the water, we are then left with pure salt. A mixture of iron and sulfur can be separated by dissolving the sulfur in liquid carbon disulfide (the iron is insoluble) or by attracting the iron to a magnet (the sulfur is not attracted).

25   We can further divide homogeneous matter into three categories: homogeneous mixtures, solutions, and pure substances. A **homogeneous mixture** is homogeneous throughout and is composed of two or more pure substances whose proportions may be *varied* in some cases without limit. The properties of the substance do not depend on what part of the material is being observed;

30   all samples of the substance look the same. One example of a homogeneous mixture is unpolluted air, which is a mixture of oxygen, nitrogen, and certain other gases.

Mixtures of gases are generally called homogeneous mixtures, but homogeneous mixtures composed of gases, liquids, or solids dissolved in *liquids* are

35   called *solutions*. A **solution** is homogeneous throughout and is composed of two or more pure substances. However, its composition usually can be varied *within certain limits*. Some common examples of solutions are sugar solutions (sugar dissolved in water), salt solutions (salt dissolved in water), carbonated water (carbon dioxide dissolved in water), alcohol solutions (ethyl alcohol dis-

40   solved in water), and vinegar (acetic acid dissolved in water). In some cases, solids may dissolve in other solids to form homogeneous mixtures called solid solutions. Brass is a solid solution consisting of zinc dissolved in copper.

From *Basic Chemistry*, 7th ed., by G. William Daub and William S. Seese. Upper Saddle River, NJ: Prentice-Hall, 1996.

Comprehension Questions

1. What is the primary difference between heterogeneous and homogeneous matter?

2. Explain the difference between a heterogeneous mixture and a homogeneous mixture.

_____

_____

_____ 3. Which of the following statements is true of mixtures?
    a. All mixtures are homogeneous.
    b. All mixtures are heterogeneous.
    c. Properties of the substances contained in mixtures usually cannot be identified.
    d. The substances contained in a mixture can often be separated.

_____ 4. Which of the following statements is true of solutions?
    a. All homogeneous mixtures are solutions.
    b. Solutions are usually heterogeneous.
    c. The amount dissolved can vary.
    d. All solutions have the same percentage of liquid.

_____ 5. Which of the following is *not* a solution?
    a. vinegar
    b. air
    c. brass
    d. carbonated water

Directions. Mark each of the following statements True (T), False (F), or Can't Tell (CT). Mark the statement Can't Tell if it is neither supported nor contradicted by the passage.

_____ 6. Heterogeneous matter is more common than homogeneous matter.

_____ 7. Solutions must always contain at least one liquid.

_____ 8. Mixtures can be heterogeneous or homogeneous.

_____ 9. Homogeneous matter consists of uniformly distributed substances in varying proportions.

_____ 10. The properties of heterogeneous mixtures vary according to the part of the mixture under observation.

Recognizing Organizational Patterns

How do the authors use comparison–contrast to organize the material in this selection?

_____

_____

Vocabulary Questions

Directions. Choose the meaning for the underlined word that best fits the context. You may consult the dictionary as needed.

_____ 1. Homogeneous matter is <u>uniform</u> in composition and properties. [Line 4]
   a. clothed or surrounded by
   b. inconsistent
   c. structured
   d. consistent

_____ 2. Homogeneous matter is uniform in composition and <u>properties</u>. [Line 4]
   a. characteristics
   b. ownership
   c. makeup
   d. structure

_____ 3. A class consisting of all women would be <u>analogous</u> to homogeneous matter.... [Lines 7–8]
   a. capable of analysis
   b. different from
   c. homogeneous
   d. comparable

_____ 4. ... the iron is <u>insoluble</u>.... [Lines 23–24]
   a. able to dissolve
   b. not able to dissolve
   c. able to solve
   d. not able to solve

_____ 5. Some common examples of solutions are sugar solutions ... <u>carbonated</u> water.... [Lines 37–39]
   a. containing suspended carbon molecules
   b. having no carbon compounds
   c. containing dissolved carbon dioxide
   d. having supplemental carbon compounds

Critical Response Questions

1. Why is it important for chemistry students to understand the difference between homogeneous and heterogeneous matter? How would this information be used by scientists?

_____

_____

_____

2. What previous knowledge is required to understand the concepts in this passage?

_____

_____

_____

3. Does the information contained in this passage have any application in daily life? Explain your answer.

_____

_____

_____

Sample Annotations for Exercise 11

COMPOSITION AND PROPERTIES OF MATTER

Regardless of its physical state, all matter is either homogeneous or heterogeneous.

Heterogeneous and Homogeneous Matter

**difference between uniform vs. not uniform

Homogeneous and heterogeneous matter differ from one another in very clear ways. **Homogeneous matter** is *uniform* in composition and properties. It is the same throughout. **Heterogeneous matter** is *not uniform* in composition and properties. It consists of two or more physically distinct *portions* or *phases* unevenly distributed. A class consisting of all women would be analogous to homogeneous matter, while a class of both men and women would be analogous to heterogeneous matter.

ex.

mixtures

Heterogeneous matter is also commonly called a *mixture*. This type of **mixture** is composed of two or more pure substances, each of which retains its identity and specific properties. The properties of the mixture depend on what part of the mixture is being observed. In many mixtures, substances can be readily identified by visual observation. For example, in a mixture of salt and sand, the human eye or a hand lens can be used to distinguish between the white salt crystals and the tan sand crystals. Similarly, in a mixture of iron and sulfur, visual observation can identify the yellow sulfur and the black iron.

ex.

can separate substances

ex.

Mixtures can usually be separated by a simple operation that does not change the composition of the several pure substances comprising the mixture. For example, a mixture of salt and sand can be separated by using water. The salt dissolves in water, but the sand does not. If, after removing the sand, we evaporate the water, we are then left with pure salt. A mixture of iron and sulfur can be separated by dissolving the sulfur in liquid carbon disulfide (the iron is insoluble) or by attracting the iron to a magnet (the sulfur is not attracted).

homogeneous mixture

proportions can vary

ex.

We can further divide homogeneous matter into three categories: homogeneous mixtures, solutions, and pure substances. A **homogeneous mixture** is homogeneous throughout and is composed of two or more pure substances whose proportions may be *varied* in some cases without limit. The properties of the substance do not depend on what part of the material is being observed; all samples of the substance look the same. One example of a homogeneous mixture is unpolluted air, which is a mixture of oxygen, nitrogen, and certain other gases.

solutions

vary within limits

Mixtures of gases are generally called homogeneous mixtures, but homogeneous mixtures composed of gases, liquids, or solids dissolved in *liquids* are called *solutions*. A **solution** is homogeneous throughout and is composed of two or more pure substances. However, its composition usually can be varied *within certain limits*. Some common examples of solutions are sugar solutions *ex.*

40

(sugar dissolved in water), salt solutions (salt dissolved in water), carbonated water (carbon dioxide dissolved in water), alcohol solutions (ethyl alcohol dissolved in water), and vinegar (acetic acid dissolved in water). In some cases, solids may dissolve in other solids to form homogeneous mixtures called solid solutions. Brass is a solid solution consisting of zinc dissolved in copper.

From *Basic Chemistry*, 7th ed., by G. William Daub and William S. Seese. Upper Saddle River, NJ: Prentice-Hall, 1996.

Biology

ELEPHANTS CALLING

Biology is the natural science by which we study living things and life processes. The Greek root *bios* means life.

The field of biology encompasses the study of all living things, from microscopic organisms to the largest mammals that have inhabited our planet. The following excerpt recounts one biologist's experiences with her study of elephants. Complete Exercise 12 to learn how she approached her study and what she discovered.

ELEPHANTS CALLING

Humans aren't the only animals to use language to communicate. Consider an elephant's extended family. An elephant clan, led by an elder female, or matriarch, and consisting of females and young males, has quite a vocabulary. Elephants communicate using infrasound, which is sound too low for human ears
5   to detect.

In 1984, Cornell University researcher Katy Payne was standing near caged elephants at a zoo when she felt a "throbbing" in the air. The sensation brought back memories of singing in the church choir as a child where the church organ pipes made a similar throbbing. "In the zoo I felt the same thing . . . , with-
10   out any sound. I guessed the elephants might be making powerful sounds like an organ's notes, but even lower in pitch," she writes in her children's book, *Elephants Calling*.

To test her hypothesis, Payne and two friends used equipment that could detect infrasound to record elephants in a circus and a zoo. Finding infrasound,
15   she moved her study to the Amboseli Plain, a salty, dusty stretch of land at the foot of Mount Kilimanjaro in Tanzania. Her lab was a truck sitting among the elephants, who grew so used to its presence that they regarded it as part of the scenery.

Living among the elephants further sharpened Payne's already highly devel-
20   oped powers of observation. She and her fellow elephant watchers soon became attuned to the subtle communications between mother and calf; the urges of a male ready to mate; and messages to move to find food or water. Writes Payne, "It is amazing how much you can learn about animals if you watch for a long time without disturbing them. They do odd things, which at
25   first you don't understand. Then gradually your mind opens to what it would

be like to have different eyes, different ears, and different taste; different needs, different fears, and different knowledge from ours."

One day, two bulls were fighting for dominance when the youngest family member, baby Raoul, slipped away. Finding a hole, Raoul stuck his trunk in-
30 side—then leapt back, bellowing, as a very surprised warthog bounded out of his invaded burrow. Raoul's mother, Renata, responded with a bellow. Payne described the scene:

> Elephants in all directions answer Renata, and they answer each other with roars, screams, bellows, trumpets, and rumbles. Male and female elephants
> 35 of all sizes and ages charge past each other and us with eyes wide, foreheads high, trunks, tails, and ears swinging wildly. The air throbs with infrasound made not only by elephants' voices but also by their thundering feet. Running legs and swaying bodies loom toward and above us and veer away at the last second.

40 The family reunited, all the animals clearly shaken. Unable to resist compar-
ing the pachyderms to people, Payne writes, "Renata does not seem angry at Raoul. Perhaps elephants don't ask for explanations."

The kind of observation that leads to new knowledge and understanding, Payne says, happens only rarely. "You have to be alone and undistracted. You
45 have to be concentrating on what's there, as if it were the only thing in the world and you were a tiny child again. The observation comes the way a dream—or a poem—comes. Being ready is what brings it to you."

From *Life*, 5th ed., by Ricki Lewis et al. New York: McGraw-Hill, 2004.

Comprehension Questions

1. How did Payne's powers of observation help her research elephant communication?

   _____

2. How did the elephant clan respond to Renata's distress call?

   _____

_____ 3. Regarding animal communication, we can conclude that
   a. elephants are the only species who communicate through infrasound.
   b. most species use infrasound to communicate.
   c. all species use complex systems of sound to communicate.
   d. human beings may not yet have discovered how all species communicate.

_____ **4.** The passage mentions *all* of the following purposes for elephant communication *except*
  a. mating.
  b. finding food.
  c. ending a fight.
  d. a mother responding to her calf.

_____ **5.** Payne seems to believe that
  a. elephant communication is as complex as human communication.
  b. elephants may experience some emotions similar to those experienced by humans.
  c. elephants are the most intelligent (nonhuman) species.
  d. scientists should not interpret animals' emotions.

Directions. Mark each of the following statements True (T), False (F), or Can't Tell (CT). Mark the statement Can't Tell if it is neither supported nor contradicted by the passage.

_____ **6.** Raoul had never seen a warthog before.

_____ **7.** Payne believes that biologists can learn a great deal about animals by observing them in their natural surroundings.

_____ **8.** The study of zoo animals often leads biologists to observe animals in their natural habitats.

_____ **9.** Raoul's mother punished him for creating an unnecessary ruckus.

_____ **10.** Payne's powers of observation improved while studying elephants in Tanzania.

Recognizing Organizational Patterns

Identify two paragraphs in the passage in which chronological order is used. Explain your answer.

_____

_____

Vocabulary Questions

Directions. Choose the meaning for the underlined word that best fits the context. You may consult the dictionary as needed.

_____ **1.** To test her hypothesis, Payne and her two friends used equipment ... [Line 13]
  a. theory
  b. research
  c. experiment
  d. research subjects

_____ **2.** ... soon became attuned to the subtle communications between mother and calf ... [Lines 20–21]
  a. frequent
  b. important
  c. obvious
  d. not obvious

_____ 3. One day, two bulls were fighting for dominance . . . [Line 28]
   a. sport
   b. authority
   c. sexual privileges
   d. independence

_____ 4. Raoul . . . leapt back, bellowing . . . [Lines 29–30]
   a. stumbling
   b. frightened
   c. roaring
   d. placing oneself in a lower position

_____ 5. Unable to resist comparing the pachyderms to people, Payne writes . . . [Lines 40–41]
   a. animals
   b. elephants
   c. animal or elephant mothers
   d. animal or elephant babies

Critical Response Questions

1. What are some advantages of observing animals in their natural environments? What are some disadvantages?

_____

_____

_____

2. What are the most important findings of Payne's research?

_____

_____

_____

3. Do you believe that animals experience emotions similar to human emotions? Explain your answer.

_____

_____

_____

Environmental Science

POPULATION GROWTH

Environmental science is a growing field. Modern concerns for protection of the environment and preservation of environmental resources have spurred an impressive amount of environmental research in the past two decades. Today, many colleges offer environmental science courses, and more colleges and universities are offering degrees in environmental science or environmental studies.

The following excerpt focuses on an issue that environmentalists believe is critical to our collective future: population growth. Complete Exercise 13 to learn more about how environmentalists are approaching this issue.

POPULATION GROWTH

Every second, on average, four or five children are born somewhere on this earth. In that same second, two other people die. This difference between births and deaths means a net gain of nearly 2.5 more humans per second in the world population. This means we are growing at a little less than 9,000 per
5 hour, 214,000 per day, or almost 78 million more people per year. In 1999, the world population passed 6 billion, making us the most numerous vertebrate species on the planet. For the families to whom these children are born, this may well be a joyous and long-awaited event. But is a continuing increase in humans good for the planet in the long run?
10 Many people worry that overpopulation will cause—or perhaps already is causing—resource depletion and environmental degradation that threaten the ecological life-support systems on which we all depend. These fears often lead to demands for immediate, worldwide birth-control programs to reduce fertility rates and to eventually stabilize or even shrink the total number of
15 humans.

Others believe that human ingenuity, technology, and enterprise can extend the world's carrying capacity and allow us to overcome any problems we encounter. From this perspective, more people may be beneficial, rather than disastrous. A larger population means a larger workforce, more geniuses, more
20 ideas about what to do. Along with every new mouth comes a pair of hands. Proponents of this worldview argue that continued economic and technological growth can both feed the world's billions and enrich everyone enough to end the population explosion voluntarily.

25   Yet another perspective on this subject derives from social justice concerns. According to this worldview, resources are sufficient for everyone. Current shortages are only signs of greed, waste, and oppression. The root cause of environmental degradation, in this view, is inequitable distribution of wealth and power rather than population size. Fostering democracy, empowering women and minorities, and improving the standard of living of the world's poorest

30   people are what are really needed. A narrow focus on population growth only fosters racism and an attitude that blames the poor for their problems, while ignoring the deeper social and economic forces at work.

Whether human populations will continue to grow at present rates and what that growth would imply for environmental quality and human life are

35   among the most central and pressing questions in environmental science.

From *Principles of Environmental Science: Inquiry and Applications*, 2nd ed., by William P. Cunningham and Mary Ann Cunningham. New York: McGraw-Hill, 2004.

Comprehension Questions

1. Why are environmental scientists concerned about human population growth?

    _____

2. How might future population growth be controlled?

    _____

_____ 3. One possible advantage of human population growth is that with increased growth
    a. diseases can be controlled more easily.
    b. more people are available to work.
    c. democracy becomes easier to achieve.
    d. resources can be shared more fairly and easily.

_____ 4. From the social justice perspective
    a. birth control is necessary if equality is to be achieved.
    b. racism results from population increase.
    c. population increases make it impossible to meet everyone's needs.
    d. if resources were divided fairly, there would be enough to meet everyone's needs.

_____ 5. We can conclude from the passage that
    a. most environmental scientists are concerned about the impact of human population growth.
    b. all environmentalists favor the use of birth control to stabilize population.
    c. social issues, such as democracy and justice, are unrelated to environmental concerns.
    d. the advantages of population increase outweigh the disadvantages.

Directions. Mark each of the following statements True (T), False (F), or Can't Tell (CT). Mark the statement Can't Tell if it is neither supported nor contradicted by the passage.

_____ 6. By 2010 Earth's human population will surpass 7 billion.

_____ 7. Human beings are the most numerous species on the planet.

_____ 8. Some people believe that human population increase is a threat to our planet's ecosystems and life support systems.

_____ 9. Some people believe that technology can help provide enough food to keep up with future increases in human population.

_____ 10. Social justice proponents believe that food shortages are a result of overpopulation.

Recognizing Organizational Patterns

Identify two cause–effect relationships discussed in the passage. Explain your answer.

_____

_____

Vocabulary Questions

Directions. Choose the meaning for the underlined word that best fits the context. You may consult the dictionary as needed.

_____ 1. Many people worry that overpopulation will cause . . . resource <u>depletion</u> and environmental degradation . . . [Lines 10–11]
   a. increase in cost
   b. scarcity
   c. reduction; using up
   d. contamination

_____ 2. Many people worry that overpopulation will cause . . . resource depletion and environmental <u>degradation</u> . . . [Lines 10–11]
   a. lowering in quality
   b. reduction in size or amount
   c. emergency; critical situation
   d. extinction or disappearance

_____ 3. Others believe that human <u>ingenuity</u>, technology, and enterprise can extend the world's carrying capacity . . . [Lines 16–17]
   a. technology
   b. wealth or capital; extensive resources

   c. cleverness
   d. information

_____ 4. <u>Proponents</u> of this worldview argue that continued economic and technological growth . . . [Lines 21–22]
   a. opponents; those against
   b. supporters; those in favor
   c. scientists or researchers
   d. people who study a given topic

_____ 5. The root cause of environmental degradation, in this view, is <u>inequitable</u> distribution of wealth and power . . . [Lines 26–28]
   a. equal
   b. unequal
   c. extensive
   d. insufficient

Critical Response Questions

1. Should birth control practices be encouraged and promoted worldwide? Why or why not?

_____

_____

_____

2. How might human ingenuity and technology help us contend with future population increases?

_____

_____

_____

3. With which of the viewpoints presented in this passage do you most agree? Why?

_____

_____

_____

Computer Science

How Private Is E-mail?

There can be no denying the impact of the digital revolution upon our culture. Consider, for example, that the parents of today's college students probably never used a computer when they were in school. Today's students, on the other hand, prepare their written assignments with a word processor and do most of their research on the Internet.

E-mail has rapidly become a taken-for-granted part of the lives of many Americans (and people in many other countries as well). The following excerpt is concerned with e-mail privacy. Complete Exercise 14 to learn about some legal and social aspects of this issue.

HOW PRIVATE IS E-MAIL?

When you drop an envelope into the corner mailbox, you probably expect it to arrive at its destination unopened, with its contents kept safe from prying eyes. When you make a phone call, you might assume that your conversation will proceed unmonitored by wiretaps or other listening devices. Can you also ex-

5 pect an e-mail message to be read only by the person to whom it is addressed?

In the United States, the Electronic Communications Privacy Act of 2000 prohibits the use of intercepted e-mail as evidence unless a judge approved a search warrant. That doesn't mean the government isn't reading your mail. Heightened security concerns after the September 11, 2001 terrorist attacks re-

10 sulted in the rapid passage of the "Patriot Act," which became law on October 26, 2001. In an effort to assist law enforcement officials, the "Patriot Act" relaxes the rules for obtaining and implementing search warrants and lowers the Fourth Amendment standard for obtaining a court order to compel an ISP to produce e-mail logs and addresses.

15 To eavesdrop on e-mail from suspected terrorists and other criminals, the FBI developed a technology called Carnivore, which scans through messages entering and leaving an ISP's e-mail system to find e-mail associated with a person who is under investigation. Privacy advocates are concerned because Carnivore scans all messages that pass through an ISP, not just those messages sent

20 to or received by a particular individual.

Although law enforcement agencies are required to obtain a court order before intercepting e-mail, no such restriction exists for employers who want to monitor employee e-mail. According to the American Management Association, 27% of U.S. businesses monitor employee e-mail. But this intentional

25   eavesdropping is only one way in which the contents of your e-mail messages might become public. The recipient of your e-mail can forward it to one or more people—people you never intended for it to reach. Your e-mail messages could pop up on a technician's screen in the course of system maintenance, up-dates, or repairs. Also, keep in mind that e-mail messages—including those you

30   delete from your own computer—can be stored on backups of your ISP's e-mail server. You might wonder if such open access to your e-mail is legal. The answer in most cases is yes.

The United States Omnibus Crime Control and Safe Streets Act of 1968 and the Electronic Communications Privacy Act of 1986 prohibit public and pri-

35   vate employers from engaging in surreptitious surveillance of employee activ-ity through the use of electronic devices. However, two exceptions to these pri-vacy statues exist. The first exception permits an employee to monitor e-mail if one party to the communication consents to the monitoring. An employer must inform employees of this policy before undertaking any monitoring. The

40   second exception permits employers to monitor their employees' e-mail if a legitimate business need exists, and the monitoring takes place within the business-owned e-mail system.

Employees generally have not been successful in defending their rights to e-mail privacy because courts have ruled that an employee's right to privacy

45   does not outweigh a company's rights and interests. Courts seem to agree that because a company owns and maintains its e-mail system, it has the right to monitor the messages it carries.

From: *Computer Concepts*, 7th ed., by June Jamrich Parsons and Dan Oja. Boston: Thomson Course Tech-nology, 2004.

Comprehension Questions

1. Who can read your e-mail?

_____

2. What is Carnivore?

_____

_____ 3. The Patriot Act of 2001
   a. caused an increase in public concern over Internet security.
   b. strengthened the protections provided by the Electronic Communications Pri-vacy Act of 2000.
   c. weakened the protections provided by the Electronic Communications Privacy Act of 2000.
   d. did not address issues relating to electronic communication.

_____ 4. An employer may secretly monitor an employee's e-mail messages
   a. only with the employee's written consent.
   b. for business purposes within the company's e-mail system.
   c. only with a court order.
   d. if the employee is using his or her own ISP on company time.

_____ 5. The authors mention all of the following ways for an e-mail message to become public *except*
   a. computer hacking.
   b. forwarding of e-mail messages.
   c. system upgrading.
   d. employer monitoring.

Directions. Mark each of the following statements True (T), False (F), or Can't Tell (CT). Mark the statement Can't Tell if it is neither supported nor contradicted by the passage.

_____ 6. The Fourth Amendment protects privacy rights of American citizens.

_____ 7. Deleted e-mails can sometimes be retrieved because they can be stored on backups of an ISP server.

_____ 8. Carnivore has been criticized because it scans messages from people who are not necessarily under suspicion.

_____ 9. Without a court order, most employee e-mail surveillance is illegal.

_____ 10. Approximately one-fourth of all work-related e-mails in the United States today are being monitored.

Recognizing Organizational Patterns

What is the primary pattern of organization used in this passage? Explain your answer.

_____

_____

Vocabulary Questions

Directions. Choose the meaning for the underlined word that best fits the context. You may consult the dictionary as needed.

_____ 1. . . . for obtaining a court order to <u>compel</u> an ISP to produce e-mail logs and addresses. [Lines 13–14]
   a. request
   b. obtain
   c. require
   d. observe

_____ 2. To <u>eavesdrop</u> on e-mail from suspected terrorists and other criminals . . . [Line 15]
   a. capture
   b. watch from a distance
   c. listen secretly
   d. pay attention

_____ 3. Privacy <u>advocates</u> are concerned because
       Carnivore scans all messages that pass
       through an ISP . . . [Lines 18–19]
       a. experts or specialists
       b. supporters
       c. opponents
       d. rights

_____ 4. . . . prohibit public and private employers
       from engaging in <u>surreptitious</u> surveillance of
       employee activity . . . [Lines 34–36]
       a. secret
       b. illegal
       c. relating to business
       d. electronic or technical

_____ 5. However, two exceptions to these privacy
       <u>statutes</u> exist. [Lines 36–37]
       a. concerns
       b. issues
       c. requirements
       d. laws

Critical Response Questions

1. What are the advantages and disadvantages of employers monitoring the e-mails of
   their employees?

   _____

   _____

   _____

2. Should the government be allowed to monitor private e-mail correspondence in the
   interest of national security?

   _____

   _____

   _____

3. How might an individual today best protect the privacy of his or her communications?

   _____

   _____

   _____

Mathematics

PROBABILITY

As you know, mathematics is much more than crunching numbers. Your college math courses will help you improve your quantitative reasoning skills and think more abstractly about numbers and their uses.

Many math topics are both abstract and practical. The concept of probability has applications in many academic disciplines and in our daily lives.

Complete Exercise 15 to learn some basic concepts related to probability.

PROBABILITY

The Latin term *a priori* means "before the fact." When studying probability *a priori*, we are arriving at valid results prior to performing any observations or experiments. This approach is called **classical probability** or *theoretical probability*. But what is probability, and why should we study it?

5   **Probability** is the likelihood that a chance event will occur. For example, if a coin is tossed, what is the probability that it will land on heads? Since there are two possible outcomes (heads or tails) and only one of them is favorable (heads), there is a 1 in 2 chance of landing on heads when flipping a coin. This result could be expressed as a fraction, decimal, or percentage as follows:

10   Probability of landing on heads $= \dfrac{1}{2}$ or 0.5 or 50%

    Tossing a coin is a **random experiment** and the event of landing on heads is an outcome of that experiment. However, in this instance, we are calculating the probability without actually flipping the coin. The probability of the event (landing on heads) is being found *a priori* or prior to any coin-tossing experiment.

15   As we imagine tossing a coin, we are assuming the coin is **fair,** meaning that it is equally likely to land on heads or tails after any toss. In this section, we can assume that all possible outcomes of an experiment are equally likely. In other words, every possible outcome has the same chance of happening.

    Imagine we have 10 names written on separate pieces of paper and dropped

20 in a hat. What does it mean to say that a name was drawn at **random** from the hat? In this context, *random* means that the paper has been mixed so that any of the 10 names has the same chance of being drawn. In general, all outcomes of a random experiment are equally likely to occur.

> ### Classical Probability of an Event
>
> If all outcomes of an experiment are equally likely to occur, then the probability of an event is the number of favorable outcomes (that result in the event occurring) divided by the number of possible outcomes.
>
> $$\text{Probability of an event} = \frac{\text{Number of favorable outcomes}}{\text{Number of possible outcomes}}$$
>
> Letting E represent an event, the probability of an event can be denoted as $P(E)$. Or, we can write
>
> $$P(E) = \frac{\text{Favorable}}{\text{Possible}}$$

The words *and*, *or*, and *not* are often used when finding the probability of an event. For example, your major area of study might have the following requirements:

- One course in math or science
- Freshman English I and Freshman English II
- Not less than 120 total credits

In the first bullet, the word *or* means that you can take either subject (math or science) or both to satisfy this requirement. The second bullet uses the word *and* to mean that both courses in English (Freshman English I and Freshman English II) must be taken. Finally, in the last bullet, *not* is used to mean that you cannot have less than 120 total credits if you want to graduate.

> In general, given events E and F, we can use **and, or,** and **not** as follows:
>
> - $P(E$ and $F)$: Denotes the probability that the event E **and** the event F both occur.
> - $P(E$ or $F)$: Denotes the probability that the event E **or** the event F occurs **or** both occur.
> - $P(not\ E)$: Denotes the probability that the event E does **not** occur.

From *Prealgebra: Journey into a Mathematical World,* by James M. Sullivan. Upper Saddle River, NJ: Prentice-Hall, 2002.

Comprehension Questions

1. What is probability?

_____

2. What is classical probability?

_____

_____

_____ 3. In a random drawing
   a. the same result is expected to occur each time the drawing or experiment is repeated.
   b. some outcomes are more likely to occur than others.
   c. all outcomes have an equal chance of occurring.
   d. probability cannot be applied.

_____ 4. The probability of a given outcome can be understood as
   a. the number of favorable outcomes divided by the number of possible outcomes.
   b. the number of favorable outcomes multiplied by the number of possible outcomes.
   c. the number of favorable outcomes added to the number of possible outcomes.
   d. the number of favorable outcomes subtracted from the number of possible outcomes.

_____ 5. Regarding the use of the words *and, not,* and *or,* in probability statements, we can conclude that
   a. *and, not,* and *or* can be used interchangeably.
   b. *or* and *and* mean the same thing.
   c. *and* is used to indicate the probability of more than one event occurring.
   d. *or* is used to indicate the probability that the event does not occur.

Directions. Mark each of the following statements True (T), False (F), or Can't Tell (CT). Mark the statement Can't Tell if it is neither supported nor contradicted by the passage.

_____ 6. Probability can be expressed as a fraction but not as a decimal.

_____ 7. Classical probability and theoretical probability are distinctly different approaches to the study of probability.

_____ 8. P(*E* or *F*) means the probability that either *E* occurs, or *F* occurs, or both *E* and *F* occur.

_____ 9. If you randomly selected a marble from a bag containing 5 blue marbles and 10 red marbles, the probability that you would select a blue marble is 50%.

_____ 10. If tomorrow morning you toss a coin 20 times, 10 tosses will be heads and 10 will be tails.

Recognizing Organizational Patterns

What is the primary pattern of organization used in this passage? Explain your answer.

_____

_____

Vocabulary Questions

Directions. Choose the meaning for the underlined word that best fits the context. You may consult the dictionary as needed.

_____ 1. When studying probability *a priori*, we are arriving at underlined valid results prior to performing any observations or experiments. [Lines 1–3]
   a. well grounded
   b. uncertain
   c. arrived at beforehand
   d. important; practical

_____ 2. This approach is called **classical probability** or *theoretical* probability. [Lines 3–4]
   a. based on previous experience
   b. reflecting traditional beliefs and values
   c. based on suggested ideas or principles
   d. imaginary

_____ 3. Tossing a coin is a **random experiment** and the event of landing on heads is an outcome of that experiment. [Lines 11–12]
   a. unusual
   b. systematic

   c. controlled
   d. not deliberate or systematic

_____ 4. In this context, random means that the paper has been mixed so that any of the 10 names has the same chance of being drawn. [Lines 21–22]
   a. experiment
   b. situation
   c. period of time
   d. probability

_____ 5. Letting *E* represent an event, the probability of an event can be denoted as $P(E)$. [Lines 28–29]
   a. determined
   b. represented
   c. studied
   d. analyzed

Critical Response Questions

1. Name two or three practical uses for the study of probability.

_____

_____

2. When conducting an experiment involving probability, why is randomness important?

_____

_____

3. Imagine that you are going to toss a coin 20 times. How many times would you predict that the coin will land heads up? Explain your answer.

_____

_____

Career-related Disciplines

Health

ADDICTION

Health studies have become popular in recent years. Many students today are choosing health-related careers. Health, as an academic discipline, is most closely associated with the natural sciences of biology and chemistry.

Complete Exercise 16 to learn how addiction is viewed by health professionals.

DEFINING ADDICTION

Addiction is continued involvement with a substance or activity despite on-going negative consequences. Addictive behaviors initially provide a sense of pleasure or stability that is beyond the addict's power to achieve in other ways. Eventually, the addicted person needs to be involved in the behavior in order
5 to feel normal.

Physiological dependence is only one indicator of addiction. Psychological dynamics play an important role, which explains why behaviors not related to the use of chemicals—gambling, for example—may also be addictive. In fact, psychological and physiological dependence are so intertwined that it is not
10 really possible to separate the two. For every psychological state, there is a corresponding physiological state. In other words, everything you feel is tied to a chemical process occurring in your body. Thus, addictions once thought to be entirely psychological in nature are now understood to have physiological components.

15 To be addictive, a behavior must have the potential to produce a positive mood change. Chemicals are responsible for the most profound addictions, not only because they alter mood dramatically, but also because they cause cellular changes to which the body adapts so well that it eventually requires the chemical in order to function normally. Yet, other behaviors, such as gam-
20 bling, spending money, working, and engaging in sex, also create changes at the cellular level along with positive mood changes. Although the mechanism is not well understood, all forms of addiction probably reflect dysfunction of certain biochemical systems in the brain.

Traditionally, diagnosis of an addiction was limited to drug addiction and
25 was based on three criteria.

1. **Withdrawal,** or the presence of an abstinence syndrome—a series of temporary physical and psychological symptoms that occurs when the addicted person abruptly stops using the drug

2. An associated pattern of pathological behavior (deterioration in work performance, relationships, and social interaction)

3. **Relapse**—the tendency to return to the addictive behavior after a period of abstinence

Until recently, health professionals were unwilling to diagnose an addiction until medical symptoms appeared in the patient. Now we know that although withdrawal, pathological behavior, relapse, and medical symptoms are valid indicators of addiction, they do not characterize all addictive behavior.

From *Health: The Basics*, 6th ed., by Rebecca J. Donatelle. New York: Pearson Education, 2005.

Comprehension Questions

1. What is addiction?

_____

2. What is an "abstinence syndrome"?

_____

____ 3. An addict is *initially* motivated by
   a. the pleasure or stability gained from the addictive substance or behavior.
   b. the fear of relapse or the avoidance of withdrawal symptoms.
   c. a sense of power over others and control over himself.
   d. the need to feel normal.

____ 4. Psychological dependence
   a. causes physiological dependence.
   b. is interconnected with physical dependence.
   c. is the result of physiological dependence.
   d. is the primary indicator or criterion for addictive behavior.

____ 5. Regarding the diagnosis of an addiction, the author suggests that
   a. only chemical addictions can be diagnosed.
   b. all addictions are diagnosed in the same way.
   c. the three traditional criteria are no longer useful.
   d. the three traditional criteria may not characterize all addictions.

Directions. Mark each of the following statements True (T), False (F), or Can't Tell (CT). Mark the statement Can't Tell if it is neither supported nor contradicted by the passage.

_____ 6. Scientists do not yet have a complete understanding of all addictive mechanisms.

_____ 7. Gambling has both a psychological and a physiological component.

_____ 8. At one time, it was believed that some addictions had no physiological component.

_____ 9. Most relapses occur because the addict cannot cope with the intensity of her physical withdrawal symptoms.

_____10. Chemical addictions are worse than behavioral addictions because behavioral addictions never cause cellular changes.

Recognizing Organizational Patterns

(1) Where is listing or enumeration used within the passage? (2) Identify one other pattern of organization (besides listing or enumeration) used in the passage and indicate in which paragraph it is used.

_____

_____

Vocabulary Questions

Directions. Choose the meaning for the underlined word that best fits the context. You may consult the dictionary as needed.

_____ 1. . . . despite ongoing negative consequences.
   [Lines 1–2]
   a. side effects
   b. results
   c. addictions
   d. relations

_____ 2. Physiological dependence is only one indicator of addiction. [Line 6]
   a. mental
   b. uncontrollable
   c. systematic
   d. physical

_____ 3. . . . of certain biochemical systems in the brain.
   [Lines 22–23]
   a. physiological
   b. psychological

   c. relating to body chemistry
   d. relating to chemicals synthesized to enhance health

_____ 4. . . . the presence of an abstinence syndrome . . .
   [Line 26]
   a. a symptom that continues to repeat itself
   b. the diagnosis of an addictive behavior pattern
   c. a group of symptoms occurring together
   d. a symptom that is the cause of other symptoms

_____ 5. An associated pattern of pathological behavior . . . [Line 29]
   a. addictive
   b. unhealthy
   c. aggressive
   d. related to depression

Critical Response Questions

1. Why is it easier to prevent an addiction than to cure it?

_____

_____

_____

2. Why have so many Americans become addicted to drugs, alcohol, or compulsive behaviors?

_____

_____

_____

3. Do you believe that some people are more prone to addiction than others? Explain your answer.

_____

_____

_____

Sample Annotations for Exercise 16

DEFINING ADDICTION

Def.

[**Addiction** is continued involvement with a substance or activity despite ongoing negative consequences.] Addictive behaviors initially provide a sense of pleasure or stability that is beyond the addict's power to achieve in other ways. Eventually, the addicted person needs to be involved in the behavior in order to feel normal.

both physiological & psychological

5

Physiological dependence is only one indicator of addiction. Psychological dynamics play an important role, which explains why behaviors not related to the use of chemicals—gambling, for example—may also be addictive. In fact, psychological and physiological dependence are so intertwined that it is not really possible to separate the two. For every psychological state, there is a corresponding physiological state. In other words, everything you feel is tied to a chemical process occurring in your body. Thus, addictions once thought to be entirely psychological in nature are now understood to have physiological components.

10

improve mood 15

chemicals and behaviors can both be addictive 20

To be addictive, a behavior must have the potential to produce a positive mood change. Chemicals are responsible for the most profound addictions, not only because they alter mood dramatically, but also because they cause cellular changes to which the body adapts so well that it eventually requires the chemical in order to function normally. Yet, other behaviors, such as gambling, spending money, working, and engaging in sex, also create changes at the cellular level along with positive mood changes. Although the mechanism is not well understood, all forms of addiction probably reflect dysfunction of certain biochemical systems in the brain.

25

Traditionally, diagnosis of an addiction was limited to drug addiction and was based on three criteria.

3 diagnostic criteria 30

1. **Withdrawal,** or the presence of an abstinence syndrome—a series of temporary physical and psychological symptoms that occurs when the addicted person abruptly stops using the drug
2. An associated pattern of pathological behavior (deterioration in work performance, relationships, and social interaction)
3. **Relapse**—the tendency to return to the addictive behavior after a period of abstinence

new understanding 35

Until recently, health professionals were unwilling to diagnose an addiction until medical symptoms appeared in the patient. Now we know that although withdrawal, pathological behavior, relapse, and medical symptoms are valid indicators of addiction, they do not characterize all addictive behavior.

From *Health: The Basics,* 6th ed., by Rebecca J. Donatelle. New York: Pearson Education, 2005.

Nursing

THEORIES ON CARING

The long-respected field of nursing continues to attract many college students. Today's nursing students must learn a great deal of theoretical and practical information regarding health and illness, medications, and patient care.

The following excerpt from a Nursing I textbook discusses caring as a central part of the nurse-client relationship. Complete Exercise 17 to learn some theoretical views regarding the role of caring within this relationship.

THEORIES ON CARING

In reading and critiquing nursing theorists' views on caring, one finds certain common themes. Caring is highly relational. The nurse and the client enter into a relationship that is much more than one person simply "doing tasks for" another. There is a mutual give and take that develops as nurse and client begin
5   to know and care for one another. Frank described a personal situation when he was suffering from cancer: "What I wanted when I was ill, was a mutual relationship of *persons* who were also clinician and client." It was important for the author to be seen as one of two fellow human beings, not the dependent client being cared for by the expert technical clinician. Caring may seem highly invisi-
10   ble at times, when a nurse and client enter a relationship of respect, concern, and support. The nurse's empathy and compassion become a natural part of every client encounter. However, the nurse–client relationship can become very visible when caring is absent. A nurse's disinterest or avoidance of a client's request, for example, will quickly convey an uncaring attitude. Benner and
15   Wrubel relate the story of one expert clinical nurse specialist who learned from a client what caring is all about:

> I felt that I was teaching him a lot, but actually he taught me. One day he said to me (probably after I had delivered some well-meaning technical in-
20   formation about his disease), "You are doing an OK job, but I can tell that every time you walk in that door you are walking out."

Clients can tell quickly when nurses fail to relate to them. In contrast, when caring is practiced, the client senses a commitment on the part of the nurse and is willing to enter into a relationship that allows the nurse to gain an under-
25   standing of the client and his or her experience of illness. This allows the nurse to become a coach and partner rather than a detached provider of care services.

Another theme that is common in the theories of caring is understanding the context of the person's life and illness. It is difficult to show caring to another individual without gaining an understanding of who they are and their perception of their illness. With experience, the nurse appreciates the value of

30   learning about the client's situation: how was the illness first recognized? How did the client feel? How does the illness affect the client's daily life practices? What values and beliefs influence the client's response? Knowing the context of a client's illness helps the professional nurse to choose and individualize interventions that will actually help the client. This approach will be more suc-

35   cessful than simply selecting interventions on the basis of the client's symptoms or disease process.

From *Fundamentals of Nursing*, 5th ed., by Patricia Potter and Anne Griffin Perry. St. Louis, MO: Mosby, 2001.

Comprehension Questions

1. Why is caring important to the nurse–client relationship?

   _____

2. How does understanding the context of a client's illness enable a nurse to better care for the client?

   _____

____ 3. When the client (referred to in the indented paragraph) said, "... I can tell that every time you walk in that door you are walking out," he was telling the nurse that
   a. she was doing a good job.
   b. he was lonely.
   c. he wanted her to show more interest in him.
   d. she hadn't provided him with enough information about his treatment.

____ 4. Which of the following *least* demonstrates a nurse's caring?
   a. The nurse asks questions about the client's life.
   b. The nurse shows empathy for the client.
   c. The nurse asks the client about his feelings.
   d. The nurse gives the client technical information about his illness.

____ 5. The passage implies that understanding a client's beliefs
   a. is the most important part of nursing care.
   b. is not relevant to caring.
   c. is the best way for a nurse to show compassion.
   d. is an important part of caring.

Directions. Mark each of the following statements True (T), False (F), or Can't Tell (CT). Mark the statement Can't Tell if it is neither supported nor contradicted by the passage.

_____ 6. All clients want a mutual relationship with their nurse.

_____ 7. Mutuality in a caring relationship implies that both parties care about one another.

_____ 8. Caring may be more visible when it is not present than when it is present.

_____ 9. Most clients cannot tell when a nurse cares about them.

_____ 10. Getting to know a client helps a nurse become more caring, but does not help her make better choices regarding the client's treatment.

Recognizing Organizational Patterns

What is the primary pattern of organization used in this passage? Explain your answer.

_____

_____

Vocabulary Questions

Directions. Choose the meaning for the underlined word that best fits the context. You may consult the dictionary as needed.

_____ 1. In reading and critiquing nursing theorists' views on caring, one finds certain common themes. [Lines 1–2]
   a. understanding
   b. debating; arguing about opposite points of view
   c. analyzing and evaluating
   d. theorizing or hypothesizing

_____ 2. There is a mutual give and take that develops as nurse and client begin to know and care for one another. [Lines 4–5]
   a. reciprocal; shared
   b. spontaneous; without planning
   c. long-lasting
   d. respectful

_____ 3. What I wanted when I was ill, was a mutual relationship of *persons* who were also clinician and client. [Lines 6–7]
   a. technician

   b. medical practitioner
   c. friend or supporter
   d. doctor

_____ 4. The nurse's empathy and compassion become a natural part of every client encounter. [Lines 11–12]
   a. knowledge; expertise
   b. ability to maintain an objective perspective within a relationship
   c. sensitivity to the feelings of others
   d. intuition

_____ 5. Knowing the context of a client's illness helps the professional nurse to choose and individualize interventions that will actually help the client. [Lines 32–34]
   a. helpful actions
   b. medications
   c. methods of conversation or interview
   d. analyses (of medical conditions)

Critical Response Questions

1. How can a patient tell if his nurse cares about him?

   _____

   _____

   _____

2. If you or someone you loved were hospitalized with a serious illness, what qualities or characteristics would you want your nurse to have?

   _____

   _____

   _____

3. In what other professions (besides nursing) might caring also be important?

   _____

   _____

   _____

Criminal Justice

AGENCIES OF CRIMINAL JUSTICE

Criminal justice is closely associated with the discipline of sociology. Criminology, the study of the causes of crime and the treatment of criminals, was originally treated as a branch of sociology. The field of criminal justice has evolved as an expansion of criminology, and includes the study of the systems that administer criminal law (police agencies, courts, and correctional facilities).

Complete Exercise 18 to learn more about America's law enforcement and court systems.

AGENCIES OF CRIMINAL JUSTICE

The contemporary structure of law enforcement, courts, and corrections institutionalizes basic notions of how law should be enforced and adjudicated and how violators should be dealt with. The nation's history as a democracy has guided the establishment of criminal justice agencies, which have been granted
5 the power to intrude into the lives of citizens only under certain circumstances. In addition, many criminal justice agencies exist on the local level, and local control helps prevent these agencies from becoming too powerful or abusive. As a result, the United States has perhaps more criminal justice agencies than any other nation, including more than 19,000 police departments, 17,000
10 courts, and 6,000 correctional facilities centered largely in local government. These agencies have in common criminal law and criminal procedure, which specify the types of acts over which the system has jurisdiction and the precise way that individual cases are to be handled.

Law Enforcement

Law enforcement agencies exist at all levels of government: federal, state, and
15 local. In each case, however, these agencies' duties are the same. We generally expect law enforcement agencies to perform four tasks: protect people and their rights, apprehend those who violate laws, prevent crimes, and provide social services. The first two responsibilities are traditionally associated with the function of **policing;** that is, enforcing the law by apprehending violators and
20 thereby protecting citizens. Crime prevention and social services such as education of the public are more recent emphases in policing.

The only difference between law enforcement agencies at different levels of government is in the types of laws they enforce. Federal law enforcement officers

25   are charged with enforcing federal laws; state police enforce state laws; and lo-
      cal police must enforce both state and local laws. The majority of police agen-
      cies and police officers are at the local level of government, which includes
      towns, cities, metropolitan districts, and counties.

Courts

      In criminal courts, legal responsibility is determined through interpretation of
      the law in relation to the circumstances of individual cases. More than 17,000
30   courts and related agencies operate in the United States, mostly at the state
      and local levels. These courts can be grouped into the federal court system
      (courts that interpret federal law) and a state court system (courts that inter-
      pret state and local laws). Both the state and the federal court systems have
      three basic types of jurisdiction. Courts of **limited jurisdiction** have narrow
35   legal authority and may arbitrate only in certain types of disputes; these in-
      clude family courts, municipal courts, and special courts such as tax courts.
      Courts of **general jurisdiction,** on the other hand, usually are referred to as
      trial courts. These are the courts in which felonies and civil cases go to trial.
      General jurisdiction courts across the country may be called county courts, cir-
40   cuit courts, and even supreme courts in some jurisdictions. The highest level of
      jurisdiction is **appellate jurisdiction.** Appellate courts review specific legal is-
      sues raised by cases in courts with general jurisdiction. An appellate court may
      reverse a conviction in a criminal case tried in a trial court. The sequence in
      which a case moves from a trial court to an appellate court occurs in every
45   state court system and in the federal court system, although the names of the
      courts vary.

From *Criminal Justice,* 3rd ed., by Jay S. Albanese. New York: Pearson Education, 2005.

Comprehension Questions

1. How are the duties of federal law enforcers different from those of local or state law enforcers?

   _____

2. Explain the difference between the three types of courts.

   _____

_____ 3. Which of the following is not a task of *enforcement* agencies?
   a. punishing offenders
   b. arresting criminals
   c. protecting the public
   d. providing public services

_____ **4.** A tax court is an example of a court of
   a. legal jurisdiction.
   b. local jurisdiction.
   c. limited jurisdiction.
   d. general jurisdiction.

_____ **5.** We can conclude from the passage that
   a. law enforcement agencies at different levels cooperate fully with one another.
   b. federal law enforcement agencies are more effective than state agencies.
   c. state police are generally not responsible for the enforcement of federal laws.
   d. appellate courts are almost always federal courts.

Directions. Mark each of the following statements True (T), False (F), or Can't Tell (CT). Mark the statement Can't Tell if it is neither supported nor contradicted by the passage.

_____ **6.** Crime prevention has always been considered the primary purpose of police work.

_____ **7.** The power of American law enforcement agencies has been limited in order to protect the rights of private citizens.

_____ **8.** Most courts in the United States are at the federal level.

_____ **9.** Most criminal trials are heard in courts of general jurisdiction.

_____**10.** Approximately 5 percent of all criminal cases are reviewed in appellate court.

Recognizing Organizational Patterns

Which pattern of organization most helped you to understand the main ideas of this passage? Explain your answer.

_____

_____

Vocabulary Questions

Directions. Choose the meaning for the underlined word that best fits the context. You may consult the dictionary as needed.

_____ **1.** ... which specify the types of acts over which the system has jurisdiction ... [Lines 11–12]
   a. procedure
   b. rights
   c. location
   d. authority

_____ **2.** ... apprehend those who violate laws ... [Line 17]
   a. understand
   b. capture
   c. punish
   d. judge the guilt or innocence of

____ 3. ...which includes towns, cities, metropolitan districts, and counties. [Lines 26–27]
   a. governmental
   b. country
   c. legal
   d. urban

____ 4. ...may arbitrate only in certain types of disputes... [Line 35]
   a. judge or decide
   b. interfere
   c. convict
   d. authorize

____ 5. These are the courts in which felonies and civil cases go to trial. [Line 38]
   a. thieves
   b. criminals
   c. serious crimes
   d. minor crimes

Critical Response Questions

1. How has our country's historical concern with the protection of citizens' rights affected the development of our criminal justice system?

_____

_____

_____

2. What are the benefits of having a multilevel court system?

_____

_____

_____

3. How might our criminal justice system be improved?

_____

_____

_____

Business

MARKETING FUNDAMENTALS

Business courses prepare business majors for careers in the business world. They also provide useful information and insights for any student in her role as consumer and participant in our commercial system. Business courses are most closely associated with the discipline of *economics*, a social science.

Complete Exercise 19 to learn about marketing, a pivotal concept and practice in the world of business.

MARKETING FUNDAMENTALS

By this point in your life, you already know quite a bit about marketing. People have been trying to sell you things for years, and you've learned something about their techniques—advertisements, price markdowns, special contests, tantalizing displays of merchandise. Despite marketing's high visibility, the term
5   is difficult to define. The American Marketing Association (AMA) recently evaluated 25 definitions before agreeing on the meaning of the word. According to AMA's definition, **marketing** is planning and executing the conception, pricing, promotion, and distribution of ideas, goods, and services to create exchanges that satisfy individual and organizational objectives.
10   As this definition implies, marketing encompasses a wide range of activities. If you set out to handle all of a firm's marketing functions, you would be very busy indeed. In fact, in most large organizations, each division has its own marketing department, staffed by a legion of specialists. Some of them conduct research to determine what consumers want to buy; some use that research to
15   design new products and services; others make decisions on how to price the firm's offerings; still others handle the transportation, storage, and distribution of the goods; and finally, some are responsible for advertising, sales, promotion, publicity, and personal selling. Marketing is involved in all decisions related to determining a product's characteristics, price, production quantities, market-
20   entry date, sales, and customer service.
    Although we generally think of marketing in connection with selling tangible products for a profit, the AMA definition applies to services and ideas as well. Social activists, religious leaders, politicians, universities, and charities of all types rely on the principles of marketing to "sell" themselves and their
25   causes to the public. **Place marketing** describes efforts to market geographic areas ranging from neighborhoods to entire countries. **Idea marketing** involves concepts that provide intellectual or spiritual benefits to the customer.

The term *product* is used in this text to refer to any "bundle of value" that can be exchanged in a marketing transaction.

The Role of Marketing in Society

30   Take another look at the AMA definition of marketing. Notice that it involves an exchange between two parties—the buyer and the selling organization—both of whom obtain satisfaction from the transaction. This definition suggests that marketing plays an important role in society by helping people satisfy their needs and wants and by helping organizations determine what to produce.

Needs and Wants

35   A **need** represents a difference between your actual state and your ideal state. You're hungry, and you don't want to be hungry; you need to eat. These needs create the motivation to buy products and are therefore at the core of any discussion of marketing.

Your **wants** are based on your needs, but they are more specific. Producers do not create needs, but they do shape your wants by exposing you to alterna-
40   tives. For instance, when you need some food, you may want a Snickers bar or an orange. A fundamental goal of marketing is to direct the customer's basic need for various products into the desire to purchase specific brands.

From *Business Today,* 8th ed., by David J. Rachman et al. Upper Saddle River, NJ: Prentice-Hall, 2000.

Comprehension Questions

1. Define *marketing.*

   _____

2. Explain the difference between a need and a want.

   _____

_____   3. Which of the following would not be an example of a marketing activity?
   a. consumer research
   b. employee fringe benefits
   c. radio advertising
   d. selling a product at a reduced price

_____   4. The authors state that ideas
   a. cannot be marketed.
   b. should not be marketed.
   c. are rarely marketed.
   d. are marketable in that they have value and can be exchanged.

_____ 5. According to the passage, marketing's primary function in society is to
   a. provide employment.
   b. facilitate exchanges that satisfy needs and wants.
   c. research consumer information.
   d. provide customers with the goods they need at the lowest possible prices.

Directions. Mark each of the following statements True (T), False (F), or Can't Tell (CT). Mark the statement Can't Tell if it is neither supported nor contradicted by the passage.

_____ 6. Marketing is basically the same thing as advertising.

_____ 7. Consumer research is an important aspect of marketing.

_____ 8. The AMA's definition of marketing is the one preferred by most American business-people.

_____ 9. Political campaigns are an example of marketing.

_____10. A product is defined as any object that can be bought and consumed.

Recognizing Organizational Patterns

Name two patterns of organization that are used in this passage, and indicate where they are used.

_____

_____

Vocabulary Questions

Directions. Choose the meaning for the underlined word that best fits the context. You may consult the dictionary as needed.

_____ 1. . . . tantalizing displays of merchandise.
   [Line 4]
   a. expensive
   b. appealing
   c. extensive
   d. taunting

_____ 2. . . . marketing is planning and executing the conception. . . . [Line 7]
   a. beginning
   b. birth
   c. promotion
   d. idea

_____ 3. . . . to create exchanges that satisfy individual and organizational objectives. [Lines 8–9]
   a. principles
   b. sales
   c. goals
   d. responsibilities

_____ 4. . . . staffed by a legion of specialists.
   [Line 13]
   a. overseas department
   b. industry
   c. multitude
   d. range

_____ 5. Although we generally think of marketing in
       connection with selling <u>tangible</u> products for
       a profit. . . . [Lines 21–22]
       a. alluring
       b. costly
       c. physical
       d. numerous

Critical Response Questions

1. Why are there so many different definitions of marketing?

   _____

   _____

   _____

2. How might consumers protect themselves from marketing campaigns?

   _____

   _____

   _____

3. Which aspects of marketing would be most important to the sale of a new product?

   _____

   _____

   _____

Business Communication

COMMUNICATING WITH CULTURES ABROAD

Communication skills are important in every career, and the improvement of communication skills should be a part of everyone's college education.

The following excerpt is taken from a business communications textbook. With today's global economy, business students must be prepared to communicate effectively with associates and customers all over the world. The excerpt focuses on the need for effective intercultural communication. Complete Exercise 20 to learn how the world of business has changed and why today's businessmen and businesswomen must be able to communicate across national and cultural boundaries.

COMMUNICATING WITH CULTURES ABROAD

In many ways, the world is becoming smaller and smaller for businesspeople. Thanks to technological advances in communication and transportation, companies can quickly and easily span the globe in search of new customers, new sources of materials, and new sources of money. Even firms that once
5   thought they were too tiny to expand into a neighboring city have discovered that they can tap the sales potential of overseas markets with the help of fax machines, the Internet, overnight delivery services, and e-mail. This rise of international business has increased international business communication by increasing exports, relaxing trade barriers, and increasing foreign competition
10   in domestic markets.

More and more businesses report that a large part of their overall sales now come from *exports* (products sold to customers in other countries). Barco, a Belgium-based maker of electronic equipment, sells 85 percent of its products to customers in other countries; Nestlé, which is based in Switzerland, sells over
15   95 percent of its products in other countries. Likewise, some U.S. companies are seeing export sales dwarf sales at home: Boston-based Gillette makes 70 percent of its sales through exports, and Seattle-based Boeing exports 80 percent of its products. U.S. firms sell more than $90 billion worth of goods and services every year to Canada alone (by far the largest U.S. trading partner, fol-
20   lowed by Japan and Mexico).

Relaxing trade barriers has also quickened the pace of international trade. Mexico, Canada, and the United States have agreed to lower trade barriers throughout the continent, creating a single market of 360 million people.

25   Moreover, discussions are under way to extend that agreement throughout the Americas. The goal is to increase *imports* (products purchased from businesses in other countries) by reducing the hassles of bringing goods across the borders. Similarly, the nations of the European Community have been eliminating trade barriers. Since 1993, capital, products, and employees have been flowing more freely across European borders, creating a unified market of 320 million people.

30   As companies move into the global marketplace, they increase the competition in domestic markets for employees, customers, and materials. They build factories abroad and buy overseas companies. In a single year, U.S. companies invested approximately $30 billion in non-U.S. facilities and equipment, employing more than 20 million people outside the United States. At the same

35   time, 30 percent of U.S. manufacturers recently reported that three of their top five competitors *in the U.S. market* are non-U.S. firms. Overall, non-U.S. corporations control nearly 15 percent of all U.S. manufacturing assets, and they employ almost 4 million people in the United States. In this fast-paced global marketplace, companies are finding that good communication skills are essential

40   for meeting customers, making sales, and working more effectively with colleagues in other countries.

From *Business Communication Today*, 5th ed., by Courtland L. Bovee and John V. Thill. Upper Saddle River, NJ: Prentice-Hall, 1998.

Comprehension Questions

1. How has technology made the world of business smaller?

   _____

2. In which continents have trade barriers been significantly reduced?

   _____

____ 3. Which of the following factors is *not* mentioned as contributing to the increase in international business communication?
   a. foreign competition in domestic markets
   b. increases in education and training
   c. increasing exports
   d. reduction of trade barriers

____ 4. We can conclude from the passage that
   a. most businesses now export the majority of their products.
   b. a business cannot succeed without exports.
   c. imports are more important to a business than exports.
   d. an increasing number of businesses are increasing their exports.

_____ 5. One important goal of reducing trade barriers is to
    a. increase imports from other nations.
    b. reduce exports to other nations.
    c. reduce competition between businesses.
    d. encourage foreign investment in foreign business.

Directions. Mark each of the following statements True (T), False (F), or Can't Tell (CT). Mark the statement Can't Tell if it is neither supported nor contradicted by the passage.

_____ 6. Small businesses are unable to compete in foreign markets.

_____ 7. The United States trades more with Canada than with Japan or Mexico.

_____ 8. Fewer trade barriers exist among North American nations than among European nations.

_____ 9. The expanding international market has led to increased competition in domestic markets.

_____10. The majority of U.S. manufacturers report that most of their competition comes from foreign businesses.

Recognizing Organizational Patterns

What is the primary pattern of organization used in this passage? Explain your answer.

_____

_____

Vocabulary Questions

Directions. Choose the meaning for the underlined word that best fits the context. You may consult the dictionary as needed.

_____ 1. ... companies can quickly and easily span the globe.... [Line 3]
    a. view from a distance
    b. control from a distance
    c. locate within a large area
    d. reach across

_____ 2. ... increasing foreign competition in domestic markets. [Lines 9–10]
    a. expanding
    b. national
    c. household
    d. foreign

_____ 3. ... in non-U.S. facilities and equipment.... [Lines 33]
    a. buildings
    b. supplies
    c. technology
    d. communications

_____ 4. ... nearly 15 percent of all U.S. manufacturing assets.... [Line 37]
    a. facilities
    b. items of value
    c. profits
    d. new products

_____ 5. . . . working more effectively with <u>colleagues</u> in
    other countries. [Lines 40–41]
    a. competitors
    b. associates
    c. companies
    d. executives

Critical Response Questions

1. What different communication skills might be needed for international business than for domestic business?

_____

_____

_____

2. What are some of the advantages of free trade between nations? What are some of the disadvantages?

_____

_____

_____

3. How does the international business market affect the typical consumer?

_____

_____

_____

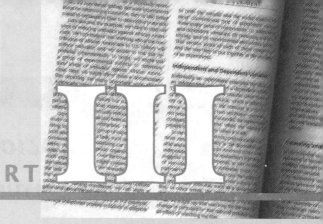

PART III

Chapter Practice

Sociology
CULTURE

Directions

1. Begin by surveying the chapter to look for answers to the following questions.

   - What is the chapter about?
   - What subtopics will be discussed?
   - What will you learn from reading and studying the chapter?
   - How interesting does the chapter look?
   - How difficult does the chapter look?
   - How familiar to you is the chapter material? That is, how much previous knowledge of the subject do you have?

   When you have completed your survey, write a summary on a separate sheet of paper of what you've learned about the chapter from the survey. Your summary should include answers to the previous questions, as well as any other information and comments you wish to add.

2. While reading the chapter, look for organizational patterns. Recognizing the patterns should help you better grasp the relationship of ideas within each paragraph and section and distinguish main ideas more easily.

   Also, form questions from the headings and subheadings (generally, write one question per heading or subheading). Write your questions on a sheet of paper. After completing each section, mentally review the main points of the section, mark the text, and write the answer(s) to your question(s), as well as any other information that seems important to you.

SAMPLE TEXTBOOK CHAPTER

From *Sociology: A Down-to-Earth Approach,* 7th ed., by James M. Henslin. New York: Pearson Education, 2005.

1   had never felt heat like this before. This was *northern* Africa, and I wondered what it must be like closer to the equator. Sweat poured off me as the temperature climbed past 110 degrees Fahrenheit.

2   As we were herded into the building—which had no air conditioning—hundreds of people lunged toward the counter at the rear of the building. With body crushed against body, we waited as the uniformed officials behind the windows leisurely examined each passport. At times like this I wondered what I was doing in Africa.

3   When I first arrived in Morocco, I found the sights that greeted me exotic—not far removed from my memories of *Casablanca, Raiders of the Lost Ark,* and other movies that over the years had become part of my memory. The men, the women, and even the children did wear those white robes that reached down to their feet. What was especially striking was that the women were almost totally covered. Despite the heat, they wore not only full-length gowns, but also head coverings that reached down over their foreheads, and veils that covered their faces from the nose down. All you could make out were their eyes—and every eye the same shade of brown.

4   And how short everyone was! The Arab women looked to be, on average, 5 feet, and the men only about three or four inches taller. As the only blue-eyed, blonde, 6-foot-plus person around, and the only one who was wearing jeans and a pullover shirt, in a world of white-robed short people I stood out like a sore thumb. Everyone stared. No matter where I went, they stared. Wherever I looked, I found brown eyes watching me intently. Even staring back at those many dark brown eyes had no effect. It was so different from home, where, if you caught someone staring at you, the person would immediately look embarrassed and glance away.

5   And lines? The concept apparently didn't even exist. Buying a ticket for a bus or train meant pushing and shoving toward the ticket man (always a man—no women were visible in any public position), who took the money from whichever outstretched hand he decided on.

6   And germs? That notion didn't seem to exist here either. Flies swarmed over the food in the restaurants and the unwrapped loaves of bread in the stores. Shopkeepers would considerately shoo off the flies before handing me a loaf. They also offered home delivery. I still remember watching a bread vendor deliver an unwrapped loaf to a woman who stood on a second-floor balcony. She first threw her money to the bread vendor, and he then threw the bread up to her. Only, his throw was off. The bread bounced off the wrought-iron balcony railing and landed in the street, which was filled with people, wandering dogs, and the ever-present, defecating burros. The vendor simply picked up the unwrapped loaf and threw it again. This certainly wasn't his day, for he missed again. But he made it on his third attempt. The woman smiled as she turned back into her apartment, apparently to prepare the noon meal for her hungry family.

7   Now, standing in the oppressive heat on the Moroccan-Algerian border, the crowd once again became unruly. Another fight had broken out. And once

And lines? The concept apparently
didn't even exist.
Buying a ticket for a bus or train meant
pushing and shoving
toward the ticket man

again, the little man in uniform appeared, shouting and knocking people aside as he forced his way to a little wooden box nailed to the floor. Climbing onto this makeshift platform, he shouted at the crowd, his arms flailing about him. The people fell silent. But just as soon as the man left, the shouting and shoving began again.

The situation had become unbearable. 8 His body pressed against mine, the man behind me decided that this was a good time to take a nap. Determining that I made a good support, he placed his arm against my back and leaned his head against his arm. Sweat streamed down my back at the point where his arm and head touched me.

Finally, I realized that I had to abandon American customs. So I pushed my 9 way forward, forcing my frame into every square inch of vacant space that I could create. At the counter, I shouted in English. The official looked up at the sound of this strange tongue, and I thrust my long arms over the heads of three people, shoving my passport into his hand.

What Is Culture?

culture the language, beliefs, values, norms, behaviors, and even material objects that are passed from one generation to the next

material culture the material objects that distinguish a group of people, such as their art, buildings, weapons, utensils, machines, hairstyles, clothing, and jewelry

nonmaterial culture (also called *symbolic culture*) a group's ways of thinking (including its beliefs, values, and other assumptions about the world) and doing (its common patterns of behavior, including language and other forms of interaction)

What is culture? The concept is sometimes easier to grasp by descrip- 10 tion than by definition. For example, suppose you meet a young woman who has just arrived in the United States from India. That her culture is different from yours is immediately evident. You first see it in her clothing, jewelry, makeup, and hairstyle. Next you hear it in her speech. It then becomes apparent by her gestures. Later, you may hear her express unfamiliar beliefs about the world or about what is valuable in life. All these characteristics are indicative of **culture**—the language, beliefs, values, norms, behaviors, and even material objects that are passed from one generation to the next.

In northern Africa, I was surrounded by a culture quite alien to my own. It 11 was evident in everything I saw and heard. The **material culture**—such things as jewelry, art, buildings, weapons, machines, and even eating utensils, hairstyles, and clothing—provided a sharp contrast to what I was used to seeing. There is nothing inherently "natural" about material culture. That is, it is no more natural (or unnatural) to wear gowns on the street than it is to wear jeans.

I also found myself immersed in a contrasting **nonmaterial culture,** that is, 12 a group's ways of thinking (its beliefs, values, and other assumptions about the world) and doing (its common patterns of behavior, including language, gestures, and other forms of interaction). North African assumptions about crowding to buy a ticket and staring in public are examples of nonmaterial culture. So are American assumptions about not doing either of these things. Like material culture, neither custom is "right." People simply become comfortable with the customs they learn during childhood, and—as in the case of my visit to northern Africa—uncomfortable when their basic assumptions about life are challenged.

Culture and Taken-for-Granted Orientations to Life

13 To develop a sociological imagination, it is essential to understand how culture affects people's lives. Meeting someone from a different culture may make us aware of culture's pervasive influence, but attaining the same level of awareness regarding our own culture is quite another matter. *Our* speech, *our* gestures, *our* beliefs, and *our* customs are usually taken for granted. We assume they are "normal" or "natural," and we almost always follow them without question. As anthropologist Ralph Linton said, "The last thing a fish would ever notice would be water." So also with people: Except in unusual circumstances, the effects of our own culture generally remain imperceptible to us.

14 Yet culture's significance is profound; it touches almost every aspect of who and what we are. We came into this life without a language, without values and morality, with no ideas about religion, war, money, love, use of space, and so on. We possessed none of these fundamental orientations that we take for granted and that are so essential in determining the type of people we become. Yet at this point in our lives we all have acquired them. Sociologists call this *culture within us*. These learned and shared ways of believing and of doing (another definition of culture) penetrate our beings at an early age and quickly become part of our taken-for-granted assumptions about what normal behavior is. *Culture becomes the lens through which we perceive and evaluate what is going on around us.* Seldom do we question these assumptions, for, like water to a fish, the framework from which we view life remains largely beyond our ordinary perception.

15 The rare instances in which these assumptions are challenged, however, can be upsetting. Although as a sociologist I should be able to look at my own culture "from the outside," my trip to Africa quickly revealed how fully I had internalized my own culture. My upbringing in Western society had given me strong assumptions about aspects of social life that had become deeply rooted in my being—staring, hygiene, and the use of space. But in this part of Africa these assumptions were useless in helping me get through daily life. No longer could I count on people to stare only surreptitiously, to take precautions against invisible microbes, or to stand in line in an orderly fashion, one behind the other.

16 As you can tell from the opening vignette, I found these assumptions upsetting, for they violated my basic expectations of "the way people *ought* to be"—although I did not know how firmly I held these expectations until they were so abruptly challenged. When my nonmaterial culture failed me—when it no longer enabled me to make sense out of the world—I experienced a disorientation known as **culture shock.** In the case of buying tickets, the fact that I was several inches taller than most Moroccans and thus able to outreach others helped me to adjust partially to their different ways of doing things. But I never did get used to the idea that pushing ahead of others was "right," and I always felt guilty when I used my size to receive preferential treatment.

17 An important consequence of culture within us is **ethnocentrism,** a tendency to use our own group's ways of doing things as they yardstick for judging others. All of us learn that the ways of our own group are good, right, proper, and even superior to other ways of life. As sociologist William Sumner, who developed this concept, said, "One's own group is the center of everything, and all others are scaled and rated with reference to it." Ethnocentrism has both positive and negative consequences. On the positive side, it creates in-group loyalties. On the negative side, ethnocentrism can lead to discrimination against the people whose ways differ from ours.

18 The many ways culture affects our lives fascinate sociologists. In this chapter, we'll examine how profoundly culture affects everything we are. This will serve as a basis from which you can start to analyze your own assumptions of reality. I should give you a warning at this point: This can result in a changed perspective on social life and your role in it. If so, life will never look the same.

culture shock the disorientation that people experience when they come in contact with a fundamentally different culture and can no longer depend on their taken-for-granted assumptions about life

ethnocentrism the use of one's own culture as a yardstick for judging the ways of other individuals or societies, generally leading to a negative evaluation of their values, norms, and behaviors

IN SUM

To avoid losing track of the ideas under discussion, let's pause for a mo-   19
ment to summarize, and in some instances clarify, the principles we have
covered.

1. There is nothing "natural" about material culture. Arabs wear gowns on
   the street and feel that it is natural to do so. Americans do the same with
   jeans.

2. There is nothing "natural" about nonmaterial culture. It is just as arbitrary to stand in line as it is to push and shove.

3. Culture penetrates deeply into our thinking, becoming a taken-for-
   granted lens through which we see the world and obtain our perception
   of reality.

4. Culture provides implicit instructions that tell us what we ought to do
   in various situations. It provides a fundamental basis for our decision
   making.

5. Culture also provides a "moral imperative"; that is, the culture that we in-
   ternalize becomes the "right" way of doing things. (I, for example, deeply
   believed that it was wrong to push and shove to get ahead of others.)

6. Coming into contact with a radically different culture challenges our basic assumptions of life. (I experienced culture shock when I discovered
   that my deeply ingrained cultural ideas about hygiene and the use of
   space no longer applied.)

7. Although the particulars of culture differ from one group of people to
   another, culture itself is universal. That is, all people have culture. There
   are no exceptions. A society cannot exist without developing shared,
   learned ways of dealing with the demands of life.

8. All people are ethnocentric, which has both positive and negative consequences.

Practicing Cultural Relativism

cultural relativism
not judging a culture but trying to understand it on its own terms

To counter our tendency to use our own culture as the standard by which we   20
judge other cultures, we can practice **cultural relativism**; that is, we can try to
understand a culture on its own terms. This means to look at how the elements
of a culture fit together, without judging those elements as superior or inferior to
our own way of life.

Because we tend to use our own culture to judge others, cultural relativism   21
presents a challenge to ordinary thinking. For example, most U.S. citizens appear to have strong feelings against raising bulls for the purpose of stabbing them
to death in front of crowds that shout "Olé!" According to cultural relativism,
however, bullfighting must be viewed from the framework of the culture in
which it takes place—*its* history, *its* folklore, *its* ideas of bravery, and *its* ideas of
gender roles.

You may still regard bullfighting as wrong, of course, if your culture, which is   22
deeply ingrained in you, has no history of bullfighting. We all possess culturally
specific ideas about cruelty to animals, ideas that have evolved slowly and match
other elements of our culture. In the United States, for example, practices that
once were common in some areas—cock fighting, dog fighting, bear–dog fighting, and so on—have been gradually weeded out.

None of us can be entirely successful at practicing cultural relativism; we sim-   23
ply cannot help viewing a contrasting way of life through the lens that our own
culture provides. Cultural relativism, however, is an attempt to refocus that lens
and thereby appreciate other ways of life rather than simply asserting, "Our way
is right."

24   Although cultural relativism helps us to avoid cultural smugness, this view has come under attack. In a provocative book, *Sick Societies,* anthropologist Robert Edgerton points out that some cultures endanger their people's health, happiness, or survival. He suggests that we should develop a scale for evaluating cultures on their "quality of life," much as we do for U.S. cities. He also asks why we should consider cultures that practice female circumcision, gang rape, or wife beating, or that sell little girls into prostitution, as morally equivalent to those that do not. Cultural values that result in exploitation, he says, are inferior to those that enhance people's lives.

25   Edgerton's sharp questions and incisive examples bring us to a topic that comes up repeatedly in this text—the disagreements that arise among scholars as they confront contrasting views of reality. It is such questioning of assumptions that keeps sociology interesting.

Section Review 1

Directions.

1. On a separate sheet of paper, write a brief summary of the main points of the sections you have just read.

2. Mark each of the following statements True (T), False (F), or Can't Tell (CT). Mark the statement Can't Tell if it cannot be determined to be either true or false based on the material in the passage. Refer to the passage as necessary to verify your answer.

_____ 1. Material culture consists of the beliefs and values of a given group.

_____ 2. People tend to assume that the beliefs and practices of their own culture are natural and normal.

_____ 3. Ethnocentrism is best understood as the disorientation one experiences when confronted with a different culture.

_____ 4. Americans are more likely to practice cultural relativism than people of other cultures.

_____ 5. All people have culture.

Directions. Write the letter of the best answer in the space provided.

_____ 1. Which of the following would *not* be a part of a group's nonmaterial culture?
   a. gestures and words used as greetings
   b. religious beliefs
   c. farming tools
   d. artistic values

_____ 2. Under which of the following circumstances would you be *least* likely to experience culture shock?
   a. You move to a different country where you don't know the native language.
   b. You move with your family to a different country where you don't know the native language.
   c. You visit a country whose culture and values are very different from your own.
   d. You visit distant relatives who live in a different state.

_____ 3. The author states that ethnocentrism
   a. should be avoided as much as possible.
   b. has become more common in recent times.
   c. cannot be modified.
   d. has both positive and negative aspects.

_____ 4. One criticism of cultural relativism is that it
   a. encourages intolerance.
   b. encourages tolerance of harmful practices.
   c. leads to ethnocentrism.
   d. is difficult to learn.

_____ 5. The author states that culture is a lens. He means that
   a. our cultural beliefs shape our perceptions and judgments.
   b. violating cultural norms leads to extreme sanctions.
   c. all people have culture.
   d. culture teaches us to communicate effectively with members of other cultures.

Components of Symbolic Culture

symbolic culture another term for nonmaterial culture

symbol something to which people attach meanings and then use to communicate with others

gestures the ways in which people use their bodies to communicate with one another

Sociologists sometimes refer to nonmaterial culture as **symbolic culture,** 26 because its central component is the symbols that people use. A **symbol** is something to which people attach meaning and that they then use to communicate. Symbols are the basis of nonmaterial culture. They include gestures, language, values, norms, sanctions, folkways, and mores. Let's look at each of these components of symbolic culture.

Gestures

Gestures, which involve using one's body to communicate with others, are use- 27 ful shorthand ways to give messages without using words. Although people in every culture of the world use gestures, a gesture's meaning may change completely from one culture to another. North Americans, for example, communicate a succinct message by raising the middle finger in a short, upward stabbing motion. I wish to stress "North Americans," for that gesture does not convey the same message in South America or most other parts of the world.

28   I was once surprised to find that this particular gesture was not universal, having internalized it to such an extent that I thought everyone knew what it meant. When I was comparing gestures with friends in Mexico, however, this gesture drew a blank look from them. After I explained its intended meaning, they laughed and showed me their rudest gesture—placing the hand under the armpit and moving the upper arm up and down. To me, they simply looked as if they were imitating a monkey, but to them the gesture meant "Your mother is a whore"—absolutely the worst possible insult in that culture.

29   Gestures not only facilitate communication but also, because they differ around the world, can lead to misunderstanding, embarrassment, or worse. One time in Mexico, for example, I raised my hand to a certain height to indicate how tall a child was. My hosts began to laugh. It turned out that Mexicans use three hand gestures to indicate height: one for people, one for animals, and another for plants. They were amused because I had ignorantly used the plant gesture to indicate the child's height.

30   To get along in another culture, then, it is important to learn the gestures of that culture. If you don't, not only will you fail to achieve the simplicity of communication that gestures allow, but also you will miss much of what is happening, run the risk of appearing foolish, and possible offend people. In some cultures, for example, you would provoke deep offense if you were to offer food or a gift with your left hand, because the left hand is reserved for dirty tasks, such as wiping after going to the bathroom. Left-handed Americans visiting Arabs, please note!

31   Suppose for a moment that you are visiting southern Italy. After eating one of the best meals in your life, you are so pleased that when you catch the waiter's eye, you smile broadly and use the standard U.S. "A-OK" gesture of putting your thumb and forefinger together and making a large "O." The waiter looks horrified, and you are struck speechless when the manager asks you to leave. What have you done? Nothing on purpose, of course, but in that culture this gesture refers to a part of the human body that is not mentioned in polite company.

32   Is it really true that there are no universal gestures? There is some disagreement on this point. Some anthropologists claim that no gesture is universal. They point out that even nodding the head up and down to indicate "yes" is not universal, because in some parts of the world, such as areas of Turkey, nodding the head up and down means "no." However, *ethologists,* researchers who study biological bases of behavior, claim that expressions of anger, pouting, fear, and sadness are built into our biology and are universal. They point out that even infants who are born blind and deaf, who have had no chance to *learn* these gestures, express themselves in the same way.

33   Although this matter is not yet settled, we can note that gestures tend to vary remarkably around the world. It is also significant that certain gestures can elicit emotions; some gestures are so associated with emotional messages that the gestures themselves summon up emotions. For example, my introduction to Mexican gestures took place at a dinner table. It was evident that my husband-and-wife hosts were trying to hide their embarrassment at using their culture's obscene gesture at their dinner table. And I felt the same way—not about *their* gesture, of course, which meant absolutely nothing to me—but about the one I was teaching them.

Language

34 Gestures and words go hand in hand, as is evident when you watch people talking. We use gestures to supplement our words, and to provide a deeper understanding of what we are communicating. In written language, we often miss the subtle cues that gestures provide. To help supply these cues in online communications,

people have developed *emoticons,* a type of "written gestures," to help convey the feelings that go with their words.

The primary way in which people communicate with one another is through 35 **language**—symbols that can be combined in an infinite number of ways for the purpose of communicating abstract thought. Each word is actually a symbol, a sound to which we have attached a particular meaning. This allows us to use it to communicate with one another. Language itself is universal in the sense that all human groups have language, but there is nothing universal about the meanings given to particular sounds. Thus, like gestures, in different cultures the same sound may mean something entirely different—or may have no meaning at all.

The significance of language for human life is difficult to overstate. As will be- 36 come apparent from the following discussion, *language allows culture to exist.*

Language Allows Human Experience to Be Cumulative 37
By means of language, we pass ideas, knowledge, and even attitudes on to the next generation, allowing it to build on experiences that it may never undergo. This building process enables humans to modify their behavior in light of what previous generations have learned. Hence the central sociological significance of language: *Language allows culture to develop by freeing people to move beyond their immediate experiences.*

Without language, human culture would be little more advanced than that of 38 the lower primates. To communicate, we would be limited to grunts and gestures, which would minimize the temporal dimension of human life. Our communications would be limited to a small time span—events that are now taking place, those that have just taken place, or those that will take place immediately—a sort of "slightly extended present." You can grunt and gesture, for example, that you want a drink of water, but in the absence of language how could you share ideas concerning past or future events? There would be little or no way to communicate to others what event you had in mind, much less the greater complexities that humans communicate—ideas and feelings about events.

Language Provides a Social or Shared Past   Without lan- 39
guage, our memories would be extremely limited, for we associate experiences with words and then use words to recall the experience. Such memories as would exist in the absence of language would be highly individualized, for only rarely and incompletely could we communicate them to others, much less discuss them and agree on something. By attaching words to an event, however, and then using those words to recall the event we are able to discuss the event. As we talk about past events, we develop shared understandings about what those events mean. In short, through talk, people develop a shared past.

Language Provides a Social or Shared Future   Language also 40
extends our time horizons forward. Because language enables us to agree on times, dates, and places, it allows us to plan activities with one another. Think about it for a moment. Without language, how could you ever plan future events? How could you possibly communicate goals, times, and plans? Whatever planning could exist would be limited to rudimentary communications, perhaps to an agreement to meet at a certain place when the sun is in a certain position. But think of the difficulty, perhaps impossibility, of conveying just a slight change in this simple arrangement, such as "I can't make it tomorrow, but my neighbor can, if that's all right with you."

language a system of symbols that can be combined in an infinite number of ways and can represent not only objects but also abstract thought

Language Allows Shared Perspectives   Our ability to speak, 41
then, provides us a social (or shared) past and future. This is vital for humanity. It is a watershed that distinguishes us from animals. But speech does much more than this. When we talk with one another, we are exchanging ideas about events;

that is, we are sharing perspectives. Our words are the embodiment of our experiences, distilled into a readily exchangeable form, mutually understandable to people who have learned that language. Talking about events allows us to arrive at the shared understandings that form the basis of social life. To not share a language while living alongside one another, however, invites miscommunication and suspicion.

42 **Language Allows Complex, Shared, Goal-Directed Behavior**   Common understandings enable us to establish a *purpose* for getting together. Let's suppose you want to go on a picnic. You use speech not only to plan the picnic but also to decide on reasons for the picnic—which may be anything from "because it's a nice day and it shouldn't be wasted studying" to "because it's my birthday." Language permits you to blend individual activities into an integrated sequence. In other words, through discussion you decide where you will go; who will drive; who will bring the hamburgers, the potato chips, the soda; where you will meet; and so on. Only because of language can you participate in such a common yet complex event as a picnic—or build roads and bridges, or attend college classes.

IN SUM

43   The sociological significance of language is that it takes us beyond the world of apes and allows culture to develop. Language frees us from the present by providing a past and future. It gives us the capacity to share understandings about the past and develop shared perceptions about the future, as well as to establish underlying purposes for our activities. Consequently, as in the case of planning a picnic, each individual is able to perform a small part of a larger activity, aware that others are carrying out related parts. In this way, language enables a series of separate activities to become united into a larger whole.

In short, *language is the basis of culture*. Like most aspects of culture, its linguistic base is usually invisible to us.

44 **Language and Perception: The Sapir-Whorf Hypothesis**   In the 1930s, two anthropologists, Edward Sapir and Benjamin Whorf, became intrigued when they noted that the Hopi Indians of the southwestern United States had no words to distinguish among the past, the present, and the future. English, in contrast, as well as German, French, Spanish, and other languages, distinguishes carefully among these three time frames. From this observation, Sapir and Whorf concluded that the commonsense idea that words are merely labels that people attach to things was wrong. *Language, they concluded, has embedded within it ways of looking at the world.* Thus thinking and perception are not only expressed through language, but also shaped by language. When we learn a language, we learn not only words, but also particular ways of thinking and perceiving.

45   The implications of the **Sapir-Whorf hypothesis** are far-reaching. *The Sapir-Whorf hypothesis reverses common sense:* It indicates that rather than objects and events forcing themselves onto our consciousness, it is our language that determines our consciousness, and hence our perception, of objects and events. Sociologist Eviatar Zerubavel gives a good example. Hebrew, his native language, does not have separate words for jam and jelly. They are classified the same, and only when Zerubavel learned English could he "see" this difference, which is "obvious" to native English speakers. Similarly, if you learn to classify students as Jocks, Goths, Stoners, Skaters, and Preps, you will perceive students in an entirely different way from someone who does not know these classifications.

Sapir-Whorf hypothesis Edward Sapir and Benjamin Whorf's hypothesis that language creates ways of thinking and perceiving

Although Sapir and Whorf's observation that the Hopi do not have tenses was 46
incorrect, they stumbled onto a major truth about social life. Learning a language
means not only learning words but also acquiring the perceptions embedded in
that language. In other words, language both reflects and shapes cultural experiences. The racial ethnic terms that our culture provides, for example, influence
how we see both ourselves and others.

Values, Norms, and Sanctions

To learn a culture is to learn people's **values,** their ideas of what is desirable in 47
life. When we uncover people's values, we learn a great deal about them, for values are the standards by which people define what is good and bad, beautiful and
ugly. Values underlie our preferences, guide our choices, and indicate what we
hold worthwhile in life.

Every group develops expectations concerning the right way to reflect its val- 48
ues. Sociologists use the term **norms** to describe those expectations, or rules of
behavior, that develop out of a group's values. The term **sanctions** refers to the
reactions people get for following or breaking norms. A **positive sanction** expresses approval for following a norm, while a **negative sanction** reflects disapproval for breaking a norm. Positive sanctions can be material, such as a prize, a
trophy, or money, but in everyday life they usually consist of hugs, smiles, a pat
on the back, or even handshakes and "high fives." Negative sanctions can also be
material—being fined in court is one example—but they, too, are more likely to
be symbolic: harsh words, or gestures such as frowns, stares, clenched jaws, or
raised fists. Getting a raise at work is a positive sanction, indicating that you have
followed the norms clustering around work values. Getting fired, however, is a
negative sanction, indicating that you have violated these norms. The North
American finger gesture discussed earlier is, of course, a negative sanction.

Because people find norms stifling, some cultures relieve the pressure through 49
moral holidays, specified times when people are allowed to break norms. Moral
holidays often center around getting drunk and being rowdy. During moral holidays, such as Mardi Gras, many norms are loosened. Some activities for which
people would otherwise be arrested are permitted—and expected—including
public drunkenness and some nudity. The norms are never completely dropped,
however—just loosened a bit. Go too far, and the police step in.

Some societies have *moral holiday places,* locations where norms are expected to 50
be broken. Red-light districts of our cities are examples. There prostitutes are allowed to work the streets, bothered only when political pressure builds. If these
same prostitutes attempt to solicit customers in adjacent areas, however, they are
promptly arrested. Lake of the Ozarks in Missouri, a fairly straight-laced area, has
"Party Cove." There, hundreds of boaters—from those operating cabin cruisers to
jet skis—moor their vessels together in a highly publicized cove, where many get
drunk and nude and dance on the boats. In one of the more humorous incidents,
boaters complained that a nude woman was riding a jet ski outside of the cove.
The water patrol investigated but refused to arrest her because the woman was
within the law—she had sprayed shaving cream on certain parts of her body. The
Missouri Water Patrol even announced in the local newspaper that it will not enter this particular cove, supposedly because "there is so much traffic that they
might not be able to get out in time to handle an emergency elsewhere."

Folkways and Mores

Norms that are not strictly enforced are called **folkways.** We expect people to 51
comply with folkways, but we are likely to shrug our shoulders and not make a
big deal about it if they don't. If someone insists on passing you on the left side

values the standards by
which people define what
is desirable or undesir-
able, good or bad, beautiful or ugly

norms the expectations,
or rules of behavior, that
develop to reflect and enforce values

sanction expressions of
approval or disapproval
given to people for up-
holding or violating norms

positive sanction a reward or positive reaction
for following norms, ranging from a smile to a prize

negative sanction an
expression of disapproval
for breaking a norm, ranging from a mild, informal
reaction such as a frown
to a formal reaction such
as a prison sentence or an
execution

folkways norms that are
not strictly enforced

of the sidewalk, for example, you are unlikely to take corrective action; although if the sidewalk is crowded and you must move out of the way, you might give the person a dirty look.

52   Other norms, however, are taken much more seriously. We think of them as essential to our core values, and we insist on conformity. These are called **mores** (MORE-rays). A person who steals, rapes, or kills has violated some of society's most important mores. As sociologist Ian Robertson put it,

> *A man who walks down a street wearing nothing on the upper half of his body is violating a folkway; a man who walks down the street wearing nothing on the lower half of his body is violating one of our most important mores, the requirement that people cover their genitals and buttocks in public.*

53   It should also be noted that one group's folkways may be another group's mores. Although a man walking down the street with the upper half of his body uncovered is deviating from a folkway, a woman doing the same thing is violating the mores. In addition, the folkways and mores of a subculture (the topic of the next section) may be the opposite of mainstream culture. For example, to walk down the sidewalk in a nudist camp with the entire body uncovered would conform to that subculture's folkways.

54   A **taboo** refers to a norm so strongly ingrained that even the thought of its violation is greeted with revulsion. Eating human flesh and having sex with one's parents are examples of such behaviors. When someone breaks a taboo, the individual is usually judged unfit to live in the same society as others. The sanctions are severe, and may include prison, banishment, or death.

mores norms that are strictly enforced because they are thought essential to core values or the well-being of the group

taboo a norm so strong that it brings revulsion if violated

Section Review 2

Directions.

1. On a separate sheet of paper, write a brief summary of the main points of the sections you have just read.

2. Mark each of the following statements True (T), False (F), or Can't Tell (CT). Mark the statement Can't Tell if it cannot be determined to be either true or false based on the material in the passage. Refer to the passage as necessary to verify your answer.

_____ 1. The terms *symbolic culture* and *nonmaterial culture* mean about the same thing.

_____ 2. One can reasonably assume that the meaning of a gesture will not change from culture to culture.

_____ 3. Language is a critical component of all human cultures.

_____ 4. Negative sanctions are much more common in most cultures than positive sanctions.

_____ 5. The norms of a society reflect its cultural values.

Cumulative Review 1 [Pages 110–121]

Directions. Write the letter of the best answer in the space provided.

_____ 1. The author suggests that culture
  a. is easy to define.
  b. is easy to understand.
  c. is easier to describe than to define.
  d. should not be defined.

_____ 2. Language contributes to culture by doing *all* of the following *except*
  a. allowing groups to pass information from generation to generation.
  b. allowing people to plan for the future.
  c. providing a means by which sanctions can be administered swiftly when norms are violated.
  d. providing a means by which people can formulate common goals.

_____ 3. We can tell from the chapter that
  a. cultural relativism is rejected by most sociologists.
  b. sociologists do not all agree on the value of cultural relativism.
  c. cultural relativism is accepted and practiced by most sociologists.
  d. sociologists do not consider their work to be scientific.

_____ 4. To avoid miscommunication with members of another culture, you should
  a. avoid the use of gestures.
  b. use only the gestures of your own culture.
  c. learn the gestures of the other culture.
  d. always explain your gestures verbally.

_____ 5. According to the Sapir-Whorf hypothesis
  a. common sense should not be applied to the study and use of language.
  b. our language provides a framework for our thoughts and perceptions.
  c. culture determines language.
  d. language's primary function is to provide a universally shared set of symbols for objects and events.

Directions. Answer each question in complete sentences, without copying word-for-word from the passage.

1. Explain the difference between material culture and nonmaterial culture.

_____

_____

_____

2. a. What is culture shock?

_____

_____

    b. Give an example of culture shock.

_____

_____

3. a. What is the purpose of moral holidays?

_____

_____

    b. Define and give an example of a moral holiday place.

_____

_____

4. Why is language essential to the development and maintenance of human culture?

_____

_____

_____

5. Explain the difference between folkways and mores.

_____

_____

_____

Vocabulary Exercise 1

Directions. Choose the meaning for the underlined word that best fits the context. You may consult the dictionary as needed.

_____ 1. . . . I found the sights that greeted me
exotic. . . . [Paragraph 3]
   a. exciting
   b. unpleasant
   c. strange and alluring
   d. difficult to understand or interpret

_____ 2. . . . standing in the oppressive heat. . . .
[Paragraph 7]
   a. excessive
   b. unusual or unfamiliar
   c. causing death or illness
   d. causing great discomfort

_____ 3. . . . to stare only surreptitiously. . . .
[Paragraph 15]
   a. secretively
   b. deliberately
   c. with curiosity
   d. in surprise

_____ 4. As you can tell from the opening vignette. . . .
[Paragraph 16]
   a. section
   b. sketch
   c. statement
   d. thesis

_____ 5. Culture also provides a "moral imperative" . . .
[Paragraph 19, point 5]
   a. grammatical form
   b. question
   c. requirement
   d. decision

_____ 6. . . . communicate a succinct message. . . .
[Paragraph 27]
   a. concise
   b. complicated
   c. difficult to understand
   d. important

_____ 7. . . . the temporal dimension of human
life. . . . [Paragraph 38]
   a. unique
   b. time-related
   c. practical
   d. of great value

_____ 8. . . . would be limited to rudimentary
communications. . . . [Paragraph 40]
   a. incomprehensible
   b. unimportant
   c. limited
   d. basic

_____ 9. It is a watershed that distinguishes us from
animals. [Paragraph 41]
   a. juncture; point where things join
   b. quality
   c. turning point; cutoff point
   d. cultural level

_____ 10. . . . even the thought of its violation is greeted
with revulsion. [Paragraph 54]
   a. surprise
   b. astonishment
   c. punishment
   d. disgust

Many Cultural Worlds: Subcultures and Countercultures

What common condition do you think this doctor is describing? Here 55
is what he said:

*[It accompanies] diaphragmatic pleurisy, pneumonia, uremia, or alcoholism ...
Abdominal causes include disorders of the stomach and esophagus, bowel diseases,
pancreatitis, pregnancy, bladder irritation, hepatic metastases, or hepatitis. Tho-
racic and mediastinal lesions or surgery may be responsible. Posterior fossa tumors or infarcts may stimulate centers in the medulla oblongata.*

My best guess is that you don't have the slightest idea what this doctor is talking
about. For most of us, he might as well be speaking Greek. Physicians who are

lecturing students in medical school, however, talk like this. This doctor is describing hiccups!

56   Physicians form a **subculture,** *a world within the larger world of dominant culture.* Subcultures consist of people whose experiences have led them to have distinctive ways of looking at life or some part of it. Even if we cannot understand the preceding quote, it makes us aware that the physician's view of life is not quite the same as ours.

57   Our society contains tens of thousands of subcultures. Some are as broad as the way of life we associate with teenagers, others as narrow as those we associate with body builders—or with doctors. Some U.S. ethnic groups also form subcultures: Their values, norms, and foods set them apart. So might their religion, language, and clothing. Occupational groups also form subcultures, as anyone who has hung out with cab drivers, artists, or construction workers can attest. Even sociologists form a subculture. As you are learning, they use a unique language for carving up the world.

58   Consider this quote from another subculture:

> *If everyone applying for welfare had to supply a doctor's certificate of sterilization, if everyone who had committed a felony were sterilized, if anyone who had mental illness to any degree were sterilized—then our economy could easily take care of these people for the rest if their lives, giving them a decent living standard—but getting them out of the way. That way there would be no children abused, no surplus population, and, after a while, no pollution. . . .*
>
> *Now let's talk about stupidity. The level of intellect in this country is going down, generation after generation. The average IQ is always 100 because that is the accepted average. However, the kid with a 100 IQ today would have tested out at 70 when I was a lad. You get the concept . . . the marching morons. . . .*
>
> *When the . . . present world system collapses, it'll be good people like you who will be shooting people in the streets to feed their families.*

Welcome to the world of Survivalists, where the message is much clearer than that of physicians—and much more disturbing.

59   The values and norms of most subcultures blend in with mainstream society. In some cases, however, such as these survivalists, some of the group's values and norms place it at odds with the dominant culture. Sociologists use the term **counterculture** to refer to such groups. Another example would be Satanists. To better see this distinction, consider motorcycle enthusiasts and motorcycle gangs. Motorcycle enthusiasts—who emphasize personal freedom and speed *and* affirm cultural values of success—are members of a subculture. In contrast, the Hell's Angels not only stress freedom and speed, but also value dirtiness and contempt toward women and work. This makes them a counterculture.

60   Countercultures do not have to be negative, however. Back in the 1800s, the Mormons were a counterculture that challenged the dominant culture's core value of monogamy.

61   An assault on core values is always met with resistance. To affirm their own values, members of the mainstream culture may ridicule, isolate, or even attack members of the counterculture. The Mormons, for example, were driven out of several states before they finally settled in Utah, which was then a wilderness. Even there the federal government would not let them practice polygamy (one man having more than one wife), and Utah's statehood was conditional on its acceptance of monogamy.

subculture the values and related behaviors of a group that distinguish its members from the larger culture; a world within a world

counterculture a group whose values, beliefs, and related behaviors place its members in opposition to the broader culture

Values in U.S. Society

An Overview of U.S. Values

As you know, the United States is a **pluralistic society,** made up of many 62 different groups. The United States has numerous religious and racial ethnic groups, as well as countless interest groups that center around such divergent activities as collecting Barbie dolls and hunting deer. This state of affairs makes the job of specifying U.S. values difficult. Nonetheless, sociologists have tried to identify the underlying core values that are shared by the many groups that make up U.S. society. Sociologist Robin Williams identified the following:

1. *Achievement and success.* Americans place a high value on personal achievement, especially outdoing others. This value includes getting ahead at work and school, and attaining wealth, power, and prestige.

2. *Individualism.* Americans have traditionally prized success that comes from individual efforts and initiative. They cherish the ideal that an individual can rise from the bottom of society to its very top. If someone fails to "get ahead," Americans generally find fault with that individual, rather than with the social system for placing roadblocks in his or her path.

3. *Activity and work.* Americans expect people to work hard and to be busily engaged in some activity even when not at work. This value is becoming less important.

4. *Efficiency and practicality.* Americans award high marks for getting things done efficiently. Even in everyday life, Americans consider it important to do things fast, and they constantly seek ways to increase efficiency.

5. *Science and technology.* Americans have a passion for applied science, for using science to control nature—to tame rivers and harness winds—and to develop new technology, from motorized scooters to talking computers.

6. *Progress.* Americans expect rapid technological change. They believe that they should constantly build "more and better" gadgets that will help them move toward that vague goal called "progress."

7. *Material comfort.* Americans expect a high level of material comfort. This comfort includes not only good nutrition, medical care, and housing, but also late-model cars and recreational playthings—from boats to computer games.

8. *Humanitarianism.* Americans emphasize helpfulness, personal kindness, aid to victims of mass disasters, and organized philanthropy.

9. *Freedom.* This core value pervades U.S. life. It inspired the American Revolution, and Americans pride themselves on their personal freedom.

10. *Democracy.* By this term, Americans refer to majority rule, to the right of everyone to express an opinion, and to representative government.

11. *Equality.* It is impossible to understand Americans without being aware of the central role that the value of equality plays in their lives. Equality of opportunity (part of the ideal culture discussed later), has significantly influenced U.S. history and continues to mark relations between the groups that make up U.S. society.

12. *Racism and group superiority.* Although it contradicts freedom, democracy, and equality, Americans value some groups more than others and have done so throughout their history. The slaughter of Native Americans and the enslaving of Africans are the most notorious examples.

pluralistic society a society made up of many different groups

CHAPTER 1 / SOCIOLOGY: CULTURE   127

63   In an earlier publication, I updated Williams's analysis by adding these three values.

1. *Education*. Americans are expected to go as far in school as their abilities and finances allow. Over the years, the definition of an "adequate" education has changed, and today a college education is considered an appropriate goal for most Americans. Those who have an opportunity for higher education and do not take it are sometimes viewed as doing something "wrong"—not merely as making a bad choice, but as somehow being involved in an immoral act.

2. *Religiosity*. There is a feeling that "every true American ought to be religious." This does not mean that everyone is expected to join a church, synagogue, or mosque, but that everyone ought to acknowledge a belief in a Supreme Being and follow some set of matching precepts. This value is so pervasive that Americans stamp "In God We Trust" on their money and declare in their national pledge of allegiance that they are "one nation under God."

3. *Romantic love*. Americans feel that the only proper basis for marriage is romantic love. Songs, literature, mass media, and "folk beliefs" all stress this value. They especially love the theme that "love conquers all."

Value Clusters

64 As you can see, values are not independent units; some cluster together to form a larger whole. In the **value cluster** surrounding success, for example, we find hard work, education, efficiency, material comfort, and individualism bound up together. Americans are expected to go far in school, to work hard afterward, to be efficient, and then to attain a high level of material comfort, which, in turn, demonstrates success. Success is attributed to the individual's efforts; lack of success is blamed on his or her faults.

Value Contradictions and Social Change

65 Not all values fall into neat, integrated packages. Some even contradict one another. The value of group superiority contradicts freedom, democracy, and equality, producing a **value contradiction.** There simply cannot be full expression of freedom, democracy, and equality, along with racism and sexism. Something has to give. One way in which Americans sidestepped this contradiction in the past was to say that freedom, democracy, and equality applied only to some groups. The contradiction was bound to surface over time, however, and so it did with the Civil War and the women's liberation movement. *It is precisely at the point of value contradictions, then, that one can see a major force for social change in a society.*

Emerging Values

66 A value cluster of four interrelated core values—leisure, self-fulfillment, physical fitness, and youthfulness—is emerging in the United States. A fifth core value— concern for the environment—is also emerging.

1. *Leisure*. The emergence of leisure as a value is reflected in a huge recreation industry—from computer games, boats, and motor homes to sports arenas, vacation homes, and travel and vacation services.

2. *Self-fulfillment*. This value is reflected in the "human potential" movement, which involves becoming "all one can be," and in books and talk shows that focus on "self-help," "relating," and "personal development."

value cluster values that together form a larger whole

value contradiction values that contradict one another; to follow the one means to come into conflict with the other

3. *Physical fitness.* Physical fitness is not a new U.S. value, but increased emphasis is moving it into this emerging cluster. This trend is evident in the "natural" foods craze; obsessive concerns about weight and diet; the joggers, cyclists, and backpackers who take to the trails; and the many health clubs and physical fitness centers.

4. *Youthfulness.* While valuing youth and disparaging old age is not new, some note a new sense of urgency. They attribute this to the huge number of aging baby boomers, who, aghast at the changes in their bodies, attempt to deny their biological fate. An extreme view is represented by a physician who claims that "aging is not a normal life event, but a disease." It is not surprising, then, that techniques for enhancing and maintaining a youthful appearance —from cosmetics to Botox injections—have become popular.

   This emerging value cluster is a response to fundamental changes in U.S. society. Americans used to be preoccupied with forging a nation and fighting for economic survival. They now have come to a point in their economic development where millions of people are freed from long hours of work, and millions more are able to retire from work at an age when they anticipate decades of life ahead of them. This value cluster centers around helping people to maintain their health and vigor during their younger years and enabling them to enjoy their years of retirement.

5. *Concern for the environment.* During most of U.S. history, the environment was viewed as something to be exploited—a wilderness to be settled, forests to be chopped down, rivers and lakes to be fished, and animals to be hunted. One result was the near extinction of the bison and the extinction in 1915 of the passenger pigeon, a bird previously so numerous that its annual migration would darken the skies for days. Today, Americans have developed a genuine and (we can hope) long-term concern for the environment.

   This emerging value of environmental concern is also related to the current stage of U.S. economic development, a point that becomes clearer when we note that people act on environmental concerns only after basic needs are met. At this point in their development, for example, the world's poor nations have a difficult time "affording" this value.

Culture Wars: When Values Clash

Changes in core values are met with strong resistance by people who hold them 67 dear. They see the change as a threat to their way of life, an undermining of both their present and their future. Efforts to change gender roles, for example, arouse intense controversy, as does support of alternative family forms and changes in sexual behavior. Alarmed at such onslaughts to their values, traditionalists fiercely defend historical family relationships and the gender roles they grew up with. The issue of socialist economic principles versus profit and private property is also at the center of controversy. Today's clash in values is so severe that the term *culture wars* has been coined to refer to it. Compared with the violence directed against the Mormons, however, today's reactions to such controversies are mild.

Values as Blinders

Just as values and their supporting beliefs paint a unique picture of reality, so they 68 also form a view of what life *ought* to be like. Americans value individualism so highly, for example, that they tend to see everyone as free to pursue the goal of success. This value blinds them to the many circumstances that impede people's efforts. The dire consequences of family poverty, parents' low education, and dead-end jobs tend to drop from sight. Instead, Americans cling to the notion that everyone can make it if they put out enough effort. And they "know" they are right, for every day, dangling before their eyes, are enticing success stories—individuals who have succeeded despite huge handicaps.

"Ideal" Versus "Real" Culture

69 Many of the norms that surround cultural values are only partially followed. Differences always exist between a group's ideals and what its members actually do. Consequently, sociologists use the term **ideal culture** to refer to the values, norms, and goals that a group considers ideal, worth aspiring to. Success, for example, is part of ideal culture. Americans glorify academic progress, hard work, and the display of material goods as signs of individual achievement. What people actually do, however, usually falls short of the cultural ideal. Compared with their abilities, for example, most people don't work as hard as they could or go as far as they could in school. Sociologists call the norms and values that people actually follow **real culture.**

ideal culture the ideal values and norms of a people, the goals held out for them

real culture the norms and values that people actually follow

Section Review 3

Directions.

1. On a separate sheet of paper, write a brief summary of the main points of the sections you have just read.

2. Mark each of the following statements True (T), False (F), or Can't Tell (CT). Mark the statement Can't Tell if it cannot be determined to be either true or false based on the material in the passage. Refer to the passage as necessary to verify your answer.

_____ 1. A counterculture is a subculture whose values conflict with those of the mainstream culture.

_____ 2. The norms of a subculture can be expected to be pretty much the same as the norms of the mainstream culture.

_____ 3. The 12 values identified by Williams have been confirmed by other sociologists.

_____ 4. Value contradictions can be an impetus to societal change.

_____ 5. Americans used to be more concerned about the environment than they are today.

Directions. Write the letter of the best answer in the space provided.

_____ 1. Which of the following is true of subcultures?
   a. There is no reliable definition of *subculture.*
   b. They are all of approximately the same size.
   c. A person can be a member of more than one.
   d. They are usually associated with ethnicity.

_____ 2. A group that practices monogamy in a culture where everyone else practices polygamy best exemplifies
   a. a subculture.
   b. a counterculture.
   c. a values cluster.
   d. traditionalism.

_____ 3. Because the United States is a pluralistic society, its values
   a. are shared by all.
   b. cannot be described.
   c. may be difficult to specify.
   d. are surprising and unexpected.

_____ 4. Which of the following is *not* identified as a value currently emerging in the United States?
   a. rugged individualism
   b. having time for recreational activities
   c. fulfilling your potential
   d. environmental protection

_____ 5. We can infer from the passage that
   a. values create an image that can be different from reality.
   b. efforts to change gender roles are welcomed readily in most cultures.
   c. traditionalists are unlikely to oppose cultural change.
   d. most subcultures have the same ideal culture but different real cultures.

Cultural Universals

With the amazing variety of human cultures around the world, are there any **cultural universals**—values, norms, or other cultural traits that are found everywhere? 70

To answer this question, anthropologist George Murdock combed through data that anthropologists had gathered on hundreds of groups around the world. He drew up a list of customs concerning courtship, marriage, funerals, games, laws, music, myths, incest taboos, and even toilet training. He found that although such activities are present in all cultures, *the specific customs differ from one group to another.* There is no universal form of the family, no universal way of disposing of the dead. Similarly, the games, rules, songs, stories, and toilet training differ from one culture to another. So do cooking and eating food. 71

Even incest is defined differently from group to group. For example, the Mundugumors of New Guinea extend the incest taboo so far that for each man, seven of every eight women are ineligible marriage partners. Other groups go in the opposite direction and allow some men to marry their own daughters. In certain circumstances, some groups *require* that brothers and sisters marry one another. The Burundi of Africa even insist that, in order to remove a certain curse, a son must have sexual relations with his mother. Such sexual relations are usually allowed only for special people (royalty) or in extraordinary situations (such 72

cultural universal a value, norm, or other cultural trait that is found in every group

sociobiology a framework of thought that views human behavior as the result of natural selection and considers biological factors to be the fundamental cause of human behavior

as when a lion hunter faces a dangerous hunt), and no society permits generalized incest for its members.

73   In short, although there are universal human activities (speech, music, storytelling, marrying, disposing of the dead, preparing food, and so on), there is no universally accepted way of doing any of them. Humans have no biological imperative that results in one particular form of behavior throughout the world. A few sociologists take the position that genes significantly influence human behavior, although almost all sociologists reject this view.

Technology in the Global Village

The New Technology

74   The gestures, language, values, folkways, and mores that we have discussed—all are part of symbolic or nonmaterial culture. Culture, as you recall, also has a material aspect: a group's *things,* from its houses to its toys. Central to a group's material culture is its technology. In its simplest sense, **technology** can be equated with tools. In its broader sense, technology also includes the skills or procedures necessary to make and use those tools.

75   We can use the term **new technology** to refer to the emerging technologies that have a significant impact on social life. People develop minor technologies all the time. Most are slight modifications of existing technologies. Occasionally, however, they develop technologies that make a major impact on human life. It is primarily to those that the term *new technology* refers. For people 500 years ago, the new technology was the printing press. For us, the new technology consists of computers, satellites, and the electronic media.

76   The sociological significance of technology goes far beyond the tool itself. *Technology sets the framework for a group's nonmaterial culture.* If a group's technology changes, so do people's ways of thinking and how they relate to one another. An example is gender relations. Through the centuries and throughout the world, it has been the custom (the nonmaterial culture of a group) for men to dominate women. Today, with instantaneous communications (the material culture), this custom has become much more difficult to maintain. For example, when women from many nations gathered in Beijing for a U.N. conference in 1995, satellites instantly transmitted their grievances around the globe. Such communications both convey and create discontent, as well as a feeling of sisterhood, motivating women to agitate for social change.

77   In today's world, the long-accepted idea that it is proper to withhold rights on the basis of someone's sex can no longer hold. What is usually invisible in this revolutionary change is the role of the new technology, which joins the world's nations into a global communication network.

Cultural Lag and Cultural Change

78   About three generations ago, sociologist William Ogburn, a functional analyst, coined the term **cultural lag.** By this, Ogburn meant that not all parts of a culture change at the same pace. When some part of a culture changes, other parts lag behind.

79   Ogburn pointed out that *a group's material culture usually changes first, with the nonmaterial culture lagging behind,* playing a game of catch-up. For example, when we get sick, we could type our symptoms into a computer and get a printout of our diagnosis and a recommended course of treatment. In fact, in some tests, computers outperform physicians. Yet our customs have not caught up with our technology, and we continue to visit the doctor's office.

technology in its narrow sense, tools; in its broader sense includes the skills or procedures necessary to make and use those tools

new technology the emerging technologies of an era that have a significant impact on social life

cultural lag Ogburn's term for human behavior lagging behind technological innovations

Sometimes nonmaterial culture never does catch up. Instead, we rigorously   80
hold on to some outmoded form—one that once was needed, but was long ago
bypassed by new technology. A striking example is our nine-month school year.
Have you ever wondered why it is nine months long, and why we take summers
off? For most of us, this is "just the way it's always been," and we've never questioned it. But there is more to this custom than meets the eye, for it is an example of cultural lag.

In the late 1800s, when universal schooling came about, the school year   81
matched the technology of the time, which was labor-intensive. For survival, parents needed their children's help at the crucial times of planting and harvesting.
Although the invention of highly productive farm machinery eliminated the
need for the school year to be so short, generations later we still live in this cultural lag.

Technology and Cultural Leveling

For most of human history, communication was limited and travel was slow.   82
Consequently, in their relative isolation, human groups developed highly distinctive ways of life as they responded to the particular situations they faced. The
unique characteristics they developed that distinguished one culture from another tended to change little over time. The Tasmanians, who lived on a remote
island off the coast of Australia, provide an extreme example. For thousands of
years, they had no contact with other people. They were so isolated that they did
not even know how to make clothing or fire.

Except in such rare instances, humans always had *some* contact with other   83
groups. During these contacts, people learned from one another, adopting some
part of the other's way of life. In this process, called **cultural diffusion,** groups
are most open to changes in their technology or material culture. They usually
are eager, for example, to adopt superior weapons and tools. In remote jungles in
South America one can find metal cooking pots, steel axes, and even bits of
clothing spun in mills in South Carolina. Although the direction of cultural diffusion today is primarily from the West to other parts of the world, cultural diffusion is not a one-way street—as bagels, woks, hammocks, and sushi bars in the
United States can attest.

With today's sophisticated technology in travel and communications, cultural   84
diffusion is occurring rapidly. Air travel has made it possible to journey around the
globe in a matter of hours. It the not-so-distant past, a trip from the United States
to Africa was so unusual that only a few hardy people made it, and newspapers
would herald their feat. Today, hundreds of thousands make the trip each year.

The changes in communication are no less vast. Communication used to be   85
limited to face-to-face speech, to written messages that were passed on from hand
to hand, and to visual signals such as smoke or light that was reflected from mir-
rors. Despite newspapers, people in some parts of the United States did not hear
that the Civil War had ended until weeks and even months after it was over. Today's electronic communications transmit messages across the globe in a matter
of seconds, and we learn almost instantaneously what is happening on the other
side of the world. During Gulf War II, reporters were "embedded" with U.S. soldiers, and for the first time in history they transmitted live video reports of bat-
tles and deaths as they occurred.

Travel and communication unite us to such an extent that there is almost no   86
"other side of the world" anymore. One result is **cultural leveling,** a process in
which cultures become similar to one another. The globalization of capitalism is
bringing not only technology but also Western culture to the rest of the world.
Japan, for example, has adopted not only capitalism but also Western forms of
dress and music. These changes, which have been superimposed on Japanese culture, have turned Japan into a blend of Western and Eastern cultures.

cultural diffusion the
spread of cultural characteristics from one group to
another

cultural leveling the
process by which cultures
become similar to one an-
other; especially refers to
the process by which U.S.
culture is being exported
and diffused into other
nations

87 Cultural leveling is occurring rapidly around the world, as is apparent to any traveler. The Golden Arches of McDonald's welcome today's visitors to Tokyo, Paris, London, Madrid, Moscow, Hong Kong, and Beijing. In Mexico, the most popular piñatas are no longer donkeys but, rather, Mickey Mouse and Fred Flintstone. In a jungle village in India—no electricity, no running water, and so remote that the only entrance was a footpath—I saw a young man sporting a cap with the Nike emblem.

88 Although the bridging of geography and culture by electronic signals and the exportation of Western icons do not in and of themselves mark the end of traditional cultures, the inevitable result is some degree of *cultural leveling,* some blander, less distinctive way of life—U.S. culture with French, Japanese, and Brazilian accents, so to speak. Although the "cultural accent" remains, something vital is lost forever.

Section Review 4

Directions.

1. On a separate sheet of paper, write a brief summary of the main points of the sections you have just read.

2. Mark each of the following statements True (T), False (F), or Can't Tell (CT). Mark the statement Can't Tell if it cannot be determined to be either true or false based on the material in the passage. Refer to the passage as necessary to verify your answer.

_____ 1. A group's symbolic culture is unlikely to be influenced by changes in technology.

_____ 2. The nine-month school year is an example of cultural lag.

_____ 3. Society improves more easily when changes in nonmaterial culture precede changes in material culture.

_____ 4. *Cultural diffusion* refers to the tendency of cultures to become similar to each other in their nonmaterial culture.

_____ 5. Cultural leveling is likely to occur more rapidly in those parts of the world in which the use of technology is growing faster.

SUMMARY and REVIEW

What Is Culture?

89 All human groups possess **culture**—language, beliefs, values, norms, and material objects that are passed from one generation to the next. **Material culture** consists of objects (art, buildings, clothing, tools). **Nonmaterial** (or **symbolic**) culture is a group's ways of thinking and patterns of behavior. **Ideal culture** is a group's ideal values, norms, and goals. **Real culture** is their actual behavior, which often falls short of their cultural ideals. Pp. 112–129.

What are cultural relativism and ethnocentrism?

90 People are naturally **ethnocentric;** that is, they use their own culture as a yardstick for judging the ways of others. In contrast, those who embrace **cultural relativism** try to understand other cultures on those cultures' own terms. Pp. 113–115.

Components of Symbolic Culture

What are the components of nonmaterial culture?

91   The central component is **symbols,** anything to which people attach meaning and that they use to communicate with others. Universally, the symbols of nonmaterial culture are **gestures, language, values, norms, sanctions, folkways,** and **mores.** Pp. 116–121.

Values in U.S. Society

What are the core U.S. values?

92   Although the United States is a **pluralistic society,** made up of many groups, each with its own set of values, certain values dominate: achievement and success, individualism, activity and work, efficiency and practicality, science and technology, progress, material comfort, equality, freedom, democracy, humanitarianism, racism and group superiority, education, religiosity, and romantic love. Some values cluster together (**value clusters**) to form a larger whole. **Value contradictions** (such as equality and racism) indicate areas of social tension, which are likely points of social change. Leisure, self-fulfillment, physical fitness, youthfulness, and concern for the environment are emerging core values. Core values do not change without opposition. Pp. 126–128.

Cultural Universals

Do cultural universals exist?

93   **Cultural universals** are values, norms, or other cultural traits that are found in all cultures. Although all human groups have customs concerning cooking, funerals, weddings, and so on, because the forms these customs take vary from one culture to another, there are no cultural universals. Pp. 130–131.

Why is language so significant to culture?

94   **Language** allows human experience to be goal-directed, cooperative, and cumulative. It also lets humans move beyond the present and share a past, future, and other common perspectives. According to the **Sapir-Whorf hyposthesis,** language even shapes our thoughts and perceptions. Pp. 117–120.

How do values, norms, sanctions, folkways, and mores reflect culture?

All groups have **values,** standards by which   95 they define what is desirable or undesirable, and **norms,** rules or expectations about behavior. Groups use **positive sanctions** to show approval of those who follow their norms, and **negative sanctions** to show disapproval of those who do not. Norms that are not strictly enforced are called **folkways,** while **mores** are norms to which groups demand conformity because they reflect core values. Pp. 120–121.

Many Cultural Worlds: Subcultures and Countercultures

How do subcultures and countercultures differ?

A **subculture** is a group whose values and re-   96 lated behaviors distinguish its members from the general culture. A **counterculture** holds some values that stand in opposition to those of the dominant culture. Pp. 124–125.

Technology in the Global Village

How is technology changing culture?

William Ogburn coined the term **cultural lag** to   97 describe how a group's nonmaterial culture lags behind its changing technology. With today's technological advances in travel and communications, **cultural diffusion** is occurring rapidly. This leads to **cultural leveling**, whereby many groups are adopting Western culture in place of their own customs. Much of the richness of the world's diverse cultures is being lost in the process. Pp. 131–133.

Cumulative Review 2 [Pages 124–134]

Directions. Write the letter of the best answer in the space provided.

_____ 1. Value clusters consist of
   a. a set of contradictory values held by members of a subculture.
   b. all primary values of a given group.
   c. a subset of related values within a given group.
   d. those values considered most important in a given subculture.

_____ 2. We can conclude from the chapter that the values of a culture
   a. remain stable unless influenced by a foreign culture.
   b. will almost certainly change and evolve over time.
   c. are not affected by changes in the material culture.
   d. are unlikely to be influenced by cultural diffusion.

_____ 3. Most Americans are likely to be members of
   a. one subculture.
   b. several subcultures.
   c. no subcultures.
   d. a counterculture.

_____ 4. Technology has an important influence on symbolic culture because
   a. it is part of the material culture.
   b. it is part of the nonmaterial culture.
   c. changes in society cannot occur without technological change.
   d. it affects the way members of society think and interact.

_____ 5. Teenagers in Japan and America wearing the same brands of jeans is an example of
   a. cultural leveling.
   b. cultural diffusion.
   c. cultural lag.
   d. cultural relativism.

Directions. Answer each question in complete sentences, without copying word-for-word from the passage.

1. How does cultural diffusion contribute to cultural leveling?

   _____

   _____

   _____

2. Explain the difference between ideal culture and real culture.

_____

_____

3. Define *values contradiction* and give an example of it.

_____

_____

_____

4. According to the author, are there any cultural universals? Explain your answer.

_____

_____

_____

5. What is technology? How do changes in technology affect a culture?

_____

_____

_____

Vocabulary Exercise 2

Directions. Choose the meaning for the underlined word that best fits the context. You may consult the dictionary as needed.

_____ 1. . . . as anyone who has hung out with cab drivers, artists, or construction workers can attest. [Paragraph 57]
   a. verify
   b. deny
   c. examine
   d. understand

_____ 2. . . . *and* affirm cultural values of success . . . [Paragraph 59]
   a. compete with
   b. support
   c. contradict
   d. develop

_____ 3. . . . challenged the dominant culture's core value of monogamy. [Paragraph 60]
   a. economic control
   b. faithfulness
   c. marriage to one partner
   d. sexual restraint

_____ 4. Americans emphasize helpfulness . . . and organized philanthropy. [Paragraph 62, point 8]
   a. charity
   b. aid
   c. cooperation
   d. economic initiative

_____ 5. ...goals that a group considers ideal, worth aspiring to. [Paragraph 69]
   a. challenging
   b. achieving
   c. seeking
   d. valuing

_____ 6. ...we rigorously hold on to some outmoded form.... [Paragraph 80]
   a. stupidly
   b. violently
   c. rigidly
   d. purposefully

_____ 7. ...human groups developed highly distinctive ways of life.... [Paragraph 82]
   a. respected
   b. respectful
   c. efficient
   d. different; distinguishable from others

_____ 8. ...the direction of cultural diffusion today.... [Paragraph 83]
   a. distinction
   b. unification
   c. tension or conflict
   d. spreading around

_____ 9. ...newspapers would herald their feat. [Paragraph 84]
   a. bravery
   b. achievement
   c. news
   d. lowest part of the body

_____ 10. ...some blander, less distinctive way of life... [Paragraph 88]
   a. less fortunate
   b. different; more different or distinct
   c. lacking distinction; flavorless
   d. old-fashioned

Critical Response Questions

1. Describe your ideal culture. What values would be primary? What norms would regulate behavior? How would those norms be enforced?

2. Why is it difficult to prevent teenagers from smoking and drinking?

3. Based on what you have read, what would you do to communicate most effectively if you were visiting a country whose culture was very different from ours?

4. How is technology changing our culture today? What changes may occur in the near future as a result of the digital revolution or other technological advancements?

5. What are the benefits of conformity for the individual and for society? What are the benefits of nonconformity for the individual and for society?

6. Why does society need moral holidays and moral holiday places?

7. Describe and analyze a subculture of which you are a member. What are its norms and values? How are they different from the norms and values of mainstream American culture?

Humanities

LOVE

Directions

1. Begin by surveying the chapter to look for answers to the following questions.

   - What is the chapter about?
   - What subtopics will be discussed?
   - What will you learn from reading and studying the chapter?
   - How interesting does the chapter look?
   - How difficult does the chapter look?
   - How familiar to you is the chapter material? That is, how much previous knowledge of the subject do you have?

   When you have completed your survey write a summary on a separate sheet of paper of what you've learned about the chapter from the survey. Your summary should include answers to the previous questions, as well as any other information and comments you wish to add.

2. While reading the chapter, look for organizational patterns. Recognizing the patterns should help you better grasp the relationship of ideas within each paragraph and section and distinguish main ideas more easily.

   Also, form questions from the headings and subheadings (generally, write one question per heading or subheading). Write your questions on a sheet of paper and, after completing each section, mentally review the main points of the section, mark the text, and write the answer(s) to your question(s), as well as any other information that seems important to you.

SAMPLE TEXTBOOK CHAPTER

From *The Art of Being Human,* 8th ed., by Richard Janaro and Thelma Altshuler. New York: Pearson Education, 2006.

Overview

1 We can scarcely overestimate the importance of love, yesterday and today, in our lives, in the world, and in the humanities. Without the theme of love, all of the arts would be diminished. Even the successive marriages of the frequently divorced

(half of all marriages now end that way) give evidence that people believe so strongly in love they keep looking for it—and that, no matter what their other achievements, they probably believe they have wasted their lives if they cannot say they have loved and been loved at some point. In countless poems, novels, operas, films, and plays, love is shown as the source of both pleasure and pain, often at the same time. Love's power has been recognized in holiday observances as well as songs about those claiming to be helpless prisoners under its spell.

2   Love is hard to describe scientifically; it may be solely the invention of the human imagination, without objective existence. Looking at love in the history of the humanities, we can see that the definition varies from era to era and from culture to culture. Artists are not united in their depictions of love. Some glorify it; others emphasize its pain; some have even tried to imagine a society whose leaders ban it entirely. This chapter offers an analysis of ways in which humanity has been affected by the myth or the mystery of love as is depicted in different cultures throughout the ages. Recognizing this obsession and its possible impact on our beliefs is crucial to the art of being human.

Body and Soul

3   Despite the sentiment in poems and songs that love is timeless, it must be considered in the context of history. Love has meant different things at different times and places, including its relative unimportance for people in desperate circumstances. Cultural anthropologists, for example, once discovered that people in a certain remote area of Africa had no word that translates as "love," though parents probably showed affection for their young by teaching them how to survive in a hostile environment. As you may have guessed, their vocabulary was filled with words that relate to survival strategies, all with favorable connotations. They seemed, however, to have little need for words that refer to tight family bonds and none for words indicating romance between adults.

4   Imagine the difficulty of having a meaningful discussion about love between people from totally different backgrounds—one waiting for romance and passion, with a wide choice of partners, the other obediently preparing to marry a stranger in a match arranged by the parents of the couple.

5   In the classical world of Greece and Rome the word *love* can be found in poetry, philosophy, and mythology, but a citizen of that world, alighting from a time machine in our era, might not understand axioms such as "Love is blind" or "Love is the answer." The time traveler, hearing the latter, might wittily retort, "To what question?"

6   The Greeks made a famous distinction between **eros,** or love as physical lust, and **agape,** in which a spiritual and intellectual relationship is more important than a strictly physical one. Though the Romans are famous for their wine-filled orgies, they recognized the distinction as well, and that distinction is still with us.

Eros

7   In the classical world passion was dangerous, responsible for endless misery. This poem by the Roman Petronius Gaius (c. 100 C.E.) offers a warning about lust and an invitation to something better:

> *Doing, a filthy pleasure is, and short;*
> *And done, we straight repent us of the sport:*
> *Let us not then rush blindly on unto it,*
> *Like lustful beasts, that only know how to do it:*
> *For lust will languish, and that heat decay.*
> *But thus, thus, keeping endless holiday,*

> *Let us together closely lie and kiss,*
> *There is no labour, nor no shame in this;*
> *This hath pleased, doth please, and long will please; never*
> *Can this decay, but is beginning ever.*

The debate continues over whether what we call *love* can mean anything   8
more than lust. Francine Prose, a contemporary author, described by a critic as
"one of our great cultural satirists," is convinced that lust is crucial to our survival.

> *Unlike the other deadly sins, lust and gluttony are allied with behav-*
> *iors required for the survival of the individual and the species. One*
> *has to eat in order to live; presumably the race would die out if lust*
> *were never permitted to work its magic.*

Physical desire is also the source of some long-lasting stories of classical   9
mythology. Typical is the account of someone—mortal or divine—caught in the
grip of uncontrollable passion. In Roman myth, the figure of Cupid, child of
Venus, is often the mischief-maker, as he aims his arrow at some unfortunate creature who is no longer able to think rationally.

One of his victims is his own mother, the goddess of love herself, who, after   10
being wounded by his arrow, becomes overcome by attraction to a mortal, Adonis. After enjoying moments of passion with a divine being, Adonis announces his
intention to go hunting. Venus pleads with him not to go in search of dangerous
game. Such advice being distinctly non-Roman, Adonis understandably ignores it
and is promptly killed by a wild boar. To perpetuate his memory and because lust
has turned into tragedy, Venus transforms his blood into a dark red flower called
the anemone. But like passion itself, the anemone is short-lived. The wind blows
the blossoms open, and all the petals suddenly are gone.

The story of Venus and Adonis lives on in powerful words and pictures. Many   11
artists, especially the Flemish Peter Paul Rubens (1577–1640), are inspired by the
myth of an impossible love between a mortal and the immortal goddess who
could not follow him to the grave. This story is not the last to show not only that
physical desire has a brief existence but also that death alone can ensure what human beings dream of and sing about: love that never ends.

In Shakespeare's dramatic poem about the pair, Venus is definitely the aggres-   12
sor, pursuing and seducing the reluctant Adonis:

> *Thrice-fairer than myself, thus she began*
> *The field's chief flower, sweet above compare,*
> *Stain to all nymphs, more lovely than a man,*
> *More white and red than doves or roses are;*
> *Nature that made thee, with herself at strife,*
> *Saith that the world hath ending with thy life.*

But in this version, after the young man dies, the goddess puts a curse on love.   13
Henceforth it shall never make anyone happy. Henceforth love shall be passion
unfulfilled or passion turned bitter.

> *It shall be fickle, false, and full of fraud,*
> *Bud and be blasted in a breathing-while;*
> *The bottom poison and the top o'erstrawed.*

Love will be "cause of war and dire events." Fathers and sons will fight each   14
other over the same woman. If any lovers are lucky enough to escape the decay of
their passion for each other, that passion will nevertheless make them miserable.
"They that love best their loves shall not enjoy."

15   Shakespeare's comedies often end with joyful lovers falling into each other's arms, but sexual love is the driving force in some of the tragedies, such as *Romeo and Juliet*. The sonnets, however, indicate that sex would be just fine if disdainful ladies would only cooperate!

16   Adonis was not alone in being radically altered following an erotic misadventure. Other mythic mortals who attract the attention of Olympian gods and goddesses either die or are changed into vegetation or heavenly bodies. In another myth, it is a woman who must die because of a god's attraction to her.

17   Persephone, daughter of Demeter, the earth mother, is so beautiful that Pluto, god of the underworld, falls in love (lust) with her, then captures and transports her to his dark kingdom. Demeter so grieves over her loss that Zeus, king of the gods, takes pity on her and allows her to share custody of the lovely daughter. During the six months that Persephone is gone, the earth mother mourns, and thus winter comes to the world. When she returns, however, the earth is reborn in spring.

18   Though a number of ancient stories tell of disaster following the passionate desires of gods for mortals, some deal with the entanglements of human beings caught in similarly dangerous passions. In mythology and in drama, Phaedra, wife of Theseus, is powerless to ward off erotic feelings for her stepson, once she too is victim of Cupid's arrow. Hippolytus, her stepson, angers Aphrodite by taking a vow of chastity. The revenge of the love goddess is to have Phaedra fall hopelessly in love with him. Reason and moderation abandon Phaedra as she pleads with Hippolytus to return her passion—but to no avail. Continuing to denounce lust, he rejects her.

19   Angry now, Phaedra tells Theseus that his son has made indecent proposals to her. She then dies by her own hand, causing her anguished husband to put a curse on his son, who is ultimately devoured by a huge sea monster. In this case we have two kinds of tragedy: one caused by unrequited passion, the other by the denunciation of love. Clearly, love is bad, no matter which road one takes! Both mother and stepson were unable to act rationally. For the classical mind, how could love be a desirable goal of human existence?

20   In classical mythology, human beings are not responsible for their tragic passions. Outside forces, personified as the gods, toy with them for amusement or the satisfaction of their own physical needs. Occasionally, the afflicted mortal is rewarded for being the target of a god's lust, but only after undergoing physical and mental torment. In one myth, which inspired a masterpiece of visual art—*Jupiter and Io,* by Italian artist Antonio Allegrio da Correggio (1494–1536), known in art history by his last name only—Io is an innocent young girl who stirs the sexual longings of the king of the gods. She runs away and is transformed into a heifer for her protection. Juno, the always jealous wife of Jupiter, does everything she can to rain destruction upon the girl but fails to kill her. Soon Jupiter is able to make love to Io, the heifer now transformed back into a girl, and the result is a son whose descendants include the great hero Hercules. This tale is probably not making a statement that lust is guaranteed to have happy consequences. Rather, it suggests—as do many classical myths—that human beings are related to the gods and in many respects are more than their equals. This explains why the gods are jealous of mortals and often affect them tragically, even if Io's fate is better than that of most women who wander into a lustful god's field of vision.

21   Physical passion and its consummation are not, therefore, always treated as evil in ancient stories. In fact, the pleasures of the flesh found their share of glorification. The Hebrew Bible, for example, contains the Song of Solomon (Song of Songs), which, though variously interpreted, appears to be a lyrical idealization of physical ecstasy. Its inclusion among sacred writings is clear evidence that to the Hebrews passion was a glorious experience, not at all inconsistent with the love of God. In this work the Lover speaks to his Beloved in sensuous terms. Her physical splendors fill him with joy. He compares her breasts to clusters of fruit and her breath to "the best wine."

During the late Middle Ages, even though Europe was strongly Christian, sec-   22
ular and erotic themes began to creep into poems and songs, which were often
written by young men studying for the priesthood. If they did not turn from their
faith, they could nonetheless be irreverent in their praise—or at least defense—of
sexual pleasure. Groups of rebellious students known as **goliards** frequented the
taverns in their leisure hours, singing songs that were anything but spiritual. The
most famous of these is *Gaudeamus Igitur* ("Let us rejoice while we are young"),
which is still played at countless college commencement ceremonies—minus the
lyrics that urge people to eat, drink, and be merry before the inevitable happens:
"Then the dust shall claim us." Many such lyrics have been discovered within the
past century, including *In Trutina* ("In my cell"), the narrator of which is a nun
who feels imprisoned in her tiny cell, longing to be outside enjoying the pleasures
to be found there.

The most famous secular author of the fourteenth century was Geoffrey   23
Chaucer (1340–1400), who, while reaffirming his devout faith, was fond of creating lusty stories and characters that shocked church authorities. In his masterpiece, *The Canterbury Tales,* he recognizes the weakness of the flesh of both
laypersons and clerics. Among the lust-driven men and women both within and
outside the church is his most unforgettable character, the aging Wife of Bath,
married five times (but always "at church door") and as lusty a creature as can be
found in the pages of literature. She sings the praises of youth and glorious sex,
culminating with a misty-eyed recognition that, as we grow old and unattractive,
we bid farewell to the joys that have made life rich and happy.

> *But lord Christ! When I remember*
> *My youth and joyful times,*
> *It tickles me to my heart's roots.*
> *Even now it does my heart good*
> *To know that I have had my world*
> *In my own time.*

As the Middle Ages waned and the Renaissance began to spread over much of   24
western Europe, bringing with it the lost glories of the classical world, the ancient
theme of lust awakened a sympathetic response in some writers, who could see it
as tragedy, and a recognition from others, who also ardently wished their lady
friends would cooperate.

In what is probably the most popular love story ever written, *Romeo and*   25
Juliet, it is quite clear that physical desire initially attracts the pair, a desire that
makes Juliet fearful. Before encouraging Romeo's suit, she warns that such an attraction is "too like the lightning" because it "ceases to be ere one can say it light-
ens." Their sexual attraction causes them to forget family duty, forget that Juliet is
promised to someone else—in short, to commit themselves with total abandon to
each other. Though their love is couched in the language of pure romance, they
too are destroyed by the curse of Venus.

The darts of the mischievous Cupid are a popular plot device, whether for ill   26
or good, and with or without him, we still have stories of people stricken with sudden, blinding passion—as if they *were* sporting arrows in their chest. Shakespeare
also saw the humorous side of the affliction in his comedy *A Midsummer Night's
Dream* (1594), when Titania, Queen of the Fairies, finds herself irresistibly drawn
to a man she would never have looked at if she were in her right mind. But she is
far from being in her right mind because a magic love potion has been administered to her that causes her to desire the first creature she looks at—in this case, a
bumbling rustic would-be actor wearing the head of a donkey and responding to
the Queen's passionate endearments with a typical donkey's bray, a sound that
drives her into absolute sexual frenzy. This is the comic flip side of the love coin for
Shakespeare. Whether you laugh or cry, passion doesn't bring much good fortune.

27   Nonetheless, Shakespeare's time was one in which passion took center stage. In England, the philosophy of hedonism, enjoyed much favor. It urged people, as the songs of the medieval goliards had, to enjoy life to the fullest because who knew what lay beyond the grave? The time of Queen Elizabeth I, who reigned until the beginning of the seventeenth century, was the heyday of celebrating the pleasures of the flesh, but usually with the darker implication that death can strike at any time. The philosopher Epicurus denounced hedonism on the grounds that its underlying obsession with death was more than enough to offset the fleeting pleasures of loving.

28   The eighteenth century, on both sides of the English Channel, was a time of polite society. Manners were extremely important, but under the surface the lusty life continued to be celebrated. One historian of the period observed that, though the drawing room was elegant and proper in all respects, behind the gilded bedroom door the rules were abandoned. Infidelity was rampant. It was expected that every well-bred gentleman of means would keep at least one mistress. Though religion kept denouncing flagrant immorality, even pious churchgoers could look the other way, especially at their own behavior.

29   By the nineteenth century the middle class was dominant, and sexual morality became a serious business. Only in marriage could sex be tolerated—at least officially. But it is no coincidence that two of the most popular hedonistic works of all time were both translated in that period. One was *A Thousand and One Nights;* the other, *The Rubáiyát of Omar Khayyám.*

30   In that century casual sexual encounters, though they happened, were not officially condoned. Marriage, at least in the West, was held to be a sacred institution between one man and one woman. The popularity of the two works just mentioned may, however, be attributed to the need for escape from rigid middle-class morality. Both reflect the exotic hedonism of foreign cultures and former times.

31   *A Thousand and One Nights* is usually, and inaccurately, referred to simply as *The Arabian Nights*. In truth, however, this vast collection of more than four hundred tales, put together from the ninth to the thirteenth centuries C.E., came from India and Persia, as well as from Arabia, and so represents a blending of several cultures. In the 1880s the stories were finally translated into English by Sir Richard Burton (1821–1890), an author and explorer, and have remained classic ever since.

32   The central character is Scheherazade, the latest wife of a much-married Sultan, who looks upon women as sexual objects with no other function than to be available at any time. Because he is all-powerful and can have any woman he desires, he has each bride executed after the wedding night. Scheherazade faces the same fate as her predecessors unless she can find a way to entertain the Sultan other than through lovemaking. The resourceful heroine decides to start telling stories, and they prove so engrossing that she dazzles her husband for a thousand and one nights, by which time we can presume the Sultan begins to see her as a human being rather than as a temporary bed partner. We can never know whether the long book was hugely popular because the ending satisfied the moral standards of the time or because the ending was overlooked in favor of the exotic tales of harem intrigues and adventures of heroes like Sinbad, Ali Baba, and Aladdin. Perhaps it offered the perfect escape into a never-never land of brilliant colors, fragrant spices, scrumptious feasting, and nights of delirious sex. Its musical counterpart, the symphonic poem *Scheherazade* by the Russian composer Nicolai Rimsky-Korsakov (1844–1908), remains a standard in the repertoire of all major orchestras and continues to enthrall listeners with its lush and sensuous tones.

33   *The Rubáiyát* (which means "quatrains," or four-line verses, in Persian) was translated by the English scholar Edward FitzGerald (1809–1883). Attributed to Omar, called Khayyám (tentmaker), a Persian poet and philosopher who lived around 1100 C.E., it is a collection of verses that celebrate both the glory and the short-lived pleasures of life, especially those of physical love. The poems tell us

that love is at once the thing that makes life exciting and the thing that, because it cannot endure, makes life ultimately a sad, futile enterprise.

> *Ah, Love! Could you and I with Him conspire*
> *To grasp this sorry Scheme of Things entire,*
> *Would we not shatter it to bits—and then*
> *Re-mould it nearer to the Heart's desire.*

Though a philosopher, Omar appears to have abandoned the life of reason in   34 favor of the life of the senses. Making love and drinking steadily may have been far more satisfying than spending sleepless nights trying to understand existence.

> *You know, my Friends, with what a brave Carouse*
> *I made a Second Marriage in my house;*
> *Divorced old barren Reason from my bed,*
> *And took the Daughter of the Vine to Spouse.*

This view of marriage may have been entertaining to Victorian husbands, but   35 the voice of conscience is there as well.

> *There was the Door to which I found no Key;*
> *There was the Veil through which I could not see;*
> *Some little talk awhile of ME and THEE*
> *There was—and then no more of THEE and ME.*

Bygone though these eras may have been, the fact remains that the theme of   36 masculine domination and women as playthings—servants of Eros, if you will— has never gone entirely out of fashion. Two of the favorite Mozart operas can be heard in almost any major opera house at any time. The Countess in *The Marriage of Figaro* (1786) is the long-suffering wife of a philandering husband who wants to exercise his right to take to bed a female servant on her wedding night—*before* the husband does! The Countess is, however, rewarded for her patience by getting to sing glorious musical laments.

Don Giovanni (1787) is actually a glorification of the most famous serial se-   37 ducer of all time. One of his victims, Zerlina, is engaged to marry someone of her own station in life and has sworn fidelity to him, a fact that makes little difference to the Don—and presumably the audience. Though the hero dies at the end and is consigned to hell, the intent of Mozart and his librettist, Lorenzo da Ponti, was probably not to make a strong case against male promiscuity.

A Chinese film of 1992, *Raise the Red Lantern*, takes place in a time when wives   38 were subject to the will of powerful masters. Each day a red lantern is hung before the house of the consort who is to be favored that night and who cannot question his wishes. The "fortunate" woman is showered with special favors during the day; more wonderful food is provided for her than for the others, and a foot massage is administered by a specially trained attendant. The woman's only obligation is to please the husband and then to bear him a son. Those who are disobedient or discovered to be having amorous relations with other men are severely punished, even executed. One wonders to what extent the film was recognized as a statement of women's rights or merely an interesting historical melodrama.

Agape

We have had much to say about the treatment of physical lust in the humanities.   39 But we should not think *love* always meant uncontrollable passion that makes people tragic victims or fools. In fact its opposite, *agape* (ah-ga-pay), is a Greek word meaning simply "love." In other words, *eros,* or lust, was not considered to be a form of love but something else altogether.

40   The most famous discourse on the subject came from Plato (427–347 B.C.E.), and agape is often called **Platonic love.** In popular usage the term *Platonic* has come to mean not only the opposite of lust but a synonym for a totally nonphysical relationship, as in the expression "They're just Platonic friends." As you will see, a truly Platonic friendship involves much more than, say, a classmate who studies with you while you both save more interesting relationships for the weekend!

41   In point of fact, Plato's ideal love may indeed include physical union with another, but the philosopher also believed the pleasures of the body can never be the highest possible good. There is no reason to believe he did not enjoy those pleasures, but he saw them only as the first rung of what we may call a ladder to the ideal.

42   In Platonic philosophy, each of us is born with a soul, the rational capacity for comprehending all of the eternal truths. The soul eventually discovers it is imprisoned in a body subject to deterioration, pain, and death. The soul, however, is immortal and will find a new home after the present body dies. The constant longing of the soul is therefore to escape from the body.

43   In his 1629 play *The New Inn,* Ben Jonson (1573?–1637) defined Platonic love as

> *A spiritual coupling of two souls*
> *So much more excellent, as it least relates*
> *Unto the body . . .*

44   For Plato, a human being's attraction to another on a strictly physical level is at least a step in the right direction because it represents a preoccupation with something other than the self—our temporary home, which, being short-lived, is of no great importance. Besides, the goal of bodily attraction is reproduction, the generation of another life; generation is likewise closer to immortality than being trapped in the trivial, everyday details of the self. Bringing into existence another life offers us a glimpse of the eternal, because we have for the time being substituted a fresh young life for a decaying, older one. Plato believed therefore that physical love can be construed as a good when it is an expression of the need for contact with what is not the self. It is not a good when physical attraction becomes obsession with the need to own, to possess, to make the other a part of oneself.

45   After a time, the soul glimpses higher visions. It longs for contact with other minds, with ideas, with art. One can therefore be in love—Platonically—with another person's mind, a painting, a sculpture, a symphony. One can fall in love with the face of another because it represents a perfect arrangement—in short, when it provides aesthetic pleasure desirable for its own sake, not for the sake of possession. One can find a painting in a museum that strongly attracts the soul and sit before it for a long time, wanting only to remain in its presence, even as one might have, at another time, longed to remain in the exciting physical presence of another person. The difference? The painting is a window through which one sees a little piece of the eternal. With the painting the soul revisits its home, beyond physical reality, where, if only for a few minutes or hours, one is in the presence of pure beauty. Platonic love is a ladder that leads past physical pleasure and upward toward the experience of pure beauty, an experience that cannot be expressed in words but only felt by the soul.

> *The true order of going, or being led . . . to things of love, is to begin*
> *from the beauties of earth and mount upwards for the sake of other*
> *beauty, using these as steps only, and from one going on to two, and*
> *from two to all fair forms, and from fair forms to fair practices, and*
> *from fair practices to fair notions, until from fair notions he arrives at*
> *the notion of absolute beauty, and at last knows what the essence of*
> *beauty is.*

For Plato, the highest form of love is therefore the love of the beautiful: in a   46
mind, in art, in life itself. The beautiful is most desired because it is unchanging,
unlike everything in the material world.

Christianity during the Middle Ages preferred Plato to Aristotle mainly be-   47
cause of his theory of agape. Christians believed the Platonic ladder leading from
physical desire to a vision of the ideal was in actuality a ladder to God. Platonic
love thus became God's love for humanity and, conversely, human spiritual, or
holy, love divorced from base passions. Whether rooted in Christianity or not, this
idea continues to influence vast numbers and forms the basis for the popular notion that to love Platonically means to refrain from sexual contact.

Almost none of us can fail to be affected by this idealism, whether overtly la-   48
beled *Platonic* or not. During a long separation, lovers may imagine each other as
they once looked, but in a reunion years later, they can face disappointment. Consider the major ideals of Plato's world: the Good, the True, and the Beautiful. Then
consider how the world of the flesh conspires against them. To be alive, to be human, is to change, eventually to be different from before, just as a flower briefly
achieves its potential. The beautiful smiling child in a photograph is for its time
the epitome of how a child should look. Part of the pleasure of seeing it is the
knowledge that the child has the potential to become something else—larger,
smarter, more agile—but different. The separated lovers may compare present reality with old photographs, noting with sadness how the actual person is no
longer the ideal person.

Platonism carries with it an ideal worth striving for and yet intrinsically dis-   49
appointing, even anti-life. (One thinks of the famous aria "The Impossible
Dream" from *Man of La Mancha,* the 1967 musical version of *Don Quixote,* in
which the virtuous knight declares he will devote his life to pure and beautiful
causes. But we note that even he admits his dream is "impossible.")

Even for the confirmed Platonist, a price must be paid for attempting to live   50
in a world higher than the physical plane. In John Keats's "Ode on a Grecian Urn"
(1820) the poet envies the inanimate lovers pictured on the urn as being superior
to human lovers because they will not suffer the pains of aging and death: "All human passion far above / The burning forehead and the parching tongue." The pictured lovers will stay the same: "Forever wilt thou love and she be fair." The poem
is just one of many, many works to make the Platonic statement that art is better
than life, because it does not change.

The Platonic concept that love in its highest form takes us to the realm of   51
pure beauty, which rules supreme at the top of this ladder, may have sounded inspiring to lovers and the artists who depict them, but they are also quick to recognize that few can withstand the rigors of the climb. Shakespeare many times com-
mented on the human weakness for sexual pleasure, once calling it "the appetite
that grows on what feeds it"—no serenity there!

In his short story "The Birthmark," Nathaniel Hawthorne recognizes the im-   52
possibility of reaching pure perfection, of experiencing ideal beauty. In the story, a
husband frequently remarks that his wife is beautiful—almost perfect, in fact—
except for the small birthmark on her cheek. He thinks he knows a way to remove
it, but this may involve danger. The wife begs him to try. She wants to appear completely beautiful for the man she loves. With the aid of his assistant, the husband
performs an experimental operation and manages to take away the ugly blemish.
As the birthmark disappears, the wife dies. Hawthorne is saying that we cannot
expect perfection in this world. Humankind is born naturally flawed and can
never attain an ideal state in which love is pure and untainted and beauty lasts forever. Is the Platonist injured by striving for it?

Section Review 1

Directions.

1. On a separate sheet of paper, write a brief summary of the main points of the sections you have just read.

2. Mark each of the following statements True (T), False (F), or Can't Tell (CT). Mark the statement Can't Tell if it cannot be determined to be either true or false based on the material in the passage. Refer to the passage as necessary to verify your answer.

_____ 1. In classical mythology, it is not unusual for a god to fall in love with a human being.

_____ 2. *Eros* and *agape* are Latin words coined by the Romans to distinguish between two types of love.

_____ 3. Geoffrey Chaucer's writings reflect the views of most of his fourteenth-century contemporaries toward sexual behavior.

_____ 4. *A Thousand and One Nights* is a hedonistic work that was popular during the nineteenth century.

_____ 5. In Plato's view, the highest form of love is the love of beauty.

Directions. Write the letter of the best answer in the space provided.

_____ 1. In the classical world, sexual passion was seen as all of the following *except*
   a. dangerous.
   b. eternal.
   c. short-lived.
   d. controlling.

_____ 2. According to the Persephone myth, spring arrives when Persephone
   a. returns from the underworld.
   b. arrives in the underworld.
   c. dies.
   d. is born.

_____ 3. During the Middle Ages
   a. attitudes toward eroticism were the same as during the Classical period.
   b. all expressions of eroticism were viewed as anti-Christian and therefore forbidden.
   c. erotic feelings were expressed in songs and poems.
   d. priests were expected to deny all sexual feelings.

_____ 4. Shakespeare's plays
   a. condemn sexuality as immoral and improper.
   b. treat passion as the highest human good.
   c. reflect both the tragic and comic view of eroticism.
   d. ignore sexual themes when focusing on romantic relationships.

_____ 5. The authors suggest that Plato's ideal
   a. makes no sense in today's world.
   b. cannot be understood without extensive study.
   c. was ultimately rejected because it conflicted with Christian values.
   d. is inspiring but difficult to achieve and maintain.

Family Love

The majority of us are born into a family circle and take for granted having sib- 53
lings, cousins, and aunts. These are the close kin who sign letters, cards, and e-mail
"with love," hug and kiss us at family gatherings, and expect loyalties and favors—
even as we expect such in return—without needing to ask why. All these actions
are performed under the rubric of the word *love.* Loyalty to the family is so much
taken for granted that juries tend to disregard a defendant's alibi that depends on
a mother's sworn oath that her child couldn't be guilty because he or she never left
her side while the crime was being committed.

Calendars are filled with reminders to demonstrate the kind of family love 54
sometimes called *togetherness.* Advertisements exhort us to "show how much you
care" with elaborate gifts and greeting cards. Supermarkets like to show a happy
assemblage of relatives around a festive table, the implication being that, if we
would only shop at Food Stuff, somehow all family ties will be restored and all
guilt washed away.

Still, we know the truth is rarely as pictured. The French satirist and social re- 55
former François Arouet, better known as Voltaire (1694–1778), once defined the
family as a "group of people who cannot stand the sight of each other but are
forced to live under the same roof." The American poet Robert Frost (1875–1963),
in his narrative poem *The Death of the Hired Man,* has one character observe

> Home is the place where, when you have to go there,
> They have to take you in.

To be sure, this is not the final word on the subject in the poem, but these 56
lines have become famous and are often quoted as if they did indeed express the
poet's philosophy. Sometimes they express the thinking of those who quote them!

How important are blood ties? The concept of family love has changed over
time. Movies and television programs can barely keep up with the new dynamics.
Nowadays schoolchildren easily master a complicated family tree expressed in visits to and from stepparents, gifts of varying value from one branch or another, and
different rules for dealing with ex-parents and former siblings, as well as the less
well-defined zone of the significant others and their offspring.

Even before the current fluid state of marriage and family, the humanities 57
dealt extensively with family love and its discontents, if only because people enjoy
reading about or watching stories about unhappy, dysfunctional families. One college instructor of playwriting told her class that "if you come from a happy home
life, you may never be able to write a play."

Think of the many unhappy children in fiction, eager to escape parents who 58
don't appreciate them or stepparents who abuse them. In popular fiction there is
usually a happy ending in which the runaways return, sometimes with a fortune.
In more serious work the ending is seldom happy, however. Literature features a
host of disappointed fathers and mothers and offspring who never manage to find
themselves. The bewildered Willy Loman, hero of Arthur Miller's *Death of a Salesman* (1949), wants his son to be more successful than his academically gifted
friend, only to be told in a wrenching confrontation scene that "a buck an hour" is
all the son believes he will ever be worth. The revelation shocks the father into a
Don Quixote–like delusion that his son is still "going to be magnificent," impelling

the poor salesman to crash his car into a wall so the son will collect the insurance and become a business triumph.

59   The humanities are full of epic struggles for family fortunes as well as hatred between brothers who have had nothing to do with each other for years. Perhaps some people find solace in reading about and seeing portrayals of families less loving than theirs. Particularly during holidays, these solace-seekers have the feeling everyone else is enjoying a festive meal complete with harmony among the generations. Though greeting cards and illustrations show Grandma setting a turkey on the table to the applause of her loving family, and though that old skinflint Scrooge comes to his senses and supplies the poverty-stricken Cratchits with more than enough food for the whole family, others are alone, eating unappetizing leftovers on a holiday that is far from merry.

60   One not-so-wonderful holiday account of family life is found in Amy Tan's *The Bonesetter's Daughter* (2001). The setting is a Chinese restaurant in San Francisco during the Festival of the Full Moon. Because of last-minute invitations, the party is larger than expected, and guests are seated at two tables. The hostess, her mother, her live-in boyfriend, and his two daughters are at one. The boyfriend's ex-wife, her parents, her husband, and their children are at another. Everyone arrives at the same time, and unity is hard to achieve. One character, noticing the non-Chinese children, asks, "Hey, are we in the white ghetto or what?"

61   Following Chinese tradition, the hostess offers the first delicacy to her mother, but the non-Chinese children squeal their disapproval of the foreign-looking food with cries of "Take it away!" The mother's boyfriend pays particular attention to his ex-wife, and Grandma shows signs of dementia. A somewhat less than happy family get-together.

62   Can something be said for societies in which men eat separately from the women, or have separate living quarters? Or societies in which the closest bonds are among children of the same age who are brought up together, without parents? In *The Republic,* for example, Plato advises that, in an ideal community, children should be taken from their parents and raised by the state. The idea has interested other utopians (people who map out plans for a perfect society). In actual society, courts and social agencies, recognizing that the mother who bore a child is not automatically endowed with the best child-rearing skills, are often called upon to judge whether a foster family or an institution guided by experts may not be in the child's best interest. Still, removing a child from its biological parent(s) may be desirable in the early years but can lead to serious problems later on. How often have adults been obsessed with the need to learn the names and the nature of their true parents? The latter may have been judged unfit early on but then undergone sobering changes, leading them to move heaven and earth to be reunited with their offspring. Yet, even if such reunions are permitted, what happens to foster parents who have established a happy home life for the children and suddenly discover that their comfortable world is about to come apart?

63   Perhaps the ancient Hebrews gave the world its first idea of the family as more than a convenient survival mechanism. In developing the father-children relationship between God and humanity, Judaism also created a model for earthly existence. First came the tribe, the larger group comprising interrelated families, governed by a patriarch, an older and presumably wiser man with great powers of judgment over all the members. The prominent biblical patriarchs Abraham and Moses are examples. Such an arrangement was logically paralleled by the idea of God as a father with the same power over human children. Strong family circles meant a strong tribe. Rules against worshipping false gods or marrying outside the tribe helped maintain coherence and unity.

64   The love accorded to God, which included fear and respect, was also demanded for the father of the earthly family. Without obedience there could be no order, and without fear, awe, and respect there could be no obedience. Fear was the means by which the children of a patriarch and all children of God showed

their love. The sometimes wrathful imposition of discipline and punishment from both fathers was *their* way of showing love.

Two biblical women, Ruth and Naomi, changed a traditional view of the fam- 65 ily when, after the death of Ruth's husband, she chose not to return to her original roots but remain instead with Naomi, her husband's mother, thus forming the basis for a new family.

> *And Ruth said, Intreat me not to leave thee,*
> *or to return from following after thee:*
> *for whither thou goest, I will go; and where*
> *thou lodgest, I will lodge: thy people shall be*
> *my people, and thy God my God.*
>
> Ruth I:16

If biblical historians are accurate, a group of Hebrew elders got together hun- 66 dreds of years after the historical events we read about in the earliest portions of the Bible, gathered up all known written accounts of Hebrew history and cultural practices, and embarked on the astonishing project of setting everything down in what they considered proper order.

The biblical story of Abraham and his covenant with God is part of Hebrew 67 history, and the Ten Commandments have been an almost endless source of analysis and commentary. One of the Commandments—Honor thy father and thy mother—has really become universally accepted, whether always acted upon or not.

To honor a parent may require specific instruction, and the Chinese sage 68 Confucius (551?–479 B.C.E.) provided exactly that. Almost every detail of living is, in fact, covered by Confucius, but none in greater detail than the rules for the treatment of one's parents and in-laws. Assuming most households included several generations, Confucius instructs children to eat whatever food is left over after their elders are finished. They must constantly inquire after the comfort of their parents, whether they are too warm or too cold, and whether they have an itch that needs scratching. There are prescribed visits morning and evening, and obedience is always foremost.

> *When sons and wives are ordered to do anything by their parents,*
> *they should immediately respond and reverently proceed to do it. In*
> *going forward or backward, or turning around, they should be careful*
> *and serious. While going out or coming in, while bowing or walking,*
> *they should not presume to belch, or cough, to yawn or stretch them-*
> *selves, to stand on one foot, or to lean against anything.*

The rules set down by Confucius may sound quaint to viewers brought up in 69 a child-centered home and nurtured with the idea that individual happiness is more important than tradition or loyalty to the family. Audiences and readers cheer when the obedient (and therefore repressed) young adult leaves home to seek a fortune far from the restrictive rules of the tribe. Nonetheless, respect for the wisdom of the strong patriarch or matriarch remains alive and well in cultures throughout the world—and even here, though it may be limited to the enjoyment of nostalgic glances backward. One of the reasons for the enduring popularity of the 1967 musical *Fiddler on the Roof* seems to be that its subject matter—the strength of the family unit and its ability to survive oppression—appeals to many who might accept the weakness of family bonds but secretly wish it were otherwise.

Two plays by Federico García Lorca illustrate the tragic consequences of 70 strong parental control. In both, mothers claim the right to steer the destiny of their daughters and to have the final say about when and whom they marry. In *Blood Wedding* (1935) the bride, promised to a man she does not love, runs off with someone else, a solution that cannot end happily in the repressed, traditional

Spanish society of Lorca's plays. *The House of Bernarda Alba* (1940) explores the tragic effect of a fiercely dominating matriarch over her daughters in a cheerless household dominated by unbreakable rules of endless mourning, forced chastity, and waiting without joy for an arranged match to materialize.

71   In a similar vein, a dominating mother in the 1993 Mexican film *Like Water for Chocolate* demands that her daughter marry no one at all in order to continue to cook and otherwise look after the household. All she can look forward to in life is becoming the caregiver of an aging parent.

72   John Steinbeck's *The Grapes of Wrath* gave the world one of the most memorable portraits of a matriarch forced to accept responsibility for keeping her family together. In the 1930s, the Joad family suffers bank foreclosure on their farm in Oklahoma and joins hundreds of other displaced Okies, as they are called, on a grueling migration to the Promised Land of California, only to discover that the "promise" (of abundant field work and high pay) was a scam. Because there are so many of them, the impoverished Okies are forced to pick fruit from sunup to sundown for a paltry salary. The four men of the family are paid *collectively* one dollar for a day's work. Ma buys a dollar's worth of hamburger from the store operated by the company and watches as her men devour the few scraps of meat, not noticing that she has none for herself. When one of the sons asks if there is any more food, she says in a voice that tries to sound pleasant and hopeful but nonetheless tears at the heart, "No, son, they ain't." The novel has attained the stature of a classic, and Ma Joad has taken her place among literature's great family protectors. Though Steinbeck has often been criticized for portraying a woman's role as solely to look after her family, the truth is that Ma Joad is heroic in the best sense of that word.

73   Not all strong parents in American literature are all as self-sacrificing as Ma Joad. One of the most overbearing fathers is the frightening creation of Henry James (1843–1915) in his 1881 novella *Washington Square*, later to become a play and film of the 1940s, both called *The Heiress*. This father makes no attempt to conceal his disappointment in his daughter, reminding her that she is far less attractive in every way than the mother who died giving birth to her. The daughter is told she lacks grace and charm and the feminine ability to flirt and make small talk. In an age when a proper marriage is the only suitable future for a physician's daughter, she is continually reminded of her sad deficiencies.

74   At length a suitor appears, a handsome, charming young man who woos her respectfully and begs her to be his wife. After meeting the man and appraising his income and career aspirations (or lack of them), the doctor decides the suitor is nothing but a fortune-hunter. Why else would such a handsome person take an interest in his daughter? The father announces his intention of bequeathing his money to a charitable institution if the marriage takes place, but the daughter is confident her suitor will marry her anyway. The two plan an elopement, but the heroine is left brokenheartedly waiting for the man who claimed to love her and who never comes for her.

75   Years later, after she inherits her father's wealth, the absent suitor, now full of apologies and renewed declarations of love, again asks the heiress to marry him. Again she agrees to an elopement, but this time she leaves him at the front door, pounding on it and begging her to forgive him. As his cries fill the empty street, she lights a lamp and goes upstairs to bed. When her aunt asks how she can be so cruel, the heiress replies with a stony face, "I have been taught by masters."

76   Often the unhappiness caused by dominating parents is treated comically. Stubborn old people making unreasonable demands on the young are simply too much fun for some writers. For thousands of years, countless stories have been built around the desire of an amorous couple to outwit the alternative marriage plans a parent has made for them. Readers and viewers are expected to be (and usually are) on the side of impetuous youths as they outwit their more unbending elders. We delight in seeing how a daughter in a Molière comedy

finds a devious a way to marry the one she loves instead of the inappropriate suitor chosen by her father.

Nor should we believe that family domination of children's destiny is limited   77
to stage and fiction. In her 1984 study of the struggle for women's independence, *The Weaker Vessel*, Antonia Fraser writes about the arranged marriage.

> *During this period, the emotion we should now term romantic love was treated with a mixture of suspicion, contempt, and outright disgust by virtually all pundits. . . . that tender passion which has animated much of the great literature of the world . . . received a hearty condemnation. Nor was this a revolutionary state of affairs in seventeenth-century England, the arranged marriage as opposed to the romantic union having been preferred by most societies.*

Friendship

Unlike Plato, his teacher, Aristotle, does not talk about love, but he is a strong be-   78
liever in friendship. He includes it among the highest goods of the happy life. For him, friendship is a strong bond between individuals sharing common interests and moral values, and it is thus similar to Plato's ideal of the perfect nonphysical relationship, except that Platonic love need not involve interaction with another person at all.

Our nature, however, seems to require, whether we like it or not, that we have ties   79
with other people who cause our lives to intertwine with theirs. Some of these ties, as in friendship, are of our own choosing; often, as in the family circle, they are not.

Even if we rarely, if ever, ascend to the top of Plato's ladder, close friendship   80
with another person is usually attainable and satisfies the Platonic requirements for a form of love that exists on a higher than physical plane. Experience shows that some of our friendships last far longer than physical obsession. Aristotle's mentor, Plato, defines *friends* as "a single soul dwelling in two bodies." Almost as strong a tribute to friendship is this statement from the Book of Revelations. "A faithful friend is a strong defense; and he that hath found one hath found a treasure."

If *kinfolk* is the traditional word for people related by blood, there ought to   81
be a designation for the friendship that has in some ways replaced the bonds of family, a new "next of kin," "super kin," or "kin by choice": people who choose to live together, starting out perhaps for economic reasons as roommates sharing the rent on an apartment. They also share their struggles to begin careers and to make important decisions about romance. Usually they find that these special kinfolk understand them in ways their parents do not. The new—usually urban—families now make appearances in movies and on Broadway and television; they find a responsive audience among young people who, overtly or otherwise, may long to substitute a self-selected family for the one into which they were born.

The 1969 international stage hit *Hair*, subtitled "The American Tribal Love   82
Rock Musical," focused on a spontaneous family of young men and women bonded by a mutual hatred of the war in Vietnam. This family was also environmentally sensitive, singing a warning about the imminent death of the planet unless active measures are taken to save it. At a performance of *Hair* on Earth Day in Chicago in 1976, the audience, customarily invited to join the actors at the curtain call in a dance celebrating life and love, was inspired to pour onto the street and help the actors dispose of litter. Well-dressed ladies and gentlemen were photographed on their hands and knees, some even in the gutter, picking up candy wrappers and cigarette butts. The dancing continued on the street for hours, tying up traffic and attracting police officers, many of whom joined this impromptu family in the common cause.

The Broadway musical *Rent,* a 1995 rock version of the opera *La Bohême,* is   83
about a group of young artists living together to ease the common burden of com-

ing up with rent money every month. Two of the roommates develop a physical relationship that is threatened when one of them is diagnosed with AIDS. How this super-kin family copes with impending tragedy provides a moving testimony to the power of self-chosen bonds. In addition to the actual lovers, all of them share the kind of love strong friendship engenders.

84   The sitcom *Friends* attracted millions of viewers each week during a 10-year run; in fact, it has been called the most successful TV show in history. Audiences ranged in age from the very young to the elderly. Clearly, it struck a responsive note, and that may have had something to do with alarming reports about the gradual erosion of the *nuclear* family. Once considered the foundation of our society, the **nuclear family,** comprising parents, children, and often one or more grandparents as well, has given way to the *extended* family, which usually includes some blood relatives as well as lifelong friends and even recent acquaintances with whom quick bonds are established. *Friends* represented an evolution to a kin-by-choice family in which no one was related, and perhaps its enormous popularity is evidence that Americans secretly fear the isolation a swiftly moving, rapidly changing society can bring.

85   When people join like-minded groups, they tend to become extreme versions of what they were originally. This could mean that consciously choosing a family is another way of affirming individuality. Because one is not living in isolation, there is group support for peculiarities, even though the *combined* peculiarities of this new family can easily result in bickering and wounded egos. At the same time, there is the tacit realization that the front door is always open.

86   In times gone by, friendship may not have been as desirable as it now seems to be in our fragmented society. In *Hamlet,* for example, Polonius gives his son Laertes paternal advice before the young man sets out to discover his place in the world: "Neither a borrower nor a lender be; for loan oft loses both itself and friend." This advice is tough-minded, isn't it? The implication is that friendship won't withstand either borrowing or lending. If the loan isn't paid back, chances are neither will ever speak to the other again.

87   Far more cynical are two recommendations about friendship made two centuries apart. In the novel *Tom Jones* by Henry Fielding (1707–1754), we are told, "[W]hen you have made your Fortune by the good Offices of a Friend, you are advised to discard him as soon as you can." In other words, what is a friend if not someone you can use to better your own station in life? One wishes that particular definition were indeed a thing of the past!

88   Just as cynical and self-centered is the presumed wit of this remark from F. Scott Fitzgerald, author of *The Great Gatsby:* "It is in the thirties that we want friends. In the forties we know they won't save us any more than love did."

89   Close in spirit to the super-kin idea of family is the buddy relationship, extolled in two classic novels, Cervantes's *Don Quixote* and Mark Twain's *Huckleberry Finn.* In both cases, we note, a close bond between two men may have something to do with one outranking the other.

90   In the former novel, the buddies are the Don, a crazed old man who believes he is a chivalrous young knight, and his faithful servant, Sancho Panza, who knows exactly what his master is but who deeply loves his idealism, however misguided it may be. If love is defined as caring more for another than for oneself, Sancho Panza, in dedicating his life to a man who has lost all contact with reality, nurturing and protecting him from the jeers of the crude world, brings us face-to-face with the veritable icon of that trait. Whether or not it exists in the real world between friends, readers may decide for themselves. The servant's love for the master is the more admirable when we consider that the master is too far gone to appreciate it, and the fragile health of the master makes it easier for the servant to devote his entire being to him.

91   That relationship has contemporary parallels, as in Alfred Uhry's 1988 Pulitzer Prize–winning play *Driving Miss Daisy.* The master in this case is a feisty

old woman who belongs to Atlanta's moneyed aristocracy. The servant is her African American chauffeur, who understands and accepts the racial barriers separating them but, like Sancho Panza, has a deep-rooted loyalty toward and genuine love for the woman. He does all he can to protect her from the knowledge that she is close to senility and will soon be utterly incapable of even feeding herself. The popularity of both the play and the movie version may be a testament to audience nostalgia for a vanished past in which such unquestioning devotion could exist. Nor can that relationship be considered racist because, like Sancho Panza, the chauffeur is superior to Miss Daisy both physically and mentally.

Huckleberry Finn begins with a continuation from an earlier novel of the   92 buddy adventures of Huck and Tom Sawyer, but the author must have realized Tom was too middle class, too much of a conformist, to fully understand the rebellious Huck. Their friendship is replaced by the bond that develops between Huck and Jim, a runaway slave. Though once more we have discrepancy in rank and ethnicity, Jim emerges as the stronger of the two, teaching Huck how to survive the hardships of life on the Mississippi River.

The age discrepancy between the fourteen-year-old Huck and the much older   93 Jim is the forerunner of many such relationships celebrated on film and television in our era. Italian film directors, in particular, are fond of pairing an old man and a young boy. The man teaches the lad about the ways of the world, offering another nostalgic glimpse of a past age when aging persons were less likely to be considered burdens on the young.

Section Review 2

Directions.

1. On a separate sheet of paper, write a brief summary of the main points of the sections you have just read.

2. Mark each of the following statements True (T), False (F), or Can't Tell (CT). Mark the statement Can't Tell if it cannot be determined to be either true or false based on the material in the passage. Refer to the passage as necessary to verify your answer.

_____ 1. Literature often reveals the discontents and tensions of family life.

_____ 2. The authors suggest that the idea of a patriarchal family may have originated with the ancient Hebrews.

_____ 3. Lorca's plays (*Blood Wedding* and *The House of Bernarda Alba*) portray patriarchs whose domination of their families leads to tragedy.

_____ 4. The popularity of the TV show *Friends* may have been related to the decline of the nuclear family.

_____ 5. Like *Huckleberry Finn*, *Driving Miss Daisy* relates the story of an older man befriending and assisting a young boy.

Cumulative Review 1 (pages 138-154)

Directions. Write the letter of the best answer in the space provided.

_____ 1. Plato viewed physical love as
   a.   positive when it expressed a need for contact outside of the self.
   b.   an obstacle to ideal love for all people at all times.
   c.   the highest form of spiritual love.
   d.   a magical force to be avoided by anyone seeking to experience beauty.

_____ 2. The theme of men's use of women as erotic playthings
   a.   is no longer evident in literature or the media.
   b.   expresses a modern version of Plato's concept of ideal love.
   c.   began during the classical era and disappeared in the nineteenth century.
   d.   is still with us today.

_____ 3. *The Grapes of Wrath* provides a memorable example of
   a.   a highly dysfunctional nuclear family.
   b.   a heroic matriarch.
   c.   an over-dominating patriarch.
   d.   the power of friendship.

_____ 4. The authors quote Antonia Fraser to show that
   a.   arranged marriages had fallen from favor by the end of the seventeenth century.
   b.   modern authors condemn romantic love.
   c.   literature has ignored romantic love.
   d.   parents have often discouraged their children's romantic relationships.

_____ 5. Judging from the literary works mentioned in this chapter, the reader can conclude that
   a.   friendship has consistently been viewed as the highest form of relationship.
   b.   the buddy relationship has been viewed as the highest form of friendship throughout history.
   c.   views of friendship have varied over time.
   d.   friendship has always been considered secondary to family.

Directions. Answer each question in complete sentences, without copying word-for-word from the passage.

1. Explain the difference between eros and agape.

_____

_____

_____

2. How were Plato's ideas about love viewed in the Middle Ages?

_____

_____

_____

3. According to the authors, why do people enjoy reading about (or watching a portrayal of) dysfunctional family relationships?

_____

_____

_____

4. What can we conclude about family relationships from Henry James's novella *Washington Square*?

_____

_____

_____

5. How is the importance of friendship illustrated in *Hair* and *Rent*?

_____

_____

_____

Vocabulary Exercise 1

Directions. Choose the meaning for the underlined word that best fits the context. You may consult the dictionary as needed.

_____ 1. To perpetuate his memory . . . Venus transforms his blood into a dark red flower . . . [Paragraph 10]
a. erase
b. continue or preserve
c. restore; revive
d. idealize; make heroic

_____ 2. Physical passion and its consummation are not, therefore, always treated as evil in ancient stories. [Paragraph 21]
a. consequences
b. fulfillment
c. difficulty
d. desire

_____ 3. . . . culminating with a misty-eyed recognition
that, as we grow old and unattractive . . .
[Paragraph 23]
   a. expressing
   b. understanding
   c. beginning
   d. concluding

_____ 4. The Countess . . . is the long-suffering wife of
a philandering husband . . . [Paragraph 36]
   a. abusive
   b. foolish; stupid
   c. cheating
   d. lacking affection

_____ 5. The beautiful smiling child in a photograph is
for its time the epitome of how a child
should look. [Paragraph 48]
   a. happy recollection
   b. person or thing that is temporary
   c. perfect example
   d. permanent impression

_____ 6. All these actions are performed under the
rubric of the word *love*. [Paragraph 53]
   a. disguise
   b. heading; category
   c. shield; protection
   d. emotion

_____ 7. Readers and viewers are expected to be . . . on
the side of impetuous youths . . .
[Paragraph 76]
   a. impulsive
   b. innocent
   c. attractive
   d. strong-willed

_____ 8. . . . treated with a mixture of suspicion, contempt, and outright disgust by virtually all
pundits . . . [Paragraph 77—quote]
   a. authorities
   b. artists
   c. older members of a family
   d. researchers

_____ 9. . . . there is the tacit realization that the front
door is always open. [Paragraph 85]
   a. unusual
   b. unspoken
   c. overwhelming
   d. insightful

_____ 10. The master in this case is a feisty old
woman . . . [Paragraph 91]
   a. wonderful
   b. unpleasant
   c. wealthy
   d . high-spirited

Romantic Love

94 We have seen how the behavior of people said to be in love is strongly influenced
by time period and cultural values. Most probably, when you, the reader, first
looked at the title of this [sample] chapter, you thought of the kind of love that we
customarily call *romantic*. For many, **romantic love** and *romance* are synonymous.

95   The contention here is that they were not always so. In fact, romantic love
cannot be located in the art and literature of the ancient world at all. Perhaps we
like to think the need for such love is inborn. When a parent insists a current
suitor is "not the right boy/girl for you," the implication is that such a person must
surely exist and will come along eventually. How many people are lost in self-pity
because Mr. or Ms. Right never shows up?

96   The "right" person is a mythic archetype indigenous to our culture, but not
necessarily universal. The arranged marriage is also an archetype, perfectly acceptable in many societies. In such places, as well as in past epochs in which the notion of romantic love did not exist, women are regarded as commodities or property, and marriage as a business transaction. Romantic love—or *true love*, as it is

sometimes known—usually needs the sense that a woman is the equal of a man, worthy of being treated with respect and adoration, and more than a sexual object or a commodity.

The prototype of romantic love is, undeniably, Shakespeare's *Romeo and* 97 *Juliet,* performed almost continually throughout the world. It is the first work that comes to mind when someone is asked to name a great love story. There are few parallels in any of the literature by Shakespeare's contemporaries, and those that come close, such as *The Duchess of Malfi* by the dramatist John Webster (1580?–1625?), are, like Shakespeare's work, considerably ahead of their time. Who knows? Webster may have been influenced by Shakespeare's story of a girl who goes against the wishes of her family, preferring a mate of whom the family disapproves, and dies for her love.

Still, as we pointed out, the famous star-crossed lovers *are* smitten by passion- 98 ate physical desires in the classical tradition. Near the end of the balcony scene, Juliet tells Romeo she must go inside now, and the anguished young man cries out, "O, wilt thou leave me so unsatisfied?" There is no mistaking what he means. Juliet answers, "What satisfaction canst thou have tonight?" The key word is *tonight.*

But there is more. Shakespeare is writing at a time when women, at least of 99 the upper classes, were no longer mere commodities. Yes, Juliet is destined for an arranged marriage, and yes, its purpose is her financial security as well as the so-cial advantages of uniting two prominent families, but Romeo, after all, is willing to have Juliet even though, if they were to marry, both would be cut off without a penny. Hence Juliet is not property in his eyes. The play tells the world that some-thing is more important than financial security or social approval—and that has come to be called "romantic" or "true" love. The language of the lovers is the lan-guage of romance, as far as subsequent eras have been concerned. Nobody is say-ing that romance is an experience entirely separate from sexual passion, but most of us would agree that romance transcends obsession with sexual union alone. Shakespeare's lovers indeed seem to believe in and share that something more, and they give up their lives for it.

Cynics believe the language of romance is all a façade and that lust is always 100 the reality. Yet the archetype has such a strong influence on all our lives—as do many other archetypes—that one must be cautious about calling it a lie or a delu-sion. Why would romance novels constitute a billion-dollar industry? Why would so many readers be lost without those heroes and heroines who think of nothing but being with each other? Poetry and songs are filled with accounts of the all-consuming emotion defined by the word *romance,* with hearts won, lost, broken, and crushed. The despairing lover in a classic popular song cries, "You took my heart and threw it away." The heart, not some other part of the body, is the loca-tion of romantic feelings.

Romance continues to be talked or written or sung about in terms that ex- 101 clude all mention of physical desire. Lovers long for one glance, for the touch of a hand, for an ascent to paradise. Romeo and Juliet elevate their passion through verse. The *West Side Story* lovers, in their version of Shakespeare's play, do so by thrilling audiences with "Maria" and "Tonight." One young soldier wrote a post-card to his beloved that said, "I'd walk around the world barefoot for one hour with you." Even if many of today's pop tunes deal with the torments of finding that one's true love is cheating, even if romance is considered a tragic state, the fact remains that it is the basis of the hopes and dreams of millions, the thing most worth striving for. It must therefore be a real force—and, if it came from the hu-manities, why, what better testament to the power of myth, art, and literature? Where would we be without them?

The language of romance is exactly what we do not find in the writings of the 102 ancient Greeks and Romans. Except for Plato, they were strictly earthbound, and they saw love as an affliction, often terrible, that drives people into desperate fires of longing. It may be fun for a time, but unless one is willing to suffer, one is better off without it. Plato, with his ladder that leads to the ideal, paved the way for the eventual emergence of the belief that ideal love transcends the flesh.

103   The notion of the love that transcends lust and lasts through and beyond time may have been glimpsed by Plato, but it grew firm roots in the Middle Ages. We can cite these sources for its growth and spread, and its continued hold on our emotions:

1. the cult that grew up around the poets and artists who celebrated the glory of the Virgin Mary

2. the *romance* itself, a sophisticate genre of literature about a (usually) high-born young man or woman for whom physical union is not allowed—one or the other may be married or have obstinate parents—but who nevertheless pledge their hearts for eternity

3. the code of chivalry, a set of elegant or courageous actions performed by a knight to honor his lady fair, including, if need be, laying down his life for her in jousting tournaments

Mariolatry

104   Although the writings of the Christian Bible do not say much about Mary, as the Christian religion spread and the Christian tradition grew during the Middle Ages, the subject of the mother of Jesus became a matter of increasing fascination. Madonna and Child became a favorite subject for medieval and, later, Renaissance painters. Poets waxed eloquent about Mary as the perfect woman, and particularly about her chastity. Though the virgin birth was not easy to comprehend, no one doubted Mary's purity—and since Mary was mortal, not divine, her purity and glory encouraged reverence for other women as well. In this view, women are deemed superior to men—literally above them if the lady in question were, like Juliet, on a balcony or in a tower from which she could wave and provide inspiration to the adoring man below.

105   Idolatry of Mary—**Mariolatry**—led to innumerable kinds of artistic expression, and it carried over into secular literature as writers borrowed the idea of the virginal heroine, worshipped for her purity as the poets worshipped Mary. Earthly love was thus presented in spiritual terms, even if lust were secretly there as well.

106   The same period saw a rebirth of interest in Plato's theory of love. It now became readily understood as the pursuit of an ideal—pure, chaste, true, and undefiled by lust—the love that cannot be destroyed, even in the grave. This ideal, we repeat, is still very much with us, despite attacks by an all-pervasive cynicism.

Romance and Chivalry

107   The word **romance** derives from the French *roman*, a long fictional narrative popular during the eleventh and twelfth centuries. In modern French, *roman* is translated as "novel." The stories were told rather than written because there was no printing press, and storytelling was an art form. Though the stories usually revolved around a man-woman relationship, the romances were not *always* about love but might include perilous journeys to distant Eastern lands at the time of the Crusades. Told from the Christian point of view, they presented dangers lying in wait for noble knights in combat with so-called infidels. Many of the best-loved romances were adventure stories about King Arthur, Camelot, and the Knights of the Round Table.

108   The word *chivalry* also had its origin in France, coming from the word *cheval*, "horse." The dashing knight on his horse had many admirable qualities, including a willingness to fight to the death in the name of his lady. All that was required of her was that she allow him to risk his life, perhaps while wearing a scarf she gave him as a token of the honor she bestowed. Thus was born the tradition of placing the lady on a pedestal and of expecting nothing in return, should she be disposed

to offer nothing. Chivalry, the knight's code, was the ancestor of the polite gestures that are often performed and expected, such as opening doors, pulling out chairs, and in general placing the lady first in any order of events. (The practice of the gentleman walking nearer to the curb is a latter-day version of chivalry, originally meant to spare the lady from being splattered with mud from carriages racing by.)

In many of the stories, even if the lady were willing to offer herself to the gal- 109
lant man, the pair could not form a lasting union because one of them was already married or otherwise unavailable. Typically such marriages were arranged by families more interested in property and financial gain than in the happiness of the off-spring. Perhaps the loving couple experienced a few moments of physical gratification in secret, but on the surface was the assumption that love denied was nobler than a loveless marriage. Love outside of marriage was made to seem as chaste.

A second assumption was that true love was made in heaven and was there- 110
fore elevated above earthly concerns such as bodily pleasure, marriages of convenience, and wealth. The belief that heaven destines each of us for another and that this person is the right and only mate persists through the centuries. Even if no union takes place between two right people, the rightness lasts forever.

One of the enduring romantic and unconsummated relationships in the 111
Middle Ages was that of Dante and the woman he called Beatrice, whom he presumably first saw when he was nine years old and whom he later immortalized in *The Divine Comedy*.

> At that moment, I say most truly that the spirit of life,
> which hath its dwelling in the secretest chamber of the heart,
> began to tremble so violently that the least pulses of my body
> shook therewith; and in trembling it said these words "Here is a
> deity stronger than I; who, coming, shall rule over me . . ."
>
> I in my boyhood often went in search of her, and found
> her so noble and praiseworthy that certainly of her might
> have been said those words of the poet Homer, "She seemed
> not to be the daughter of a mortal man, but of God."

Dante's overwhelming attraction toward Beatrice was, he said, the inspiration 112
behind the hundred **cantos** of *The Divine Comedy*. It is the reason he as the narrator of the poem is willing to undertake the arduous journey through the Inferno and Purgatory before reaching Paradise. It is understood that they will never be able to enjoy their love in any mortal way.

In Canto V of his poem, Dante visits the circle of hell (the Inferno) in which 113
are the souls of damned, carnal sinners who suffer eternal punishment for their unsanctified lust. Because illicit passion literally swept them off their feet, they can now find no rest. Still, in the tragic tale of Paolo and Francesca, two of the doomed lovers, the poet, while not justifying their sin, nonetheless is compassionate toward them. In fact, the reason he does not place them in lower circles where punishment is far more severe is that, even though they were misguided, at least they *loved*. The lowest circle is reserved for Satan, who represents the total absence of love.

Paolo is the brother of a man in an arranged marriage to Francesca, sent to 114
inform the lady of the parents' wishes. One day, however, they are so strongly affected by reading about the passion of an Arthurian knight that they fall into each other's arms, unable to keep from enjoying the strong sexual feelings that overwhelm them. Francesca explains to the poet-narrator:

> We were alone and without any dread.
> Sometimes our eyes, at the word's secret call,
> Met, and our cheeks a changing color wore.
> But it was one page only that did all.

When we read how that smile, so thirsted for,
Was kissed by such a lover, he that may
Never from me be separated more
All trembling kissed my mouth. . . .[14]

115   Yearning and aspiration toward an unreachable beloved is a feature of romantic love. Domesticity is not. Romantic love tends to feature not wedding anniversaries and visits from in-laws and grandchildren, but rather the death of one or both lovers. Those in the grip of an overwhelming passion—whether or not induced by a magic arrow or love potion—tend not to live moderately. Lovers of music are the beneficiaries of all that suffering, as, for example, in the erotic yet also spiritual "Liebestod" ("Love-Death") from the opera *Tristan and Isolde,* composed between 1857 and 1859 by Richard Wagner to celebrate his love for a married woman. Isolde, the heroine, is promised to King Mark, but she is escorted to the wedding by the king's nephew Tristan. On the ship they drink a love potion that creates feelings too powerful to resist. Like much romantic art, the opera carries the implicit message that illicit love is short-lived but wonderful enough to make early death worthwhile. Ordinary mortals who live by the rules are shown to live safe but dull lives. True love is therefore often combined with death. In the final scene, Isolde kneels by the body of her lover and sings the "Liebestod," perhaps the most sexually explicit as well as passionately romantic music ever written, its rising melodic line and crescendo, its sonorous chords becoming a musical parallel to the sex act itself (according to many interpretations)—reaching a glorious high note of ecstasy before resolving itself in a serene aftermath that brings peace and death to Isolde as she rests on the body of her lover.

116   If, as cynics like to say, romantic love is pure balderdash, we must be proud of a human tradition that can so nobly celebrate and create its reality.

Courtly Love

117   During the twelfth century Queen Eleanor of Aquitaine, wife of England's King Henry II and mother of Richard the Lionhearted, inaugurated a form of entertainment that eventually spread to other royal courts and became known as **courtly love.** In order to amuse themselves, Eleanor and her circle of aristocratic female friends held mock trials in which the defendant, a young man who declared his passionate longing for a reluctant young woman, was given a series of difficult tasks to perform in order to win her approval. The "jury" heard the case—that is, listened to the young man's account of all he had done to win the lady's favor—and then decided whether or not the favor should be granted. Most of the time it was not, an outcome that was in no way expected to diminish the plaintiff's devotion.

118   Courtly love became known more precisely as a set of rules for the proper conduct of courtship, rules based on the recommendations of Eleanor and others as they developed this "harmless" diversion. The idea that a high-bred woman was born to be adored and a man to be her virtual slave was implicit, if not directly stated, in the romances, so by the time rules were actually set down, there was little objection from the masculine side.

119   Earlier in this chapter we mentioned Cervantes's *Don Quixote* and the deep friendship between the hero and his servant. In addition, Cervantes created his own version of courtly love. The mad hero, who imagines himself a courageous knight, invents a fair lady he names Dulcinea; she is actually a peasant girl named Aldonza. In his delusion he imagines she is pure and unreachable and makes himself her slave. This letter to the imaginary lady fair is the epitome of romantic love carried to absurd extremes. The Don invites her to ask anything of him, even his very life:

. . . I am thine, and if not, do what thou likest, for by ending of my
life, I shall both satisfy thy cruelty and my desires.

He signs the letter, self-effacingly, The Knight of the Ill-Favored Face.

The model for Don Quixote's cruel lady may well have been a real person, de-   120
scribed in a relatively obscure book of the thirteenth century called *Freudenliest*
("The Service of Women") by an actual knight with the unique name of Ulrich
von Lichtenstein. The book contains 30,000 lines of narrative verse, all claiming to
constitute the autobiography of a man who sacrificed nearly his entire existence
for a princess who for years did not know he existed.

When he was twelve, Ulrich, knowing that if he were to become a knight he   121
must adopt the role of courtly lover, became a page in the court of a certain
princess. He was so much in love that he would steal a basin of water in which the
lady had washed her hands, then reverently drink it. Later, he fought in tournaments, developing a reputation as a brave knight willing to defeat all others in the
name of his all-consuming obsession.

His only reward for these efforts was a series of insulting rebuffs. Even when   122
he cut off his finger and sent it to her in a velvet-lined box, the princess was unimpressed. After a number of years, the lady finally agreed to allow the poor suffering man to visit her, but only if he came as a leper in the company of other lepers.
After spending a long, rainy night outside in a ditch, he was finally allowed to
climb a ladder and peer into the window of the lady's chamber, only to find a hundred candles burning and eight maids standing by her bed. After making a few
crude remarks about his appearance and stupid devotion, she then pushed him
and the ladder back into the moat surrounding the castle. *Freudenliest* concludes
with some pretty cynical observations about women—rare for the time but perhaps understandable in this case.

In 1507, the long-standing rules of courtly love were altered in a book called   123
The Courtier, by Baldassare Castiglione (1478–1529), in which the tempering effect
of the Renaissance begins to be felt. The woman, though still powerful, is now less
cruel; instead, she is well-educated, charming, witty, and sophisticated. She requires
a suitor to be her match—or nearly so. She still refuses to lose control no matter
how much she secretly admires the man, and while he is expected to sue for a physical encounter, she is not supposed to grant it. The grounds, however, have
changed. To surrender to him would coarsen what was thought to be an entirely
civilized relationship. (She has begun to sound like some of Shakespeare's wittiest
and most independent heroines, who adore privately but hurl insults publicly!)

Love as a Game

The Roman poet Ovid (43 B.C.E.–18 C.E.), who specialized in writing about the sub-   124
ject, defined love as "a game of seduction." Whether readers of Castiglione agreed
and privately enjoyed physical encounters behind bedroom doors we cannot be entirely sure, but during the seventeenth century—again, among the high born and
well bred—the game of seduction became quite fashionable, often as a way of making the satisfaction of lust more delicious, as Ovid no doubt had in mind, but often
as a sparring match between two people who really loved each other romantically.
Courtship began as a verbal match between educated and witty partners and ended
in physical or physical-romantic union, but only if preceded by stylish playfulness
and earnest competition. The game of love provides us with some of drama's most
memorable dialogue and charming characters. (Whether it will continue to do so
depends on the willingness of playwrights and scriptwriters to provide clever
talk—and whether audiences have the patience to listen.)

In England, especially during the period known as the Restoration (begin-   125
ning in 1661, when the monarchy was reinstated after twenty years of unsuccessful democracy), the sexes reached an equality exceeding even that of the late Middle Ages. Charles II adored women and encouraged them to show their
independence. In this period women took two steps forward—before the nineteenth century took them three steps back.

126   English theater sparkled with plays about the game of seduction, all carried out in high style and delightful banter. Mirabell and Millamant were the most glittering couple to grace the stage of that time in William Congreve's *The Way of the World* (1700). They manage to hide their feelings for each other behind a dazzling display of linguistic skill, yet manage not to hide the truth of their deep feelings for each other. The play combines the purity of romantic love with the sophistication of courtly love.

127   Rules of the love game are observed by the couple, who openly scorn sentimentality and sincere vows. They speak in mutually curt tones and throw challenges to each other that would never be understood by people unaware of the game they are playing. Millamant sounds downright cruel when she laughs at her lover's serious face and talks of using his letters to roll up her hair. She is reluctant to entertain a proposal of marriage, despite the fact that she has never wanted to marry anyone else. Yet, according to the fashion of the day, she declares that she really would not want to surrender her cherished solitude. Besides, she has a host of other admirers. (Her name means "a thousand lovers" in French.)

128   For his part, Mirabell is no saint, and she knows it. He was the lover of other women in the play, one of whom accuses him of fathering her child (which he probably did). Nor is he foolish enough to suggest to Millamant that they elope without the approval of her aunt and guardian, who would withhold the lady's fortune if marriage were to take place without her consent. Instead, he uses his wits and ingenuity to embarrass the guardian and gain both her approval and her fortune. Neither Millamant nor the audience would have expected Mirabell to be morally perfect. In this sophisticated, essentially hardboiled society one had to be a tough survivor, and true love had to accommodate the fact that it could exist only as a game played for high stakes by skillful players.

129   The play is over three centuries old, yet audiences today find it way ahead of its time, particularly in the Act IV scene when the lovers draw up a marriage contract, or prenuptial agreement, as it is now called. Millamant demands that, even after the wedding, her husband must respectfully request sexual favors from her, not regard them as an automatic right. She will sleep as late as she wants in the morning, nor will she endure being called pet names such as joy, jewel, sweetheart, "and the rest of that nauseous cant" when they are in public. She insists on her privacy and refuses to be "intimate with fools, because they may be your relations." Mirabell insists that she limit what she drinks (no strong liquor) and the confidences she shares with her female friends; he commands her not to smear her face with creams and oils at bedtime and reminds her not to squeeze her body into corsets when she becomes pregnant as a result of their "endeavors"—to which Millamant cries, "Odious endeavors!" (But there is every indication that both are looking forward to them.)

130   "These provisos admitted," he concludes, "I may prove a tractable and complying husband." She replies, "These articles subscribed, if I continue to endure you a little longer, I may by degrees dwindle into a wife." Then she adds hastily, "[H]ere, kiss my hand, though."

131   Allowing for changes in language during the three centuries since *The Way of the World* first appeared, couples determined not to make public parade of their strong feelings for each other no doubt still enjoy the banter of Congreve's famous lovers. They stand as icons of how sophisticated people can hold their own in an unsentimental environment and yet not forego the pleasures of romance. Despite today's high divorce rate and the competition between men and women for success and recognition, there may currently be more Mirabells and Millamants— closet romantic lovers, so to speak—than we might suppose.

132   In fact, love-as-a-game remains a popular theme, especially with audiences who like to show their sophisticated taste by sounding cynical about romantic love but who secretly long for its existence. Sparring couples like the gender-equal characters portrayed by Spencer Tracy and Katharine Hepburn in films of the 1940s and

1950s, who know very well that they really love each other; the Billy Crystal–Meg Ryan pair in *When Harry Met Sally* (1989), who don't know it; and, more recently, Julianne Moore and Pierce Brosnan as the unlikely lovers in *Laws of Attraction* (2004), all enjoy putting each other down and wanting to show disdain for a conventional middle-class life together. They quarrel more than they kiss or display outward signs of affection. In the latter film, apparent hostility between the lovers is raised to another level when they wake up in a bedroom and suddenly remember that, after over-imbibing the night before, they had "accidentally" gotten married.

Section Review 3

Directions.

1. On a separate sheet of paper, write a brief summary of the main points of the sections you have just read.

2. Mark each of the following statements True (T), False (F), or Can't Tell (CT). Mark the statement Can't Tell if it cannot be determined to be either true or false based on the material in the passage. Refer to the passage as necessary to verify your answer.

_____ 1. The need to find the right person to love and marry is a universal instinct.

_____ 2. Some people believe that romantic love is nothing more than a disguise for sexual desire.

_____ 3. In the Middle Ages, reverence for Mary led to increased respect for women in general and promoted the idea of the virginal heroine.

_____ 4. Dante, the author of *The Divine Comedy*, was inspired by a woman named Beatrice, whom he eventually married.

_____ 5. Don Quixote was a fictional character whose author believed in the ideals of courtly love.

Directions. Write the letter of the best answer in the space provided.

_____ 1. The idea of romantic love probably originated in
  a. ancient Greece.
  b. the Biblical era.
  c. the Middle Ages.
  d. the twentieth century.

_____ 2. Shakespeare's *Romeo and Juliet* can be considered a genuine romantic love story for all of the following reasons *except* that
  a. both lovers are willing to sacrifice everything for their love.
  b. their attraction is sexual, yet is also more than sexual.
  c. they regard each other as equal human beings rather than property.
  d. they both come from families of property.

_____ 3. Generally, in a chivalrous relationship
  a. the lady was expected to give herself to the knight in return for his protection.
  b. the knight and lady would eventually marry.
  c. the knight would act in the lady's behalf without expecting any reward from her.
  d. both parties were expected to remain chaste forever.

_____ 4. The courtly love tradition provided
  a. rules for courtship for upper-class men and women.
  b. rules to help married couples maintain loving relationships.
  c. witty conversational rules to stimulate sexual appetite.
  d. guidelines to ensure that marriages would be based on love.

_____ 5. According to this reading, equality of the sexes was greatest during the
  a. nineteenth century.
  b. seventeenth-century Restoration.
  c. late Middle Ages.
  d. early Middle Ages.

Love and Marriage

133 Notice that marriage is mentioned sparingly thus far in the chapter. It deserves its own special treatment, because sometimes convenience or prearrangements outweigh love in importance; sometimes romantic love is present at the outset but diminishes as time goes on; and often, quite often, differences of opinion about **gender roles** interfere with the course of true love. And yes, true love *can* remain throughout the course of a lifetime. Clearly, no institution, especially in modern society, is quite so complex.

The Victorian Model

134 We begin with the period of history in which the code of morality grew strong on both sides of the Atlantic: Queen Victoria's reign in England (1837–1901). The Victorian era was the heyday of the upper middle class, which decided to forget its humble past and start living "correctly" in the manner of the aristocracies of old. It also created the most stringent code of behavior any society had ever known, and the huge "middle" middle class, looking to its "betters" for role models, followed the code even more strictly.

135   As it was first conceived, the Victorian model saw marriage as not only the goal but also the duty of respectable men and women, the prime—really, the only—source of true happiness. Specific gender roles were assigned. The husband was the breadwinner. The status of men thus became elevated, and women now saw their importance diminished. Even when the wife's inheritance was the source of a family's income, the husband was still the dominant figure in the household, making the big decisions about where the family would live, what kind of education the children would receive, and, of course, when and whom they would marry. If daughters were likely to be married off to promising future executives, sons were frequently earmarked for wives who would bring with them generous dowries.

The wife's job was to run a good household, to deal with the servants, to 136
choose the menus (always with an eye to pleasing her husband's tastes), and, on
appropriate occasions, to show off her husband's net worth. The still common
phrase **conspicuous consumption** was coined in 1901 by the economist Thorsten
Veblen (1857–1929) to describe the spending habits of the money-conscious society, which included the wife's costly apparel and display of fine jewelry as demonstrations of her husband's success.

Out of this society emerged the **double standard** whereby the woman, but 137
not the man, was expected to remain a virgin until the wedding night. The groom
had the right to wed a bride untouched by other men, regardless of his own past
(or present) escapades. An adulterous wife was ostracized forever by polite society; but a husband suspected of indulging in extramarital affairs usually incurred
only mischievous winks from other men. Wives were not supposed to mention the
subject. Novel after novel, play after play in the Victorian Age showed the disasters
that befell women who broke the moral code.

Remnants of the double standard remain today, with varying degrees of ac- 138
ceptance. More than one hundred years later it continues to be influential, even
admired, especially among those who value traditional institutions, such as carefully specified gender roles that provide clear rules about the obligations of each
member of the household. Throughout the world today, in some societies, the patriarchal system remains in place. Marriages are arranged for children, educational
opportunities are minimal or nonexistent for girls, women are prevented from
showing their face in public, and in custody disputes, children are expected to remain with their father.

In the 1930s, when the family unit was in danger of splitting apart because of 139
economic instability, an American play set in the Victorian era was a long-running
success. *Life with Father,* adapted in 1938 by Howard Lindsay and Russell Crouse
from the memoir of the same name by Clarence Day, provided a genial and nostalgic visit to what many considered the good old days. Father Day, stubborn and
tyrannical, is the acknowledged ruler of the family domain, believing that his
word is law, almost by divine right. Mother Day—perhaps for the pleasure of the
modern wives—appears to accept her subordinate role while managing by devious strategies to get her way, but never by bickering or direct confrontation.
Sometimes she pretends not to understand what her husband is saying and talks
in a disorganized manner that spins Father's head until he backs down. The play
became a successful movie in 1947, mainly because in the post–World War II period marriage and the family were threatened by shifting gender roles and nostalgia for a more stable past grew even stronger than it had been a decade earlier. And
what about now?

The film version was recently released on DVD and received this Internet 140
comment from a young viewer: "This movie is too stupid for me to relate to."

New Versions and Continued Misgivings

Despite current cynicism about the way family life used to be shown, as voiced by 141
the DVD viewer quoted above, different attitudes toward love, reviewed in this
chapter, *including* the Victorian model, continue to influence our hopes and expectations. In discussing a recently announced engagement, overtly or discreetly,
friends usually want to know if a bride or groom has made a good choice economically, and there are nods of approval (or envy) on hearing that one or the other
has "married well."

Books and movies are still described as aimed for male or female audiences, 142
and the handsome, brave hero with smoldering eyes is still a good catch. Even in a
freer age in which the more productive moneymaker may be the wife, the house-
husband who takes the children to the park and who prepares dinner is apt to
cause talk among some members of the older generation, who also may count

backward the number of months between the birth of a first baby and the day wedding vows were exchanged. The "frank, equal, and open" discussions recommended in so many marriage manuals and by experts on daytime television shows still seem, to many people, less desirable in practice, than softer, more "feminine" ways of resolving conflicts.

143   At the same time, the twenty-first century has brought greater freedom to choose. Newspaper announcements of recent weddings (or commitment ceremonies) are not confined to members of the same ethnic group, class level, or even gender. Accounts of how the couple met and were attracted to each other may often include shared trips and apartments long before a public exchange of vows.

144   Feminist thinking sees no reason not to be frank and open in matters of intimate relationships, even if it means denying that love alone makes life complete. The heroine of Wendy Wasserstein's Pulitzer Prize–winning play *The Heidi Chronicles* (1988) learns that love need not be the pivotal event in anyone's life. After a disappointing relationship with a gay doctor, Heidi, in a final scene that is anything but poignant, feels totally free to continue her life without a long-term commitment to anyone.

145   HBO's *Sex and the City* enjoyed a long run and appealed to audiences of both sexes and all ages because it covered all the bases. The friendship among the four main characters—one of whom is over forty and another who is pushing forty—came close to illustrating Aristotle's definition of friends as "two [in this case, four] souls in a single body," as they meet almost daily for lunch and share the most intimate secrets of their lives. Each of the women, however, has her own personal needs, ranging from the satisfaction of pure lust to a desire for a more traditional middle-class wedding and marriage to the balancing of marriage and a career to the need to combine both good sex and a truly caring relationship. As the series neared its conclusion, there was public speculation about whether the final episode would show each of the four women with her need satisfied. Opinion polls (yes, some were actually conducted) revealed that most viewers believed the main character, Carrie Bradshaw, would turn down all possibilities of marriage and be strong in the realization that a truly caring relationship need not exist. After all, the object of her sexual needs is Mr. Big, generally described in today's parlance as a hunk, a promiscuous being who runs every time he hears the word *commitment*. Several versions of the episode were filmed, and even the cast was not told which would finally be shown. The polls proved wrong. Mr. Big was suddenly transformed into the caring, committed husband Carrie dreamed of, evidently suggesting the writers' or producers' belief that, at heart, the American public is tender and sentimental and likes to think the archetype of the one and only is alive and well.

146   The classical idea of love-as-lust continues to exert the strong influence it has always had both in periods of moral repression and in more permissive societies such as our own. Literature, drama, film, and television can be as graphic as they want and use language that was once forbidden. The assumption that sexual passion is uppermost in everybody's mind lies behind ads and commercials seeking to make consumers want products that often have nothing to do with the illustrations and text. Some of the products, however, directly address sexual needs and problems, including cures for impotence. Standup comics no longer need speak in euphemisms for parts of the body and intimacy. Women like the four friends in *Sex and the City*, who speak frankly about their sexual needs, are no longer presented only as outlandishly comical characters.

147   Still, *every* kind of romantic or anti-romantic story is out there for anyone to read or see. If we want, we can even enjoy a modern fairy tale, such as *Don't Bet on the Prince* (1986) by Jack Zipes, which begins as a wise and witty (not shy, maidenly, and dimwitted) princess is introduced to a prince from a nearby kingdom. Sitting next to her at a royal banquet, he is swept away by her beauty and charm and falls instantly in love. The families are delighted and look forward to a

wedding. When the couple rises to dance, however, he is appalled to discover that she is taller than he, and the next day, when he shows off on horseback and expects her admiration for jumping hedges and ditches, she gives instead a superior display of equestrianism. After the prince calls off the wedding, she loses the use of her legs and takes to bed. Feeling superior to the princess once more, the prince condescends to visit her but rejects her again when he discovers that she converses as skillfully as she had ridden horses. Forlorn, the princess loses her voice, and now that she can neither move nor speak, she becomes an acceptable candidate for marriage. Not to worry! *This* princess decides to reject his offer and accept a different suitor, one who is shorter and less articulate than she but admires her for all her accomplishments. Her health restored, they live happily ever after—but on *her* terms.

One can even find negative views of the new definition of gender roles. Feminist author Shulamith Firestone warns that the new freedoms and rejection of the old rules can bring hazards to women. 148

> *By convincing women that the usual female games and demands were despicable, unfair, prudish, old-fashioned, puritanical, and self-destructive, a new reservoir of available females was created . . . for traditional sexual exploitation, disarming women of even the little protection they had so painfully acquired.*

Love in a Time of Health Hazards

The pairing of love and disease has a long history in the humanities. Some new works may remind us of the romantic operas of the nineteenth century, such as Verdi's *La Traviata,* in which the heroine dies, usually from tuberculosis or consumption, as it used to be called. We have already discussed Jonathan Larson's *Rent,* a modern adaptation of Puccini's *La Bohême,* in which AIDS substitutes for consumption. 149

AIDS has had a tremendous effect on the entertainment world. Many actors and dancers succumbed quickly to the disease, especially during the 1980s, when medical treatments were less advanced than they are now. Writers gave us plays and films about love that strengthens and deepens under the shadow of inevitable death, about dying men cared for by lovers who might otherwise have never shown the ability to care more for another than they do for themselves. 150

Larry Kramer's 1985 play *The Normal Heart,* revived in 2004, contains a powerful and heartbreaking scene. The caregiving lover of a man near death from AIDS returns home with a bag of groceries, hoping to induce his dying partner to eat something, only to find him on the floor, shaking from an unstoppable fever. The caregiver's profound grief suddenly erupts into anger at death and at his lover for leaving him and at the complacent society that pretends none of this is happening. In his rage he hurls groceries at the pitiable figure on the floor, screaming invectives through his tears. An equally memorable scene occurs at the end of Craig Lucas's *Longtime Companion* (1990), when a man holds his dying lover in his arms and gives him permission to "let go," even though it means leaving him forever. 151

Perhaps we can say that the health hazards of the world today unexpectedly turned many writers away from the cynical attitudes toward love that flourished in less troublesome times. Perhaps the shadow of death has led to the realization that we cannot afford to abandon a precious ideal. In the 1992 musical *Kiss of the Spider Woman,* two prisoners in a South American jail, one gay and one straight, share a cell, and though death is all around, they transcend their fears through a relationship that at first seemed impossible. The straight prisoner loses his distaste for homosexuality, at least for one night in which he finds that *any* form of love is better than loneliness and abandonment. 152

Love and Older People

153   If thousands upon thousands of younger people have been lost to AIDS, thousands of older people have found their life spans greatly lengthened with the emergence of new drugs and medical treatments. In addition to experiencing unexpected and continued health, many senior citizens now face a different kind of problem: how to overcome society's and their own stereotyped notions of what is and is not acceptable behavior for people past sixty. Years ago, one never heard, "Sorry. Grandmother can't baby-sit tonight because she has a date."

154   According to Colombian-born (1928) Nobel Prize winner Gabriel García Márquez, one is never too old to love and be loved. His 1988 novel *Love in the Time of Cholera* deals with both disease and aging. In the beginning of the story, Florentino Diaz, a rather nondescript and awkward young man, is overwhelmingly attracted to Fermina Daza. The lady, however, marries a successful doctor, partly because she finds her relentless suitor Florentino peculiar, if not repulsive. Nonetheless, the ardent admirer is loyal to his lady for over fifty years. When at length Fermina's husband dies, Florentino renews his suit, though by now both have reached an age when there should be no question of sexual attraction.

155   Nonetheless, Fermina agrees to marriage, if only out of weariness from having repelled Florentino's advances for so long. At first she has no intention of sharing her body with him as they set sail on a long voyage to escape the cholera epidemic that is ravaging the country. One night, however, Fermina submits to his ceaseless demands:

> *Then he looked at her and saw her naked to the waist, just as he had imagined her. Her shoulders were wrinkled; her breasts sagged, her ribs were covered by a flabby skin as pale and cold as a frog's. She covered her chest with the blouse she had just taken off, and she turned out the light. Then he sat up and began to undress in the darkness, throwing everything at her that he took off, while she threw it back, dying of laughter.*

156   So what is love in this instance? We cannot say the word is inappropriate or has no sexual connotations, for this geriatric couple indulge in passionate sex incessantly after their wedding night. It is their saving grace. Their love is not Platonic, for, having lost touch for over fifty years, they know almost nothing of each other's mind. Whatever they have together is assuredly good and seems to be the author's almost mystic answer to the world's problems.

157   It certainly beats hate, doesn't it?

Imagining a World in Which Only Sex Exists

158   Warnings about separating love and sex are evident in three works of fiction that attack **utopianism,** the belief that there are ideal ways to plan and run a society. This belief goes all the way back to *The Republic* of Plato, who describes a society in which parents give their newborns into the care of the State, which will raise them to become rational human beings, free of emotional ties, and understanding that marriage is for reproduction only.

159   In Aldous Huxley's 1932 novel *Brave New World*, there are no emotional quandaries that cannot be solved by popping a pill called "soma." Sex is easily available for pleasure alone, without guilt or responsibility. Couples get together briefly, enjoy themselves, and move on to other partners. This is not only condoned but demanded by the State. Skilled scientists take care of reproduction through in vitro fertilization. Children are thus conceived and born in the laboratory. The babies have no connection with parents; they all immediately become wards of the State, to be carefully conditioned and monitored as productive citizens of the future.

The only taboo is affection for another person. In other words, sex yes, love   160
no. In a world carefully engineered for efficiency, love in the romantic sense would
only get in the way. Something inside Huxley's main character, however, tells him
that there is more to life than this, that he is missing out on something. He manages to escape the utopia and wanders far away, where he finds and joins a group
of people living as a nuclear family. For the first time in his life he is happy.

In George Orwell's *1984* (written in 1948), love is again forbidden on   161
grounds of being contrary to the interests of the State, ruled by the unseen Big
Brother, who watches everybody constantly. The novel gave rise to the immortal
phrase "Big Brother is watching you," now used to describe surveillance technology in public buildings, the monitoring of protest marches, and the proliferation
of bugging devices on telephones. The hero and heroine break all rules by falling
in love and indulging in sexual relations, only to have their most intimate moments and private conversations discovered and exposed. Their punishment is to
be sent for brainwashing to a rehabilitation center, called, ironically, the Ministry
of Love. When Orwell wrote the novel, World War II had just ended, and Soviet
communism was being declared the next great enemy. The book remains a powerful anti-utopian statement, but more than that, a powerful warning against government intrusion into the right of individual privacy.

In Margaret Atwood's 1986 *The Handmaid's Tale,* all rights except that of re-   162
production have been taken from women. Each woman is given a designation that
indicates her service to the State. Women are denied education, careers of their
choice, and the ability to choose a mate based on love. The handmaid of the title
is a slave who must always wear an identifying garment; her name, Offred, means
"of Fred," the man who owns her. When Fred and Offred have sex, as is required
when a woman is in her fertile period, Fred's wife is present to oversee the process.
The resulting child will belong to the husband and wife. Once again, the author is
fearful that the powers of the state, even in a democracy, can be used as instruments of oppression against those deemed undesirable.

The statement running through all of these novels is that love is a natural in-   163
stinct and cannot be denied or controlled by outside forces. Some may argue that
this version of love is still based only on sexual passion. Or is there more to it than
that?

One of the major lessons of the humanities is that all of us are free to choose,   164
and that includes the freedom to define love in a way most meaningful for us.

Will chivalry be an important component? or a return to the stability of un-   165
breakable family ties? or a game that is not expected to last? or an ad in the Per-
sonals column?

We may choose to remain single, without feeling the need to travel with or   166
arrive at a social event with a recognizable lifetime partner.

We may be comfortable behaving according to the traditional rules requiring   167
us to marry someone from a background acceptable to our family and friends and
fitting into accepted gender roles.

We may make our own rules, unconcerned about which partner earns more   168
money, which one is considerably older or younger than the other, or even whether
a relationship that seems so right at the moment will or must last a lifetime.

Or we may decide love is not to be defined, only to be experienced, as the   169
poet Hannah Kahn would have us believe.

SIGNATURE

If I sing because I must
being made of singing dust,

and I cry because of need
being made of watered seed,

and I grow like twisted tree
having neither symmetry

nor the structure to avert
the falling axe, the minor hurt,

yet of one thing I am sure
that this bears my signature

that I knew love when it came
and I called it by its name.

Section Review 4

Directions.

1. On a separate sheet of paper, write a brief summary of the main points of the sections you have just read.

2. Mark each of the following statements True (T), False (F), or Can't Tell (CT). Mark the statement Can't Tell if it cannot be determined to be either true or false based on the material in the passage. Refer to the passage as necessary to verify your answer.

_____ 1. The phrase *conspicuous consumption* refers to the double standard of sexual morality for men and women.

_____ 2. The Victorian marriage model influences the attitudes of many Americans today.

_____ 3. Some modern thinkers believe that happiness is not dependent upon marriage or having a long-term romantic relationship.

_____ 4. Plays about AIDS have shown that with death approaching, love can grow stronger.

_____ 5. Utopian novels like *Brave New World* and *1984* portray a world in which sex is forbidden to most individuals.

Key Terms

canto a division of a long poem, such as *The Divine Comedy*, corresponding to a chapter in a book
conspicuous consumption phrase coined by Thorsten Veblen to explain the economic habits of the Victorian-era middle and upper classes, connoting the desire to make a public display of one's wealth

courtly love an artificial and codified set of rules governing the mating behavior of the upper classes during the late Middle Ages and the Renaissance; principal among these was the right of the lady to make any demands she wished in order to test the loyalty and devotion of her suitor

double standard originally a reference to the right of the husband, but not the wife, during the Victorian period to have sex before—and often outside—marriage
gender role the way society defines the rights and responsibilities of each sex, especially within marriage

goliard a medieval troubadour, usually a young man training for the priesthood, who sang lyrics extolling the hedonistic life and encouraging others to enjoy themselves before entering austere holy orders

Mariolatry the idealization of the Virgin Mary as practiced by a late medieval cult of poets and painters; not only did it ennoble the life and characteristics of the mother of Jesus but it also tended to elevate the status of upper-class women and women in holy orders

nuclear family the traditional family unit of father, mother, and children; once included grandparents, but less apt to now

Platonic love originally, an ideal relationship between two compatible minds that may have begun as physical passion but moved to a higher plane involving mutual intellectual and aesthetic interests; it can also define one's love for an idea or work of art or the physical beauty of another, divorced from any desire to possess it; in popular usage, it simply connotes a relationship without sex

romance a genre of fiction, originating in the Middle Ages, featuring the exploits of a dashing knight and his pure love for a lady fair for whom he is willing to die—and often does

romantic love a relationship that may or may not include sex, which is less important in any case than tender feelings and a desire to be with the other person for the sake of that person, rather than for the satisfaction of personal desires

utopianism the belief that the ideal society can be planned and rationally administered

Topics for
Writing and Discussion

1. Platonic love is sometimes defined is as a ladder beginning with delight in a physical union and leading upward to the oneness of two minds. Do you believe Plato's definition of the highest form of love is still valid? Why or why not?

2. Is genuine friendship more or less important to you than a satisfying, if temporary, physical relationship? Pretend you are forced to choose.

3. Parents, unhappy because they believe their children show them insufficient gratitude, have been known to say, "After all, look what we have done for you. Don't you think you owe us something?" Is *owe* a verb that should be used in discussions of family love?

4. Despite feminism and the fact that a husband frequently needs assistance from his working wife, cite evidence, from your own observations, that the Victorian gender role models are still around.

5. Tap your creative energies. Write a little story in which two of the characters you read about in this chapter meet each other. What might Romeo, for example, say to Ulrich von Lichtenstein? What might the father of James's heiress say to Tristan? Or what might Mirabell say to Juliet on the balcony?

6. Still tapping your creative energies, write a dialogue between two people who both use the word *love* to describe their relationship that somehow makes clear that each is operating according to a different definition of the word.

7. If, when some people declare love for each other, they really mean they have physical desires and nothing else, would it help matters if one simply said to the other, "I am in lust"? Or do we need to disguise the actual meaning? If we do, explain why.

8. Does romantic love figure in your expectations of a relationship? Or a marriage? Or both? Or is it only a figment of the imagination?

9. Watch two or three television sitcoms that deal, in one way or another, with relationships that can be classified under the heading "love." Report on the different meanings you find. Talk about the handling of gender roles.

10. Imagine you are living next door to an elderly and single man or woman who suddenly takes in a live-in companion, and the two of them party nightly into the wee hours. Suppose, further, that the neighbors, including your parents, sign a petition asking the police to put an end to this disgraceful blight on the neighborhood. Write a speech you would make either to the partying couple, explaining why their behavior is inappropriate, *or* to the petitioners, explaining why their attitude is inappropriate.

11. The text says that the language of Romeo and Juliet has become the language of romance ever since. Pretend that you are listening to the excerpt from the play with a very young person who doesn't understand what you mean by "It's so romantic." What do you answer?

Cumulative Review 2 (pages 157-172)

Directions. Write the letter of the best answer in the space provided.

_____ 1. Which of the following is *not* true of romantic love?
   a. It is more than physical desire.
   b. It has been popularized in modern songs and films.
   c. It has lost popularity in modern times.
   d. It implies equality between lovers.

_____ 2. The "game of love" refers to
   a. seductive verbal exchanges preceding and enhancing physical love.
   b. procedures and rules for the selection of suitable marriage partners.
   c. the courtly love traditions established under Eleanor of Aquitaine.
   d. the chivalric code of medieval knights.

_____ 3. The producers' decision to change Mr. Big into a caring husband for the final episode of *Sex and the City* is an indication of
   a. the public's continued preference for the one-true-love concept.
   b. the return of Victorian values to today's TV programs.
   c. the writers' lack of respect for feminist values.
   d. today's audiences' preference for love as lust.

_____ 4. Shulamith Firestone's quote (p. 168) makes the point that today's new gender roles
   a. are helping women find more satisfying relationships.
   b. are making it harder for women to avoid sexual exploitation.
   c. are making it harder for women to find suitable partners.
   d. are helping women to be more in touch with their real needs.

_____ 5. At the conclusion of the chapter, the authors suggest that
   a. traditional gender roles will continue to guide the choices of most adults.
   b. soon no one will need traditional gender roles.
   c. in the near future, more people are likely to choose to remain single.
   d. each person has the freedom to define love as he or she chooses.

Directions. Answer each question in complete sentences, without copying word-for-word from the passage.

1. What evidence do the authors cite to support their claim that the archetype of romantic love still strongly influences all of our lives?

   _____

   _____

   _____

2. What is Mariolatry? How did Mariolatry contribute to the growth of romantic love?

_____

_____

_____

3. Describe the Victorian marriage model.

_____

_____

_____

4. What point(s) do the authors make regarding love and older people?

_____

_____

_____

5. What point about love is made by the poem that concludes the chapter?

_____

_____

_____

Vocabulary Exercise 2

Directions. Choose the meaning for the underlined word that best fits the context. You may consult the dictionary as needed.

_____ 1. The "right" person is a mythic archetype in-digenous to our culture . . . [Paragraph 96]
   a. fundamental idea, model, or pattern
   b. detailed explanation
   c. written or graphic illustration
   d. category that is subdivided into several subcategories

_____ 2. The "right" person is a mythic archetype indigenous to our culture . . . [Paragraph 96]
   a. imported
   b. native
   c. external
   d. contrary or opposite

_____ 3. Poets waxed eloquent about Mary as the perfect woman . . . [Paragraph 104]
   a. practiced
   b. spoke
   c. grew or became
   d. wrote

_____ 4. Yearning . . . is a feature of romantic love. Domesticity is not. [Paragraph 115]
   a. strong desire
   b. marriage
   c. home life; household affairs
   d. reason

_____ 5. ... he concludes, "I may prove a <u>tractable</u> and complying husband." [Paragraph 130]
   a. stubborn
   b. easily managed
   c. affectionate
   d. calm; hard to upset

_____ 6. It also created the most <u>stringent</u> code of behavior any society had ever known ... [Paragraph 134]
   a. complete
   b. uniform; consistent
   c. complex
   d. strict; rigid

_____ 7. An adulterous wife was <u>ostracized</u> forever by polite society ... [Paragraph 137]
   a. criticized
   b. ridiculed
   c. looked down upon
   d. banished; excluded

_____ 8. ... the <u>complacent</u> society that pretends none of this is happening. [Paragraph 151]
   a. at large; external
   b. irresponsible; immoral
   c. prejudiced; biased
   d. self-satisfied; smug

_____ 9. Nonetheless, the <u>ardent</u> admirer is loyal to his lady for over fifty years. [Paragraph 154]
   a. intense in feeling; passionate
   b. persistent; long-lasting
   c. stubborn
   d. old; aged

_____ 10. ... there are no emotional <u>quandaries</u> that cannot be solved by popping a pill ... [Paragraph 159]
   a. difficulties
   b. strong feelings
   c. negative feelings
   d. boundaries or limits

Critical Response Questions

1. What is love?

2. What is needed for a successful, lasting marriage? Why is the divorce rate so high nowadays?

3. Do men and women enjoy genuine equality today, or does the double standard still influence our relationships? Explain your answer.

4. What is friendship? Why is friendship important? Is friendship a kind of love?

5. How important is the nuclear family in today's society? How important is the extended family?

6. In this chapter, the authors make frequent reference to literary works and the popular media. How do these references enhance our understanding of the important concepts and issues addressed in the chapter?

7. Does the chapter provide a complete picture of love? Are there aspects of love or types of loving relationships that are not discussed in the chapter?

CHAPTER

Criminal Justice

PERPETRATORS AND VICTIMS OF CRIME

Directions

1. Begin by surveying the chapter to look for answers to the following questions.

   - What is the chapter about?
   - What subtopics will be discussed?
   - What will you learn from reading and studying the chapter?
   - How interesting does the chapter look?
   - How difficult does the chapter look?
   - How familiar to you is the chapter material? That is, how much previous knowledge of the subject do you have?

   When you have completed your survey, write a summary on a separate sheet of paper of what you've learned about the chapter from the survey. Your summary should include answers to the previous questions, as well as any other information and comments you wish to add.

2. While reading the chapter, look for organizational patterns. Recognizing the patterns should help you better grasp the relationship of ideas within each paragraph and section and distinguish main ideas more easily.

   Also, form questions from the headings and subheadings (generally, write one question per heading or subheading). Write your questions on a sheet of paper and, after completing each section, mentally review the main points of the section, mark the text, and write the answer(s) to your question(s), as well as any other information that seems important to you.

SAMPLE TEXTBOOK CHAPTER

From *Criminal Justice*, 3rd ed., by Jay S. Albanese. New York: Pearson Education, 2005.

Who Are the Victims and Perpetrators of Crime?
Age
Gender
Race and Ethnicity
Socioeconomic Status

What Is Crime Profiling?
Offender Profiles
Victim Profiles
Crime Scene Profiles

THAT'S A FACT
Perspectives on Partner Violence

MEDIA AND CRIMINAL JUSTICE
Superheroes and Crime Prevention

CRITICAL THINKING EXERCISES
The Characteristics of Homicide
Preventing School Shootings

Lisa Duy entered Doug's *Shoot'n*

1   *Sports* in Salt Lake City to buy a Smith & Wesson 9-millimeter semiautomatic pistol. In accordance with the law, the store manager called the Utah Bureau of Criminal Identification to run a background check on Ms. Duy. She was quickly approved because no record was found of any felony convictions or mental illness. The store manager showed Ms. Duy how to hold and fire the heavy stainless-steel gun in the basement shooting range before she left the store. The only unusual circumstance, the store manager later recalled, was that she left the store wearing the ear protectors he had loaned her.

Learning Objectives

Explain how data on demographic factors can help prevent and solve crimes.

Identify factors of age and gender in offenders and victims of crime.

Analyze differences between male and female offending and victimization and the role of victim–offender relationships.

Evaluate factors of race, ethnicity, and socioeconomic status in offending and victimization.

Define and describe three types of crime profiling and explain their uses.

Give a specific example of a profile for one of the Index crimes.

2   Less than two hours after leaving the store, Lisa Duy walked into a local television station and began firing the gun. She took about fifty shots, killing a young mother and wounding the building manager. As it turned out, Ms. Duy had a long history of psychiatric problems. A year earlier she had been committed to a mental hospital for paranoid schizophrenia after she had threatened to kill an FBI agent, but this information was not available for the background check because laws in most states protect the privacy of the mentally ill to avoid stigma. Lisa Duy's delusions involved the belief that the television station was broadcasting information about her sex life.[1]

3   Are incidents like these common? What kinds of people typically commit serious crimes of violence and crimes against property? A better understanding of the types of persons likely to become involved in these crimes as victims or offenders helps us to evaluate the circumstances of crime and provide clues for prevention.

Who Are the Victims and Perpetrators of Crime?

Information about the nature of criminal incidents comes from the 4 reports of citizens to the National Crime Victimization Survey (NCVS) and from the FBI Uniform Crime Reports, which gather information about persons arrested. The new NIBRS program* will gather more information about the circumstances of crimes known to police once that program becomes nationwide in scope.

Age

There is often little relation between an individual's fear of crime 5 and the actual chances that person will be a victim of a crime. The elderly have been found to be most fearful of crime, yet they are victimized less often than any other age group. Figure 3.1 summarizes the distribution of crime victims by age. The figure indicates that in general, from age sixteen onward the younger the person, the greater the likelihood of being victimized by a violent crime (rape, robbery, assault). People age sixty-five or older are victimized by rape, robbery, aggravated assault, and personal larceny at a rate of less than 4 per 1,000. This is nearly twenty times lower than the victimization rate for the same crimes of sixteen- to nineteen-year-olds, the highest-risk group. It appears that one of the advantages of aging is a reduction in one's likelihood of being a crime victim. The risk is highest during the teenage and young adult years, but it drops dramatically after age twenty-five.

The reasons for these discrepancies based on age are not difficult to understand. Young people are more active and mobile and expose themselves to risk more often. They also visit more dangerous places, at later hours, and take fewer security precautions than do older people. In fact, although they own considerably less property than older people, they expose themselves to risk much more often and hence are victimized more often.

According to the Uniform Crime 7 Report, 17 percent of all persons arrested nationally are under eighteen

Figure 3.1
Age of Distribution of Crime Victims for Violent Crimes (age twelve and older)

SOURCE: Compiled from Callie Marie Rennison, *Crime Victimization 2002* (Washington, DC: Bureau of Justice Statistics, 2003).

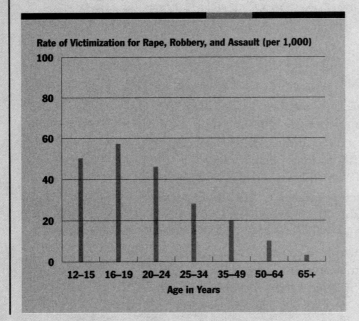

Rate of Victimization for Rape, Robbery, and Assault (per 1,000)

Age in Years

*The National Incident-Based Reporting System collects data on criminal incidents for 22 categories of offenses.

and 46 percent are under age twenty-five. This age pattern does not vary much by type of crime, with 46 percent of violent crime arrests (including homicide) and 58 percent of property crime arrests involving people under age twenty-five.[2] This finding suggests that the majority of crimes are committed by young people, although not necessarily juveniles. Juveniles represent less than 20 percent of all arrests, a number that has been dropping steadily.

Figure 3.2 illustrates trends in arrests of those under age eighteen. The graph illustrates that juvenile arrests dropped in every major crime category over the five years shown for an overall decline of 20 percent. Nevertheless, those aged eighteen to twenty-four are the most likely to be arrested. Violent and property crimes require some combination of force and/or stealth and therefore are most easily carried out by younger people. Older people disposed to violence or theft are much more likely to be arrested for forgery, fraud, embezzlement, and offenses against the family, crimes in which the victims either are tricked or have little chance of escape.

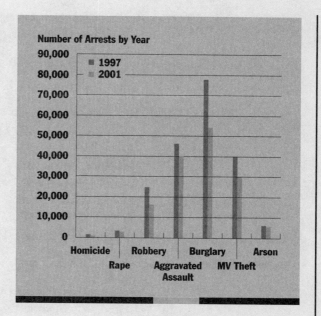

Figure 3.2
Five-Year Trends in Arrests of Juveniles (number of arrests by year)

SOURCE: Federal Bureau of Investigation, *Uniform Crime Report* (Washington, DC: U.S. Government Printing Office, published annually).

JUVENILE
OFFENDERS

8

Section Review 1

Directions.

1. On a separate sheet of paper, write a brief summary of the main points of the sections you have just read.

2. Mark each of the following statements True (T), False (F), or Can't Tell (CT). Mark the statement Can't Tell if it cannot be determined to be either true or false based on the material in the passage. Refer to the passage as necessary to verify your answer.

_____ 1. The store manager who sold Lisa Duy a pistol had followed proper procedures when checking her background.

_____ 2. The elderly are more likely to be crime victims than teenagers or middle-aged adults.

_____ 3. An eleven-year-old is as likely to be a crime victim as a thirteen-year-old.

_____ 4. One reason that young people are more exposed to crime is that they own more property worth stealing.

_____ 5. In 1997, approximately 50,000 juvenile arrests were made for burglary.

Gender

Women make up 22 percent of all those arrested in the United States. Men make up 83 percent of individuals arrested for violent crimes and 71 percent of those arrested for property crimes. Women are most frequently arrested for larceny, although they account for only 32 percent of all larceny arrests.[3] It is clear that serious crimes are far more likely to be committed by men than by women. Nevertheless, trends in female criminal activity are increasing. For the ten-year period 1992–2002, female arrests rose 18 percent (compared to a 9 percent decrease for males). Likewise, female arrests for violent crimes rose by 12 percent during that period, while male arrests for crimes of violence decreased by 12 percent. In general, although female involvement in crime has been increasing in recent years, males still are arrested five times more often than women.

The same is not true for victims, however. Victimization rates for men and women show that property crimes affect women as often as men. The rate of personal theft against men is 0.6 per 1,000 population, virtually the same rate as for women. However, women are victimized by violent crimes at a rate of 21 per 1,000 population, whereas the rate for men is 26 per 1,000.[4] Except for the crime of rape, however, women are significantly less likely than men to be victims of serious crime. This is illustrated in Figure 3.3, which shows that women suffer the vast majority of sexual assaults. For other types of assaults men are far more likely to be victimized. Overall, women are overrepresented among crime victims in relation to the rates of arrests of females. This suggests that for virtually all serious crimes, men victimize women in disproportionate numbers.

A significant factor in these patterns of victimization is the victim–offender relationship. More than half of violent crime victims know the offender. In cases of rape and sexual assault, 72 percent of victims knew the offender: Female victims of sexual assault are most likely to be victimized by friends/acquaintances (47 percent), intimates (22 percent), and relatives (2 percent).

VICTIMIZATION RATES FOR WOMEN

Figure 3.3
Gender and Victimization

SOURCE: Callie Marie Rennison, *Criminal Victimization 2002* (Washington, DC: Bureau of Justice Statistics, 2003).

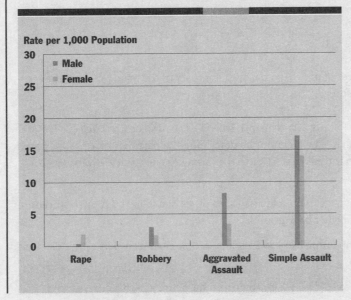

9

10

11

12   **Intimate Partner Violence**   Violence between intimate partners (current or former spouses, boyfriends, or girlfriends) is a growing problem that disproportionately victimizes women. The NCVS estimates that approximately 1 million violent crimes are committed annually by current or former intimate partners, about 85 percent of which are against women. This represents 22 percent of all violent crime against women, whereas only 3 percent of all violence against men is committed by intimate partners.[5]

13   A **National Violence Against Women (NVAW) Survey** was sponsored by the National Institute of Justice and the Centers for Disease Control and Prevention to obtain more information about the circumstances of offenses against women. The survey consisted of telephone interviews with 8,000 women and 8,000 men in a nationally representative sample. The survey concluded that "intimate partner violence is pervasive in U.S. society," with nearly 25 percent of surveyed women and 8 percent of men reporting they were physically assaulted or raped by a current or former spouse, a cohabiting partner, or a date at some point in their lives.[6] During the preceding twelve months 1.5 percent of women and 0.9 percent of men said they had been physically assaulted or raped by a partner. The survey also found that stalking by intimate partners is more prevalent than once thought. Nearly 5 percent of women and 0.6 percent of men reported being stalked by a current or former spouse, date, or intimate partner during their lifetime. Based on these estimates, approximately 500,000 women and 185,000 men are stalked by an intimate partner annually.

14   These findings suggest that crimes by persons known to the victim are both common and serious. Violence by intimates is difficult to detect due to the low visibility of these incidents and the low likelihood of their being reported to police. Crime prevention programs historically have not strongly emphasized crimes within intimate relationships, but greater public education and awareness are needed to encourage reporting of these crimes to authorities and to enable persons in abusive relationships to recognize their situation and take steps to remove themselves from a dangerous situation. Studies have found that the causes of **intimate partner violence** are distinct from the causes of general crime, and that the effectiveness of existing partner abuse interventions have not been evaluated extensively.[7] Therefore, more needs to be learned about the dynamics of how relationships deteriorate and result in criminal violence. On the positive side, the rate of intimate partner violence has fallen from 9.8 to 7.5 per 1,000 women according to the NCVS. In 2000, approximately 1,700 murders were attributable to intimate partners, a substantial decrease from 3,000 murders of this kind in 1976.[8] This might be a reflection of the drop in crime rates in general in recent years.

15   **Characteristics of Female Offenders**   Female offenders have several distinct characteristics that distinguish their offending patterns

VICTIM–OFFENDER RELATIONSHIPS

STALKING

National Violence Against Women (NVAW) Survey
Interviews a national sample of 16,000 men and women regarding the circumstances of crimes against women

intimate partner violence
Physical assaults between current or former spouses, boyfriends, or girlfriends.

© 2007 Pearson Education, Inc.

DIFFERENCES IN FEMALE OFFENDING

from those of males. For example, female-to-female violence occurs in about 75 percent of all cases of violent female offending (rape, robbery, assault). This compares to male-to-male violence, which occurs in 70 percent of male violence. The result is that about 29 percent of violent offenders overall had a victim of a different gender, and nine-tenths of these were male offenders with female victims.[9]

The location of violent offending by women is also different from men. Approximately half of female offenders committed their offense at or near the victim's home or at school. Less than a third of male offenders committed crimes at these locations. This difference reflects the fact that women are more likely to commit crimes against intimates, relatives, or acquaintances than are men. About 62 percent of female violent offenders had a prior relationship with the victim, whereas only 36 percent of male violent offenders knew the victim.[10] Females also use weapons in their crimes about half as often as males, which may be a reflection of the unplanned nature of many of these incidents. 16

Explaining the differences in female versus male offending is difficult. A recent study looked at both property and violent crimes committed by males and females, examining the impact of poverty, income inequality, joblessness, and female-headed households. These factors were found to be equally important to both female and male offending, although they could not explain why males committed crimes at much higher rates than females.[11] The causes and consequences of female offending are likely to be found only after examining the circumstances and context of individual incidents. Such an analysis will shed light on the relationship between crime and factors that are not easy to measure, such as stress, emotional abuse, and failure to recognize noncriminal alternatives in highly charged situations. 17

Section Review 2

Directions.

1. On a separate sheet of paper, write a brief summary of the main points of the sections you have just read.

2. Mark each of the following statements True (T), False (F), or Can't Tell (CT). Mark the statement Can't Tell if it cannot be determined to be either true or false based on the material in the passage. Refer to the passage as necessary to verify your answer.

_____ 1. Women commit larceny more often than men.

_____ 2. Men are victims of violent crime more often than women.

_____ 3. The NVAW survey found that one out of every four women reported that within the past year she had been raped or assaulted by an intimate partner.

_____ 4. Violent crimes by women often occur near their homes or schools, with the victim often being someone known to the perpetrator.

_____ 5. Men commit more crimes than women because they are more susceptible to economic pressures.

Cumulative Review 1 (pages 176-182)

Directions. Write the letter of the best answer in the space provided.

_____ 1. Which of the following age groups is at greatest risk for crime victimization?
   a. 12–19
   b. 20–34
   c. 35–49
   d. 50 and older

_____ 2. We can tell from the chapter that
   a. juvenile arrests have been decreasing.
   b. juvenile arrests have been increasing.
   c. most crimes are committed by persons under 21 years of age.
   d. violent crime by persons between the ages of 18 and 24 has decreased by 20 percent.

_____ 3. From 1992 to 2002, the rate of female arrest for violent crime has
   a. decreased steadily.
   b. decreased drastically.
   c. remained unchanged.
   d. increased significantly.

_____ 4. Regarding intimate partner violence, the author suggests that
   a. stronger punishments are needed to protect partners from harm.
   b. it has been increasing at an alarming rate.
   c. more needs to be learned about its causes.
   d. detection of intimate partner violence has improved since people have become more willing to report it.

_____ 5. The author suggests that stress and emotional abuse
   a. are not factors in criminal activity.
   b. may play a role in criminal activity.
   c. are usually very important factors in criminal activity.
   d. often cause criminals to overlook nonviolent alternatives.

Directions. Answer each question in complete sentences, without copying word-for-word from the passage.

1. Why was Lisa Duy sold a gun, despite the fact that she had a long history of psychiatric problems?

_____

_____

_____

2. Why are young people more likely to be crime victims?

_____

_____

_____

3. What are the reasons why violence by intimate partners is hard to detect?

_____

_____

_____

4. How common is stalking? Compare stalking rates for men and women.

_____

_____

_____

5. What conclusions can be drawn regarding the differences between crimes committed by women and crimes committed by men?

_____

_____

_____

Vocabulary Exercise 1

Directions. Choose the meaning for the underlined word that best fits the context. You may consult the dictionary as needed.

_____ 1. ...laws in most states protect the privacy of the mentally ill to avoid <u>stigma</u>. [Paragraph 2]
   a. investigation
   b. something that detracts from a person's reputation
   c. public disclosure of a criminal activity
   d. discrimination

_____ 2. People age sixty-five or older are victimized by...personal <u>larceny</u> at a rate of less than 4 per 1,000. [Paragraph 5]
   a. assault
   b. theft
   c. burglary
   d. violent beating or battery

_____ 3. The reasons for these <u>discrepancies</u> based on age are not difficult to understand.
   [Paragraph 6]
   a. differences
   b. causes
   c. actions
   d. crimes

_____ 4. Violent and property crimes require some combination of force and/or <u>stealth</u>...
   [Paragraph 8]
   a. skill or cleverness
   b. strength
   c. previous planning
   d. secrecy

_____ 5. The rate of personal theft against men is... <u>virtually</u> the same rate as for women.
   [Paragraph 10]
   a. theoretically
   b. occasionally
   c. practically
   d. frequently

_____ 6. This suggests that for virtually all serious crimes, men victimize women in <u>disproportionate</u> numbers. [Paragraph 10]
   a. comparable
   b. unequal
   c. of the same ratio
   d. increasing at a constant proportion

_____ 7. The survey concluded that "intimate partner violence is <u>pervasive</u> in U.S. society,"...
   [Paragraph 13]
   a. indefinite
   b. destructive
   c. spread throughout
   d. infrequent

_____ 8. The survey also found that stalking by intimate partners is more <u>prevalent</u> than once thought. [Paragraph 13]
   a. common
   b. rare
   c. dangerous
   d. unknown or unstudied

_____ 9. Studies have found that the causes of intimate partner violence are <u>distinct</u> from the causes of general crime... [Paragraph 14]
   a. related to
   b. similar; corresponding
   c. different
   d. understood or explained

_____ 10. In 2000, approximately 1,700 murders were <u>attributable</u> to intimate partners...
   [Paragraph 14]
   a. leading to
   b. vulnerable
   c. reported by
   d. caused by

Race and Ethnicity

18   Whites account for 70 percent of all arrests, while blacks are arrested for 28 percent of all crimes. For Index crimes, whites comprise 58 percent of arrests for violent crimes and 65 percent of arrests for property crimes.[12] These police statistics count only those offenders who are caught, however, and the NCVS asks respondents who see their attacker in cases of rape, robbery, and assault to identify the perceived race of the offender. The differences are striking and are dis-

Table 3.1   Race of Offenders in Violent Crimes
(rape, robbery, assault)

RACE	ARRESTED BY POLICE	IDENTIFIED BY VICTIM
White	58%	45%
Black	40	26
Other or Unknown	2	30

SOURCE: FBI Uniform Crime Report, *Crime in the United States* (Washington, DC: U.S. Government Printing Office, 2002); *Criminal Victimization in the United States, 2001: Statistical Tables* (Washington, DC: Bureau of Justice Statistics, 2003).

RACE AND OPPORTUNITY

played in Table 3.1, which shows significant discrepancy in the racial composition of offenders from the two data sources. These differences can be accounted for by the fact that most offenders are not caught, so those arrested may not represent offenders in general. It also is true that victims are sometimes mistaken about the race of the offender, given the circumstances of the crime (e.g., darkness, a very brief look at the offender, or a masked offender), and that there are a significant number of cases where the victim is unsure about the race of the offender.

African Americans   Blacks are victims of violent crime at higher 19 rates than any other race. Their victimization rate for rape, robbery, and assault is 42 per 1,000, compared to a victimization rate of 32 per 1,000 for whites. In a similar way, black households are victimized by property crimes (burglary, larceny, and motor vehicle theft) at a rate more than 30 percent higher than that of whites (250 property crimes per 1,000 households versus 190 per 1,000 households for whites).[13] As noted in the previous section, victimization is related to age. The median age for blacks in the United States is 30 years whereas the average age for whites is 36.3 years. This age difference would be expected to increase the involvement of blacks in Index crimes. Victimization also is strongly influenced by the opportunity for crime. In the case of motor vehicle theft, for example, whites own 170 million vehicles in the United States, whereas blacks own 17.3 million vehicles. Accounting for this huge difference in the opportunity for theft (i.e., the tenfold greater availability of stealing a car owned by a white), the victimization rate for blacks is still three times higher than it is for whites (16 thefts per 1,000 motor vehicles owned for blacks versus 5 thefts per 1,000 for whites).[14]

Hispanics   Hispanics constitute a small but growing segment of 20 victims of serious crimes. People of Hispanic origin constitute about 8 percent of the U.S. population, and may be of any race. They are immigrants from Spanish-speaking countries such as Mexico (62 percent), Puerto Rico (13 percent), and Central and South America (12 percent). Their rate of victimization by violent crimes is 35 per 1,000 population, 9 percent higher than the rate for other whites but 20 percent lower than that for blacks.

In the case of the property crimes of burglary, larceny, and motor 21 vehicle theft, Hispanic households are victimized at a rate of 232 per 1,000 households, a rate that is 22 percent higher than that of whites and 8 percent lower than that of blacks.[15] This reflects the general trend that Hispanics have crime victimization rates somewhere between those of whites and blacks.

22   The good news is that the overall rate of victimizations has been declining for all races and ethnicities. From 1993 to 2001 both property crime and violent crime rates have dropped significantly for all races. The drop in violent crime victimization is illustrated in Figure 3.4. For property crimes, black households had the largest drop in victimization from 1993 to 2001.

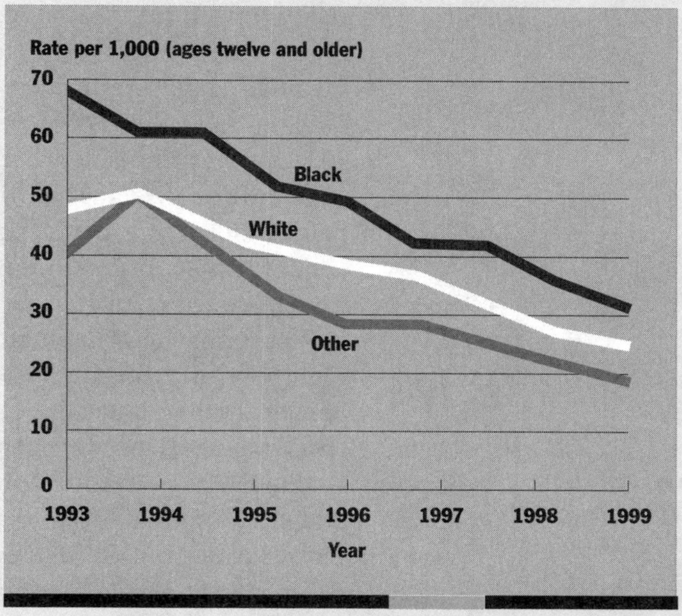

Figure 3.4
Rate of Violent Crime Victimizations by Race, 1993–2001 (per 1,000 persons age 12 and older)

SOURCE: Callie Marie Rennison, *Criminal Victimization 2001* (Washington, DC: Bureau of Justice Statistics, 2002).

23   **Native Americans**   Native Americans constitute about 1 percent of the total U.S. population, or 2.4 million people. This group consists of Alaska Natives, Aleuts, and American Indians. Historically, this group has not received systematic attention from the American criminal justice system. Native Americans comprise 1.3 percent of all arrests in the United States, and their low median age, 27.4 years, is the youngest of any population group in the United States. As noted earlier, young adults are much more likely to be involved in Index crimes than are those past age 30. This is reflected in NCVS data, which show that Native Americans experience the highest per capita rate of violence of any group (about 1 violent crime for every person aged 18 to 24). Overall, victimization rates for Native Americans are about twice that of the rest of the U.S. population.[16]

24   Issues of particular concern for Native Americans are interracial violence and arrests for alcohol-related offenses. More than 70 percent of violent crime victimizations of Native Americans are committed by persons of other races. This is markedly different from whites, for whom 70 percent of victimizations are white-on-white crimes, and for blacks, for whom 80 percent of victimizations are black-on-black crimes. The high proportion of victimizations of Native Americans by persons of other races suggests that underlying social and racial problems may be at the root of some of this violence. Second, alcohol use was a factor in 38 percent of violent crime victimizations of Native Americans, compared to 29 percent for whites and 21 percent for blacks.[17] Disproportionate levels of alcohol abuse also are suggested by the fact that arrest rates of Native Americans for alcohol-related offenses (i.e., driving under the influence, liquor law violations, and public drunkenness) are more than double that for all races. These factors help to explain the high crime and victimization rate for Native Americans.

ALCOHOL-RELATED OFFENSES

Asian Americans   Asian Americans are another diverse population   25
group that is beginning to receive attention in American criminal
justice. Asian Americans include Hawaiian Natives and Pacific Islanders, as well as those whose ancestors came from countries in
Asia, such as China, Japan, Korea, and Vietnam. There are currently
10.4 million "Asians" in the United States, comprising nearly 4
percent of the U.S. population. Asian Americans constitute 1.2 percent of those arrested in the United States annually, and they have
a median age of thirty-one years. Their victimization rate is the
lowest of any racial or ethnic group in the United States, with 29 violent victimizations per 1,000 persons.[18] The rate for whites is 70
percent higher; blacks have twice the victimization rate, and Native Americans 4 times the victimization rate of Asian Americans.

RACIAL
TENSION AND
VICTIMIZATION

Important issues for Asian Americans are interracial violence   26
and the circumstances of murders involving Asians. Similar to
Native Americans, a high percentage (about 68 percent) of their violent victimizations involve offenders of other races. This suggests underlying racial tension that may affect victimization rates.
Second, Table 3.2 illustrates that although murders involving
Asians are far fewer than for most groups, homicides involving
Asians are much more likely to result from violent felonies than
is found for any other race. On the other hand, Asian Americans
are significantly less likely than any other race to be involved in
murders that involve fights under the influence of alcohol or
drugs. Clearly, Asian Americans use alcohol and drugs at very low
levels, but the incidence of homicides resulting from violent
felonies suggests possible problems with gangs, extortion, and
other serious social problems.

It should be kept in mind, of course, that race itself does not pre-   27
dispose a person to crime. In the United States, race and ethnicity
are closely tied to age, income, and residence in cities (where crime
rates are higher). Whites tend to be older and have higher incomes

Table 3.2   Circumstances of Murder by Race

MURDERS WITH KNOWN CIRCUMSTANCES	WHITE	BLACK	NATIVE AMERICAN	ASIAN AMERICAN
Violent felony	16%	11%	11%	27%
Other felony	10	11	5	8
Suspected felony	4	3	4	3
Brawl under the influence of alcohol or drugs	6	4	13	2
Arguments	38	50	45	35
Other circumstances	27	21	22	25
Total number	181,043	156,203	2,515	4,545

SOURCE: Lawrence A. Greenfeld and Steven K. Smith, *American Indians and Crime* (Washington, DC: Bureau of
Justice Statistics, 1999); FBI Supplemental Homicide Reports.

than blacks and Hispanics. Whites are also more likely to live out-side cities. These factors contribute greatly to the differences in rates of victimization by race.

Socioeconomic Status

28   The influence of income on the risk of victimization is illustrated by the fact that the risk of household burglary declines as income rises. Households with incomes below $15,000 per year are more likely to be burglarized than those with incomes above $15,000. Middle-income households ($25,000 to $75,000) have the lowest property crime victimization rates, but the rate increases for those households with incomes more than $75,000 per year.[19] Higher property crime rates at the high and low ends of income levels can be explained by several factors. First, victimization rates are significantly higher in cities, where most low-income households are located. Second, those with higher incomes own more property, thereby increasing the opportunities for victimization.

29   For violent crimes, persons with higher incomes have the lowest rate of victimization, and those with the lowest incomes (less than $7,500 annually) experience the highest rate of violence (58 per 1,000 persons). This is accounted for primarily by location of residence (higher income allows for housing in lower crime areas). Also, the fact that those with higher incomes are able to move about in safer (low crime) areas reduces their exposure to victimization risk.

VICTIMIZATION RATES FOR LOW-INCOME HOUSEHOLDS

Section Review 3

Directions.

1. On a separate sheet of paper, write a brief summary of the main points of the sections you have just read.

2. Mark each of the following statements True (T), False (F), or Can't Tell (CT). Mark the statement Can't Tell if it cannot be determined to be either true or false based on the material in the passage. Refer to the passage as necessary to verify your answer.

_____ 1. NCVS data reveal that victims of violent crime identify their attackers as white more than half of the time.

_____ 2. Blacks are victims of violent crimes more often than whites or any other race.

_____ 3. Hispanic households are robbed less often than black households but more often than white households.

_____ 4. According to Table 3.2, Asian Americans have the lowest percentage of murders associated with violent felonies.

_____ 5. The richer you are, the less likely you are to be a property crime victim.

What Is Crime Profiling?

crime profiling
Analysis of criminal incidents to isolate the precise characteristics of offenders, victims, and situations in order to better understand and prevent crime.

Crime profiling involves analysis of criminal incidents to isolate 30 the precise characteristics of offenders, victims, and situations in order to better understand and prevent crime. Behavioral profiling focuses on the characteristics and conduct of offenders and victims (e.g., demographic characteristics, prior history, and current conduct), while crime scene profiling involves examination of the physical and situational characteristics of criminal incidents (e.g., place, time, and physical evidence). In both cases the objective is to assess numerous incidents of similar kinds in order to develop typologies, or models, to explain and predict how crimes occur. This information is used to help police in surveillance and crime prevention activities and also help educate the public and policymakers about individuals and situations at high risk for crime.

Offender Profiles

offender profiles
Examination of offender backgrounds (e.g., physical and social characteristics, prior history, and method of conduct) to look for common patterns.

STUDY OF
BURGLARS

Offender profiles are developed by examining a large number of 31 similar crimes to look for common patterns. The offender's physical characteristics, prior history, and method of conduct are all relevant in creating the profile.[20] Information that is commonly used is from the NCVS and UCR, which provide national data on known incidents. More detailed data about offender motivations and specialization is taken from studies conducted by researchers on smaller groups of known offenders.

In the case of burglary, for example, UCR arrest statistics reveal 32 that 70 percent of those arrested are white and 28 percent are black, and two-thirds of burglaries are committed by offenders over eighteen years of age. Nearly 90 percent of burglary arrestees are males. The U.S. Bureau of Justice Statistics tracks felony defendants in large counties, which provides additional detailed information about those formally charged with burglary. Sixty-six percent have a prior felony arrest, and 67 percent had prior convictions. A total of 39 percent were on probation, parole, or on pretrial release at the time of their arrest.[21] Studies of burglars, based on interviews with known offenders and police, have found that most burglars do not specialize in burglary as a crime. They tend to commit a variety of offenses, but only rarely commit violent crimes. Burglars do not appear to escalate into more serious crimes, although they may specialize in certain types of burglary (e.g., jewelry stores or vacation houses) for short periods.[22] Combining different sources of information like these enables the investigator to develop leads in cases where the suspect is unknown, and to form offender profiles for use in detection and prevention efforts.

Victim Profiles

33   **Victim profiles** are analogous to offender profiles in looking at a large number of criminal incidents to find patterns of the types of persons who are victimized under certain circumstances. The primary source of data for victim profiles is the NCVS, because it encompasses a large national sample of citizens who are interviewed about their victimization experiences. Continuing with our burglary profile, the NCVS counts only household burglaries, but these are much more common than commercial burglaries. Despite the fact that there are approximately 13.3 million black households in the United States versus 90 million white households, blacks are victimized at a rate of 53 per 1,000 households. The rate for whites and other races is 32 per 1,000 households. In cases where the head of the household is 20 to 49 years of age, burglaries occur 50 percent more often than if the head of the household is 50 or older. Households headed by teenagers are burglarized at an even higher rate—more than four times the rate of those 50 and over. Poor households are at the highest risk (a victimization rate ranging between 44 and 67 per 1,000 for incomes under $15,000) versus wealthier households where the victimization rate is 24 per 1,000 (for incomes $50,000 and up). The Northeast has a significantly lower per-capita burglary rate than do other regions of the country, and urban households are significantly more likely than rural or suburban households to be victimized. Likewise, rented dwellings are almost twice as likely to be burglarized as owned homes.[23] Interviews with burglars have found that the extent to which the household can be seen by passersby or neighbors, has good area lighting, shows no obvious displays of wealth, and displays signs of occupancy all lower the risk of victimization.[24] Organizing these common elements, a profile of a typical burglary victim can be constructed to form the basis for crime prevention programs.

■ **victim profiles**
Examination of a large number of similar criminal incidents to find patterns in the types of persons who are victimized under certain circumstances.

HOUSEHOLD VICTIMIZATION

Crime Scene Profiles

34   **Crime scene profiles** examine the circumstances that surround criminal incidents in a search for patterns associated with criminal offending. One important source of this information is the NCVS, because that survey asks victims about the situation in which they were victimized. A crime scene profile for burglary would include the fact that household burglaries involving unlawful entry without the use of force are by far the most common. Forcible entries and attempted forcible entries occur about half as often. This suggests that unlocked and open doors and windows are a primary entry point for burglars. The NCVS also reveals that the risk of victimization for burglary increases as the number of people living in the household increases. Households with six or more members have a burglary victimization rate twice that of households with

■ **crime scene profiles**
Examination of the circumstances surrounding criminal incidents in a search for patterns associated with criminal offending.

only two or three members. In an analogous way, the number of housing units or apartments in the building is related to the risk of victimization. Buildings with between five and nine units have the highest rate of victimization, compared to those with fewer units, or those with ten or more units. The lowest risk of burglary is in single-family homes. The longer a person lives in the same dwelling also lowers the likelihood of burglary.

35 In 90 percent of burglaries the losses are not recovered, although the typical loss is valued at less than $250. The most common items stolen are personal effects, such as jewelry, clothing, portable electronic gear and cameras, household furnishings, and wallets. Most burglaries occur during the day between 6:00 A.M. and 6:00 P.M.[25] Research studies help to put this data in context. Interviews with burglars show that most engage in the crime due to a need for money. They look for attractive targets (dwellings likely to have money or property that can be sold), no sign of occupants or other guardians present (e.g., dogs, neighbors), and convenience (ease of entry and exit).[26] Therefore, the circumstances around which offenders decide to act can be determined from close scrutiny of past incidents. A burglary profile based on the information presented here is summarized in Table 3.3.

36 The case of Lisa Duy described at the beginning of this chapter had not ended at the time of this writing. She was placed in the Utah State Hospital to be treated for paranoid schizophrenia. She has been found mentally incompetent to stand trial for murder, although if her condition improves a trial could proceed.[27] The Critical Thinking exercise on homicide illustrates how better knowledge of the circumstances of homicide, combined with profiling techniques, could be used to predict and prevent such tragedies in the future by providing more accurate understanding of the perpetrators and victims of crime.

BURGLARY PROFILE

Table 3.3   Crime Profile for Burglary (high-risk factors associated with past)

OFFENDER	VICTIM	CRIME SCENE
Male	Black household	Unforced entry
White	Headed by teenager or young person (under 50)	Five to nine units in building
Prior felony arrest(s)	Rented dwelling	Loss under $250
Prior convictions	Household income under $15,000	Occurred during the day
Little crime specialization	Urban location	Attractive target
Violence rare		No occupants or guardians

Section Review 4

Directions.

1. On a separate sheet of paper, write a brief summary of the main points of the sections you have just read.

2. Mark each of the following statements True (T), False (F), or Can't Tell (CT). Mark the statement Can't Tell if it cannot be determined to be either true or false based on the material in the passage. Refer to the passage as necessary to verify your answer.

_____ 1. Predicting and preventing crime are two important goals of crime profiling.

_____ 2. Most burglars specialize in burglary and rarely commit other crimes.

_____ 3. Commercial burglaries generally occur in poor, black communities.

_____ 4. An apartment building with twelve units is more likely to be victimized by burglary than a similar building with eight units.

_____ 5. Lisa Duy will never be tried for murder.

critical thinking exercises

The Characteristics of Homicide

The homicide rate has fallen in recent years to its lowest level in three decades.[a] This good news is mitigated by the apparent randomness of homicide and our inability to predict and prevent its occurrence. An analysis by the *New York Times* closely examined the circumstances of 100 rampage murders (sudden killings without apparent motive). It found that "most of the killers spiraled down a long slow slide, mentally and emotionally."[b] This kind of homicide is quite rare, but careful review of these cases shows that red flags existed in most cases, such as the accumulation of weapons, talking openly of committing violence, and sudden dramatic changes in behavior. This suggests that even homicides that appear random and without motive might be preventable if closer attention is paid to the circumstances surrounding criminal incidents.

Consider five important facts about more typical homicides in the United States:

- More than half of all homicides occur in cities with populations over 100,000.

- Blacks are disproportionately involved as both homicide victims and offenders, and 94 percent of black homicide victims are killed by blacks.

- Males are nine times more likely than females to commit homicide, although most homicides by females involve male victims.

- Only 4 percent of homicides involve multiple victims, while 17 percent involve multiple offenders.

- The circumstances of many homicides are unknown, although arguments are still the leading known cause, followed by deaths caused during the commission of a felony.[c]

CRITICAL THINKING QUESTIONS

1. Given what you've learned in this chapter about the factors associated with crime, offenders, and victims, explain why you believe each of the five facts about homicide listed above is true.

2. How would you attempt to change the disproportionate involvement of blacks in homicides as victims and offenders, given what you know about the factors associated with crime?

NOTES

a. James Alan Fox and Marianne W. Zawitz, *Homicide Trends in the United States: 1998 Update* (Washington, DC: Bureau of Justice Statistics, 2000).

b. Laurie Goodstein and William Glaberson, "The Well-Marked Roads to Homicidal Rage," *New York Times* (April 9, 2000), p. 1.

c. *Homicide Trends in the U.S.* (Washington, DC: Bureau of Justice Statistics, 2000), www.ojp.usdoj.gov/bjs/homicide.

Preventing School Shootings

n 1999, the Federal Bureau of Investigation's National Center for the Analysis of Violent Crime invited 160 educators, mental health professionals, and members of the law enforcement community to a symposium on school shootings and threat assessment. Among the attendees was someone who knew the shooter at each of eighteen separate incidents of school shootings in the United States and the investigators who worked on each case.

A report was published in 2000 based on this symposium that identified a series of "warning signs" involving the student's personality, family dynamics, school dynamics, and social dynamics. The report cautioned that these warning signs should not be considered in isolation from one another, but "if all or most of them" occur together with a threat made by a student, the threat must be taken seriously and acted upon.

1. **Personality**—leakage of violent thoughts or feelings in words or pictures; low tolerance for frustration, poor coping skills; lack of resiliency; failed love relationship; resentment over perceived injustices; signs of depression, narcissism, or alienation; dehumanizing attitudes; lack of empathy, exaggerated sense of entitlement, attitude of superiority, exaggerated or pathological need for attention; externalized blame; masked low self-esteem; anger management problems; intolerance; inappropriate humor; manipulative; lack of trust; closed social group; change of behavior; rigid and opinionated; unusual interest in sensational violence; fascination with violence-filled entertainment; negative role models; behavior relevant to carrying out a threat.

2. **Family dynamics**—turbulent parent–child relationship; acceptance of pathological behavior; access to weapons; lack of intimacy; few limits on the child's conduct; no limits or monitoring of television and Internet.

3. **School dynamics**—student is "detached" from school; school tolerates disrespectful behavior; student perceives inequitable discipline; school culture is inflexible; students have a pecking order; a code of silence; and unsupervised computer access.

4. **Social dynamics**—easy access to media/entertainment with themes of extreme violence; extremist peer group or peers fascinated with violence; use of drugs and alcohol; unusual nature of students' interests outside school; copycat behavior.[a]

CRITICAL THINKING QUESTIONS

1. As a former high-school student, what do you see as the pros and cons in applying these criteria to assess threats made in school settings?

2. School shootings occur infrequently despite their dreadfulness, and the more infrequent an event, the more difficult it is to predict. Would it be possible to predict which students are at high risk of such conduct based on these, or other, factors?

NOTES

a. Mary Ellen O'Toole, *The School Shooter: A Threat Assessment Perspective* (Quantico, VA: FBI Academy, 2000).

SUMMARY

WHO ARE THE VICTIMS AND PERPETRATORS OF CRIME?

- Information about the nature of criminal incidents and crime victims comes from the reports of citizens to the National Crime Victimization Survey (NCVS).

- The FBI Uniform Crime Reports gathers information about the characteristics of persons arrested.

- Most property and violent crime offenders are young—between the ages of eighteen and twenty-five.

- Males comprise 83 percent of all arrests, although the rate of female arrests is rising slowly.

- Women are more likely to commit crimes against intimates, relatives, or acquaintances than are men.

- Whites account for 68 percent of all arrests, while blacks are arrested for 30 percent of all crimes.
- Except for the crime of rape, males are victimized by violent crimes at a rate almost twice that for women.
- Women are the victims of property crimes at a rate similar to that for men.
- Approximately 1 million violent crimes are committed annually by current or former intimate partners, about 85 percent of which are against women.
- About 29 percent of violent offenders overall had a victim of a different gender, and nine in ten of these were male offenders with female victims.
- Blacks are victims of violent crime at higher rates than any other race.
- Hispanics have crime victimization rates at a rate somewhere between that of whites and blacks.
- Victimization rates for Native Americans are about twice that of the rest of the U.S. population.
- The victimization rate for Asians is the lowest of any racial or ethnic group in the United States, with 29 violent victimizations per 1,000 persons.
- For violent crimes, persons with higher incomes have the lowest rate of victimization, and those with the lowest incomes (less than $7,500 annually) experience the highest rate of violence.

WHAT IS CRIME PROFILING?

- Crime profiling involves analysis of criminal incidents to isolate the precise characteristics of offenders, victims, and situations in order to better understand and prevent crime.
- Behavioral profiling focuses on the characteristics and conduct of offenders and victims (e.g., demographic characteristics, prior history, and current conduct).
- Crime scene profiling involves examination of the physical and situational characteristics of criminal incidents (e.g., place, time, and physical evidence).

KEY TERMS

National Violence Against Women (NVAW) Survey 181
intimate partner violence 181
crime profiling 190

offender profiles 190
victim profiles 191
crime scene profiles 191

QUESTIONS FOR REVIEW AND DISCUSSION

1. Where does information about the nature of criminal incidents come from?
2. How does age affect rates of offending and victimization in the United States?
3. How does gender affect rates of offending and victimization?

4. What does research show about offenders and their victims in instances of violent crime?

5. How common or rare is intimate partner violence in the United States, and who are the victims?

6. How do male and female offenders differ in their crimes?

7. How do rates of offending and victimization vary by race and ethnicity?

8. How common or rare is race-based crime in the United States, and who are the victims?

9. What is the influence of income on the risk of victimization?

10. What kinds of profiling can help in the prevention of crime?

NOTES

1. Fox Butterfield, "The Mentally Ill Often Skirt a Landmark Federal Gun Control Law," *New York Times* (April 11, 2000), p. 1.

2. Compiled from Federal Bureau of Investigation, *Crime in the United States* (Washington, DC: U.S. Government Printing Office, 2002), p. 210.

3. Ibid.

4. Callie Marie Rennison, *Criminal Victimization 2002* (Washington, DC: Bureau of Justice Statistics, 2003).

5. Callie Marie Rennison, *Intimate Partner Violence* (Washington, DC: Bureau of Justice Statistics, 2003).

6. Patricia Tjaden and Nancy Thoemnes, *Extent, Nature, and Consequences of Intimate Partner Violence: Findings from the National Violence Against Women Survey* (Washington, DC: National Institute of Justice, 2000).

7. Terrie E. Moffitt, Robert F. Krueger, Avshalom Caspi, and Jeff Fagan, "Partner Abuse and General Crime: How Are They the Same? How Are They Different?," *Criminology*, vol. 38 (February, 2000), pp. 199–232; Rosemary Chalk and Patricia A. King, *Violence in Families: Assessing Prevention and Treatment Programs* (Washington, DC: National Academy Press, 1998).

8. Rennison, p. 2.

9. Lawrence A. Greenfeld and Tracy L. Snell, *Women Offenders* (Washington, DC: Bureau of Justice Statistics, 1999).

10. Greenfeld and Snell, p. 3.

11. Darrell Steffenmeier and Dana Haynie, "Gender, Structural Disadvantage, and Urban Crime: Do Macrosocial Variables Also Explain Female Offending Rates?," *Criminology*, vol. 38 (May, 2000), pp. 403–38.

12. Federal Bureau of Investigation, *Crime in the United States* (Washington, DC: U.S. Government Printing Office, 2002).

13. Rennison, p. 5.

14. *Criminal Victimization in the United States, 2001: Statistical Tables* (Washington, DC: Bureau of Justice Statistics, 2003).

15. Rennison, p. 5.

16. Lawrence A. Greenfeld and Steven K. Smith, *American Indians and Crime* (Washington, DC: Bureau of Justice Statistics, 1999).

17. Greenfeld and Smith, pp. 7–9.

18. Ibid.

19. Rennison, p. 6.

20. Terance D. Miethe and Richard McCorkle, *Crime Profiles: The Anatomy of Dangerous Persons, Places, and Situations* (Los Angeles: Roxbury, 1998).

21. Brian A. Reaves, *Felony Defendants in Large Urban Counties, 1998* (Washington, DC: Bureau of Justice Statistics, 2001).

22. Richard Wright and Scott Decker, *Burglars on the Job: Streetlife and Residential Break-ins* (Boston: Northeastern University Press, 1994); R. I. Mawby and Hazell Croall, eds. *Burglary* (Willan Publishing, 2002); Jan M. Chaiken and Marcia R. Chaiken, *Varieties of Criminal Behavior* (Santa Monica, CA: Rand Corporation, 1982).

23. Rennison, p. 9.

24. Paul Cromwell, James Olson, and D'Aunn Wester Avery, *Breaking and Entering: An Ethnographic Analysis of Burglary* (Thousand Oaks, CA: Sage Publications, 1991); George Rengert and John Wasilchick, *Suburban Burglary: A Time and Place for Everything* (Springfield, IL: Charles C. Thomas, 1985); Neal Shover, *Great Pretenders: Pursuits and Careers of Persistent Thieves* (Boulder, CO: Westview Press, 1996).

25. *Criminal Victimization in the United States, 1998: Statistical Tables* (Washington, DC: Bureau of Justice Statistics, 2000).

26. Cromwell, Olson, and Avery; Rengert and Wasilchick.

27. Stephen Hunt, "Accused Killer of AT&T Worker Is Ordered to Undergo More Treatment," *The Salt Lake Tribune* (August 22, 2000), p. 1.

Cumulative Review 2 (Pages 185-196)

Directions. Write the letter of the best answer in the space provided.

_____ 1. Which two racial/ethnic groups are most often victimized by members of other groups?
   a. Hispanics and blacks
   b. blacks and Asian Americans
   c. Asian Americans and Native Americans
   d. Hispanics and Native Americans

_____ 2. The author states that the overall rate of violent crimes
   a. has been increasing steadily for all racial/ethnic groups.
   b. has been decreasing noticeably for all racial/ethnic groups.
   c. has increased for some groups while decreasing for others.
   d. has remained about the same for most groups.

_____ 3. White Americans
   a. have the lowest crime rates of all racial/ethnic groups.
   b. have the highest victimization rates of all racial/ethnic groups.
   c. commit 70 percent of the violent crimes in the U.S. annually.
   d. are arrested for almost six of every ten violent crimes.

_____ 4. Which of the following households would most likely be victimized by burglary?
   a. an urban apartment building in the West
   b. a suburban apartment building in the Northeast
   c. a privately owned rural home in the Northeast
   d. a privately owned suburban home in the Midwest

_____ 5. Most burglaries occur between 6:00 A.M. and 6:00 P.M. because
   a. this is when burglars expect homes to be unoccupied.
   b. police surveillance increases at night.
   c. homeowners lock doors more at night.
   d. the need for money is the primary motivation for burglary.

Directions. Answer each question in complete sentences, without copying word-for-word from the passage.

1. According to the author, why do the statistics comparing white and black arrest rates (reported in Table 3.1) differ significantly from the statistics obtained from interviewing crime victims?

_____

_____

_____

2. What is the relationship between socioeconomic status and crime victimization?

_____

_____

_____

3. What is crime profiling?

_____

_____

_____

4. Why do Asian Americans have a high incidence of homicides resulting from violent felonies?

_____

_____

_____

5. Who is most likely to be victimized by a burglar?

_____

_____

_____

Vocabulary Exercise 2

Directions. Choose the meaning for the underlined word that best fits the context. You may consult the dictionary as needed.

_____ 1. For Index crimes, whites comprise 58 percent of arrests for violent crimes . . . [Paragraph 18]
   a. explain
   b. make up
   c. report
   d. exercise

_____ 2. The median age for blacks in the United States is 30 years . . . [Paragraph 19]
   a. dividing line
   b. in the middle of a range of numbers
   c. primary; at maximum potential
   d. most important or best

_____ 3. Hispanics constitute a small but growing segment of victims of serious crimes. [Paragraph 20]
   a. contribute
   b. create
   c. organize
   d. represent

_____ 4. Asian Americans are another <u>diverse</u> population group that is beginning to receive attention in American criminal justice.
[Paragraph 25]
a. varied
b. odd or unusual
c. minority
d. cultural

_____ 5. ... suggests possible problems with gangs, <u>extortion</u>, and other serious social problems.
[Paragraph 26]
a. theft associated with violence
b. wrongdoing
c. getting money through threats
d. selling or trade of illegal drugs

_____ 6. Behavioral profiling focuses on the characteristics and conduct of offenders and victims (e.g., <u>demographic</u> characteristics ...)
[Paragraph 30]
a. having to do with the study of human populations
b. having to do with the study of crime and criminals
c. geographic
d. democratic

_____ 7. This information is used to help police in <u>surveillance</u> and crime prevention activities ...
[Paragraph 30]
a. capture of suspects
b. accumulation of evidence
c. close watch or observation
d. analysis of a crime scene

_____ 8. Victim profiles are <u>analogous</u> to offender profiles in looking at a large number of criminal incidents ... [Paragraph 33]
a. analyzed carefully
b. comparable
c. different from
d. useful; used for a specific purpose

_____ 9. Therefore, the circumstances around which offenders decide to act can be determined from close <u>scrutiny</u> of past incidents. [Paragraph 35]
a. examination
b. repetition
c. simulation (imitation)
d. similarity

_____ 10. She has been found mentally <u>incompetent</u> to stand trial for murder ... [Paragraph 36]
a. inflexible
b. lacking in normal intelligence
c. not legally qualified
d. capable

Critical Response Questions

1. Is Lisa Duy responsible for her actions? If not, who is? Explain your answer.

2. What can you do to avoid becoming a crime victim?

3. Should gun control laws be stricter? Why or why not?

4. Why might crimes committed by women be increasing? How can this problem be best addressed?

5. What are some reasons why the overall crime rate has been declining in recent years? Is there more that we can do to continue this decrease, or to make it happen faster?

6. What might be some reasons for intimate partner violence? How can we prevent these incidents from occurring?

7. What are the advantages of profiling? What are the disadvantages?

CHAPTER

Chemistry

INTRODUCTION TO CHEMISTRY

Directions

1. Begin by surveying the chapter to look for answers to the following questions.

   - What is the chapter about?
   - What subtopics will be discussed?
   - What will you learn from reading and studying the chapter?
   - How interesting does the chapter look?
   - How difficult does the chapter look?
   - How familiar to you is the chapter material? That is, how much previous knowledge of the subject do you have?

   When you have completed your survey, write a summary on a separate sheet of paper of what you've learned about the chapter from the survey. Your summary should include answers to the previous questions, as well as any other information and comments you wish to add.

2. While reading the chapter, look for organizational patterns. Recognizing the patterns should help you better grasp the relationship of ideas within each paragraph and section and distinguish main ideas more easily.

   Also, form questions from the headings and subheadings (generally, write one question per heading or subheading). Write your questions on a sheet of paper and, after completing each section, mentally review the main points of the section, mark the text, and write the answer(s) to your question(s), as well as any other information that seems important to you.

SAMPLE TEXTBOOK CHAPTER

From *Basic Chemistry*, 7th ed., by G. William Daub and William S. Seese. Upper Saddle River, NJ: Prentice-Hall, 1996.

GOALS FOR CHAPTER 4

1. To gain an understanding of science and the scientific method and of chemistry's place among the sciences (Section 4.1).
2. To classify a chemist's research interests or research papers as being in one of the five subfields of chemistry (Section 4.2).
3. To trace the development of chemistry as a science (Section 4.3).

1   What do you think of when you hear the word "chemical"? You probably think of some foul-smelling substance in a laboratory. Certainly such items are chemicals, but chemicals are everywhere. The soap and bleach you use to wash your clothes are chemicals. So are the metal and plastic that form the washer and dryer. Your body is a collection of chemicals, the most abundant of which is water (60% of your weight).

2   Studying chemistry, then, is studying *life*. As you study this book, you will learn about the most basic structures and interactions behind things that you take for granted: the water you drink, the air you breathe, and the food you eat. You will see how generations of chemists have given the world not only a better understanding of itself but also many products that improve our lives. Such products include plastics, polymers such as nylon and Orlon, synthetic rubber, fertilizers, and many pharmaceutical agents.

3   Before you can appreciate the work that went into designing these products, however, you need to know more about chemistry: its methods, its history, and its study.

4.1 Science and the Scientific Method

4   You already know one of the most important things about chemistry: it is a science. **Science** is organized or systematized knowledge gathered by the scientific method. Chemists and other scientists approach their studies in an organized manner known as the scientific method. The **scientific method** involves three steps:

1. Collect facts and data by observing natural events under carefully controlled conditions—**experimentation.**
2. Examine and correlate these facts and propose a hypothesis. A **hypothesis** is a tentative theory to explain the data.
3. Plan and execute *further experimentation* to support or refute the hypothesis, and propose a scientific theory or law if possible.

5   You use a loose form of the scientific method whenever you play a video game. The first time you play the game you observe what happens as you move around the screen and push different combinations of buttons—you *experiment*. When the game ends, you consider the meaning of your observations in an attempt to figure out how to improve your score—you form a *hypothesis* to explain the events you noted. You then play again to see if you have made any progress in mastering the game. This *further experimentation* either supports your hypothesis or causes you to revise it.

6   Scientists follow and use these same three steps: experimentation, hypothesis formation, and further experimentation. They sometimes add one last step when repeated experiments confirm a hypothesis under certain conditions with no exceptions; they propose a *scientific law* (see Figure 4.1).

7   Some experiments result in hypotheses, a few in theories, and even fewer in scientific laws. Many times a hypothesis has to be modified or even discarded after further experimentation. Theories may stand unchallenged for years before new experimental data reveal them to be unacceptable. New theories then arise, and the process continues.

8   Workers in all sciences formulate hypotheses and theories and rely on mathematics to express their findings as precisely as possible. Research workers in the *abstract sciences* (mathematics and logic), the *biological sciences* (botany, zoology, physiology, and microbiology), and the *physical sciences* (chemistry, geology, and physics) can often exert careful control of their experiments and come to precise conclusions. Those exploring the *social sciences* (archaeology, economics, history, political science, psychology, and sociology) cannot usually perform highly controlled experiments. The biological sciences, in their attempt to become more precise, have become more chemically oriented in the explanation of health and disease.

Science   Organized or systematized knowledge gathered by the scientific method.

Scientific method Procedure for studying the world in three organized steps: experimentation, hypothesis proposal, and further experimentation.

Experimentation Collection of facts and data by observing natural events under carefully controlled conditions.

Hypothesis   Tentative explanation of the results of experimentation; it is subject to verification or rejection in further experiments.

FIGURE 4.1
The scientific method and the development of a scientific law.

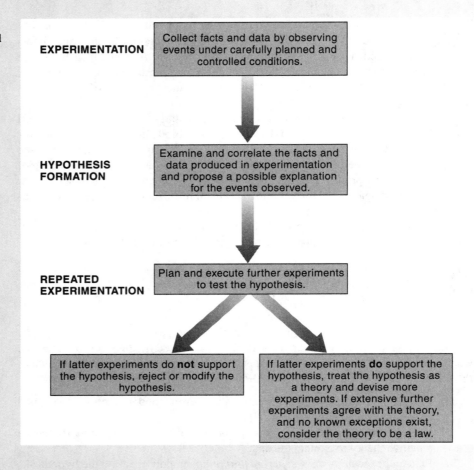

For example, a psychologist seeking to learn how people solve problems must allow for personal differences among the individuals tested. In contrast, a chemist studying the strength of a new material designed to be a glue can duplicate the glue and try it on different materials to determine how well it works.   9

Study Exercise 4.1

Suppose you decide to do some home cooking. You find a recipe for old-fashioned   10 vegetable soup in your mom's cookbook. After reading the recipe, you think the soup sounds "flat" but that a little chili powder would spice it up. You make the soup and add a small amount of chili powder to it. You serve it to your family, and they consider it very good. You repeat the preparation of the soup but this time record the amount of chili powder you add to the recipe. Again, your family likes it. What is the experimentation? What is the hypothesis? What is the further experimentation? What would you need to do before making your conclusions a law?

Experimentation: Adding chili powder to the vegetable soup.   11
Hypothesis: Chili powder will improve the flavor of the vegetable soup.
Further experimentation: Repeat the preparation of the soup with a given amount of chili powder and see if your family continues to like it. Before making the recipe a law, vary the amount and type of chili powder and also serve the soup during various seasons of the year—summer, winter, and so on. You may also want to try it out on some of your friends.

Work Problem 3.

Section Review 1

Directions.

1. On a separate sheet of paper, write a brief summary of the main points of the section you have just read.

2. Mark each of the following statements True (T), False (F), or Can't Tell (CT). Mark the statement Can't Tell if it cannot be determined to be either true or false based on the material in the passage. Refer to the passage as necessary to verify your answer.

_____ 1. Water is the most prevalent chemical in the human body.

_____ 2. A hypothesis is the same thing as a theory.

_____ 3. The first and third steps of the scientific method both involve experimentation.

_____ 4. Only one out of every thousand theories becomes a scientific law.

_____ 5. Social scientists have less control over their fields of study than chemical researchers.

Directions. Write the letter of the best answer in the space provided.

_____ 1. The authors mention fertilizers and plastics as examples of
   a. chemicals.
   b. important breakthroughs in the history of chemistry.
   c. discoveries that would have been impossible without the scientific method.
   d. useful products developed by chemists.

_____ 2. Science is defined as
   a. the use of experimentation to confirm hypotheses.
   b. knowledge obtained through the use of the scientific method.
   c. an organized and precise approach to self-understanding.
   d. a discipline in which highly controlled experimentation is required.

_____ 3. We can conclude that the three steps of the scientific method
   a. may be performed in any order.
   b. must be performed in proper sequence.
   c. usually result in the formulation of a scientific law.
   d. are necessary for the enjoyment of video games.

_____ 4. A scientist has proposed a hypothesis regarding the sleeping habits of the platypus. Her next step is to
   a. collect preliminary, general data about the lifestyle of the platypus.
   b. contact other scientists to obtain their opinions of her hypothesis.
   c. formulate and prove a scientific law regarding the platypus's sleeping patterns.
   d. collect data to confirm or disprove her hypothesis.

© 2007 Pearson Education, Inc.

_____ 5. The biological sciences have become more chemically oriented because
   a. mathematics cannot be applied to biological research.
   b. biologists are unable to perform controlled experiments.
   c. chemistry enables biologists to be more precise in their findings.
   d. biology cannot be considered a science without the application of chemistry.

4.2 The Science of Chemistry

Chemistry Study of the composition of substances and the changes they undergo.

Chemistry is the science concerned with the *composition* of substances and the *changes* they undergo. For example, chemistry is concerned with the components of water (composition) and the interactions between water and other substances (transformations). 12

Within the field of chemistry, chemists work on many types of problems. These problems can be categorized broadly as belonging to one of the five subfields of chemistry: (1) organic chemistry, (2) inorganic chemistry, (3) analytical chemistry, (4) physical chemistry, and (5) biochemistry. These subfields are presented in Table 4.1 along with some simple examples of problems within each subfield. 13

There is a certain amount of overlap among these subfields. In fact, some of the most exciting work in chemistry today involves problems related to more than one of the areas listed in Table 4.1. For example, a chemist studying the structure and nature of high-temperature superconductors draws on data and techniques from inorganic, analytical, and physical chemistry. 14

Organic chemistry Study of the substances containing carbon.

Inorganic chemistry Study of all substances other than those containing carbon.

Analytical chemistry Study of the quantitative and qualitative analysis (examination) of elements and compound substances.

Physical chemistry Study of the structures of substances, how fast they change, and the role of heat in chemical changes.

Biochemistry Study of the chemical reactions that occur in living organisms.

Table 4.1	The Five Subfields of Chemistry	
SUBFIELD	SUBJECT	EXAMPLE
Organic chemistry	Study of substances containing carbon, symbol C	Preparation of aspirin ($C_9H_8O_4$) or Tylenol ($C_8N_9NO_2$)
Inorganic chemistry	Study of all substances that do not contain carbon	Understanding how a car battery works
Analytical chemistry	Study of what is in a sample (*qualitative*) and how much of it is there (*quantitative*)	Measuring the amount of a particular pesticide in groundwater
Physical chemistry	Study of the structures of substances, how fast substances change (*kinetics*), and the role of heat in chemical change (*thermodynamics*)	Understanding the changes that occur when ice melts to give liquid water
Biochemistry	Study of the chemical reactions in living systems	Understanding how saliva breaks down some of the foods we eat as we chew

Work Problems 4 and 5.

Study Exercise 4.2
Listed below are the research interests of some international chemists. Using the definitions of the branches of chemistry listed in Table 4.1, classify these research interests as organic, inorganic, analytical, physical, or biochemical. 15
   a. Ring compounds of carbon that also contain sulfur
      Gardner W. Stacy   (organic)
   b. Chemical composition of seeds of Ohio buckeyes
      Booker T. White   (biochemical)
   c. Kinetics of transition metal reactions
      Nancy Rowan   (physical or inorganic)

Section Review 2

Directions.

1. On a separate sheet of paper, write a brief summary of the main points of the section you have just read.

2. Mark each of the following statements True (T), False (F), or Can't Tell (CT). Mark the statement Can't Tell if it cannot be determined to be either true or false based on the material in the passage. Refer to the passage as necessary to verify your answer.

_____ 1. Organic chemistry was the first important subfield discovered by chemists.

_____ 2. Analytical chemistry is concerned with determining what is contained in a sample.

_____ 3. A research chemist today may encounter problems that require knowledge of several chemistry subfields.

_____ 4. The change of water to vapor would mainly concern biochemistry.

_____ 5. Carbon-containing substances are the primary concern of inorganic chemistry.

Cumulative Review 1 [Pages 200–204]

Directions. Write the letter of the best answer in the space provided.

_____ 1. The main point of the passage's first paragraph (p. 201) is that
   a. all chemicals have unpleasant smells.
   b. not all chemicals have unpleasant smells.
   c. everything is made of chemicals.
   d. water is the most abundant chemical in the human body.

_____ 2. A scientific law is proposed when
   a. the scientific process requires another step.
   b. the last round of experimentation has been evaluated.
   c. a theory is considered important enough to warrant further research.
   d. a theory is confirmed by a substantial amount of research.

_____ 3. We can conclude from the passage that
   a. an archaeologist and a psychologist use the same research methods.
   b. a geologist has less control over her studies than a biologist.
   c. social scientists avoid studies where they cannot control all the variables.
   d. a physicist has more control over his research than a sociologist.

_____ 4. Regarding the subfields of chemistry, the authors suggest that
   a. they cannot be further subdivided.
   b. they are interrelated.
   c. they are best understood as separate, unrelated disciplines.
   d. organic and inorganic chemistry are the most important subfields.

_____ 5. Research on plant growth would probably fall into which of the following subfields?
  a. biochemistry
  b. physical chemistry
  c. analytical chemistry
  d. inorganic chemistry

Directions. Answer each question in complete sentences, without copying word-for-word from the passage.

1. What is chemistry?

   _____

   _____

   _____

2. In your own words, explain the steps of the scientific method.

   _____

   _____

   _____

3. What is the difference between a hypothesis and a theory?

   _____

   _____

   _____

4. When does a theory become a scientific law?

   _____

   _____

   _____

5. How is research in the natural sciences different from research in the social sciences?

   _____

   _____

   _____

Vocabulary Exercise 1

Directions. Choose the meaning for the underlined word that best fits the context. You may consult the dictionary as needed.

_____ 1. Such products include plastics, polymers . . . <u>synthetic</u> rubber. . . . **[Paragraph 2]**
   a. natural in origin
   b. of various uses
   c. made by combining
   d. fibrous in texture

_____ 2. . . . and many <u>pharmaceutical</u> agents. **[Paragraph 2]**
   a. unknown
   b. artificial
   c. disease-fighting
   d. drug

_____ 3. Science is organized or <u>systematized</u> knowledge. . . . **[Paragraph 4]**
   a. organized
   b. objective
   c. abstract
   d. complicated

_____ 4. Examine and <u>correlate</u> these facts. . . . **[Paragraph 4, point 2]**
   a. study
   b. compare
   c. calculate
   d. confirm

_____ 5. A hypothesis is a <u>tentative</u> theory. . . . **[Paragraph 4, point 2]**
   a. logical
   b. proposed
   c. probable
   d. based on research

_____ 6. A hypothesis is a tentative <u>theory</u>. . . . **[Paragraph 4, point 2]**
   a. proposal to take action
   b. organized collection of data
   c. explanation of how things or facts are related
   d. scientific investigation or inquiry

_____ 7. . . . to support or <u>refute</u> the hypothesis. . . . **[Paragraph 4, point 3]**
   a. disprove
   b. confirm
   c. question
   d. break down

_____ 8. Research workers in the <u>abstract</u> sciences. . . . **[Paragraph 8]**
   a. experimental
   b. practical
   c. logical
   d. conceptual

_____ 9. . . . can often <u>exert</u> careful control of their experiments. . . . **[Paragraph 8]**
   a. lose
   b. exercise
   c. design
   d. ensure

_____ 10. . . . high-temperature <u>superconductors</u>. . . . **[Paragraph 14]**
   a. rare chemicals
   b. chemicals used to conduct scientific research
   c. metals that conduct electricity without resistance
   d. elements that have no conduction properties

4.3 Brief History of Chemistry

The many areas under investigation by chemists today reflect the explosion of interest   16
in and understanding of chemical processes. Some of these processes have been
known for a long time. For example, the ancient Egyptians and Chinese were well acquainted with the process of fermentation in the production of alcoholic beverages.
Some of the foundations of modern chemistry trace back to the early Greeks and
Arabs. Democritus (about 460–370 B.C.), a Greek, proposed a theory on the atomic
structure of substances that preceded John Dalton's atomic theory by 2200 years. Al-
Khowarizmi, an Arab mathematician, devised the number zero in about A.D. 825, providing the mathematical expression so essential to modern science. In the medieval
period, European alchemists experimented endlessly in a fruitless attempt to turn lead
and other common metals into gold. Only recently, in the twentieth century, have scientists been able to transform platinum into gold (at great cost).

Two of the most important names in the founding of chemistry as a science are   17
Robert Boyle (1627–1691) and Antoine Laurent Lavoisier (1743–1794). Boyle
strongly advocated experimentation in the search for knowledge. Boyle's study of the
effect of pressure on the volume of a gas is an example of the scientific method.
Lavoisier is often considered the father of the science of chemistry. He demonstrated
that combustion is the result of the combination of a fuel with oxygen from the air.
Lavoisier used the scientific method to reveal that the popular theory of combustion
was wrong and opened the door to a new way of looking at substances.

Since the time of Lavoisier, individuals in virtually every nation in the world have   18
made contributions to our understanding of chemistry. Table 4.2 lists just a few of the
major discoveries since that time. Many of these individuals have received the Nobel
Prize in chemistry, the greatest single honor a scientist can receive.* These men and
women came from many different nations and ethnic backgrounds and a variety of
cultural and economic circumstances.

While Western Europeans dominated chemistry until World War I, American   19
chemists have increasingly come to the forefront since 1920. In the aftermath of
World War II, the United States became the world leader in all aspects of chemistry,
from research and development to production. Efforts in Japan and the former Soviet
Union have made both of these countries increasingly influential in the chemical
community. The future influence of the countries of the former Soviet Union, particularly Russia, in the advancement of science remains to be seen. Possibly China will
play a more influential role in the future.

*The Nobel Prize was established in 1901 form the estate of Alfred Bernhard Nobel (1833–1896), the in-
ventor of dynamite. Six Nobel Prizes are customarily awarded annually for outstanding contributions to
physics, chemistry, physiology or medicine, literature, economic sciences, and the promotion of world
peace.

Table 4.2		**Important Discoveries in Chemistry Since the Time of Lavoisier**	
NAME	DATES	COUNTRY OF ORIGIN	CONTRIBUTION
Charles Goodyear	1800–1860	United States	Discovered process for vulcanizing rubber using sulfur
Marie Curie[a]	1867–1934	Poland	Discovered radium
Gilbert Lewis	1875–1946	United States	Contributed to knowledge of chemical bonds
Otto Hahn[a]	1879–1968	Germany	Discovered nuclear fission, the process used in nuclear reactors
Niels Bohr[a]	1885–1962	Denmark	Developed model for the structure of the atom
Sir Robert Robinson[a]	1886–1975	United Kingdom	Prepared many useful medicinal agents
Albert von Szent-Gyorgi[a]	1893–1986	Hungary	Studied chemistry of muscle contractions
Wallace Carothers	1896–1937	United States	Discovered nylon
Percy Julian	1899–1975	United States	Developed process for mass-producing cortisone
Linus Pauling[a]	1901–1994	United States	Contributed to knowledge of chemical bonds and to world peace
Dorothy Crowfoot Hodgkin[a]	1910–1994	United Kingdom	Determined the structures of vitamin B_{12}, penicillin, and insulin
Melvin Calvin[a]	b. 1911	United States	Explained process of photosynthesis
Glenn Seaborg[a]	b. 1912	United States	Studied nuclear chemistry
Rosalind Franklin	1920–1958	United Kingdom	Studied structure of deoxyribonucleic acid (DNA), which controls the genetic code
Francis Crick[a]	b. 1916	United Kingdom	Proposed structure for DNA
Robert Woodward[a]	1917–1979	United States	Developed syntheses of various organic compounds such as quinine, lysergic acid, strychnine, reserpine, chlorophyll, vitamin B_{12}
Frederick Sanger[a]	b. 1918	United Kingdom	Identified chemical structure of insulin and investigated DNA
James Watson[a]	b. 1928	United States	Proposed structure of DNA

[a]Received the Nobel Prize. Marie Curie, Linus Pauling, and Frederick Sanger all received the prize twice. Rosalind Franklin did not receive a Nobel Prize because she died of cancer before her work could be recognized. Her research played an important part in the deoxyribonucleic acid structure proposed by Francis Crick and James Watson.

Section Review 3

Directions.

1. On a separate sheet of paper, write a brief summary of the main points of the section you have just read.

2. Mark each of the following statements True (T), False (F), or Can't Tell (CT). Mark the statement Can't Tell if it cannot be determined to be either true or false based on the material in the passage. Refer to the passage as necessary to verify your answer.

_____ 1. China will play an increasingly important role in chemical research in the next decade.

_____ 2. The Nobel Prize is the most prestigious award a chemist can achieve.

_____ 3. James Watson received the Nobel Prize in 1928.

_____ 4. Charles Goodyear was the first chemist.

_____ 5. European alchemists believed that it was possible to turn lead into gold.

4.4 The Study of Chemistry

You will get the most out of your efforts if you use a systematic approach to your stud- 20
ies. It is better to study six days a week for one hour than one day a week for six hours.
As chemists, we have a prejudice: we want you not only to understand chemistry but to
like it, too! Thus, we have written this text for you. We hope that analogies and applications to everyday life will make chemistry interesting and fun to learn.

Finally, chemistry is not always easy. In fact, its challenges are what keep chemists 21
excited about their field. By learning chemistry, you will be learning about a systematic approach to meeting challenges, which is a skill you can use whether your future
in chemistry is as a teacher, a laboratory technician, a nurse, a technical sales representative, or a reader of the daily newspaper. Chemistry is an important part of your
life and the future of our planet.

 ## Summary

This chapter considered the scientific method and its basis in experimentation; it de- 22
scribed the various fields of science; and it classified chemistry as a physical science
(Section 4.1). Chemistry is the study of the composition of substances and the
changes they undergo. The chapter presented the various subfields of chemistry (Section 4.2) and a brief history of chemistry (Section 4.3). Finally, the chapter offered
some insight into why you might want to learn chemistry (Section 4.4).

 ## Exercises

1. Define or explain the following terms (the number in parentheses refers to
the section in the text where the term is mentioned):
   a. science (4.1)   b. experimentation (4.1)
   c. hypothesis (4.1)   d. scientific law (4.1)
   e. scientific method (4.1)   f. abstract sciences (4.1)
   g. physical sciences (4.1)   h. biological sciences (4.1)
   i. chemistry (4.2)   j. organic chemistry (4.2)
   k. inorganic chemistry (4.2) l. analytical chemistry (4.2)
   m. physical chemistry (4.2)   n. biochemistry (4.2)

2. Distinguish between
   a. biological and physical sciences   b. hypothesis and scientific law
   c. inorganic and organic chemistry   d. organic chemistry and biochemistry

 ## Problems

Science and the Scientific Method (see Section 4.1)

3. Imagine that you want to know the fastest route to the ice cream parlor. You
begin by driving routes A, B, C, and D at the same speed on four successive
evenings and seeing how long each takes. You compare the results and decide which is faster. You then repeat each of the measurements several times
over the next few weeks to confirm your initial judgment. Which of the
steps is experimentation? Hypothesis formation? Further experimentation?
What would you need to do before making your conclusion a law?

The Science of Chemistry (see section 4.2)

4. Listed below are the research interests of some international chemists. Using the definitions of the branches of chemistry listed in Table 4.1, classify each of these research interests as organic, inorganic, analytical, physical, or biochemical.
   a. Chemical kinetics and mechanisms of electrochemical reactions and dynamics of membrane function—William D. Weir
   b. Trace analysis of pollutants—Basil H. Vassos
   c. Bacterial metabolism; metabolism of radioactive purines in bacteria and animals; chemotherapy—Gertrude B. Elion
   d. Synthetic and theoretical organophosphorus chemistry—Sheldon Buckler

5. The following is a list of research papers published in various scientific journals. Using the definitions of the branches of chemistry, classify each of these research papers as organic, inorganic, analytical, physical, or biochemical.
   a. "Thermochromism in Copper(II) Halide Salts"—Darrell R. Bloomquist, Mark R. Pressprich, and Roger D. Willett
   b. "A New Procedure for Regiospecific Synthesis of Benzopyran-1-ones [$C_9H_6O_2$]"—Frank M. Hauser and Vaceli M. Baghdanov
   c. "Gas-Phase Chemistry of Pentacoordinate Silicon Hydride Ions"—David J. Hajdasz, Yeunghaiu Ho, and Robert R. Squires
   d. "Multiple Forms of the Nerve Growth Protein and Its Subunits"—Andrew P. Smith
   e. "The Nature of Soluble Copper(I) Hydride [CuH]"—J. A. Dilts
   f. "The Preparation and Properties of Peroxychromium(III) Species [$Cr_2O_2^{4+}$ and $Cr_3(O_2)_2^{5+}$]"—Edward L. King
   g. "Thermodynamics of Proton Ionization in Dilute Aqueous Solution"—James L. Christensen

✓ Chapter Quiz

1. What do we call the study of the composition of substances and the changes they undergo?

2. Listed below are the research interests of some international chemists. Using the definitions of the branches of chemistry, classify each of these research interests as organic, inorganic, analytical, physical, or biochemical.
   a. Propellant chemistry and thermodynamics—Frank I. Tanczos
   b. Structure of molecules by X-ray methods—Dorothy Hodgkin
   c. Chemistry of carbon-containing polymers—Carl S. Marvel

3. A child strikes out in a baseball game three times in a row. The child then changes to a lighter bat and gets a hit. The child subsequently uses the lighter bat and gets three more hits in five tries. Which of the steps is experimentation? Hypothesis formation? Further experimentation? What would need to be done before making the conclusions a law?

Cumulative Review 2 [Pages 208–211]

Directions. Write the letter of the best answer in the space provided.

_____ 1. The ancient Egyptians
  a. had a more advanced understanding of chemistry than the ancient Greeks and Romans.
  b. understood some of the chemical processes that remain in use today.
  c. made important contributions to modern research procedures.
  d. were highly skilled mathematicians.

_____ 2. The alchemists' attempts to change base metals into gold
  a. have been partially achieved in modern times.
  b. were foolish, superstitious, and misguided.
  c. may be realized in the next century.
  d. led to the development of other important theories.

_____ 3. Lavoisier and Boyle are important figures in chemistry because they
  a. discovered how to safely perform experiments with oxygen and other gases.
  b. invented the scientific method.
  c. exposed incorrect theories.
  d. utilized the scientific method and made important discoveries.

_____ 4. We can tell from Table 4.2 that
  a. Niels Bohr made important contributions to our understanding of the atom.
  b. most important modern chemists were born in the United States.
  c. James Watson is not alive today.
  d. Rosalind Franklin and Francis Crick collaborated on DNA research.

_____ 5. The authors believe that
  a. the United States will continue to dominate the field of chemistry throughout the twenty-first century.
  b. Western European chemists no longer play an important role in chemical research.
  c. China and Russia may play increasingly important roles in the future.
  d. American chemists were unimportant until after World War II.

Directions. Answer each question in complete sentences, without copying word-for-word from the passage.

1. List some of the contributions to the field of chemistry made by the ancient Egyptians and Greeks.

_____

_____

_____

2. Why is Lavoisier considered the father of the science of chemistry?

_____

_____

_____

3. List two twentieth-century American chemists and describe their contributions to modern chemistry.

_____

_____

_____

4. According to the authors, what is the best way to study chemistry?

_____

_____

_____

5. What do the authors believe are the main benefits of studying chemistry?

_____

_____

_____

Vocabulary Exercise 2

Directions. Choose the meaning for the underlined word that best fits the context. You may consult the dictionary as needed.

_____ 1. . . . the ancient Egyptians and Chinese were well acquainted with the process of fermentation. . . . [Paragraph 16]
   a. agriculture
   b. agitation
   c. derivation of one substance from another
   d. breakdown of complex molecules

_____ 2. Boyle strongly advocated experimentation. . . . [Paragraph 17]
   a. made a practice of
   b. challenged
   c. recommended
   d. developed

_____ 3. He demonstrated that <u>combustion</u> is the result of.... [Paragraph 17]
    a. rust
    b. chemical interaction
    c. explosion
    d. burning

_____ 4. These men and women came from many different nations and <u>ethnic</u> backgrounds.... [Paragraph 18]
    a. racial
    b. cultural
    c. national
    d. familial

_____ 5. Discovered process for <u>vulcanizing</u> rubber.... [Table 4.2]
    a. inventing
    b. synthesizing
    c. extracting
    d. strengthening

Critical Response Questions

1. Why do the authors believe that chemistry is an important subject for all students to study? Do you agree? Why or why not?

2. Is it essential for all chemists to adhere to the scientific method described in this chapter? Why or why not?

3. Are social sciences necessarily less "scientific" than the natural sciences? Discuss.

4. Imagine that a chemist and a psychologist both wanted to help a baseball player become a better fielder. How might their approaches differ? Which one do you think would be more helpful? Why?

5. Which of the contributions of the ancient Egyptian and Greeks are most important to our understanding of chemistry today. Why?

6. What advancements in the field of chemistry are likely to occur in your lifetime?

7. The authors suggest that it is better to study for one hour on six different days than to study for six hours on one day. In your experience, is it better to spread out your study time, or to study for fewer, longer periods? Explain your answer.

Psychology

HEALTH AND STRESS

Directions

1. Begin by surveying the chapter to look for answers to the following questions.

   - What is the chapter about?

   - What subtopics will be discussed?

   - What will you learn from reading and studying the chapter?

   - How interesting does the chapter look?

   - How difficult does the chapter look?

   - How familiar to you is the chapter material? That is, how much previous knowledge of the subject do you have?

   When you have completed your survey, write a summary on a separate sheet of paper of what you've learned about the chapter from the survey. Your summary should include answers to the previous questions, as well as any other information and comments you wish to add.

2. While reading the chapter, look for organizational patterns. Recognizing the patterns should help you better grasp the relationship of ideas within each paragraph and section and distinguish main ideas more easily.

   Also, form questions from the headings and subheadings (generally, write one question per heading or subheading). Write your questions on a sheet of paper. After completing each section, mentally review the main points of the section, mark the text, and write the answer(s) to your question(s), as well as any other information that seems important to you.

SAMPLE TEXTBOOK CHAPTER

From *The World of Psychology*, 5th ed., by Samuel Wood, Ellen Green Wood, and Denise Boyd. New York: Pearson Education, 2005.

Sources of Stress

- *What was the Social Readjustment Rating Scale designed to reveal?*

- *What roles do hassles and uplifts play in the stress of life, according to Lazarus?*

- *How do approach–approach, avoidance–avoidance, and approach–avoidance conflicts differ?*

- How do the unpredictability and lack of control over a stressor affect its impact?
- For people to function effectively and find satisfaction on the job, what nine variables should fall within their comfort zone?
- How do people typically react to catastrophic events?
- How might historical racism affect the health of African Americans?

Responding to Stress

- What is the "general adaptation syndrome"?
- What are the roles of primary and secondary appraisals when a person is confronted with a potentially stressful event?

- What is the difference between problem-focused and emotion-focused coping?

Health and Illness

- How do the biomedical and biopsychosocial models differ in their approaches to health and illness?
- What are the Type A and Type B behavior patterns?
- How do psychological factors influence cancer patients' quality of life?
- What are the effects of stress on the immune system?
- What four personal factors are associated with health and resistance to stress?
- What are the relationships among gender, ethnicity, and health?

How would you react to the news that you had a life-threatening disease?

Lifestyle and Health

- What is the most dangerous health-threatening behavior?
- What are some health risks of alcohol abuse?
- What are some benefits of regular aerobic exercise?
- What are the benefits and risks associated with alternative medicine?

Perhaps you remember Michael J. Fox as Alex P. Keaton, an endearing teenager on the hit 1980s TV series *Family Ties*. Or you may have seen him first as Marty McFly, who raced back and forth in time in the *Back to the Future* trilogy. Or you might have come to know him when he returned to prime-time television, portraying Michael Flaherty, New York's deputy mayor, on ABC's *Spin City*.

In 1998, many were stunned when this popular star announced that he had Parkinson's disease, and had been battling it in secret for 7 years. Parkinson's is a debilitating degenerative disease that strikes the neural circuits and the inner workings of the neurons in the brain that control movement. Symptoms include slow or jerky movements, tremors that range from mild to uncontrollable shaking, and garbled speech. Clearly, this is a particularly devastating disease for an actor. Can you imagine the stress Fox had to endure in keeping his illness a secret? Concerns about someone finding out, or about how long he could physically and emotionally continue as an actor, must have weighed heavily on him. Acting was his living, the way he supported his family.

3   Fox was deeply stressed, but not devastated. In fact, he didn't even slow down. He even wrote a book about his life titled *Lucky Man: A Memoir* (Fox, 2002). How could a person struggling with an ever-worsening, debilitating chronic disease consider himself lucky? Fox knows that his joys far outweigh his troubles. Not only has he had a very successful career in a highly competitive field, but more importantly, he has the love and support of his wife, actress Tracy Pollan, and their children.

4   Michael J. Fox is more than a successful actor who has been stricken with a terrible disease. He has turned tragedy into triumph and now spends his time, his financial resources, and his talents trying to help others. He chairs the Michael J. Fox Foundation for Parkinson's Disease Research to raise awareness of the disease and secure funds to help find a cure. And he knows, firsthand, that one's health is far more important than fame and fortune.

5   In this chapter, we explore many aspects of health and stress. We begin our exploration by looking at stress, which is necessary for survival, but which, if chronic and excessive, can become disabling or even deadly.

Sources of Stress

6   What do you mean when you say you are "stressed out"? Most psychologists define **stress** as the physiological and psychological response to a condition that threatens or challenges an individual and requires some form of adaptation or adjustment. Stress is associated with the **fight-or-flight response,** in which the body's parasympathetic nervous system triggers the release of hormones that prepare the body to fight or escape from a threat. Most of us frequently experience other kinds of **stressors,** which are stimuli or events that are capable of producing physical or emotional stress.

Holmes and Rahe's Social Readjustment Rating Scale

7   Researchers Holmes and Rahe (1967) developed the **Social Readjustment Rating Scale (SRRS)** to measure stress by ranking different life events from most to least stressful and assigning a point value to each event. Life events that produce the greatest life changes and require the greatest adaptation are considered the most stressful, regardless of whether the events are positive or negative. The 43 life events on the scale range from death of a spouse (assigned 100 stress points) to minor law violations such as getting a traffic ticket (11 points). Find your life stress score by completing *Try It 5.1* (on page 219).

8   Holmes and Rahe claim that there is a connection between the degree of life stress and major health problems. People who score 300 or more on the SRRS, the researchers say, run about an 80% risk of suffering a major health problem within the next 2 years. Those who score between 150 and 300 have a

■ **stress**
The physiological and psychological response to a condition that threatens or challenges a person and requires some form of adaptation or adjustment.

■ **fight-or-flight response**
A response to stress in which the parasympathetic nervous system triggers the release of hormones that prepare the body to fight or flee.

■ **stressor**
Any stimulus or event capable of producing physical or emotional stress.

■ **Social Readjustment Rating Scale (SRRS)**
Holmes and Rahe's measure of stress, which ranks 43 life events from most to least stressful and assigns a point value to each.

What was the Social Readjustment Rating Scale designed to reveal?

What roles do hassles and uplifts play in the stress of life, according to Lazarus?

50% chance of becoming ill within a 2-year period. More recent research has shown that the weights given to life events by Holmes and Rahe continue to be appropriate for adults in North America and that SRRS scores are correlated with a variety of health indicators.

Some researchers have questioned whether a high score on the 9 SRRS is a reliable predictor of future health problems. One of the main shortcomings of the SRRS is that it assigns a point value to each life change without taking into account how an individual copes with that stressor. One study found that SRRS scores did reliably predict disease progression in multiple sclerosis patients. But the patients who used more effective coping strategies displayed less disease progression than did those who experienced similar stressors but coped poorly with them.

Daily Hassles and Uplifts

■ **hassles**
Little stressors, including the irritating demands that can occur daily, that may cause more stress than major life changes do.

■ **uplifts**
The positive experiences in life, which may neutralize the effects of many hassles.

■ **approach–approach conflict**
A conflict arising from having to choose between equally desirable alternatives.

■ **avoidance–avoidance conflict**
A conflict arising from having to choose between undesirable alternatives.

■ **approach–avoidance conflict**
A conflict arising when the same choice has both desirable and undesirable features.

Which is more stressful—major life events or those little problems and frustra- 10 tions that seem to crop up every day? Richard Lazarus believes that the little stressors, which he calls **hassles,** cause more stress than major life events do. Daily hassles are the "irritating, frustrating, distressing demands and troubled relationships that plague us day in and day out." Kanner and others developed the Hassles Scale to assess various categories of hassles. Unlike the Holmes and Rahe scale, the Hassles Scale takes into account the facts that items may or may not represent stressors to individuals and that the amount of stress produced by an item varies from person to person. People completing the scale indicate the items that have been a hassle for them and rate those items for severity on a 3-point scale. Table 5.1 shows the 10 hassles most frequently reported by college students.

DeLongis and others studied 75 American couples over a 6-month period 11 and found that daily stress (as measured on the Hassles Scale) related significantly to present and future "health problems such as flu, sore throat, headaches, and backaches." Research also indicates that minor hassles that accompany stressful major life events, such as those measured by the SRRS, are better predictors of a person's level of psychological distress than the major events themselves.

According to Lazarus, **uplifts,** or positive experiences in life, may neutralize 12 the effects of many hassles. Lazarus and his colleagues also constructed an Uplifts Scale. As with the Hassles Scale, people completing this scale make a cognitive appraisal of what they consider to be an uplift. Items viewed as uplifts by some people may actually be stressors for others. For middle-aged people, uplifts are often health- or family-related, whereas for college students uplifts often take the form of having a good time.

Making Choices

How do approach–approach, avoidance–avoidance, and approach–avoidance conflicts differ?

What happens when you have to decide which movie to see or which new restau- 13 rant to try? Simply making a choice, even among equally desirable alternatives (an **approach–approach conflict**), can be stressful. Some approach-approach conflicts are minor, such as deciding which movie to see. Others can have major consequences, such as the conflict between building a promising career or interrupting that career to raise a child. In an **avoidance–avoidance conflict,** a person must choose between two undesirable alternatives. For example, you may want to avoid studying for an exam, but at the same time you want to avoid failing the test. An **approach– avoidance conflict** involves a single choice that has both desirable and undesirable features. The person facing this type of conflict is simultaneously

Try It 5.1   Finding a Life Stress Score

To assess your level of life changes, check all of the events that have happened to you in the past year. Add up the points to derive your life stress score.

Rank	Life Event	Life Change Unit Value	Your Points
1	Death of spouse	100	____
2	Divorce	73	____
3	Marital separation	65	____
4	Jail term	63	____
5	Death of close family member	63	____
6	Personal injury or illness	53	____
7	Marriage	50	____
8	Getting fired at work	47	____
9	Marital reconciliation	45	____
10	Retirement	45	____
11	Change in health of family member	44	____
12	Pregnancy	40	____
13	Sex difficulties	39	____
14	Gain of new family member	39	____
15	Business readjustment	39	____
16	Change in financial state	38	____
17	Death of close friend	37	____
18	Change to different line of work	36	____
19	Change in number of arguments with spouse	35	____
20	Taking out loan for major purchase (e.g., home)	31	____
21	Foreclosure of mortgage or loan	30	____
22	Change in responsibilities at work	29	____
23	Son or daughter leaving home	29	____
24	Trouble with in-laws	29	____
25	Outstanding personal achievement	28	____
26	Spouse beginning or stopping work	26	____
27	Beginning or ending school	26	____
28	Change in living conditions	25	____
29	Revision of personal habits	24	____
30	Trouble with boss	23	____
31	Change in work hours or conditions	20	____
32	Change in residence	20	____
33	Change in schools	20	____
34	Change in recreation	19	____
35	Change in church activities	19	____
36	Change in social activities	18	____
37	Taking out loan for lesser purchase (e.g., car or TV)	17	____
38	Change in sleeping habits	16	____
39	Change in number of family get-togethers	15	____
40	Change in eating habits	15	____
41	Vacation	13	____
42	Christmas	12	____
43	Minor violation of the law	11	____

Life stress score: ____

TABLE 5.1	The Ten Most Common Hassles for College Students	
HASSLE		**PERCENTAGE OF TIMES CHECKED**
1. Troubling thoughts about future		76.6
2. Not getting enough sleep		72.5
3. Wasting time		71.1
4. Inconsiderate smokers		70.7
5. Physical appearance		69.9
6. Too many things to do		69.2
7. Misplacing or losing things		67.0
8. Not enough time to do the things you need to do		66.3
9. Concerns about meeting high standards		64.0
10. Being lonely		60.8

Source: Kanner et al. (1981).

drawn to and repelled by a choice—for example, wanting to take a wonderful vacation but having to empty a savings account to do so.

Unpredictability and Lack of Control

"Good morning, class. Today, we are going to have a pop quiz," your professor 14 says. Do these words cause a fight-or-flight response in your body? Such reactions are common, because unpredictable stressors are more difficult to cope with than predictable stressors. Laboratory tests have shown that rats receiving electric shocks without warning develop more ulcers than rats given shocks just as often but only after receiving a warning. Likewise, humans who are warned of a stressor before it occurs and have a chance to prepare themselves for it experience less stress than those who must cope with an unexpected stressor.

How do the unpredictability and lack of control over a stressor affect its impact?

Our physical and psychological well-being is profoundly influenced 15 by the degree to which we feel a sense of control over our lives. Langer and Rodin studied the effects of control on nursing-home residents. Residents in one group were given some measure of control over their lives, such as choices in arranging their rooms and in the times they could see movies. They showed improved health and well-being and had a lower death rate than another group who were not given such control. Within 18 months, 30% of the residents given no choices had died, compared with only 15% of those who had been given some control over their lives. Control is important for cancer patients, too. Some researchers suggest that a sense of control over their daily physical symptoms and emotional reactions may be even more important for cancer patients than control over the course of the disease itself.

Several studies suggest that we are less subject to stress when we have the 16 power to do something about it, whether we exercise that power or not. Glass and Singer subjected two groups of participants to the same loud noise. Participants in one group were told that they could, if necessary, terminate the noise by pressing a switch. These participants suffered less stress, even though they never did exercise the control they were given. Friedland and others suggest that when people experience a loss of control because of a stressor, they are motivated to try to reestablish control in the stressful situation. Failing this, they often attempt to increase their sense of control in other areas of their lives.

Stress in the Workplace

17   Perhaps there is no more troublesome source of stress than the workplace. Everyone who works is subject to some job-related stress, but the amount and sources of the stress differ, depending on the type of job and the kind of organization. Albrecht suggests that if people are to function effectively and find satisfaction on the job, the following nine variables must fall within their comfort zone.

For people to function effectively and find satisfaction on the job, what nine variables should fall within their comfort zone?

- *Workload.* Too much or too little to do can cause people to feel anxious, frustrated, and unrewarded.
- *Clarity of job description and evaluation criteria.* Anxiety arises from confusion about job responsibilities and performance criteria or from a job description that is too rigidly defined to leave room for individual initiative.
- *Physical variables.* Temperature, noise, humidity, pollution, amount of workspace, and the physical positions (standing or sitting) required to carry out job duties should fall within a person's comfort zone.
- *Job status.* People with very low-paying, low-status jobs may feel psychological discomfort; those with celebrity status often cannot handle the stress that fame brings.
- *Accountability.* Accountability overload occurs when people have responsibility for the physical or psychological well-being of others but only a limited degree of control (air-traffic controllers, emergency room nurses and doctors); accountability underload occurs when workers perceive their jobs as meaningless.
- *Task variety.* To function well, people need a comfortable amount of variety and stimulation.
- *Human contact.* Some workers have virtually no human contact on the job (forest-fire lookouts); others have almost continuous contact with others (welfare and employment office workers). People vary greatly in how much interaction they enjoy or even tolerate.
- *Physical challenge.* Jobs range from being physically demanding (construction work, professional sports) to requiring little to no physical activity. Some jobs (firefighting, police work) involve physical risk.
- *Mental challenge.* Jobs that tax people beyond their mental capability, as well as those that require too little mental challenge, can be frustrating.

18   Workplace stress can be especially problematic for women because of gender-specific stressors, including gender discrimination and sexual harassment in the workplace and difficulties in combining work and family roles. These added stressors have been shown to increase the negative effects of occupational stress on the health and well-being of working women.

19   Job stress can have a variety of consequences. Perhaps the most frequently cited is reduced effectiveness on the job. But job stress can also lead to absenteeism, tardiness, accidents, substance abuse, and lower morale. However, as you might predict, unemployment is far more stressful for most people than any of the variables associated with on-the-job stress. Given a choice between a high-stress job and no job at all, most of us would choose the former.

Catastrophic Events

Catastrophic events such as the terrorist attacks of September 11, 2001, and the   20
crash of the space shuttle *Columbia* in early 2003 are stressful both for those who
experience them directly and for people who learn of them via news media. Most
people are able to manage the stress associated with such catastrophes. However, for some, these events lead to **post-traumatic stress disorder
(PTSD),** a prolonged and severe stress reaction to a catastrophic event
(such as a plane crash or an earthquake) or to severe, chronic stress (such
as that experienced by soldiers engaged in combat or residents of neighborhoods in which violent crime is a daily occurrence).

*How do
people typically
react to catastrophic
events?*

■ **post-traumatic
stress disorder
(PTSD)**

A prolonged and severe
stress reaction to a catastrophic event or to severe,
chronic stress.

The potential impact of catastrophic events on the incidence of   21
PTSD is illustrated by surveys conducted before and after September 11,
2001. Prior to the terrorist attacks, most surveys found that between 1% and 2%
of Americans met the diagnostic criteria for PTSD. Two months after the attacks,
about 17% of Americans surveyed by researchers at the University of California–Irvine reported symptoms of PTSD. When the researchers conducted follow-up interviews with survey participants 6 months after the attacks, 6% of
them were still experiencing distress. Other researchers have found additional
lingering effects associated with September 11 (see Figure 5.1, below).

People with post-traumatic stress disorder often have flashbacks, nightmares,   22
or intrusive memories that make them feel as though they are actually re-experi-
encing the traumatic event. They suffer increased anxiety and startle easily, particularly in response to anything that reminds them of the trauma. Many sur-
vivors of war or catastrophic events experience *survivor guilt* because they lived
while others died; some feel that perhaps they could have done more to save others. Extreme combat-related guilt is a risk factor for suicide or preoccupation
with suicide in Vietnam veterans. One study of women with PTSD revealed that
they were twice as likely as women without PTSD to experience first-onset

---

FIGURE 5.1   **Americans' Stress Levels after September 11, 2001**

Researchers have found that Americans continued to experience increased levels of stress and anxiety several
months after the terrorist attacks of September 11, 2001.

Sources: Clay (2002), Clay et al. (2002), Schlenger et al. (2002), Silver et al. (2002).

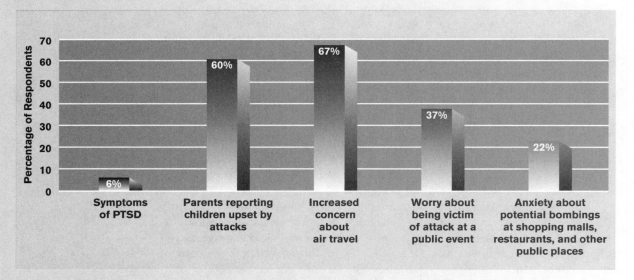

depression and three times as likely to develop alcohol problems. PTSD sufferers also experience cognitive difficulties, such as poor concentration.

Racism and Stress

23 A significant source of chronic stress is being a member of a minority group in a majority culture. A study of white and African American participants' responses to a questionnaire about ways of managing stress revealed that a person may experience racial stress from simply being one of the few or only members of a particular race in any of a variety of settings, such as a classroom, the workplace, or a social situation. The feelings of stress experienced in such situations can be intense, even in the absence of racist attitudes, discrimination, or any other overt evidence of racism.

24 Some theorists have proposed that a phenomenon called *historical racism*—experienced by members of groups that have a history of repression—can also be a source of stress. Researchers interested in the effects of historical racism have focused primarily on African Americans. Many of these researchers claim that the higher incidence of high blood pressure among African Americans is attributable to stress associated with historical racism. Surveys have shown that African Americans experience more race-related stress than members of other minority groups do. Those African Americans who express the highest levels of concern about racism display higher levels of cardiovascular reactivity to experimentally induced stressors, such as sudden loud noises, than do peers who express less concern. Thus, there may indeed be a link between perceptions of historical racism and high blood pressure.

25 However, African Americans are also more likely than members of other minority groups to have a strong sense of ethnic identity, a factor that helps moderate the effects of racial stress. Some studies show that personal characteristics, such as hostility, may increase the effects of racial stress. The relationship between historical racism and cardiovascular health is probably fairly complex and varies considerably across individuals. Moreover, some researchers believe that the association must be studied more thoroughly in other historically repressed groups, such as Native Americans, before firm conclusions can be drawn.

How might historical racism affect the health of African Americans?

Remember It 5.1

1. According to Holmes and Rahe, health may be adversely affected if a person experiences many stressful _____ in a short period of time.

2. According to Lazarus, _____ typically cause more stress than major life events do.

3. Rich cannot decide whether to go out with friends or stay home and study for tomorrow's test. This is an example of an _____ conflict.

4. The belief that one has _____ over a situation can moderate the effects of stress.

5. The nine variables proposed by Albrecht to account for most job-related stress are

_____, _____, _____,

_____, _____, _____,

_____, _____, and _____.

6. _____ is a prolonged and severe stress reaction that can result from experiencing a catastrophic event.

7. Some researchers have found links between _____ and high blood pressure in African Americans.

ANSWERS: 1. life events; 2. hassles; 3. approach-avoidance; 4. control; 5. workload, job status, physical variables, clarity of job description, accountability, task variety, human contact, physical challenge, mental challenge; 6. post-traumatic stress disorder; 7. historical racism

Section Review 1

Directions.

1. On a separate sheet of paper, write a brief summary of the main points of the sections you have just read.

2. Mark each of the following statements True (T), False (F), or Can't Tell (CT). Mark the statement Can't Tell if it cannot be determined to be either true or false based on the material in the passage. Refer to the passage as necessary to verify your answer.

_____ 1. The authors imply that the ideal life would contain no stress.

_____ 2. According to the SRRS, becoming wealthier is more stressful than moving into a new home.

_____ 3. The Hassles Scale is a better predictor of health problems than the SRRS.

_____ 4. Two months after the attacks of September 11, 2001, most Americans were suffering from PTSD.

_____ 5. Approach–avoidance conflicts are more stressful than avoidance–avoidance conflicts.

Directions. Write the letter of the best answer in the space provided.

_____ 1. The authors use Michael J. Fox's story to show that
   a. stress often causes illness.
   b. fame often leads to stress.
   c. how a person responds to stress is of great importance.
   d. more research is needed to understand Parkinson's disease.

_____ 2. According to Holmes and Rahe
   a. people with high SRRS ratings are more vulnerable to serious health problems.
   b. how you cope with stress is more important than the stress itself.
   c. individuals with low SRRS ratings can be assured of a healthy life.
   d. conflicts are the major source of stress in most people's lives.

_____ 3. Regarding workplace stress, the authors state that
   a. men and women experience equal amounts of workplace stress.
   b. too great a workload is the most significant contributor to workplace stress.
   c. the stress of unemployment is usually worse than job-related stress.
   d. job-related stress is worse for many people than unemployment stress.

_____ 4. Historical racism theorists believe that
   a. all minorities experience equal degrees of stress associated with racism.
   b. racism in America is declining.
   c. African Americans who have not experienced discrimination are unlikely to have high blood pressure or other stress-related symptoms.
   d. high blood pressure among African Americans is associated with historical racism.

_____ 5. Which of the following statements regarding stress and control is *not* true?
   a. Having a greater sense of control over your life can contribute to a longer life.
   b. Being warned about a stressor can reduce the stress associated with it.
   c. Knowing you have control reduces stress even if you don't exercise that control.
   d. When a stressor causes lack of control in one part of a person's life, most people typically respond by giving up control in other parts of their life as well.

Responding to Stress

26   How do you respond to stress? Psychologists have different views of the ways in which people respond to stressful experiences. Each approach can help us gain insight into our own experiences and, perhaps, deal more effectively with stress.

Selye and the General Adaptation Syndrome

27   Hans Selye (1907–1982), the researcher most prominently associated with the effects of stress on health, established the field of stress research. At the heart of Selye's concept of stress is the **general adaptation syndrome (GAS),** the predictable sequence of reactions that organisms show in response to stressors. It consists of three stages: the alarm stage, the resistance stage, and the exhaustion stage. (See Figure 5.2, below.)

28   The first stage of the body's response to a stressor is the **alarm stage,** in which the adrenal cortex releases hormones called *glucocorticoids* that increase heart rate, blood pressure, and blood sugar levels, supplying a burst of energy that helps the person deal with the stressful situation. Next, the organism enters the **resistance stage,** during which the adrenal cortex continues to release glucocorticoids to help the body resist stressors. The length of the resistance stage depends both on the intensity of the stressor and on the body's power to adapt. If the organism finally fails in its efforts to resist, it reaches the **exhaustion stage,** at which point all the stores of deep energy are depleted, and disintegration and death follow.

■ **general adaptation syndrome (GAS)**
The predictable sequence of reactions (alarm, resistance, and exhaustion stages) that organisms show in response to stressors.

What is the general adaptation syndrome?

■ **alarm stage**
The first stage of the general adaptation syndrome, in which the person experiences a burst of energy that aids in dealing with the stressful situation.

FIGURE 5.2 The General Adaptation Syndrome

The three stages in Selye's general adaptation syndrome are (1) the alarm stage, during which there is emotional arousal and the defensive forces of the body are mobilized for fight or flight; (2) the resistance stage, in which intense physiological efforts are exerted to resist or adapt to the stressor; and (3) the exhaustion stage, when the organism fails in its efforts to resist the stressor.
Source: Selye (1956).

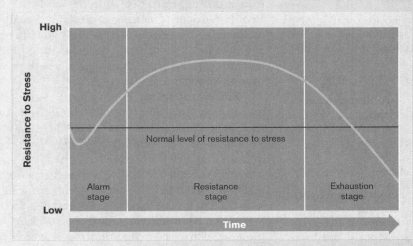

■ **resistance stage**
The second stage of the general adaptation syndrome, when there are intense physiological efforts to either resist or adapt to the stressor.

■ **exhaustion stage**
The third stage of the general adaptation syndrome, which occurs if the organism fails in its efforts to resist the stressor.

■ **primary appraisal**
A cognitive evaluation of a potentially stressful event to determine whether its effect is positive, irrelevant, or negative.

What are the roles of primary and secondary appraisals when a person is confronted with a potentially stressful event?

■ **secondary appraisal**
A cognitive evaluation of available resources and options prior to deciding how to deal with a stressor.

■ **coping**
Efforts through action and thought to deal with demands that are perceived as taxing or overwhelming.

■ **problem-focused coping**
A direct response aimed at reducing, modifying, or eliminating a source of stress.

■ **emotion-focused coping**
A response involving reappraisal of a stressor to reduce its emotional impact.

Selye found that the most harmful effects of stress are due to the prolonged 29 secretion of glucocorticoids, which can lead to permanent increases in blood pressure, suppression of the immune system, weakening of muscles, and even damage to the hippocampus. Thanks to Selye, the connection between extreme, prolonged stress and certain diseases is now widely accepted by medical experts.

Lazarus's Cognitive Theory of Stress

Is it the stressor itself that upsets us, or the way we think about it? Richard Lazarus 30 contends that it is not the stressor that causes stress, but a person's perception of it. According to Lazarus, when people are confronted with a potentially stressful event, they engage in a cognitive process that involves a primary and a secondary appraisal. A **primary appraisal** is an evaluation of the meaning and significance of the situation—whether its effect on one's well-being is positive, irrelevant, or negative. An event appraised as stressful could involve (1) harm or loss, that is, damage that has already occurred; (2) threat, or the potential for harm or loss; or (3) challenge, that is, the opportunity to grow or to gain. An appraisal of threat, harm, or loss can occur in relation to anything important to you—a friendship, a part of your body, your property, your finances, or your self-esteem. When people appraise a situation as involving threat, harm, or loss, they experience negative emotions such as anxiety, fear, anger, and resentment. An appraisal that sees a challenge, on the other hand, is usually accompanied by positive emotions such as excitement, hopefulness, and eagerness.

During **secondary appraisal,** if people judge the situation to 31 be within their control, they make an evaluation of available resources—physical (health, energy, stamina), social (support network), psychological (skills, morale, self-esteem), material (money, tools, equipment), and time. Then, they consider the options and decide how to deal with the stressor. The level of stress they feel is largely a function of whether their resources are adequate to cope with the threat, and how severely those resources will be taxed in the process. Figure 5.3 summarizes the Lazarus and Folkman psychological model of stress. Research supports their claim that the physiological, emotional, and behavioral reactions to stressors depend partly on whether the stressors are appraised as challenging or threatening.

Coping Strategies

If you're like most people, the stresses you have experienced have helped you 32 develop some coping stratgies. **Coping** refers to a person's efforts through action and thought to deal with demands perceived as taxing or overwhelming. **Problem-focused coping** is direct; it consists of reducing, modifying, or eliminating the source of stress itself. If you are getting a poor grade in history and appraise this as a threat, you may study harder, talk over your problem with your professor, form a study group with other class members, get a tutor, or drop the course.

Emotion-focused coping involves reappraising a stressor in order to reduce 33 its emotional impact. If you lose your job, you may decide that it isn't a major tragedy and instead view it as a challenge, an opportunity to find a better job with a higher salary. Despite what you may have heard, ignoring a stressor—one form of emotion-focused coping—can be an effective way of managing stress. Researchers studied 116 people who had experienced heart attacks. All of the participants reported being worried about suffering another attack. However, those who tried to ignore their worries were less likely to exhibit anxiety-related symptoms such as nightmares and flashbacks. Other emotion-focused strategies, though, such as keeping a journal in which you write about your worries and track how they change over time, may be even more effective.

FIGURE 5.3   Lazarus and Folkman's Psychological Model of Stress

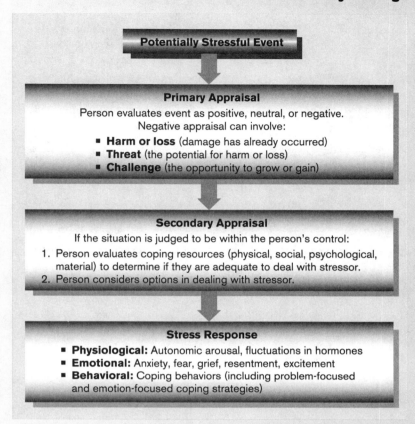

Potentially Stressful Event

Primary Appraisal
Person evaluates event as positive, neutral, or negative.
Negative appraisal can involve:
- **Harm or loss** (damage has already occurred)
- **Threat** (the potential for harm or loss)
- **Challenge** (the opportunity to grow or gain)

Secondary Appraisal
If the situation is judged to be within the person's control:
1. Person evaluates coping resources (physical, social, psychological, material) to determine if they are adequate to deal with stressor.
2. Person considers options in dealing with stressor.

Stress Response
- **Physiological:** Autonomic arousal, fluctuations in hormones
- **Emotional:** Anxiety, fear, grief, resentment, excitement
- **Behavioral:** Coping behaviors (including problem-focused and emotion-focused coping strategies)

Lazarus and Folkman emphasize the importance of a person's perceptions and appraisal of stressors. The stress response depends on the outcome of the primary and secondary appraisals, whether the person's coping resources are adequate to cope with the threat, and how severely the resources are taxed in the process.
Source: Folkman (1984).

■ **proactive coping**
Active measures taken in advance of a potentially stressful situation in order to prevent its occurrence or to minimize its consequences.

34   A combination of problem-focused and emotion-focused coping is probably the best stress-management strategy. For example, a heart patient may ignore her anxiety (emotion-focused coping) while conscientiously adopting recommended lifestyle changes such as increasing exercise (problem-focused coping).

35   Some stressful situations can be anticipated in advance, allowing people to use a strategy called **proactive coping,** which consists of efforts or actions taken in advance of a potentially stressful situation to prevent its occurrence or to minimize its consequences. Proactive copers anticipate and then prepare for upcoming stressful events and situations, including those that are certain and those that are only likely.

36   *Review and Reflect 5.1* summarizes the key aspects of the various theories concerning humans' response to stress.

What is the difference between problem-focused and emotion-focused coping?

R E V I E W *and* R E F L E C T 5.1

Theories of Stress Responses

THEORY	DESCRIPTION
Selye's general adaptation syndrome (GAS)	Three stages: alarm, resistance, and exhaustion
Lazarus's cognitive theory	Primary appraisal (evaluation of stressor), followed by secondary appraisal (evaluation of resources and options)
Coping strategies	Problem-focused coping, directed toward stressor; emotion-focused coping, directed toward the emotional response to the stressor

Remember It 5.2

1. Selye focused on the _____ aspects of stress, but Lazarus focused on its _____ aspects.

2. Match each stage of the GAS with its description.

    ____ (1) alarm stage   a. depletion of all stores of deep energy

    ____ (2) resistance stage   b. intense physiological efforts to adapt to the stressor

    ____ (3) exhaustion stage   c. emotional arousal and preparation for fight or flight

3. During _____ appraisal, a person evaluates his or her coping resources and considers options for dealing with a stressor.

4. _____ coping involves adjusting one's emotions to deal with a stressor, while _____ coping involves modifying or eliminating a particular stressor.

ANSWERS: 1. physiological, psychological; 2. (1) c, (2) b, (3) a; 3. secondary; 4. Emotion-focused, problem-focused

Section Review 2

Directions.

1. On a separate sheet of paper, write a brief summary of the main points of the sections you have just read.

2. Mark each of the following statements True (T), False (F), or Can't Tell (CT). Mark the statement Can't Tell if it cannot be determined to be either true or false based on the material in the passage. Refer to the passage as necessary to verify your answer.

    ____ 1. Resistance to stress reaches its highest level during the second stage (resistance stage) of the GAS.

    ____ 2. During a primary appraisal, a person determines how best to use his or her resources to deal with a stressor.

    ____ 3. Ignoring a stressor is never an effective way to manage stress because it results in increased anxiety.

    ____ 4. Most people use problem-focused coping and emotion-focused coping with equal frequency and with equal success.

    ____ 5. According to Hans Selye, stress is caused by a person's perception of a stressor rather than the stressor itself.

Cumulative Review 1 (pages 215-227)

Directions. Write the letter of the best answer in the space provided.

_____ 1. Which of the following is an example of an approach–approach conflict?
    a. wanting to buy a new car but not having enough money to afford it
    b. choosing between two desirable majors
    c. deciding whether or not to quit a job when you have no other income source
    d. deciding whether or not to go to the dentist when you have a toothache

_____ 2. Taking extra vitamin C to avoid catching cold would be an example of
    a. problem-focused coping.
    b. emotion-focused coping.
    c. proactive coping.
    d. primary appraisal.

_____ 3. Which of the following statements is _not_ true regarding the secretion of glucocorticoids?
    a. Glucocorticoids mobilize the body's resources in response to a stressor.
    b. Their prolonged secretion leads to harmful effects.
    c. Their prolonged secretion can do permanent bodily damage.
    d. They are produced in equal amounts throughout the three stages of the GAS.

_____ 4. Post-traumatic stress disorder is best understood as
    a. the sequence of stages an organism experiences in response to stress.
    b. the normal response to catastrophic events.
    c. a powerful stressor that cannot be managed.
    d. an extreme, extended stress response to a catastrophe or to severe, chronic stress.

_____ 5. The reader can conclude that
    a. an individual's personality can affect his or her response to a stressor.
    b. people who like their jobs do not experience job-related stress.
    c. young adults tend to have poor coping skills.
    d. two employees with the same job status will experience the same degree of job stress.

Directions. Answer each question in complete sentences, without copying word-for-word from the passage.

1. What is stress?

_____

_____

_____

2. What are the typical consequences of job stress?

_____

_____

_____

3. What are the symptoms of post-traumatic stress disorder?

_____

_____

_____

4. Why is stress dangerous?

_____

_____

_____

5. Explain the differences between a primary appraisal and a secondary appraisal of a stressful circumstance. Give an example of each.

_____

_____

_____

Vocabulary Exercise 1

Directions. Choose the meaning for the underlined word that best fits the context. You may consult the dictionary as needed.

_____ 1. Parkinson's is a <u>debilitating</u> degenerative disease that strikes the neural circuits . . .
[Paragraph 2]
a. incurable
b. weakening
c. terminal
d. painful

_____ 2. Parkinson's is a debilitating <u>degenerative</u> disease that strikes the neural circuits . . .
[Paragraph 2]
a. incurable
b. weakening
c. terminal
d. worsening

_____ 3. We begin our exploration by looking at stress, which is necessary for survival, but which, if chronic and excessive . . . [Paragraph 5]
   a. more than is necessary
   b. painful
   c. lasting a long time
   d. unusual or extraordinary

_____ 4. . . . SRRS scores are correlated with a variety of health indicators. [Paragraph 8]
   a. associated
   b. studied
   c. important; having an effect
   d. analyzed

_____ 5. According to Lazarus, uplifts, or positive experiences in life, may neutralize the effects of many hassles. [Paragraph 12]
   a. counteract
   b. emphasize
   c. improve
   d. clarify

_____ 6. . . . from a job description that is too rigidly defined to leave room for individual initiative . . . [Paragraph 17, point 2]
   a. reward
   b. satisfaction
   c. coming up with new ideas
   d. doing more than is necessary

_____ 7. But job stress can also lead to absenteeism, tardiness . . . and lower morale. [Paragraph 19]
   a. knowledge of right and wrong
   b. appropriate behavior
   c. poor job performance
   d. spirit or enthusiasm

_____ 8. The potential impact of catastrophic events on the incidence of PTSD is illustrated by surveys . . . [Paragraph 21]
   a. importance
   b. frequency
   c. data
   d. study

_____ 9. People with post-traumatic stress disorder often have flashbacks, nightmares, or intrusive memories . . . [Paragraph 22]
   a. extremely unpleasant; agitating
   b. interfering
   c. unfamiliar or unrecognized
   d. repeating over and over

_____ 10. . . . in the absence of racist attitudes, discrimination, or any other overt evidence of racism. [Paragraph 23]
   a. prejudiced
   b. unclear; hidden
   c. obtained by research
   d. open, unconcealed

Health and Illness

37 Have you heard the term *wellness* and wondered exactly what was meant by it? This word is associated with a new approach to thinking about health, used by both professionals and laypersons. This approach encompasses a growing emphasis on lifestyle, preventive care, and the need to maintain wellness rather than thinking of health matters only when the body is sick. Health psychologists are discovering how stress, through its influence on the immune system, may affect people's health. They are also examining how personal and demographic factors are related to both illness and wellness.

How do the biomedical and biopsychosocial models differ in their approaches to health and illness?

Two Approaches to Health and Illness

38 For many decades, the predominant view in medicine was the **biomedical model,** which explains illness in terms of biological factors. Today, physicians and psychologists alike recognize that the **biopsychosocial model** provides a fuller

FIGURE 5.4   The Biopsychosocial Model of Health and Illness

The biopsychosocial model focuses on health as well as on illness and holds that both are determined by a combination of biological, psychological, and social factors. Most health psychologists endorse the biopsychosocial model.

Source: Green & Shellenberger (1990).

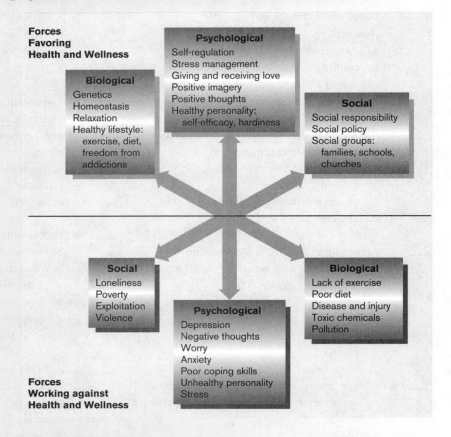

biomedical model
A perspective that explains illness solely in terms of biological factors.

biopsychosocial model
A perspective that focuses on health as well as illness and holds that both are determined by a combination of biological, psychological, and social factors.

health psychology
The subfield within psychology that is concerned with the psychological factors that contribute to health, illness, and recovery.

explanation of both health and illness (see Figure 5.4). This model considers health and illness to be determined by a combination of biological, psychological, and social factors.

Growing acceptance of the biopsychosocial approach has given rise to a new   39
subfield, **health psychology,** which is "the field within psychology devoted to understanding psychological influences on how people stay healthy, why they become ill, and how they respond when they do get ill." Health psychology is particularly important today because several prevalent diseases, including heart disease and cancer, are related to unhealthy lifestyles and stress.

Coronary Heart Disease

In order to survive, the heart muscle requires a steady, sufficient supply of oxygen   40
and nutrients carried by the blood. Coronary heart disease is caused by the narrowing or the blockage of the coronary arteries, the arteries that supply blood to the heart muscle. Although coronary heart disease remains the leading cause of death in the United States, responsible for 31% of all deaths, deaths due to this cause have declined 50% during the past 30 years.

A health problem of modern times, coronary heart disease is largely attribut-   41
able to lifestyle and is therefore an important field of study for health psychologists. A *sedentary lifestyle*—one that includes a job at which one spends most of the time sitting and less than 20 minutes of exercise three times per week—is the primary modifiable risk factor contributing to death from coronary heart disease. Other modifiable risk factors are high serum cholesterol level, cigarette smoking, and obesity.

Though not modifiable, another important risk factor is family history. The   42
association between family history and coronary heart disease is both genetic and behavioral. For instance, individuals whose parents have high blood pressure, but

who have not yet developed the disorder themselves, often exhibit the same kinds of emotional reactivity and poor coping strategies as their parents.

43   High levels of stress and job strain have also been associated with increased risk for coronary heart disease and stroke. Apparently, the effects of stress enter the bloodstream almost as if they were injected intravenously. Malkoff and others report that after an experimental group of participants had experienced laboratory-induced stress, their blood platelets (special clotting cells) released large amounts of a substance that promotes the buildup of plaque in blood vessels and may lead to heart attack and stroke. No changes were found in the blood platelets of unstressed control-group participants.

44   Personality type is also associated with an individual's risk of heart disease. After extensive research, cardiologists Meyer Friedman and Ray Rosenman concluded that there are two types of personality: Type A, associated with a high rate of coronary heart disease, and Type B, commonly found in persons unlikely to develop heart disease. Do you have characteristics similar to those of a Type A or a Type B person? Before reading further, complete *Try It 5.2* and find out.

45   People with the **Type A behavior pattern** have a strong sense of time urgency and are impatient, excessively competitive, hostile, and easily angered. They are "involved in a chronic, incessant struggle to achieve more and more in less and less time." Type A's would answer "true" to most or all of the questions in the *Try It*. In contrast, people with the **Type B behavior pattern** are relaxed and easygoing and are not driven by a sense of time urgency. They are not impatient or hostile and are able to relax without guilt. They play for fun and relaxation rather than to exhibit superiority over others. Yet, a Type B individual may be as bright and ambitious as a Type A person, and more successful as well. Type B's would answer "false" to most or all of the *Try It* questions.

46   Using meta-analysis, Miller and others found that 70% of middle-aged men with coronary heart disease exhibited the Type A behavior pattern, compared to 46% of healthy middle-aged men. Research indicates that the lethal core of the

What are the Type A and Type B behavior patterns?

■ **Type A behavior pattern**
A behavior pattern marked by a sense of time urgency, impatience, excessive competitiveness, hostility, and anger; considered a risk factor in coronary heart disease.

■ **Type B behavior pattern**
A behavior pattern marked by a relaxed, easygoing approach to life, without the time urgency, impatience, and hostility of the Type A pattern.

Try It 5.2   Type A or Type B?

Answer (T) or (F) for each of the statements below. (Adapted from Friedman & Rosenman, 1974.)

_____ 1. I forcefully emphasize key words in my everyday speech.

_____ 2. I usually walk and eat quickly.

_____ 3. I get irritated and restless around slow workers.

_____ 4. When talking to others, I get impatient and try to hurry them along.

_____ 5. I get very irritated, even hostile, when the car in front of me drives too slowly.

_____ 6. When others are talking, I often think about my own concerns.

_____ 7. I usually think of or do at least two things at the same time.

_____ 8. I get very impatient when I have to wait.

_____ 9. I usually take command and move the conversation to topics that interest me.

_____ 10. I usually feel guilty when I relax and do nothing.

_____ 11. I am usually too absorbed in my work to notice my surroundings.

_____ 12. I keep trying to do more and more in less time.

_____ 13. I sometimes punctuate my conversation with forceful gestures such as clenching my fists or pounding the table.

_____ 14. My accomplishments are due largely to my ability to work faster than others.

_____ 15. I don't play games just for fun. I play to win.

_____ 16. I am more concerned with acquiring things than with becoming a better person.

_____ 17. I usually use numbers to evaluate my own activities and the activities of others.

Type A personality is not time urgency but anger and hostility, which fuel an aggressive, reactive temperament. Hostility is not only highly predictive of coronary heart disease but also associated with ill health in general.

How do psychological factors influence cancer patients' quality of life?

Cancer

Cancer is the second-leading cause of death in the United States, ac- 47 counting for 23% of all deaths. Cancer strikes frequently in the adult population, and about 30% of Americans—over 75 million people— will develop cancer at some time in their lives. The young are not spared the scourge of cancer, for it takes the lives of more children aged 3 to 14 than any other disease.

Cancer, a collection of diseases rather than a single illness, can invade cells in 48 any part of a living organism—humans, other animals, and even plants. Normal cells in all parts of the body divide, but fortunately they have built-in instructions about when to stop dividing. Unlike normal cells, cancer cells do not stop dividing. And, unless caught in time and destroyed, they continue to grow and spread, eventually killing the organism. Health psychologists point out that an unhealthy diet, smoking, excessive alcohol consumption, promiscuous sexual behavior, or becoming sexually active in the early teens (especially for females) are all behaviors that increase the risk of cancer.

The more than 1 million people in the United States who are diagnosed 49 with cancer each year have the difficult task of adjusting to a potentially life-threatening disease and the chronic stressors associated with it. Thus, researchers claim that cancer patients need more than medical treatment. Their therapy should include help with psychological and behavioral factors that can influence their quality of life. Carver and others found that 3 months and 6 months after surgery, breast cancer patients who maintained an optimistic outlook, accepted the reality of their situation, and maintained a sense of humor experienced less distress. Patients who engaged in denial—refusal to accept the reality of their situation—and had thoughts of giving up experienced much higher levels of distress. Dunkel-Schetter and others found that the most effective elements of a strategy for coping with cancer were social support (such as through self-help groups), a focus on the positive, and distraction. Avoidant coping strategies such as fantasizing, denial, and social withdrawal were associated with more emotional distress.

The Immune System and Stress

What are the effects of stress on the immune system?

Composed of an army of highly specialized cells and organs, the immune sys- 50 tem works to identify and search out and destroy bacteria, viruses, fungi, parasites, and any other foreign matter that may enter the body. The key components of the immune system are white blood cells known as **lymphocytes**, which include B cells and T cells. *B cells* are so named because they are produced in the bone marrow. *T cells* derive their name from the thymus gland, where they are produced. All cells foreign to the body, such as bacteria, viruses, and so on, are known as *antigens*. B cells produce proteins called *antibodies*, which are highly effective in destroying antigens that live in the bloodstream and in the fluid surrounding body tissues. For defeating harmful foreign invaders that have taken up residence inside the body's cells, however, T cells are critically important.

■ **lymphocytes**
The white blood cells—including B cells and T cells—that are the key components of the immune system.

The immune system may turn against healthy cells or specific organs and at- 51 tack them, as happens in autoimmune diseases such as juvenile diabetes, multiple sclerosis, rheumatoid arthritis, and lupus. Moreover, the system itself may be the target of a disease-causing organism. For example, *acquired immune deficiency syndrome (AIDS)* is caused by the *human immunodeficiency virus (HIV)*. The virus attacks the T cells, gradually but relentlessly weakening the immune system until it is essentially nonfunctional.

52   **Psychoneuroimmunology** is a field of study in which psychologists, biologists, and medical researchers combine their expertise to learn the effects of psychological factors—emotions, thinking, and behavior—on the immune system. Researchers now know that the immune system is not just a means for fighting off foreign invaders. Rather, it is an incredibly complex, interconnected defense system working with the brain to keep the body healthy.

53   Psychological factors, emotions, and stress are all related to immune system functioning. The immune system exchanges information with the brain, and what goes on in the brain can apparently enhance or suppress the immune system. In one study, researchers gave volunteers nasal drops containing a cold virus. Within the next few days, symptoms of the viral infection rose sharply in some of the 151 women and 125 men who participated in the study, but less so or not at all in others. Participants with a rich social life in the form of frequent interactions with others—spouses, children, parents, co-workers, friends, and volunteer and religious groups—seemed to enjoy a powerful shield of protection against the virus infection. This pattern of protection held across age and racial groups, for both sexes, at all educational levels, and at every season of the year.

54   Close social ties—to family, friends, and others—apparently have good effects on the immune system. Ill effects often come from stress. Periods of high stress are correlated with increased symptoms of many infectious diseases, including oral and genital herpes, mononucleosis, colds, and flu. Stress can cause decreased levels of the immune system's B and T cells. Kiecolt-Glaser and others found that elderly men and women experiencing chronic stress as a result of years of caring for a spouse with Alzheimer's disease showed an impaired immune response to flu shots. Physicians have long observed that stress and anxiety can worsen autoimmune diseases. And "if fear can produce relapses [in autoimmune diseases], then even the fear of a relapse may become a self-fulfilling prophecy." Stress is also associated with an increase in illness behaviors—reporting physical symptoms and seeking medical care.

55   Stress has the power to suppress the immune system long after the stressful experience is over. An experimental group of medical students who were enduring the stress of major exams was compared with a control group of medical students who were on vacation from classes and exams. When tested for the presence of disease-fighting antibodies, participants in the exam group, but not those in the control group, had a significant reduction in their antibody count because of the stress. The lowered antibody count was still present 14 days after the exams were over. At that point, the students were not even aware that they were still stressed and reported feeling no stress.

56   In addition to academic pressures, poor marital relationships and sleep deprivation have been linked to lowered immune response. Several researchers have reported that severe, incapacitating depression is also related to lowered immune system activity. For several months after the death of a spouse, the widow or widower suffers weakened immune system function and is at a higher risk of mortality. Severe bereavement weakens the immune system, increasing a person's chance of suffering from a long list of physical and mental ailments for up to 2 years following a partner's death.

Personal Factors Reducing the Impact of Stress and Illness

57   There are several personal factors that seem to offer protection against the effects of stress and illness.

■ **psychoneuro–immunology**
(sye-ko-NEW-ro-IM-you-NOLL-oh-gee) A field in which psychologists, biologists, and medical researchers combine their expertise to study the effects of psychological factors on the immune system.

Optimism   People who are generally optimistic tend to cope more effectively with   58
stress, and this, in turn, may reduce their risk of illness. An important characteristic
optimists share is that they generally expect good outcomes. Such positive expectations help make them more stress-resistant than pessimists, who tend to expect bad
outcomes. An especially lethal form of pessimism is hopelessness. A longitudinal
study of a large number of Finnish men revealed that participants who reported feeling moderate to high hopelessness died from all causes at two to three times the
rates of those reporting low or no hopelessness.

Hardiness   Studying male executives with high levels of stress, psychologist   59
Suzanne Kobasa found three psychological characteristics that distinguished those
who remained healthy from those who had a high incidence of illness. The three
qualities, which she referred to collectively as **hardiness,** are *commitment, control,*
and *challenge.* Hardy individuals feel a strong sense of commitment to both their
work and their personal life. They see themselves not as victims of whatever
life brings, but as people who have control over consequences and outcomes. They act to solve their own problems, and they welcome challenges in life, viewing them not as threats but as opportunities for
growth and improvement.

*What four
personal factors are
associated with health
and resistance
to stress?*

Florian and others found that commitment and control alone are   60
apparently sufficient to produce hardiness. In stressful situations, commitment and control are compatible, complementary attributes. Commitment ensures a continuing involvement in the situation and provides the
staying power to see it through. A person who is committed does not give up.
Control provides confidence that the person is in charge of the situation and is
capable of finding the right solution to solve the problems at hand.

■ **hardiness**
A combination of three
psychological qualities—
commitment, control, and
challenge—shared by
people who can handle
high levels of stress and
remain healthy.

Religious Involvement   Another personal factor that contributes to resistance   61
to stress and illness is religious faith. One longitudinal study (conducted over a
period of 28 years) revealed that frequent attendance at religious services is correlated with better health habits. A meta-analysis of 42 separate studies combined
data on some 126,000 individuals and revealed that religious involvement is positively associated with measures of physical health and lower rates of cancer, heart
disease, and stroke. Also, measures of religious involvement were reliable predictors of greater longevity when all causes of mortality were considered. The specific measures of religious involvement most closely related to a lower mortality
rate were regular attendance at worship services, religious orthodoxy, and a personal sense of comfort and strength from one's religion. This study and others
have found the association between religious involvement and lower mortality to
be stronger for women than for men.

Why is religious involvement linked to health? Researchers are currently ex-   62
amining a number of hypotheses. One proposal is that individuals who frequent
religious services experience proportionately more positive emotions than those
who do not attend. Another is that religious involvement provides people with a
stronger form of social support than is available to those who are not religious.
Essentially, this hypothesis claims that social support may be more meaningful,
and more effective, when it comes from others who share your worldview. Researchers have also proposed that religious practices, specifically meditation and
prayer, may have positive effects on health-related physiological variables such as
blood pressure.

■ **social support**
Tangible and/or emotional
support provided in time of
need by family members,
friends, and others; the
feeling of being loved, valued, and cared for by those
toward whom we feel a
similar obligation.

Social Support   Another factor contributing to better health is **social support.**   63
Social support is support provided, usually in time of need, by a spouse, other family
members, friends, neighbors, colleagues, support groups, or others. It can involve

tangible aid, information, and advice, as well as emotional support. It can also be viewed as the feeling of being loved, valued, and cared for by those toward whom we feel a similar obligation.

64   Social support appears to have positive effects on the body's immune system as well as on the cardiovascular and endocrine systems. Social support may help encourage health-promoting behaviors and reduce the impact of stress so that people are less likely to resort to unhealthy methods of coping, such as smoking or drinking. Further, social support has been shown to reduce depression and enhance self-esteem in individuals who suffer from chronic illnesses such as kidney disease. And a large study of soldiers who had enlisted in the U.S. Army showed that a high level of social support from peers was an essential ingredient in reducing stress. People with social support recover more quickly from illnesses and lower their risk of death from specific diseases. Social support may even increase the probability of surviving a heart attack because it buffers the impact of stress on cardiovascular function. A longitudinal study of 4,775 people over a 9-year period found that those low in social support died at twice the rate of those high in social support.

65   In recent years, social support researchers have begun to distinguish between *perceived support*, the degree to which a person believes help is available when needed, and *received support*, the actual help a person receives from others. Interestingly, many have found that perceived support is more important than received support. Other research has shown that high levels of perceived social support are associated with lower levels of depression and even with recovery from depression. Such perceived support may be more a function of individual personality than of the actual availability of family and friends who can offer help. One longitudinal study found that college-aged participants who had sociable, outgoing personalities were more likely to report having high levels of perceived social support later in adulthood. These results underscore the importance of psychological variables in health.

Gender, Ethnicity, and Health

66 The degree of wellness and the leading health risk factors are not the same for all Americans, but rather differ across gender and among various cultural and ethnic groups. The good news is that efforts to erase the gender and race disparities in medical research and treatment are under way.

67 **The Gender Gap**   Researchers have found that women are more likely than men to seek medical care. Nevertheless, most medical research in the past, much of it funded by the U.S. government, rejected women as participants in favor of men. One area where the failure to study women's health care needs has been particularly evident is in research examining mortality risk following open-heart surgery. Women are more likely to die after such surgery than are men. To date, studies have shown that the gender gap in surgical survival narrows with age, but researchers are still investigating why women's postsurgical mortality rate is higher than men's.

68   Women are also slighted in general health care and treatment. Physicians are more likely to see women's health complaints as "emotional" in nature rather than due to physical causes. The AMA released a major report in 1991 revealing that of men and women who received an abnormal reading on a heart scan, 40% of the men but only 4% of the women were referred for further testing and possible bypass surgery. Women are less likely than men to receive kidney dialysis or a kidney transplant.

What are the relationships among gender, ethnicity, and health?

African Americans   African Americans make up 12% of the U.S. population. They 69
are represented in every socioeconomic group, from the poorest to the richest, but
their overall poverty rate is about three times higher than that of white Americans. As
a result, many African Americans are at higher risk for disease and death and are more
likely to suffer from inadequate health care. Their life expectancy trailed behind that
of the total U.S. population throughout the 20th century. African American infants
are at twice the risk of death within their first year of life as white American infants.

Compared to white Americans, African Americans have higher rates of dia- 70
betes, arthritis, and, as you learned earlier in this chapter, high blood pressure.
African Americans are 40% more likely than white Americans to die of heart disease and 30% more likely to die of cancer. Even when African and white Americans of the same age suffer from similar illnesses, the mortality rate of African
Americans is higher. Also, the rate of AIDS is more than three times higher
among African Americans than among white Americans.

Hispanic Americans   By the end of the 20th century, Hispanic Americans, the 71
fastest-growing U.S. minority group, represented about 13% of the total population. However, Hispanic Americans account for more than 20% of new tuberculosis
cases in the United States. Hypertension and diabetes are also more prevalent
among Hispanic Americans than among non-Hispanic white Americans, but heart
problems are less prevalent. Cigarette smoking and alcohol abuse are more common
among Hispanic American teenagers than among teenagers in other U.S. ethnic
groups. Further, Hispanic Americans are at high risk of death from accidental injuries (automobile accidents and other causes), homicide, cirrhosis and other chronic
liver diseases, and AIDS.

Native Americans   Native Americans, the smallest of all minority groups in the 72
United States, number about 2 million. The fact that a large proportion of Native
Americans die before the age of 45 partly accounts for their statistically low rates of
heart disease and cancer, which are more common among older people. Alcohol
represents another serious risk factor for Native Americans and plays a leading role
in their high homicide and suicide rates. Native Americans under age 35 are at least
10 times more likely than other Americans to die from diseases directly related to alcoholism. Rates of diabetes are also dramatically higher among Native Americans
than for other groups.

Asian Americans   Asian Americans, who make up 3.6% of the U.S. population, are 73
comparatively very healthy. The overall age-adjusted death rate for Asian American
males is 40% lower than that for white American males, but their death rate from
stroke is 8% higher. Of all U.S. ethnic groups, infant mortality is lowest for Chinese
Americans, at 3 deaths per 1,000 births, compared with 7 per 1,000 for the overall
population.

Remember It 5.3

1. The biomedical model focuses on _____;
the biopsychosocial model also emphasizes

_____.

2. Research suggests that the most harmful component of the Type A behavior pattern is

_____ .

3. Quality of life is associated with _____
among cancer patients.

4. HIV attacks the _____ cells of the immune system.

5. Lowered immune response has been associated
with _____.

6. Hardiness includes _____, _____,
and _____.

ANSWERS: 1. illness, health; 2. hostility; 3. optimism; 4. T; 5. stress; 6. commitment, control, challenge

Section Review 3

Directions.

1. On a separate sheet of paper, write a brief summary of the main points of the sections you have just read.

2. Mark each of the following statements True (T), False (F), or Can't Tell (CT). Mark the statement Can't Tell if it cannot be determined to be either true or false based on the material in the passage. Refer to the passage as necessary to verify your answer.

_____ 1. The biopsychosocial model of health and illness is more widely accepted by psychologists than by physicians.

_____ 2. People with Type A personalities are more prone to heart attack because they are impatient and always in a hurry.

_____ 3. Research has determined that the human immune system is a complex network of defenses that is influenced by psychological factors.

_____ 4. Social support is associated with lower stress levels and better health.

_____ 5. Middle-aged women have a greater mortality risk after open-heart surgery than middle-aged men.

Directions. Write the letter of the best answer in the space provided.

_____ 1. All of the following are modifiable risk factors for heart disease *except*
   a. exercise.
   b. cholesterol level.
   c. smoking.
   d. family history.

_____ 2. The authors state that compared with those who accept it, cancer patients who deny the reality of their illness
   a. live longer.
   b. live a shorter time.
   c. experience more stress.
   d. experience less stress.

_____ 3. Stress can affect the immune system by
   a. decreasing levels of B and T cells.
   b. increasing levels of B and T cells.
   c. blocking communication between B and T cells.
   d. increasing communication between B and T cells.

_____ 4. The authors suggest that hardiness
   a. is inherited.
   b. cannot be learned.
   c. helps people avoid illness.
   d. combines three qualities found in people with religious lifestyles.

_____ 5. The authors state that higher disease and mortality rates among African Americans are a result of
   a. lack of research.
   b. economic differences.
   c. inherited characteristics.
   d. differences in education.

Lifestyle and Health

What is the most dangerous health-threatening behavior?

Think about your own health for a moment. What do you think is the greatest threat to your personal well-being and longevity? For most Americans, health enemy number one is their own habits—lack of exercise, too little sleep, alcohol or drug abuse, an unhealthy diet, and overeating. What can make someone change an unhealthy lifestyle? Perhaps vanity is the key. Researchers have found that people are more likely to adopt healthy behaviors if they believe behavioral change will make them look better or appear more youthful than if they simply receive information about the health benefits of the suggested change. Still, there are some health-threatening behaviors that carry such grave risks that everyone ought to take them seriously. The most dangerous unhealthy behavior of all is smoking. 74

Smoking and Health

Smoking remains the foremost cause of preventable diseases and deaths in the United States. That message appears to be taking root because the prevalence of smoking among American adults has been decreasing and is currently under 25%. Moreover, smoking is more likely to be viewed as a socially unacceptable behavior now than in the past. There are wide variations in smoking habits according to gender and ethnic group. The highest rates of smoking are found among Native American men (41%) and women (29%), while the lowest rates are reported for Asian American men (18%) and women (11%). 75

Even though the prevalence of smoking is decreasing, every year more than 1 million young Americans become regular smokers, and more than 400,000 American adults die from diseases related to tobacco use. Smoking increases the risk for heart disease, lung cancer, other cancers that are smoking-related, and emphysema. It is now known that smoking suppresses the action of T cells in the lungs, increasing susceptibility to respiratory tract infections and tumors. 76

Other negative consequences from smoking include a widespread incidence of chronic bronchitis and other respiratory problems; deaths and injuries from fires caused by smoking; and low birthweight and retarded fetal development in babies born to smoking mothers. Furthermore, mothers who smoke during pregnancy tend to have babies who are at greater risk for anxiety and depression and are five times more likely to become smokers themselves. Millions of nonsmokers engage in *passive smoking* by breathing smoke-filled air—with proven ill effects. Research indicates that nonsmokers who are regularly exposed to *secondhand smoke* have twice the risk of heart attack of those who are not exposed. 77

Because smoking is so addictive, smokers have great difficulty breaking the habit. Even so, 90% of ex-smokers quit smoking on their own. The average 78 smoker makes five or six attempts to quit before finally succeeding. Some aids, such as nicotine gum and the nicotine patch, help many people kick the habit. A meta-analysis involving 17 studies and over 5,000 participants revealed that 22% of people who used the nicotine patch stopped smoking compared with only 9% of those who received a placebo. Twenty-seven percent of those receiving the nicotine patch plus antismoking counseling or support remained smoke-free. But even with the patch, quitting is difficult, because the patch only lessens withdrawal symptoms, which typically last 2 to 4 weeks. Half of all relapses occur within the first 2 weeks after people quit, and relapses are most likely when people are experiencing stressful negative emotions or are using alcohol. It takes just one cigarette, sometimes only one puff, to cause a relapse.

79   Researchers have found smoking rates to be high in people suffering from drug and alcohol abuse and schizophrenia. Furthermore, a link has been found between smoking and major depression, both of which are thought to be influenced by genetic factors. Some smokers who try to quit are at higher risk for major depression. Withdrawal brings on depression in more than 85% of those with a history of depression, compared with only 20% of those with no such history. Consequently, depressed smokers are much less likely to succeed at quitting.

Alcohol Abuse

80 Do you use alcohol regularly? Many Americans do. *Substance abuse* is defined as continued use of a substance that interferes with a person's major life roles at home, in school, at work, or elsewhere and contributes to legal difficulties or psychological problems. Alcohol is perhaps the most frequently abused substance of all, and the health costs of alcohol abuse are staggering—in fatalities, medical bills, lost work, and family problems.

81   Approximately 10 million Americans are alcoholics. Alcohol abuse is three times more prevalent in males than in females. People who begin drinking before age 15 are four times more likely than those who begin later to become alcoholics. For many, alcohol provides a method of coping with life stresses they feel otherwise powerless to control. As many as 80% of men and women who are alcoholics complain of episodes of depression. A large study of almost 3,000 alcoholics concluded that some depressive episodes are independent of alcohol, whereas others are substance-induced.

What are some health risks of alcohol abuse?

82   Alcohol can damage virtually every organ in the body, but it is especially harmful to the liver and is the major cause of cirrhosis, which kills 26,000 people each year. Other causes of death are also more common in alcoholics than in nonalcoholics. One Norwegian longitudinal study involving more than 40,000 male participants found that the rate of death prior to age 60 was significantly higher among alcoholics than nonalcoholics. Alcoholics are about three times as likely to die in automobile accidents or of heart disease as nonalcoholics, and they have twice the rate of deaths from cancer.

83   Shrinkage in the cerebral cortex of alcoholics has been found by researchers using MRI scans. CT scans also show brain shrinkage in a high percentage of alcoholics, even in those who are young and in those who show normal cognitive functioning. Moreover, heavy drinking can cause cognitive impairment that continues for several months after the drinking stops. The only good news in recent studies is that some of the effects of alcohol on the brain seem to be partially reversible with prolonged abstinence.

84   Alcoholism's toll goes beyond the physical damage to the alcoholic. In 1995, alcohol was involved in 41% of the traffic fatalities in the United States, which numbered almost 17,300. Alcohol has been implicated in 20–36% of suicides, 53% of falls, and 48% of burns.

Since the late 1950s, the American Medical Association has maintained that   85
alcoholism is a disease, and once a percon becomes an alcoholic, he or she is always an alcoholic. According to this view, even a small amount of alcohol can
cause an irresistible craving for more, leading alcoholics to lose control of their
drinking. Thus, total abstinence is seen as the only acceptable and effective
method of treatment. Alcoholics Anonymous (AA) endorses both the disease concept and the total abstinence approach to treatment. There is a drug that may
make abstinence somewhat easier. German researchers report that the drug
acamprosate helps prevent relapse in recovering alcoholics.

Some studies suggest a genetic influence on alcoholism and lend support to   86
the disease model. For example, neuroscientist Henri Begleiter and his colleagues
have accumulated a large body of evidence suggesting that the brains of alcoholics respond differently to visual and auditory stimuli than those of nonalcoholics. Further, many relatives of alcoholics, even children and adults who have
never consumed any alcohol in their lives, display the same types of response patterns. The relatives of alcoholics who do display these patterns are more likely to
become alcoholics themselves or to suffer from other types of addictions. Consequently, Begleiter has suggested that the brain-imaging techniques he uses in his
research may someday be used to determine which relatives of alcoholics are ge-
netically predisposed to addiction.

Exercise

How much exercise do you get? Many studies show that regular exercise pays rich   87
dividends in the form of physical and mental fitness. However, many people still
express reluctance to exercise. Some simply prefer not to be physically active;
others blame such factors as the cost of joining a health club or even the unpredictability of the weather for their lack of physical activity. Such individuals are
missing out on one of the simplest and most effective ways of enhancing
one's health.

What are some benefits of regular aerobic exercise?

■ **aerobic exercise**
(ah-RO-bik) Exercise that
uses the large muscle
groups in continuous,
repetitive action and in-
creases oxygen intake and
breathing and heart rates.

Aerobic exercise (such as running, swimming, brisk walking, bi-   88
cycling, rowing, and jumping rope) is exercise that uses the large muscle
groups in continuous, repetitive action and increases oxygen intake and
breathing and heart rates. To improve cardiovascular fitness and endurance
and to lessen the risk of heart attack, an individual should perform aerobic exercise regularly—three or four times a week for 20–30 minutes, with additional
5- to 10-minute warm-up and cool-down periods. Less than 20 minutes of aerobic exercise three times a week has "no measurable effect on the heart," and more
than 3 hours per week "is not known to reduce cardiovascular risk any further."
However, individuals who engage in more than 3 hours of aerobic activity each
week are more successful at losing excess weight and keeping it off than are those
who exercise less.

In case you are not yet convinced, consider the following benefits of exercise: 89

■ Increases the efficiency of the heart, enabling it to pump more blood with
  each beat; and reduces the resting pulse rate and improves circulation

■ Raises levels of HDL (the good blood cholesterol), which (1) helps rid the
  body of LDL (the bad blood cholesterol) and (2) removes plaque buildup on
  artery walls

■ Burns up extra calories, enabling you to lose weight or maintain your weight

■ Makes bones denser and stronger, helping to prevent osteoporosis in women

■ Moderates the effects of stress

■ Gives you more energy and increases your resistance to fatigue

■ Benefits the immune system by increasing natural killer cell activity

Alternative Medicine

90   Do you take vitamins or herbal supplements in hopes of positively influencing your health? According to surveys, Americans spend billions of dollars each year on unconventional treatments—herbs, massage, self-help groups, megavitamins, folk remedies, and homeopathy—for a variety of illnesses and conditions. In one such survey, the National Science Foundation found that 88% of Americans believe that there are valid ways of preventing and curing illnesses that are not recognized by the medical profession. College-educated Americans are more likely to use unconventional treatments than those who have less education.

91   The National Science Foundation defines **alternative medicine** as any treatment or therapy that has not been scientifically demonstrated to be effective. Even a simple practice such as taking vitamins sometimes falls into this category. For instance, *scurvy* (a condition whose symptoms include bleeding gums and easy bruising) has been scientifically determined to be caused by vitamin C deficiency. So, taking vitamin C to prevent or cure scurvy is not considered an alternative therapy. However, if you take vitamin C to protect yourself against the common cold, you are using alternative medicine because vitamin C has not been scientifically proven to prevent colds.

■ **alternative medicine**
Any treatment or therapy that has not been scientifically demonstrated to be effective.

92   If alternative treatments lack scientific support, why do so many people believe in them? One possibility is that it is easier to take a vitamin than to make a lifestyle change. But it is also true that people who do their own research about alternative therapies may happen upon effective treatments of which their physicians are unaware. However, most patients who use alternative treatments do not inform their physicians about them. Health professionals cite this tendency toward secrecy as a major risk factor in the use of alternative medicine. They point out that many therapies, especially those that involve food supplements, have pharmacological effects that can interfere with treatments prescribed by physicians. Consequently, individuals who use alternative treatments should tell their physicians about them. While doctors may be skeptical about the utility of the alternative treatments, they need to have this information about their patients in order to practice conventional medicine effectively. Moreover, faith in an alternative treatment may cause an individual to delay seeking necessary conventional medical treatment.

What are the benefits and risks associated with alternative medicine?

93   Although it is true that some alternative therapies may be helpful in both preventing and treating illness, most health professionals agree that lifestyle changes bring greater health benefits than do any type of alternative medicine. Unfortunately, many people resist making lifestyle changes because they see them as taking too long to be effective or being too difficult to carry out. A smoker may think, "I've been smoking so long, quitting now won't make a difference." An obese person may be so overwhelmed by the amount of weight loss necessary to attain an ideal weight that she or he gives up. However, the benefits of various lifestyle changes, some of which are fairly easy to achieve, can be well worth the effort. And remember, to be healthier, you don't have to make *all* of the changes. You might consider starting with just one. Even if you never make another change, you are likely to live longer and be healthier than you would have otherwise.

Remember It 5.4

1. The greatest threat to Americans' health and longevity is a(n) _____.

2. _____ is the leading preventable cause of disease and death.

3. Excessive intake of _____ can damage virtually every organ in the body.

4. Cardiovascular fitness and endurance can be improved through _____.

ANSWERS: 1. unhealthy lifestyle; 2. Smoking; 3. alcohol; 4. aerobic exercise

Section Review 4

Directions.

1. On a separate sheet of paper, write a brief summary of the main points of the sections you have just read.

2. Mark each of the following statements True (T), False (F), or Can't Tell (CT). Mark the statement Can't Tell if it cannot be determined to be either true or false based on the material in the passage. Refer to the passage as necessary to verify your answer.

_____ 1. Children of mothers who smoke during pregnancy are more likely to become smokers than children whose mothers are nonsmokers.

_____ 2. Teenage girls who drink are more likely to become alcoholics than teenage boys who drink.

_____ 3. Both the American Medical Association and Alcoholics Anonymous view alcoholism as a disease whose only cure is complete abstinence.

_____ 4. One hour of aerobic exercise five times a week is more effective than 30 minutes of aerobic exercise four times a week for reducing the risk of heart attack.

_____ 5. The authors imply that alternative health treatments are a complete waste of time and money.

Summary and Review

Sources of Stress   p. 217

What was the Social Readjustment Rating Scale designed to reveal? p. 217

The SRRS assesses stress in terms of life events, positive or negative, that necessitate change and adaptation. Holmes and Rahe found a relationship between degree of life stress (as measured on the scale) and major health problems.

What roles do hassles and uplifts play in the stress of life, according to Lazarus? p. 218

According to Lazarus, daily hassles typically cause more stress than major life changes. Positive experiences in life—uplifts—can neutralize the effects of many of the hassles, however.

How do approach—approach, avoidance—avoidance, and approach—avoidance conflicts differ? p. 218

In an approach-approach conflict, a person must decide between equally desirable alternatives. In an avoidance-avoidance conflict, the choice is between two undesirable alternatives. In an approach–avoidance conflict, a person is both drawn to and repelled by a single choice.

How do the unpredictability and lack of control over a stressor affect its impact? p. 220

Stressors that are unpredictable and uncontrollable have greater impact than those that are predictable and controllable.

For people to function effectively and find satisfaction on the job, what nine variables should fall within their comfort zone? p. 221

The nine variables that should fall within a worker's comfort zone are workload, clarity of job description and evaluation criteria, physical variables, job status, accountability, task variety, human contact, physical challenge, and mental challenge.

How do people typically react to catastrophic events?   p. 222

Most people cope quite well with catastrophic events. However, some people develop post-traumatic stress disorder (PTSD), a prolonged, severe stress reaction, often characterized by flashbacks, nightmares, or intrusive memories of the traumatic event.

How might historical racism affect the health of African Americans? p. 223

Some researchers believe that African Americans have higher levels of high blood pressure than members of other groups because of stress due to historical racism. African Americans who express high levels of concern about racism display larger cardiovascular responses to experimentally induced stressors than do their peers in other ethnic groups, who express lower levels of concern.

Responding to Stress   p. 225

What is the general adaptation syndrome? p. 225

The general adaptation syndrome (GAS) proposed by Selye is the predictable sequence of reactions that organisms show in response to stressors. It consists of the alarm stage, the resistance stage, and the exhaustion stage.

What are the roles of primary and secondary appraisals when a person is confronted with a potentially stressful event? p. 226

Lazarus maintains that, when confronted with a potentially stressful event, a person engages in a cognitive appraisal process consisting of (1) a primary appraisal, to evaluate the relevance of the situation to one's well-being (whether it will be positive, irrelevant, or negative), and (2) a secondary appraisal, to evaluate one's resources and determine how to cope with the stressor.

What is the difference between problem-focused and emotion-focused coping?   p. 226

Problem-focused coping is a direct response aimed at reducing, modifying, or eliminating the source of stress; emotion-focused coping involves reappraising a stressor in order to reduce its emotional impact.

Health and Illness   p. 231

How do the biomedical and biopsychosocial models differ in their approaches to health and illness?   p. 231

The biomedical model focuses on illness rather than on health and explains illness in terms of biological factors. The biopsychosocial model focuses on health as well as on illness and holds that both are determined by a combination of biological, psychological, and social factors.

What are the Type A and Type B behavior patterns?   p. 233

The Type A behavior pattern, often cited as a risk factor for coronary heart disease, is characterized by a sense of time urgency, impatience, excessive competitive drive, hostility, and easily aroused anger. The Type B behavior pattern is characterized by a relaxed, easygoing approach to life, without the time urgency, impatience, and hostility of the Type A pattern.

How do psychological factors influence cancer patients' quality of life? p. 234

Cancer patients can improve their quality of life by maintaining an optimistic outlook, accepting the reality of their situation, and maintaining a sense of humor. Social support and psychotherapy can help them do so.

What are the effects of stress on the immune system?   p. 234

Stress has been associated with lowered immune response and with increased symptoms of many infectious diseases.

What four personal factors are associated with health and resistance to stress?   p. 235

Personal factors related to health and resistance to stress are optimism, hardiness, religious involvement, and social support.

What are the relationships among gender, ethnicity, and health? p. 237

Women are more likely than men to seek medical care, but women's needs have often been ignored by medical researchers and health care providers. African Americans, Hispanic Americans, and Native Americans have higher rates of many diseases than do white Americans. Asian Americans are comparatively very healthy.

Lifestyle and Health   p. 240

What is the most danger-ous health-threatening behavior?   p. 240

Smoking is considered the most dangerous health-related behavior because it is directly related to over 400,000 deaths each year, including deaths from heart disease, lung cancer, respiratory diseases, and stroke.

What are some health risks of alcohol abuse? p. 241

Alcohol abuse damages virtually every organ in the body, including the liver, stomach, skeletal muscles, heart, and brain. Alcoholics are three times as likely to die in motor vehicle accidents as are non-alcoholics.

What are some benefits of regular aerobic exercise?   p. 242

Regular aerobic exercise reduces the risk of cardiovascular disease, increases muscular strength, moderates the effects of stress, makes bones denser and stronger, and helps one maintain a desirable weight.

What are the benefits and risks associated with alternative medicine? p. 243

Alternative medicine—the use of any treatment that has not been proven scientifically to be effective—can benefit individuals who find alternative treatments that are effective. However, many patients increase their risk of poor outcomes by not telling their physicians about their use of alternative treatments. And some people delay seeking necessary conventional medical treatment because they believe that alternative approaches will work.

Key Terms

aerobic exercise, p. 242
alarm stage, p. 225
alternative medicine, p. 243
approach–approach conflict, p. 218
approach–avoidance conflict, p. 218
avoidance–avoidance conflict, p. 218
biomedical model, p. 232
biopsychosocial model, p. 232
coping, p. 226
emotion-focused coping, p. 226
exhaustion stage, p. 226

fight-or-flight response, p. 217
general adaptation syndrome (GAS), p. 225
hardiness, p. 236
hassles, p. 218
health psychology, p. 232
lymphocytes, p. 234
post-traumatic stress disorder (PTSD), p. 222
primary appraisal, p. 226
proactive coping, p. 227
problem–focused coping, p. 226

psychoneuroimmunology, p. 235
resistance stage, p. 226
secondary appraisal, p. 226
Social Readjustment Rating Scale (SRRS), p. 217
social support, p. 236
stress, p. 217
stressor, p. 217
Type A behavior pattern, p. 233
Type B behavior pattern, 233
uplifts, p. 218

Cumulative Review 2 (pages 231–246)

Directions. Write the letter of the best answer in the space provided.

_____ 1. In the biopsychosocialmodel of health and illness, all of the following are considered psychological forces *except*

a. stress.

b. self-regulation.

c. hardiness.

d. loneliness.

_____ 2. The authors state that Americans are more likely to change an unhealthy lifestyle if
   a. their doctor recommends the change.
   b. they believe it will improve their appearance.
   c. they've seen advertisements or infomercials endorsing the change.
   d. they are provided additional health information.

_____ 3. The immune system benefits from all of the following *except*
   a. positive social interaction.
   b. feelings of aggression.
   c. a sense of commitment.
   d. an optimistic attitude.

_____ 4. Regarding individuals who are trying to quit smoking, we can infer that
   a. most people who try to quit are successful.
   b. nicotine patches have no real benefits.
   c. stress increases the chances of a relapse.
   d. individuals who are unsuccessful in their first attempts to quit are highly unlikely to succeed in later attempts.

_____ 5. People who use alternative health treatments
   a. should inform their doctors of what they are using.
   b. should not use alternative treatments at the same time as conventional treatments.
   c. tend to be less educated than individuals who use only conventional treatments.
   d. tend to avoid exercise and healthy food choices.

Directions. Answer each question in complete sentences, without copying word-for-word from the passage.

1. What is wellness?

   _____

   _____

   _____

2. What are the main differences between Type A personalities and Type B personalities?

   _____

   _____

   _____

3. What significant gender and racial inequalities exist in American health care?

_____

_____

_____

4. What are the health benefits of exercise?

_____

_____

_____

5. What evidence supports the conclusion that alcoholism has a genetic component?

_____

_____

_____

Vocabulary Exercise 2

Directions. Choose the meaning for the underlined word that best fits the context. You may consult the dictionary as needed.

_____ 1. . . . several prevalent diseases . . . are related to unhealthy lifestyles and stress. [Paragraph 39]
   a. deadly
   b. recent; modern
   c. contagious
   d. common; widespread

_____ 2. A sedentary lifestyle . . . is the primary modifiable risk factor contributing to death from coronary heart disease. [Paragraph 41]
   a. sitting or stationary
   b. stressful
   c. modern
   d. busy; productive

_____ 3. They are "involved in a chronic, incessant struggle to achieve more and more in less and less time." [Paragraph 45]
   a. without stopping
   b. filled with tension
   c. combative or aggressive
   d. unsuccessful

_____ 4. An especially lethal form of pessimism is hopelessness. [Paragraph 58]
   a. unfortunate
   b. unusual
   c. hurtful
   d. deadly

_____ 5. It can involve tangible aid, information, and advice, as well as emotional support. [Paragraph 63]
   a. helpful
   b. invisible
   c. concrete; material
   d. financial

_____ 6. The good news is that efforts to erase the gender and race disparities in medical research and treatment are under way. [Paragraph 66]
   a. differences
   b. problems
   c. prejudices
   d. points of disagreement

_____ 7. ... 22% of people who used the nicotine patch stopped smoking, compared with only 9% of those who received a placebo. [Paragraph 78]
a. medication
b. harmless substance containing no real medication
c. reward for participation in an experiment
d. substance containing a new, experimental medication

_____ 8. ... 88% of Americans believe that there are valid ways of preventing and curing illnesses that are not recognized by the medical profession. [Paragraph 90]
a. inexpensive; affordable
b. legitimate; effective
c. unsafe; not trustworthy
d. new

_____ 9. While doctors may be skeptical about the utility of the alternative treatments ... [Paragraph 92]
a. curious
b. confident
c. doubtful
d. uninformed

_____ 10. While doctors may be skeptical about the utility of the alternative treatments ... [Paragraph 92]
a. expense
b. safety
c. design
d. usefulness

Critical Response Questions

1. In your opinion, what are the best ways to cope with stress? What are the worst ways?

2. Why is the workplace such a high source of stress for so many Americans? What might be done to make our workplaces less stressful?

3. Given the health hazards that smoking poses for smokers and nonsmokers, should the sale of cigarettes be made completely illegal? Why or why not?

4. Do you agree with Lazarus's theory that stress is caused by a person's perception of a stressor rather than the stressor itself? Explain your answer.

5. Why do so many Americans abuse alcohol? What can be done to encourage more moderate use of alcoholic beverages?

6. Do you believe that there are valid ways of preventing and curing illnesses that are not recognized by the medical profession? What alternative health treatments do you believe are valid? Support your answer.

7. What should be done to erase the gender and racial inequalities that exist in our health systems?

Media

THE WEB

Directions

1. Begin by surveying the chapter to look for answers to the following questions.

   - What is the chapter about?
   - What subtopics will be discussed?
   - What will you learn from reading and studying the chapter?
   - How interesting does the chapter look?
   - How difficult does the chapter look?
   - How familiar to you is the chapter material? That is, how much previous knowledge of the subject do you have?

   When you have completed your survey, write a summary on a separate sheet of paper of what you've learned about the chapter from the survey. Your summary should include answers to the previous questions, as well as any other information and comments you wish to add.

2. While reading the chapter, look for organizational patterns. Recognizing the patterns should help you better grasp the relationship of ideas within each paragraph and section and distinguish main ideas more easily.

   Also, form questions from the headings and subheadings (generally, write one question per heading or subheading). Write your questions on a sheet of paper. After completing each section, mentally review the main points of the section, mark the text, and write the answer(s) to your question(s), as well as any other information that seems important to you.

SAMPLE TEXTBOOK CHAPTER

From *The Media of Mass Communication*, 7th ed., 2006 Update, by John Vivian. New York: Pearson Education, 2006.

1 **Single-handedly,** Tim Berners-Lee invented the **World Wide Web.** Then, unlike many entrepreneurs who have used the Web to amass quick fortunes, Berners-Lee devoted his life to refining the Web as a medium of communication open to everyone for free.

2   Berners-Lee, an Oxford engineer, came up with the web concept because he couldn't keep track of all his notes on various computers in various places. It was 1989. Working at **CERN,** a physics lab in Switzerland, he proposed a system to facilitate scientific research by letting scientists' computers tap into each other. In a way, the software worked like the brain. In fact, Berners-Lee said that the idea was to keep "track of all the random associations one comes across in real life and brains are supposed to be so good at remembering, but sometimes mine wouldn't."

3   Working with three software engineers, Berners-Lee had a demonstration up and running within three months. As Berners-Lee traveled the globe to introduce the Web at scientific conferences, the potential of what he had devised became clear. The Web was a system that could connect all information with all other information.

4   The key was a relatively simple computer language known as **HTML,** short for **hyptertext markup language,** which, although it has evolved over the years, remains the core of the Web. Berners-Lee also developed the addressing system that allows computers to find each other. Every Web-connected computer has a unique address, a **universal resource locator (URL).** For it all to work, Berners-Lee also created a protocol that actually links computers: **HTTP,** short for **hypertext transfer protocol.**

5   In 1992 leading research organizations in the Netherlands, Germany and the United States committed to the Web. As enthusiasm grew in the scientific research community, word spread to other quarters. In one eight-month period in 1993, Web use multiplied 414 times. Soon "the Web" was a household word.

6   As you would expect, Berners-Lee had offers galore from investors and computer companies to build new ways to derive profits from the Web. He said no. Instead, he has chosen the academic life. At the Massachusetts Institute of Technology he works out of spartan facilities as head of the **W3 consortium,** which sets the protocol and coding standards that are helping the World Wide Web realize its potential.

7   It's hard to overrate Berners-Lee's accomplishment. The Web is the information infrastructure that likely will, given time, eclipse other media. Some liken Berners-Lee to Johannes Gutenberg, who 400 years earlier had launched the age of mass communication with the movable type that made mass production of the written word possible.

World Wide Web

8   ● **Study Preview** The World Wide Web has emerged as the eighth major mass medium. Many newspaper and magazine companies are delivering colorful, often expanded editions electronically to people at computer screens. The Web is more flexible than other media. Users can navigate paths among millions of on-screen messages.

In this chapter you will learn:

- The World Wide Web is emerging as a major mass medium.
- The Web operates on a global Internet that links many far-flung computer networks.
- Advertising is becoming the primary revenue source for Web services.
- Transistors and fiber-optic cable have increased the capacity for exchanging data.
- The Web is based on a nonlinear communication form called hypertext.
- Hypertext is revolutionizing news-telling, but its effect on other storytelling forms is uncertain.
- Evaluating Web content requires its own measures.
- Digitization is impelling the transition of some traditional media to the Web.
- Should government assure universal Web access? Can privacy be protected? Can cyberpornography be curbed?

Tim Berners-Lee ○ Devised protocols and codes for the World Wide Web.

World Wide Web ● System that allows global linking of information modules in user-determined sequences.

media ● online

Time 100: Profile of Tim Berners-Lee as part of *Time's* 100 Most Important People of the 20th Century. www.time.com/time/time100/scientist/profile/bernerslee.html

Internet and Web

1945 Vannevar Bush proposed Memex, a machine for associative links among all human knowledge.	**1978** Mead introduced Nexis full-text online news database.	**1997** Rob Malda, a college student, created slashdot.org, "news for news," one of the first blogs.
1969 U.S. military created ARPAnet to link contractors and researchers	**1979** CompuServ began online service to consumers.	**1999** Larger capacity Internet2 introduced.
1973 Mead Data Central launched Lexis, the first full-text online legal database.	**1989** Tim Berners-Lee devised coding that made the Web possible.	**2003** Amazon.com demonstrated new speed of search engines with Search Inside a Book.
	1993 Marc Andreessen created predecessor to Netscape browser.	

CERN ● European particle physics research facility in Geneva, Switzerland.

hypertext markup language (HTML) ● Language that is the coding for messages on the Web.

universal resource locator (URL) ● The addresses assigned to a page on the Web.

hypertext transfer protocol (HTTP) ● The coding that allows Web-linked computers to communicate with each other.

W3 consortium ● Organizations that use the Web work through the W3 consortium (World Wide Web, 3Ws, get it?) to update Web coding.

website ● Where an institution establishes its Web presence.

New Mass Medium

From a dizzying array of new technologies, the World Wide Web emerged in the mid-1990s as a powerful new mass medium. What is the Web? It is where ordinary people can go on their computer screens and, with a few clicks of a mouse button, find a vast array of information and entertainment that originates all over the world. Make no mistake, though: The Web is not just singular on-screen pages. The genius of the Web is that on-screen pages are linked to others. It is the *people* browsing the Web, not editors and programmers, who choose which on-screen pages to go to, and which to pass by, and in what sequence. People don't need to go linearly from Newscast Story 1 to Newscast Story 2. By using all kinds of on-screen indexing and cross-referencing, they can link instantly to what interests them. It's an almost seamless journey from a Disney promotion message for a new movie to a biography of the movie's leading lady in the *USA Today* archives to things as disparate as L. L. Bean's mail-order catalog and somebody's personal collection of family snapshots. In short, the Web is an interface for computers that allows people anywhere to connect to any information anywhere else on the system. 9

Every major mass-media company has put products on the Web. Thousands of start-up companies are establishing themselves on the ground floor. The technology is so straightforward and access is so inexpensive that millions of individuals have set up their own websites. 10

How significant is the Web as a mass medium? Estimates are that the number of Web users in the United States is approaching 100 million—six times the number in 1995, roughly 30 percent of the U.S. population. The percentage of people familiar with the Web is mushrooming, as personal computers become standard household equipment and as virtually every schoolchild becomes computer literate. 11

The significance of the Web is measurable in other ways too. There are people who have given up reading the print edition of newspapers and instead browse through the Web edition. Some of the news sites are updated constantly. Almost every U.S. magazine and newspaper has a **website,** from the venerable but tech-savvy *New York Times* to local papers in the hinterlands. 12

The Web in Context

The terms Web and *Internet* are often tossed around loosely, leading to lots of confusion. The fundamental network that carries messages is the Internet. It 13 dates to a military communication system created in 1969. The early Internet carried mostly text.

14   The Web is a structure of codes that permits the exchange not only of text but also of graphics, video, and audio. Web codes are elegantly simple for users, who don't even need to know them to tap into the Web's content. The underlying Web codes are accepted universally, which makes it possible for anyone with a computer, a modem, and a Web connection to tap into anything introduced from anywhere on the global Web. The term *Web* comes from the spidery links among millions of computers that tap into the system—a maze that not even a spider could visualize and that becomes more complex all the time.

15   For most practical purposes it is the Web that's a mass medium, with messages posted for mass audiences. Other messages on the Web, mostly e-mail, are more point-to-point communication than mass communication.

16   The prefix *cyber-* is affixed almost casually to anything involving communication via computer. *Cyberspace* is the intangible place where the communication occurs. *Cyberporn* is sexual naughtiness delivered on screen. A *cyberpunk* is a kid obsessed with computer protocols and coding. The term *cyberspace* was introduced by science fiction novelist **William Gibson** in his book *Neuromancer.* At that point, in 1984, he saw a kind of integration of computers and human beings. Paraphrasing a bit, here is Gibson's definition of *cyberspace:* "A consensual hallucination experienced daily by billions of people in every nation. A graphic representation of data abstracted from the banks of every computer in the human system. Unthinkable complexity. Lines of light ranged in the nonspace of the mind. Clusters and constellations of data."

Bandwidth Limitations

17   The first newspaper and magazine forays onto the Web were mostly text. Gradually, simple graphics and small photos joined the mix. Why not full-blown graphics, intense in color and detail? In a word: **bandwidth.** Bandwidth is the capacity available on a cable for transmission. There's only so much room. It's the same issue that prevents an unlimited number of television stations from being on the air—not enough channel room. On the Internet, text and simple graphics take up relatively little bandwidth. Fancy graphics take more, which means that they require more time to transmit. Super-detailed photos can take several minutes. Music and video require lots of bandwidth.

18   **Fiber-Optic Cable**   In the 1990s telephone and cable TV companies began replacing their cables with high-capacity lines made of **fiber-optic cable.** With fiber-optic cable, messages now are sent as pulses of light—theoretically at 186,000 miles a second—rather than as much slower electrical pulses. The increases in capacity have been dramatic.

19   **Multiplexing**   With **multiplexing** technology a message is broken into bits for transmission through whatever cable pipelines have room at the moment. Then the bits are reassembled at the delivery point. So instead of a message getting clogged in a pipeline that's already crammed, the messages move in small bits called packets, each packet going through whatever pipeline has room. The message ends up at its destination faster.

20   **Compression**   Technology has been devised that screens out nonessential parts of messages so that they need less bandwidth. This is especially important for graphics, video, and audio, which are incredibly code-heavy. Coding for a blue sky in a photo, for example, need not be repeated for every dot of color. Even without redundant coding, the sky still appears blue. Unless compressed, audio is also loaded with redundant coding.

media online

A Little History of the World Wide Web: From 1945 to 1995. www.w3.org/History.html

24 Hours in Cyberspace: Bradley University hosts this site showcasing highlights of a day in the life of the Web. www.bradley.edu/24hours

The Internet: One company that sells Internet connection services offers this short summary of how bandwidth works for the average Internet user. www.bandwidthplace.com/speedtest/info.php?a=internet

cyber- Prefix for human connection via computers.

William Gibson Science fiction writer who coined the term *cyberspace.*

bandwidth Space available in a medium, such as cable or the electromagnetic spectrum, to carry messages.

fiber-optic cable Glass strands capable of carrying data as light.

multiplexing Technology to transmit numerous messages simultaneously.

	Dial-up Modem 56 kilobits per second	Future Modem, Upgraded Bandwith 4 megabits per second
Simple image 2 megabits	35.7 seconds	0.5 seconds
Short animation 72 megabits	21.5 minutes	18 seconds
Long animation 4.3 gigabits	21.4 hours	18 minutes

Improving Download Time.
The more complex a graphical Web message, the longer it takes to download it with dial-up modems. Video takes forever, it seems. Download times will improve as people acquire faster modems for their computers and as more capacity is built into the Internet. An interim solution is *streaming*, which downloads content into your computer while you're doing other things. You can begin watching while the download is still in progress.

Some **compression** technology further streamlines a message by eliminating 21 details that the human eye or ear will not miss. For example, compression drops sound on a CD that would start dogs howling but that humans cannot hear.

Streaming   When a message is massive with coding, such as audio and video, 22 the message can be segmented and the segments stored in a receiving computer's hard drive for replay even before all segments of the message have been received. This is called **streaming.** Most audio and video today is transmitted this way, which means some downloading delay—but often only seconds. The more complex the coding, the longer it takes. Also, the type of connection makes a difference. For example, Web access by satellite is much faster than a dial-up telephone connection.

The Internet

● **Study Preview**   The Internet is the wired infrastructure on which Web mes- 23 sages move. It began as a military communication system, which expanded into a government-funded civilian research network. Today, the Internet is a user-financed system tying institutions of many sorts together into an "information superhighway."

Information Highway

Some historians say that the most important contribution of Dwight Eisen- 24 hower's presidency in the 1950s was the U.S. **interstate highway system.** It was a massive project, easily surpassing the scale of such previous human endeavors as the Panama Canal. Eisenhower's interstates bound the nation together in new ways and facilitated major economic growth by making commerce less expensive. Today, an **information superhighway** has been built—an electronic network that connects libraries, corporations, government agencies, and individuals. This electronic superhighway is called the **Internet,** and it is the backbone of the World Wide Web.

compression ○ Technology that makes a message more compact by deleting nonessential underlying code.

streaming ● Technology that allows playback of a message to begin before all the components have arrived.

interstate highway system
● Frequent analogy for the Internet.

information superhighway
● Loose term for Internet.

25   The Internet had its origins in a 1969 U.S. Defense Department computer network called **ARPAnet,** which stood for Advanced Research Projects Agency Network. The Pentagon built the network so military contractors and universities doing military research could exchange information. In 1983 the **National Science Foundation,** whose mandate is to promote science, took over.

26   This new National Science Foundation network attracted more and more institutional users, many of which had their own internal networks. For example, most universities that joined the NSF network had intracampus computer networks. The NSF network, then, became a connector for thousands of other networks. As a backbone system that interconnects networks, **Internet** was a name that fit.

Internet2

27   By 1996 the Internet had become clogged with exponential growth in traffic. University network engineers designed a new high-speed backbone to connect research networks. Called **Internet2,** the new backbone was up and running by 1999, carrying data as fast as 2.4 gigabits per second—four times faster than its predecessors. The consortium that owns Internet2 grew to include 203 research universities, 526 four-year colleges, and 551 community colleges. Its use grew beyond sharing research information to include distance learning. Even with a 2003 upgrade to 10 gigabits per second, clogging again was a problem.

28   One solution, an even faster Internet3, may not be financially possible. An interim possibility is to lease **dark fiber,** the unused fiber-optic capacity of commercial telecommunications companies that overbuilt in the late 1990s. Already Internet2 is too costly for many colleges. Basic connection and membership fees range from $160,000 to $450,000 a year. Internet3 would cost even more.

Online Services

29   The World Wide Web became operational in the 1990s, but commercial online services go back another 20 years. **Mead Data Central,** an Ohio company, offered **Lexis,** the first online full-text database, in 1973. Lexis carried state and federal statutes, court decisions and other legal documents. A lawyer could tap into Lexis for research and cut back on maintaining and updating the traditional expensive office law library. Because Lexis was delivered via telephone lines whose capacity precluded data-intensive graphics, there was nothing fancy about how Lexis looked—like simple text on the computer screen. But it was just what lawyers and legal scholars needed, and they paid handsomely for the service.

30   Building on its Lexis success, Mead launched **Nexis** in 1978. Nexis was the first online database with national news organizations, including the *New York Times,* the *Washington Post,* the Associated Press, and *U.S. News & World Report.* Nexis proved invaluable to researchers, who could search not only recent editions of participating newspapers and magazines but also back issues. Today, Nexis includes thousands of publications from around the world.

31   Lexis and Nexis remain full-text services, with massive amounts of unadorned, gray content. While they are still important to many people, especially as a research source, they have been eclipsed by flashy, graphic-oriented services designed for mass audiences. Nexis comes nowhere near the glitz of America Online.

media online

Internet2: Re-creating the partnership among academia, industry and government that fostered today's Internet in its infancy.
www.internet2.org

LexisNexis: Online database service.
www.lexisnexis.com

America Online
www.aol.com

Internet ○ The backbone network for Web communication.

ARPAnet ○ Military network that preceded the Internet.

National Science Foundation ○ Developed the current Internet to give scholars access to supercomputers.

Internet ○ A network of computer networks.

Internet2 ○ A network consortium owned by research institutions for fast data transfer.

dark fiber ○ Excess telecommunication capacity available for data transfer.

Mead Data Central ○ Created Lexis and Nexis.

Lexis ● First online full-text database; carries legal documents.

Nexis ● First online database with national news.

Commerce and the Web

● **Study Preview**   The Web has emerged as a commercial medium. Some   32
sites are built around products. Others, in a more traditional vein, are designed to attract an
audience with content, such as news. The sites sell access to that audience to advertisers.

Advertising-Free Origins

Before the Web, the Internet was a pristine, commerce-free medium. If some-   33
body put out a message that had even a hint of filthy lucre, purists by the
dozens, even hundreds, deluged the offender with harsh reminders that commerce was not allowed. By and large, this self-policing worked.

When the Web was introduced as an advanced Internet protocol, its poten-   34
tial for commerce was clear almost right away. The World Wide Web Consortium, which sets standards for Web protocols, created the dot-com suffix to
identify sites that existed to do business. That decision transformed the Web
and our lives.

Web Commerce

Today, nearly two decades after Tim Berners-Lee invented the Web, no self-   35
respecting major retailer is without a Web presence.

Point of Purchase   Web retailers display their wares on-screen, take orders,   36
and ship the products. The old **point-of-purchase** concept, catching consumers
at the store with displays and posters, has taken on a whole new meaning. In
the cyberworld the point of purchase is not the merchant's shop but the consumer's computer screen.

Business to Business   Another form of Web commerce goes by the buzzword   37
B2B, short for business-to-business commerce. Businesses that service other
businesses have taken to the Web to supplement their traditional means of
reaching their customers.

Advertising Forms   The Web also carries advertising. At many sites the ad-   38
vertising is like a traditional ad that promotes a product or service and steers
potential customers either to more information or to a place to make a purchase. These ads are akin to those in magazines, newspapers, radio, and television. At these **dot-coms,** the noncommercial content is the attraction. You
won't find usatoday.com touting that it has great ads. Rather, the dominant
consumer product is news. Just as in the print editions of *USA Today,* the site
sells advertisers on the access it provides them to an audience attracted by the
news content.

Less traditional are dot-coms whose thrust is the product, like music sites   39
that sell recordings. The site is one big advertisement, often dolled up with fac-
toids, games, and trivia to keep customers at the site and prolong exposure to
the product, thus increasing the probability of sales. These sites are like a jazzy
catalog.

Web Advertising

Many retailing dot-coms were profitable early on, but the going was slow for   40
media companies that looked to advertising to pay the freight for expensive
content like news. Not until 1997 was any profit reported from a website that

point-of-purchase ○
In-store advertising to catch
buyers.

B2B ○   Short for business-
to-business advertising. More
focused than most consumer
advertising.

dot-coms ●   Commercial
websites, so named because
their Web addresses end with
the suffix *.com.*

was intending to be advertising supported. The first was the Channel 4000 site, operated by Minneapolis television station WCCO.

41   The lure of advertising revenue was at the heart of many business plans for news sites in the late 1990s. Venture capitalists poured billions of dollars into these sites. Building these sites into revenue producers took longer than expected. Some sites, like Microsoft's highbrow slate.com, stopped free access and began charging a subscription fee to supplement the disappointing advertising revenue stream. However, disappointing results caused slate.com to revert to free access. At some sites, investors pulled the plug. At the award-winning criminal justice site APB.com, investors decimated the staff in 2000 to stem the outflow of cash. Others quietly went out of business.

42   When the bubble burst for so many dot-coms, most remaining sites looked to advertising rather than venture capitalists to sustain them economically. With more than 100 million people with Web access in the United States by 2000, and the number growing, the potential for dot-coms to be advertising supported was clear. But many advertisers were hesitant. Advertisers were never quite sure what they were buying. Measuring and categorizing Web audiences was not easy.

Section Review 1

Directions.

1. On a separate sheet of paper, write a brief summary of the main points of the sections you have just read.

2. Mark each of the following statements True (T), False (F), or Can't Tell (CT). Mark the statement Can't Tell if it cannot be determined to be either true or false based on the material in the passage. Refer to the passage as necessary to verify your answer.

_____ 1. HTTP is a computer language that is used for nearly all Web-based instructions.

_____ 2. Pictures require more bandwidth than text and are slower to transmit.

_____ 3. Fiber-optic cable allows faster transmission of data because it sends messages in light pulses rather than electrical pulses.

_____ 4. The creation of the information superhighway, or Internet, during the 1950s is considered one of the most important achievements of the Eisenhower presidency.

_____ 5. Consumers are more responsive to Web ads than to ads in traditional publications.

Directions. Write the letter of the best answer in the space provided.

_____ 1. Tim Berners-Lee created the World Wide Web in order to
   a.   amass a quick fortune.
   b.   promote international peace.
   c.   assist scientific research.
   d.   assist the U.S. military.

_____ 2. Bandwidth is best understood as
   a. the speed at which information can be transmitted.
   b. the capacity of a cable to transmit data.
   c. the requirements for the transmission of graphic material.
   d. the distance an electronic impulse must travel to be transmitted.

_____ 3. The author states that Internet2
   a. is inexpensive but not fast enough.
   b. was only a small improvement over the original Internet.
   c. was significantly faster than the original Internet, but not fast enough.
   d. was initially designed by the Pentagon but later taken over by the NSF.

_____ 4. Initially, the Internet
   a. had no advertisements.
   b. was viewed as an excellent vehicle for advertising.
   c. allowed advertising on a restricted scale.
   d. was used to design support systems for dot-com enterprises.

_____ 5. The first online services were used primarily for
   a. industrial sales.
   b. consumer reports.
   c. experimental scientific research.
   d. legal and news research.

Measuring the Web Audience

● **Study Preview**   The Web's growing reach has fueled interest in cyber-   43
space as an effective place for advertisers to reach consumers. A problem, however, is that
nobody has solid data on how many people are surfing to websites that carry ads.

Inconsistent Data

The difficulty of measuring Web audiences is illustrated by a numbers war that   44
broke out in 1998 between news rivals cnn.com and msnbc.com.

The upstart MSNBC site, a spin-off of the Microsoft-NBC television net-   45
work, claimed in news releases and advertisements that it had beaten CNN. A
New York measurement firm, Media Metrix, had found that MSNBC had almost 4.3 million unique visitors a month with 7.4 percent reach. (Reach is the
percentage of all Web users who visit a site.) Somewhere in the dust, said Media Metrix, was CNN, with 3.4 million unique visitors and 6.9 percent reach.

CNN fired back that the comparison was unfair because it rated only CNN   46
Interactive and not related sites: cnnfn.com, cnnsi.com, and allpolitics.com.
MSNBC, said CNN executives, covers finance, sports, and politics all on one
site. CNN's claim: We're Number One.

Numbers are tricky for other reasons too. Different survey companies use   47
different methods to gather data. Furthermore, the companies haven't agreed
on definitions. Some separate out workplace users, foreign users, and others.
Some don't. Consider the discrepancies from three companies who measured
CNN in May 1998:

- **@4Plan:** 11.8 million
- **RelevantKnowledge:** 5.6 million
- **Media Metrix:** 2.5 million

48   Advertisers, of course, want solid numbers on which to base decisions about placing their ads. To that end, the Internet Advertising Bureau and the Advertising Research Foundation are scrambling to come up with measurement guidelines that will compare apples with apples, not with oranges.

The Web's Advertising Reach

49   Despite upbeat Nielsen data about people who use the Web, there remains a hitch in developing the Web as a major advertising medium. Nobody has devised tools to measure traffic at a website in meaningful ways. Such data are needed to establish advertising rates that will give advertisers confidence that they're spending their money wisely. For traditional media, advertisers look to standard measures like **cost per thousand** (CPM) to calculate the cost effectiveness of ads in competing media. Across-the-board comparisons aren't possible with the Web, however—at least not yet. In some ways, buying space for cyberads is a crap shoot.

50   The most-cited measure of Web audiences is the **hit.** Every time someone browsing the Web clicks an on-screen icon or on-screen highlighted section, the computer server that offers the Web page records a hit. Some companies that operate websites tout hits as a measure of audience, but savvy advertisers know hits are a misleading indicator of audience size. The online edition of *Wired* magazine, *HotWired,* for example, records an average of 100 hits from everybody who taps in. *HotWired*'s 600,000 hits on a heavy day come from a mere 6,000 people.

51   Another measure of Web usage is the **visit,** a count of the people who visit a site. But visits too are misleading. At *Playboy* magazine's website, 200,000 visits are scored on a typical day, but that doesn't mean that *Playboy* cyber-ads are seen by 200,000 different people. Many of the same people visit again and again on a given day.

52   Some electronic publications charge advertisers by the day, others by the month, others by the hit. But because of the vagaries of audience measurements, there is no standard pricing. Knowing that the Web cannot mature as an advertising medium until advertisers can be given better audience data, electronic publications have asked several companies, including Nielsen, to devise tracking mechanisms. But no one expects data as accurate as press runs and broadcast ratings any time soon. In the meantime advertisers are making seat-of-the-pants assessments as to which websites are hot.

Web Technology

53   ● **Study Preview** The 1947 invention of the transistor led to data digitization and compression. Without transistors the Web would never have come into being. Nor would the other mass media be anything like we know them today. Another invention, Corning Glass's fiber-optic cable, makes it possible to transmit huge amounts of digitized data.

Transistors

54   Three researchers at AT&T's **Bell Labs** developed the **semiconductor** switch in 1947. **Walter Brattain, Jack Bardeen** and **William Shockley,** who would receive the 1956 Nobel Prize, took pieces of glasslike silicon (just sand, really) and

cost per thousand (CPM) ◐ Advertising industry measure of an ad's reach.

hit ◐ Tallies every click on a Web page.

visit ◐ Tallies every person who visits a website.

Bell Labs ● AT&T facility where transistor was invented.

semiconductor ● Tiny sand-based transistor that responds to weak on–off charges.

William Shockley, Jack Bardeen, Walter Brattain ● Codevelopers of transistor.

devised a way to make them respond to a negative or positive electrical charge. These tiny units, first called **transistors,** now more commonly called **semi-conductors** or *chips,* functioned very rapidly as on–off switches. The on–off technology, in which data are converted to on–off codes, is called **digitization** because data are reduced to a series of digits, 1 for on, 0 for off.

Digitization   As might be expected, Bell researchers tried applying the junc-   55
tion transistor to telephone communication. Soon they found ways to convert the human voice to a series of coded pulses for transmission on telephone lines to a receiver that would change them into a simulation of the voice. These pulses were digital on–off signals that were recorded so quickly at one end of the line, and reconstructed so quickly at the other, that they sounded like the real thing. The rapid on–off signals worked like the persistence of vision phenomenon that creates the illusion of movement in motion pictures.

A milestone event occurred in 1962 when AT&T sent a message to Chicago   56
from suburban Skokie using transistor technology—the first digital telephone call. Until that moment telephone communication was based on sound waves being converted to varying electrical currents for transmission. At the receiving end, the currents were changed back to sound waves. With digital transmission voices were instead converted to an incredibly fast-moving stream of discrete on–off digital pulses.

Compression   Bell Labs also devised techniques to squeeze different calls onto   57
the same line simultaneously, which increased the capacity of the nation's telephone network. With traditional telephone technology, dating to Alexander Graham Bell's 1876 invention of the telephone, only one message could be carried at a time on a telephone line. With digitization, however, a new process called **multiplexing** became possible. Tiny bits of one message could be interspersed with tiny bits of other messages for transmission and then sorted out at the other end.

AT&T introduced multiplex telephone services in 1965. People marveled   58
that 51 calls could be carried at the same time on a copper wire with on–off digital switching technology. The capacity of the nation's telephone communication system was dramatically increased without laying even a single new mile of wire.

Few people foresaw that digitization and compression would revolutionize   59
human existence, let alone do it so quickly. The Web wasn't even a glimmer in anyone's eye back then. Nonetheless, the building blocks for the Web were being created.

Miniaturization   Radio and television were the first mass-media beneficiaries   60
of the transistor. In the 1940s broadcast equipment was built around electrical tubes, which looked somewhat like light bulbs. These tubes heated up and eventually burned out. In addition, they consumed massive amounts of electricity. Transistors, on the other hand, could perform the same functions with hardly any electricity and no heat. Important, too, was that transistors were much, much smaller than tubes and much more reliable.

Consumers began benefiting directly from transistor **miniaturization** in the   61
mid-1950s. Until then, even the smallest radios, called "table models," were hunky pieces of furniture. Then came a new product: handheld, battery-powered transistor radios that people could carry anywhere. Those tiny radios, however, were merely glimpses at the mass communication revolution that transistors were ushering in.

Not only did the use of transistors dramatically reduce the size and weight of   62
broadcast equipment, the size of computers shrank as well. In the 1940s early computers, based on tube technology, were so big that it took entire buildings to

transistor ● Semiconductor.

digitization ● Converting on–off coding for storage and for transmission.

multiplexing ● Compressing messages for simultaneous transmission on same line or radio wave.

miniaturization ● Reducing the size of devices for data recording, storage, or retrieval.

house them and large staffs of technicians to operate them. Today, the Marquardt Corporation estimates that all the information recorded in the past 10,000 years can be stored in a cube six feet by six feet by six feet. All twelve million books in the Library of Congress would occupy fewer than two cubic inches.

63   There seems no end to miniaturization. IBM has developed a computer drive that, using **giant magneto-resistance** technology, crams an incredible 100 million digital characters on a thumbtack-size disk. IBM now expects to be producing GMR disks that can accommodate 2 billion characters on a thumbtack. That's equivalent to two thousand novels.

64   **Efficiencies**   Transistor-based equipment costs less to manufacture and operates with incredible efficiency. The National Academy of Science estimates that it cost $130,000 to make 125 multiplications when the forerunners of today's computers were introduced in the 1940s. By 1970 the cost was a mere $4. Today, it can be done for pennies.

Fiber Optics

65   While AT&T was building on its off–on digital technology to improve telephone service in the 1960s, **Corning Glass** developed a cable that was capable of carrying light at incredible speeds—theoretically 186,000 miles per second. It was apparent immediately that this new fiber-optic cable could carry far more digitized multiplex messages than could copper. The messages were encoded as light pulses rather than as the traditional electrical pulses for transmission.

66   By the 1980s new equipment to convert data to light pulses for transmission was in place, and long-distance telephone companies were replacing their copper lines with fiber optics, as were local cable television systems. Today, using semiconductor switching combined with optical fiber cable, a single line can carry 60,000 telephone calls simultaneously. In addition to voice, the lines can carry all kinds of other messages that have been broken into digitized pulses. With fiber-optic cable the entire *Oxford English Dictionary* can be sent in just seconds. Such speed is what has made the Web a mass medium that can deliver unprecedented quantities of information so quickly.

Nonlinear Communication

67   ● **Study Preview**   Hypertext, a relatively recent concept for creating messages, is the heart of the Web as a mass medium. With hypertext the people who receive messages can influence the sequence of the messages they receive. Once, it was only the senders who had such power.

Vannevar Bush's Memex

68   Until recently, we were all accustomed to mass messages flowing from start to finish in the sequence that mass communicators figured would be most effective for most people. Many mass messages still flow linearly. Newscasts, as an example, start with the most important item first. A novel builds climactically to the final chapter. A television commercial catches your attention at the start and names the advertiser in the sign-off. This is **linear communication.**

69   **Vannevar Bush,** a leading thinker of his time, noted to *Atlantic* magazine readers in 1945 that knowledge had expanded exponentially in the twentieth century, but the means for "threading through" the maze were "the same as used in the days of square-rigged ships." Bush proposed a machine he called

giant magneto-resistance (GMR) ○ Allows super-miniaturization.

Corning Glass ○ Company that developed fiber-optic cable.

linear communication ● Messages presented in a specified start-to-end sequence.

Vannevar Bush ● Proposed a machine for relational information retrieval.

memex to mimic human thinking in organizing material. With his memex people could retrieve information through automated association with related information.

Alas, Bush's memex was never built, but a generation later, technologist **Ted Nelson,** who may have heard his grandfather read Bush's article aloud, picked up on the idea. In his 1962 book *Literary Machines,* Nelson coined the term **hypertext** for an alternate way for people to send and receive information. Nelson also used the term *nonsequential writing,* but it was *hypertext* that stuck. 70

With the Web, people can proceed linearly or nonlinearly through material. You can read straight through from beginning to end. That would be linear. Or you can use your mouse to click highlighted words, called *hot spots,* and transport yourself beyond the text to related material existing elsewhere on the Web and not even part of the text. This linking capability lets you roam the whole world nonlinearly to pursue what you regard as important. The Web empowers you to choose your own course, going beyond what any individual author has to offer. 71

In primitive ways people have done a kind of hypertext learning for centuries. In the library a researcher may have two dozen books open and piled on a desk, with dozens more reference books handy on a shelf. Moving back and forth among the books, checking indexes and footnotes, and fetching additional volumes from the library stacks, the researcher is creating new meanings by combining information in new sequences. The computer has accelerated that process and opened up thousands of resources, all on-screen, for today's scholars. 72

memex ○ Machine proposed by Vannevar Bush for nonlinear information access.

Ted Nelson ○ Coined the term *hypertext* for nonlinear communication.

hypertext ● Method of interrelating messages so that users control their sequence.

Section Review 2

Directions.

1. On a separate sheet of paper, write a brief summary of the main points of the sections you have just read.

2. Mark each of the following statements True (T), False (F), or Can't Tell (CT). Mark the statement Can't Tell if it cannot be determined to be either true or false based on the material in the passage. Refer to the passage as necessary to verify your answer.

_____ 1. In 1998, MSNBC's website became more popular than CNN's .

_____ 2. Most advertisers consider hits to be the most reliable measure of Web audience response.

_____ 3. The telephone company used digitization to change the human voice into a series of digital on–off signals.

_____ 4. Transistor radios became widely available to consumers in the 1940s.

_____ 5. Vannevar Bush built a machine called the *memex* that mimicked human thought and enabled people to retrieve information nonlinearly for the first time.

Cumulative Review 1 (pages 250-262)

Directions. Write the letter of the best answer in the space provided.

_____ 1. One important problem for companies who wish to advertise on the Web is that
   a. advertisers do not yet have reliable ways to measure the size of Web audiences.
   b. the cost of Web advertising is impossible to determine.
   c. there is no way to count visits to websites.
   d. the cost of Web advertising is very high compared to advertising in other media.

_____ 2. Compression is a method for
   a. digitizing graphic data.
   b. compacting data by eliminating nonessential code.
   c. transmitting several messages simultaneously.
   d. converting data into light pulses.

_____ 3. Which of the following is an example of nonlinear thinking?
   a. reading a novel straight through from beginning to end
   b. watching a movie without pausing or rewinding
   c. listening to a song on the radio
   d. moving back and forth between two research sources

_____ 4. Which of the following can we conclude regarding the dot.-com businesses of the 1990s?
   a. They rarely earned a profit.
   b. Retailing sites were profitable before sites that relied on advertising.
   c. Most of them are still making large profits today.
   d. Venture capitalists invested in retail sites rather than advertising-supported sites.

_____ 5. Fiber-optic cable is important to Web technology because it
   a. transmits a much greater amount of information than earlier cable material.
   b. stores huge amounts of data in tiny spaces.
   c. automatically digitizes graphic input.
   d. made possible the miniaturization of computer components.

Directions. Answer each question in complete sentences, without copying word-for-word from the passage.

1. Explain the difference between the Web and the Internet.

_____

_____

_____

2. What is cyberspace?

    _____

    _____

    _____

3. Why is multiplexing critical to computer technology?

    _____

    _____

    _____

4. Briefly summarize the progress that has been made since the 1940s in miniaturization.

    _____

    _____

    _____

5. Why is the size of Web audiences difficult to measure?

    _____

    _____

    _____

Vocabulary Exercise 1

Directions. Choose the meaning for the underlined word that best fits the context. You may consult the dictionary as needed.

_____ 1. Then, unlike many entrepreneurs who have used the Web to amass quick fortunes . . . [Paragraph 1]
  a. researchers
  b. businessmen
  c. scientists
  d. Web designers

_____ 2. . . . he proposed a system to facilitate scientific research by letting scientists' computers tap into each other. [Paragraph 2]
  a. begin
  b. make easier
  c. support financially
  d. build; construct

_____ 3. ... he works out of <u>spartan</u> facilities as head of the W3 consortium ... [Paragraph 6]
   a. urban; citified
   b. Greek
   c. simple, plain
   d. clean

_____ 4. ... to things as <u>disparate</u> as L. L. Bean's mail-order catalog and somebody's personal collection of family snapshots. [Paragraph 9]
   a. strange or odd
   b. similar
   c. dissimilar
   d. interesting; arousing curiosity

_____ 5. ... from the <u>venerable</u> but tech-savvy *New York Times* to local papers in the hinterlands. [Paragraph 12]
   a. highly respected
   b. popular
   c. highly profitable
   d. urban

_____ 6. By 1996 the Internet had become clogged with <u>exponential</u> growth in traffic. [Paragraph 27]
   a. increasing slowly but steadily
   b. unexpected
   c. mathematical
   d. increasing dramatically

_____ 7. Before the Web, the Internet was a <u>pristine</u>, commerce-free medium. [Paragraph 33]
   a. pure; unspoiled
   b. expensive
   c. priceless
   d. immature

_____ 8. ... investors <u>decimated</u> the staff in 2000 to stem the outflow of cash. [Paragraph 41]
   a. drastically reduced
   b. completely and immediately eliminated
   c. replaced
   d. reduced the salaries of

_____ 9. ... but <u>savvy</u> advertisers know hits are a misleading indicator of audience size. [Paragraph 50]
   a. experienced
   b. highly paid
   c. technically oriented
   d. shrewd

_____ 10. With digital transmission voices were instead converted to an incredibly fast-moving stream of <u>discrete</u> on–off digital pulses. [Paragraph 56]
   a. tactful
   b. silent
   c. separate
   d. electronic

Hypertext

73   ● **Study Preview**   Major news media are creating hypertext products that are revolutionizing how news is told. Whether hypertext will revolutionize other forms of storytelling, such as the novel, is unclear.

Pre-Hypertext Innovations

74 Although hypertext itself is not new, the shift to hypertext from linear presentation in traditional media has been gradual. A preliminary stage was merely casting text in digital form for storage and transmission. This is what other early on-line services like Nexis did, providing linear full-text content of news stories from cooperating newspapers. While a major step forward at the time, full-text is derisively called **shovelware** by hypertext enthusiasts because it simply moves content from a traditional medium to a new one without much adaptation to the unique characteristics of the new medium. Shovelware falls short of the potential of the Web.

shovelware ○ Computer-delivered products that are not modified from the linear original.

The **Media Lab** at the Massachusetts Institute of Technology came up with   75
the next refinement: the *Daily Me,* an experimental digital newspaper that
provided subscribers with information only on subjects they specified in advance. Take, for example, a car buff who follows baseball and who earns a living running a grocery store in Spokane, Washington. For this person a customized *Daily Me* would include news on the automobile industry, the American and National Leagues and the Spokane Indians farm club, livestock and produce market reports, news summaries from the Spokane area and neighboring British Columbia and Idaho, and a brief summary of major national and world news.

MIT's *Daily Me* innovation took commercial form at the *Wall Street Jour-*   76
nal, which in 1995 launched the first customizable electronic newspaper. It was
called **Personal Journal,** with the subtitle: "Published for a Circulation of
One." *Personal Journal,* which cost $18 a month plus 50 cents per update, offered whatever combination a subscriber wanted of business and general coverage by category, market tables and selected quotes, sports, and weather. Such customization, matching content to a user's interest, is now common.

Hypertext News

The potential of digital news was realized with the Web. When *USA Today*   77
established a website, it offered a hypertext product—not shovelware. *USA To-*
day webmasters broke the newspaper's content into Web page-size components,
updated them 24 hours a day as events warranted, and linked every page with
others. Every day, readers can choose among thousands of connections, in effect creating their own news package by moving around among the entire content of the newspaper. Hot spots include links to archived material from previous coverage that *USA Today*'s webmasters think some readers would want to draw on for background.

All the major news products coming online today are state-of-the-art hy-   78
pertext ventures. Some websites offer users an opportunity to communicate immediately back to the creators of the products.

Hyperfiction

While digital technology is revolutionizing many aspects of human communi-   79
cation, it is unclear whether all literary forms will be fundamentally affected.
There have been experiments with hypertext fiction. For example, the computer games *Myst* and *Riven* put players in dreamlike landscapes where they wander through adventures in which they choose the course of events. Options, of course, are limited to those the authors put into the game, but the player has a feeling of creating the story rather than following an author's plot. *Myst* and *Riven* represent a new dimension in exploration as an experiential literary form.

Some futurists see interactivity overtaking traditional forms of human sto-   80
rytelling, and the term **hyperfiction** has been applied to a few dozen pioneer
hypertext novels. One hyperfiction enthusiast, Trip Hawkins, who creates video games, laid out both sides in a *New York Times* interview: "Given the choice, do viewers really want to interact with their entertainment? Watching, say, *Jurassic Park,* wouldn't they prefer to have Steven Spielberg spin the tale of dinosaurs munching on their keepers in an island theme park?" For himself, however, Hawkins says, "I want to be on the island. I want to show that I could have done better than those idiots did. I could have gotten out of that situation."

Evaluating the Web

81   ● **Study Preview**   The traditional gatekeeping process that filters media content for quality is less present on the Web. Web users need to take special care in assessing the merit of what they find on the Web.

Accuracy on the Web

82   The Web has been called a democratized mass medium because so many people create Web content. Almost anybody can put up a site. A downside of so much input from so many people is that the traditional media gatekeepers aren't necessarily present to ensure accuracy. To be sure, there are many reliable sites with traditional gatekeeping, but the Web is also littered with junk.

83   Of course, unreliable information isn't exclusive to the Web. But among older media, economic survival depends on finding and keeping an audience. Unreliable newspapers, for example, eventually lose the confidence of readers. People stop buying them, and they go out of business. The Web has no such intrinsic economic imperative. A site can be put up and maintained with hardly any capital—in contrast to a newspaper, which requires tons of newsprint and barrels of ink, not to mention expensive presses, to keep coming out. Bad websites can last forever.

84   To guard against bad information, Web users should pay special heed to the old admonition: Consider the source. Is the organization or person behind a site reliable? If you have confidence in *USA Today* as a newspaper, you can have the same confidence in its website. Another news site, no matter how glitzy and slick, may be nothing more than a lunatic working alone in a dank basement somewhere recasting the news with perverse twists and whole-cloth fiction.

85   In research reports, footnotes or endnotes need to be specific on Web sources, including URL addresses. This allows people who read a report to go to the Web source to make their own assessment—just as traditional footnotes allow a reader to go to the library and check a source.

86   Even with notations, a report that cites Web sources can be problematic. Unlike a book, which is permanent once it's in print, Web content can be in continuing flux. What's there today can be changed in a minute—or disappear entirely. To address this problem at least in part, notation systems specify that the date and time of the researcher's Web visit be included.

87   In serious research, you can check whether an online journal is refereed. A mission statement will be on the site with a list of editors and their credentials and a statement on the journal's editorial process. Look to see whether articles are screened through a **peer review** process.

Attributes of Excellent Web Sites

88   Several organizations issue awards to excellent websites. The most prestigious are the **Webby** awards, a term contrived from the nickname for the somewhat parallel Emmy awards of television. Many Web awards, though, are for design and graphics, not content, although there are many measures of a site's excellence.

89   **Content**   The heart of all mass-media messages is the value of the content. For this, traditional measures of excellence in communication apply, such as accuracy, clarity, and cohesion.

peer review ● A screening mechanism in which scholarly material is reviewed by leaders in a discipline for its merits, generally with neither the author nor the reviewers knowing each other's identity.

Webby ● A major award of excellence for websites.

Navigability   Does the site have internal links so you can move easily from page to page and among various points on the site? Among the mass media, navigability is a quality unique to the Web.   90

External Links   Does the site connect to related sites on the Web? The most distinctive feature of the Web as a mass medium is interconnectivity with other sites on the global network. Good sites exploit this advantage.   91

Intuitive to Use   The best sites have navigational aids for moving around a site seamlessly and efficiently. These include road signs of many sorts, including clearly labeled links.   92

Loading Times   Well-designed sites take advantage of the Web as a visual medium with images. At the same time, pages should load quickly so users don't have to wait and wait and wait for a page to write itself to their screens. This means the site needs a balance. Overdoing images, which require lots of bandwidth, works against rapid downloads. Absence of images makes for dull pages.   93

Media Melding

● **Study Preview**   Many mass media as we know them are converging into digitized formats. Complementing and hastening this technological melding are ownership conglomeration and joint ventures. Government deregulation is contributing to a freer business environment that encourages new ventures.   94

Technological Convergence

Johannes Gutenberg brought mass production to books, and the other primary print media, magazines and newspapers, followed. People never had a problem recognizing differences among books, magazines, and newspapers. When sound recording and movies came along, they too were distinctive, and later so were radio and television. Today, the traditional primary media are in various stages of transition to digital form.   95

The cable television systems and the Internet are consolidating with companies in the forefront, such as AT&T. This **technological convergence** is fueled by accelerated miniaturization of equipment and the ability to compress data into tiny digital bits for storage and transmission. And all the media companies, whether their products traditionally relied on print, electronic, or photographic technology, are involved in the convergence.   96

As the magazine *The Economist* noted, once-discrete media industries "are being whirled into an extraordinary whole." Writing in *Quill* magazine, *USA Today*'s Kevin Manay put it this way: "All the devices people use for communicating and all the kinds of communication have started crashing together into one massive megamedia industry. The result is that telephone lines will soon carry TV shows. Cable TV will carry telephone calls. Desktop computers will be used to watch and edit movies. Cellular phone-computers the size of a notepad will dial into interactive magazines that combine text, sound and video to tell stories."   97

Unanticipated consequences of the new technology are not better illustrated than by **Search Inside a Book,** a service offered by Amazon.com. Readers   98

technological convergence
○ Melding of print, electronic, and photographic media into digitized form.

Search Inside a Book ●
Amazon.com search engine that can find a term or phrase in every book that has been scanned into a database, initially 120,000 titles.

can type a phrase into a search box on the Amazon site, and an Amazon computer scans a database of in-print books in their entirety for matches. In 2003, when the service began with 120,000 titles, a search for the phrase "weapons of mass destruction" found 1,690 uses of the phrase and gave the reader an option to download images of the pages on which the phrase appears, as well as half a dozen surrounding pages. Amazon, in the business of selling books, won't let people download whole books, but the service demonstrates possibilities for the library of the future. And what future can indexers possibly find in a world of search engines that flip through so much so quickly?

Transition Ahead

99   Nobody expects the printed newspaper to disappear overnight or for movie houses, video rental shops, and over-air broadcasters to go out of business all at once. But all the big media companies have established stakes on the Web, and in time, digitized messages delivered over the Web will dominate.

100   Outside of the Web itself, major media companies also are trying to establish a future for themselves in reaching audiences in new digital ways. Companies that identify voids in their ability to capitalize on new technology have created joint ventures to ensure they won't be left out. The NBC television network, for example, provides news on Microsoft's MSN online service. All of the regional telephone companies have picked up partners to develop video delivery systems. Cable companies are gearing for telephone-like two-way interactive communication systems that will, for example, permit customers not only to receive messages but also to send them.

Government Deregulation

101   Until recent years a stumbling block to the melding of digital media was the U.S. government. Major components of today's melded media—the telephone, television and computer industries—grew up separately, and government policy kept many of them from venturing into the others' staked-out territory of services. Telephone companies, for example, were limited to being common carriers. They couldn't create their own media messages, just deliver other people's. Cable companies were barred from building two-way communication into their systems.

102   In the 1970s government agencies began to ease restrictions on business. In 1984 President **Ronald Reagan** stepped up this **deregulation,** and more barriers came down. The pro-business Reagan administration also took no major actions against the stampede of media company mergers that created fewer and bigger media companies. George H. W. Bush, elected in 1988, and Bill Clinton, elected in 1992, continued Reagan's deregulation initiatives and also his soft stance on mergers. The Clinton position, however, was less ideological and more pragmatic. Clinton's thinking was based on the view that regulation and antitrust actions would disadvantage U.S. media companies, and other enterprises too, in global competition.

103   In 1996 Congress approved a new telecommunications law that wiped out many of the barriers that impeded full-bore exploitation of the potential of new media. The law repealed a federal ban against telephone companies providing video programming. Just as significant, cable television systems were given a green light to offer two-way local telephone service. The law, the **Telecommunications Act of 1996,** accelerated the competition that had been emerging between telephone and cable television companies to rewire communities for higher-quality, faster delivery of new audio and video services.

Ronald Reagan ○ President who pushed deregulation.

deregulation ○ Government policy to reduce regulation of business.

Telecommunications Act of 1996 ○ Repealed many limits on services that telephone and cable companies could offer.

Section Review 3

Directions.

1. On a separate sheet of paper, write a brief summary of the main points of the sections you have just read.

2. Mark each of the following statements True (T), False (F), or Can't Tell (CT). Mark |the statement Can't Tell if it cannot be determined to be either true or false based on the material in the passage. Refer to the passage as necessary to verify your answer.

_____ 1. Users of *USA Today*'s website can communicate immediately back to the site's creators.

_____ 2. Shovelware is text placed online without hypertext linkage.

_____ 3. One problem with the citation of a Web source in a research paper is that the content of a website can easily change.

_____ 4. Virtually all Web awards emphasize content over design.

_____ 5. Before 1996, telephone companies were prohibited from providing video programming.

Directions. Write the letter of the best answer in the space provided.

_____ 1. Regarding hyperfiction, the author suggests that
    a. the future of hyperfiction is uncertain.
    b. most people prefer to interact with their entertainment.
    c. thus far, experiments with hypertext fiction have all been failures.
    d. eventually, hypertext fiction will replace traditional entertainment.

_____ 2. The author advises Web users to
    a. avoid online news sources.
    b. use online journals only if they are refereed.
    c. double-check any information obtained from one website against the information on another website.
    d. obtain information from websites known to be reliable.

_____ 3. Which of the following is probably *not* true of a good website?
    a. It contains both internal and external links.
    b. It relies on images rather than words.
    c. It is easy to use.
    d. Its content is cohesive.

_____ 4. One important reason why websites can be less reliable sources of information than traditional print sources is that
    a. there is less competition among websites.
    b. websites are inexpensive to create and maintain.
    c. Web users are less educated than traditional print users.
    d. websites are rarely designed with profit in mind.

_____ 5. One important consequence of the increasing digitization of traditional media is that

    a. the different media are becoming less distinct.

    b. the different media are becoming more distinct.

    c. the media have become less important for mass communication.

    d. the government has increased regulation of the mass media.

Public Policy and the Web

104   ● **Study Preview** The Web is a content-neutral medium whose content is more directly user-driven than the traditional media. This makes the Web hard to regulate, which has created new privacy issues. The ease with which messages can be created has resulted in problems for moralists concerned about indecent material. Authoritarian governments find censorship of the Web difficult.

Universal Access

105   Although Web use is growing dramatically, the fact is that not everybody has access. Those who can afford computers and access fees have benefited tremendously. What about everybody else? This is a profound public policy question, especially in a democracy that prides itself on ensuring equality for every citizen on basic matters like access to information.

106   One line of reasoning is that the government should not guarantee **universal access**. This rationale draws on the interstate highway system as an analogy. The government builds the roads, but individuals provide the vehicles to drive around on the system.

107   The counterargument is that access to information will become so essential to everyone's well-being that we could end up with a stratified society of info-rich and info-poor people. Such a knowledge gap hardly is the democratic ideal.

Global Inequities

108   The exchange of information facilitated by the Web boosted the United States into unprecedented prosperity going into the twenty-first century. One measure of efficiency, **diffusion of innovation**, improved dramatically. The time that innovations take to be widely used, which was once ten years, dropped to one year.

109   A problem, though, is that much of the world isn't well plugged in. Even in Japan, a major industrial nation, only 17 percent of the population uses the Web—in contrast, by some estimates, to more than 40 percent in North America. All of the Middle East and Africa have only 7.5 million Web users in total.

110   In short, the United States stands to realize more of the economic advantages of the Web than other countries, creating new international inequities. Aside from other oases such as Canada, Britain, and Scandinavia, the rest of the world is falling further and further behind.

111   If maximum U.S. prosperity depends on free trade in a global economy, as many economists argue, then the rest of the world must be folded fully into the Web.

MEDIA LITERACY

1. How does bandwidh affect the Web's ability to realize its potential?

2. What examples can you give of the technological convergence of older media and the Web?

3. What makes hypertext a revolutionary tool in mass communication?

---

universal access ● Giving everyone the means to use the Web.

diffusion of innovation ● Process through which news, ideas, values, and information spread.

Privacy and the Web

The genius of Tim Berners-Lee's original web concept was its openness. Information could be shared easily by anyone and everyone. Therein too was a problem. During the Web's commercialization in the late 1990s, some companies tracked where people ventured on the Web. The tracking was going on silently, hidden in the background, as people coursed their way around the Web. Companies gathering information were selling it to other companies. There was fear that insurance companies, health-care providers, lenders, and others had a new secret tool for profiling applicants.   112

Government agencies began hinting at controls. Late in 1999, Berners-Lee and the Web protocol-authoring consortium he runs came up with a new architecture, **P3P,** short for Platform for Privacy Preferences, to address the problem. With P3P people could choose the level of privacy they wanted for their Web activities. Microsoft, Netscape and other browser operators agreed to screen sites that were not P3P-compliant. In effect, P3P automatically bypassed websites that didn't meet a level of privacy expectations specified by individual Web users.   113

Yet to be determined is whether P3P, an attempt at Web industry self-regulation, can effectively protect consumers from third parties sharing private information. If P3P fails, Congress and federal agencies might follow through with backup protections.   114

Cyberpornography

Moralists, many in elected offices, are trying to eradicate indecency from cyberspace, especially if children have access. How serious is the problem? No one is certain how much **cyberpornography** is out there. Although a lot of Web traffic is to porn sites, Vanderbilt University business professors Donna Hoffman and Thomas Novak estimate that only one-half of 1 percent of the files available on the Internet could be described as pornographic. How often kids visit those sites is impossible to measure. Some people would argue that even a single child's exposure to pornography is too much and justifies sanctions.   115

Policing the Internet, including websites, presents unique challenges. The nature of the Web is that it is unstructured and unregulated, and the available material is in ongoing flux. The anarchy of the Web is its inherent virtue. The immensity of cyberspace is another problem for would-be regulators. The Web system that Tim Berners-Lee and his associates devised has infinite capacity.   116

Among alternatives to protect children are desktop programs that have come on the market to identify objectionable Internet bulletin boards and websites. **SurfWatch,** for example, blocks access to such sites as soon as they are discovered. Bill Duvall of Los Altos, California, who created SurfWatch, hires college students to monitor cyberspace for sexual explicitness and updates SurfWatch regularly. He identifies five to ten new smut sites a day.   117

Commercial online services keep close tabs on what goes on in their bulletin boards and chatrooms, and occasionally excise bawdy material. In addition, the industry is working on a ratings system, somewhat like Hollywood's movie ratings, to help parents to screen things they deem inappropriate for the kids. Since 1993, however, the commercial online services have been able to give their subscribers access to the unregulated Internet. Once out of an online service's gate, subscribers are beyond the protection of the service's in-house standards of acceptability.   118

P3P ○ A Web protocol that allows users to choose a level of privacy. Short for Platform for Privacy Preferences.

cyberpornography ● Indecency delivered by computer.

SurfWatch ● Software that intercepts indecent material.

Media Future: The Web

119 Futurists are scrambling, fruitlessly it seems, to sort through technological breakthroughs to figure out where the Web is going. Their vision extends only a few months ahead at best. Amid all the haze, two realities are clear. First, bandwidth improvements will exponentially expand capacity for transmission and exchange of messages. Second, the Web is beginning to untether itself from landlines as wireless networks, *wi-fi* for short, continue to proliferate. A wireless future will make the Web a medium of ultimate portability. The possibilities that will come with further miniaturization of equipment and compression of messages are mind-boggling.

120 As the technological breakthroughs leapfrog each other, we will see the traditional media shift increasingly to the Web. Don't expect to wake up one morning, though, and find the world is paperless and that local television stations have vanished. Just as horses and buggies and the automobile coexisted for forty years, so will e-books and p-books. Television will still be television as we know it today, with many people satisfied with living-room sets pretty much as now—although with bigger screens, sharper pictures, and movie-house sound quality.

121 In short, media companies will need to use two redundant modes to maximize the audience. Already we see this with over-air radio stations that stream online, magazines and newspapers on paper and on the Web, and recordings available at the record store and also downloadable.

122 Could the Web lose its diversity? Media mogul Barry Diller, well regarded for his crystal ball on media trends, sees ownership consolidation ahead for the Web, just like the other media. Citing cable giant Comcast, he said in a 2003 *Newsweek* interview: "You can already see at Comcast and others the beginning of efforts to control the home pages that their consumers plug into. It's for one reason: To control a toll bridge or turnstile through which others must pay to go. The inevitable result will be eventual control by media giants of the Internet in terms of independence and strangulation. This is a situation where history is absolutely destined to repeat itself." Most Web users hope Diller is wrong.

Section Review 4

Directions.

1. On a separate sheet of paper, write a brief summary of the main points of the sections you have just read.

2. Mark each of the following statements True (T), False (F), or Can't Tell (CT). Mark the statement Can't Tell if it cannot be determined to be either true or false based on the material in the passage. Refer to the passage as necessary to verify your answer.

_____ 1. The term *diffusion of innovation* refers to corporate profit-taking on the Internet.

_____ 2. Most Americans believe that the government should ensure universal access to the Internet for all citizens.

_____ 3. P3P is a government-sponsored effort to protect the privacy rights of Web users.

_____ 4. Though no one knows exactly how much pornography can be found on the Internet, estimates suggest that less than one of every 100 available Internet files are pornographic.

_____ 5. Barry Diller believes that the Internet will become increasingly controlled by large corporations.

Chapter Wrap-Up

The Web utilizes the global Internet, so computers anywhere can exchange digitized data—including text, visuals and audio. Many media companies are investing heavily in cyberspace, and the expansion of high-capacity fiber-optic cable networks will increase capacity tremendously so that audio and moving visuals are on tap live on any computer screen connected to the Internet. Two-way communication via the Web already is standard fare. With every passing day, more mass communication is occurring on the Web.

Questions for Review

1. How can the Web be defined as a new and distinctive mass medium?
2. How is the Web related to the Internet?
3. What is the difficulty with the Web as an advertising medium?
4. What is the effect of digitization and fiber-optic cable on mass communication?
5. What is the connection between the Web and hypertext?
6. Will hypertext change the way that human beings create stories and receive them?
7. Why was digitizing a necessary prelude to the Web?
8. Should public policy guarantee everyone, including children, total access to the Web?

Questions for Critical Thinking

1. Will it ever be possible to condense all human knowledge into an area smaller than the 36-square-foot cube described by the Marquardt Corporation?
2. What makes books, magazines, newspapers, sound recordings, movies, radio, and television different from one another? What will become of these distinctions in coming years?
3. Trace the development of the technology that has made the Web possible.
4. What were the innovations that Tim Berners-Lee introduced that are revolutionizing mass communication?
5. How does hypertext depart from traditional human communication? And does hypertext have a future as a literary form?
6. What obstacles would you have in designing public policy to assure access for every citizen to the Web?
7. Some people say there is no point in trying to regulate cybersmut. Do you agree? Disagree? Why?
8. Some mass media may be subsumed by the Web. Pretend you are a futurist and create a timeline for this to happen.

Keeping Up to Date

Industry Standard is the main trade journal of e-commerce.

The magazine *Wired* offers hip coverage of cyberdevelopments, issues, and people.

Trade journals *Editor & Publisher, Advertising Age,* and *Broadcasting & Cable* have excellent ongoing coverage of their fields.

InfoWorld covers the gamut of cybernews.

Widely available news media that explore cyberissues include *Time, Newsweek,* the *Wall Street Journal,* and the *New York Times.*

Don't overlook surfing the Web for sites that track Web developments.

Cumulative Review 2 (pages 265–275)

Directions. Write the letter of the best answer in the space provided.

_____ 1. Downloading images of book pages on the Web is an example of
   a. diffusion of innovation.
   b. deregulation.
   c. technological convergence.
   d. hypertext fiction.

_____ 2. The author suggests that website awards
   a. are pretty much meaningless.
   b. should be more carefully regulated by Internet authorities.
   c. overemphasize navigability.
   d. often recognize design and graphics rather than content.

_____ 3. Increased use of the Internet in other countries would probably
   a. hurt the U.S. economy.
   b. help the U.S. economy.
   c. have no effect on the U.S. economy.
   d. ensure economic equity among nations.

_____ 4. The author suggests that children's access to pornography on the Web
   a. is not a serious problem.
   b. can be restricted by some software programs.
   c. should be restricted by state law.
   d. will not be a problem in the future as Web-policing efforts improve.

_____ 5. Which is the safest conclusion to draw regarding the future of the Internet?
   a. Web use will becoming increasingly wireless.
   b. Web use will be controlled by one or two giant corporations.
   c. Many media companies will be forced out of business.
   d. Most traditional media, like television and radio, will disappear.

Directions. Answer each question in complete sentences, without copying word-for-word from the passage.

1. How does hyperfiction differ from traditional forms of entertainment?

_____

_____

_____

2. Compare the policies of the Reagan and Clinton administrations regarding deregulation. How were they similar? How were they different?

_____

_____

_____

3. Briefly explain the arguments for and against a government guarantee of universal Internet access.

_____

_____

_____

4. Why is it difficult to police the Internet for pornography?

_____

_____

_____

5. How does P3P help to protect the privacy of Web users?

_____

_____

_____

Vocabulary Exercise 2

Directions. Choose the meaning for the underlined word that best fits the context. You may consult the dictionary as needed.

_____ 1. . . . full-text is <u>derisively</u> called shovelware by hypertext enthusiasts . . . [Paragraph 74]
   a. accurately
   b. mistakenly
   c. in an original manner
   d. mockingly

_____ 2. To guard against bad information, Web users should pay special heed to the old <u>admonition</u>: Consider the source. [Paragraph 84]
   a. popular idea
   b. source of information
   c. logical error
   d. warning

_____ 3. The most <u>prestigious</u> are the Webby awards . . . [Paragraph 88]
   a. well researched
   b. lucrative; producing wealth
   c. well respected; esteemed
   d. oldest; going back in time

_____ 4. For this, traditional measures of excellence in communication apply, such as accuracy, clarity and <u>cohesion</u>. [Paragraph 89]
   a. standard of judgment
   b. completeness of information
   c. logical consistency
   d. brevity; shortness of words

_____ 5. The Clinton position, however, was less ideological and more <u>pragmatic</u>. [Paragraph 102]
   a. practical
   b. based upon theory
   c. idealistic
   d. financial

_____ 6. . . . we could end up with a <u>stratified</u> society of info-rich and info-poor people. [Paragraph 107]
   a. democratic
   b. unequal; containing higher and lower social classes
   c. lacking in education
   d. unable to change, grow or develop; rigidified

_____ 7. Moralists, many in elected offices, are trying to <u>eradicate</u> indecency from cyberspace . . . [Paragraph 115]
   a. locate
   b. control
   c. remove
   d. outlaw

_____ 8. The <u>anarchy</u> of the Web is its inherent virtue. [Paragraph 116]
   a. size; magnitude
   b. usefulness
   c. flexibility
   d. lack of order

_____ 9. . . . wireless networks, *wi-fi* for short, continue to <u>proliferate</u>. [Paragraph 119]
   a. appear
   b. multiply rapidly
   c. compete fiercely
   d. operate without regulation

_____ 10. In short, media companies will need to use two <u>redundant</u> modes to maximize the audience. [Paragraph 121]
   a. more than is needed
   b. having no noticeable differences
   c. working together; coordinated
   d. backup; substitute

Critical Response Questions

1. How has the Web changed the world in which we live? How has it changed American culture?

2. How can Web users best evaluate the quality of the websites they visit? How can they best ensure that the information they encounter is accurate?

3. Why is universal Internet access important to our, or any, democracy? What are some ways to promote and support universal access?

4. To what extent, if any, should the government regulate Internet business?

5. Do you prefer traditional entertainment or interactive entertainment? Explain your answer.

6. How should the problem of cyberpornography be addressed?

7. To what extent should students rely on Web sources when completing research papers? Explain your answer.

CHAPTER

Health

INFECTIOUS AND NONINFECTIOUS CONDITIONS

Directions

1. Begin by surveying the chapter to look for answers to the following questions.

   - What is the chapter about?
   - What subtopics will be discussed?
   - What will you learn from reading and studying the chapter?
   - How interesting does the chapter look?
   - How difficult does the chapter look?
   - How familiar to you is the chapter material? That is, how much previous knowledge of the subject do you have?

   When you have completed your survey, write a summary on a separate sheet of paper of what you've learned about the chapter from the survey. Your summary should include answers to the previous questions, as well as any other information and comments you wish to add.

2. While reading the chapter, look for organizational patterns. Recognizing the patterns should help you better grasp the relationship of ideas within each paragraph and section and distinguish main ideas more easily.

   Also, form questions from the headings and subheadings (generally, write one question per heading or subheading). Write your questions on a sheet of paper and, after completing each section, mentally review the main points of the section, mark the text, and write the answer(s) to your question(s), as well as any other information that seems important to you.

SAMPLE TEXTBOOK CHAPTER

From *Health: The Basics*, Sixth Edition, by Rebecca J. Donatelle. San Francisco: Benjamin Cummings, 2005.

Objectives

- Discuss the risk factors for infectious diseases.

- Describe the most common pathogens infecting humans today.

- Explain how your immune system works to protect you and what factors may make it less effective.

- Explain the major emerging and resurgent diseases affecting humans;

discuss why they are increasing in incidence and what actions are being taken to reduce risks.

- Discuss the various sexually transmitted infections, their means of transmission, and actions that can be taken to prevent their spread.

- Discuss human immunodeficiency virus and acquired immune defi-

ciency syndrome, trends in infection and treatment, and the impact on special populations, such as women and members of the international community.

- Discuss the chronic lung diseases, common neurological disorders, diabetes and other digestion-related disorders, and the varied musculo-skeletal diseases.

E very moment of every day, you are in contact with microscopic organisms   1
that have the ability to cause illness or even death. These disease-causing agents, known as **pathogens,** are found in air and food and on nearly every object or person with whom you come in contact. Although new varieties of pathogens arise all the time, scientific evidence indicates that many have existed for as long as there has been life on the planet. Fossil evidence shows that infections, cancer, heart disease, and a host of other ailments afflicted the earliest human beings. At times, infectious diseases wiped out whole groups of people through epidemics such as the Black Death, or bubonic plague, which killed half the population of Europe in the 1300s. A pandemic, or global epidemic, of influenza killed more than 20 million people in 1918, while strains of tuberculosis and cholera continue to cause premature death throughout the world.

In spite of our best efforts to eradicate them, these diseases are a continuing   2
menace to all of us. The news isn't all bad, however. Even though we are bombarded by potential pathogenic threats, our immune systems are remarkably adept at protecting us. *Endogenous microorganisms* are those that live in peaceful coexistence with their human host most of the time. For people in good health and whose immune systems are functioning properly, endogenous organisms are usually harmless. But in sick people or those with weakened immune systems, these normally harmless pathogenic organisms can cause serious health problems.

Exogenous microorganisms are organisms that do not normally inhabit the   3
body. When they do, however, they are apt to produce an infection and/or illness. The more easily these pathogens can gain a foothold in the body and sustain themselves, the more **virulent,** or aggressive, they may be in causing disease. However, if your immune system is strong, you will often be able to fight off even the most virulent attacker. Several factors influence your susceptibility to disease.

Assessing Your Disease Risks

Most diseases are **multifactorial diseases**—that is, they are caused by the interac-   4
tion of several factors from inside and outside the person. For a disease to occur, the *host* must be *susceptible,* which means that the immune system must be in a

| **Pathogen**   A disease-causing agent. |
| **Virulent**   Strong enough to overcome host resistance and cause disease. |
| **Multifactorial disease**   Disease caused by interactions of several factors. |

The New York Times
In the News

H.I.V. Secrecy Is Proving Deadly

By Howard Markel

With the progress in the medical treatment for HIV over the past decade, unsafe sexual practices have risen and prevention efforts stalled.

And when it comes to being infected with HIV, the truth still remains shrouded in secrecy.

Today, many public health experts say that failure to disclose HIV infection to partners, whether unintentionally or intentionally, is a significant but underreported factor in the continued spread of the virus in the United States.

The Centers for Disease Control and Prevention estimates that as many as 33 percent of the 900,000 Americans infected with the virus may not know it.

Dr. Robert Klitzman, a psychiatrist, and Dr. Ronald Bayer, an ethicist, both professors at Columbia, have explored the prevailing range of views and practices concerning HIV disclosure in a newly published book, *Mortal Secrets: Truth and Lies in the Age of AIDS*.

Using oral history interviews, the book explores the sexual practices of 49 men and 28 women in New York City.

Read the complete article online in the eThemes section of this book's website: www.aw-bc.com/donatelle.

Original article published November 25, 2003. Copyright © 2003 The New York Times. Reprinted with permission.

weakened condition; an *agent* capable of transmitting a disease must be present; and the *environment* must be hospitable to the pathogen in terms of temperature, light, moisture, and other requirements. Other risk factors also apparently increase or decrease susceptibility.

Risk Factors You Can't Control

5 Unfortunately, some risk factors are beyond our control. Here are some of the most common.

6 **Heredity** Perhaps the single greatest factor influencing longevity is the longevity of a person's parents. Being born into a family in which heart disease, cancer, or other illnesses are prevalent seems to increase risk. Still other diseases are caused by direct chromosomal inheritance. For example, **sickle-cell anemia,** an inherited blood disease that primarily affects African Americans, is often transmitted to the fetus if both parents carry the sickle-cell trait. It is often unclear whether hereditary diseases occur as a result of inherited chromosomal traits or inherited insufficiencies in the immune system.

7 **Aging** After age 40 we become more vulnerable to most of the chronic diseases. Moreover, as we age, our immune systems respond less efficiently to invading organisms, thus increasing risk for infection and illness. The same flu that produces an afternoon of nausea and diarrhea in a younger person may cause days of illness or even death in an older person. The very young are also at risk for many diseases, particularly if they are not vaccinated against them.

8 **Environmental Conditions** Unsanitary conditions and the presence of drugs, chemicals, and hazardous pollutants and wastes in food and water probably have a great effect on our immune systems. It is well documented that poor environmen-

Sickle-cell anemia Genetic disease commonly found among African Americans; results in organ damage and premature death.

tal conditions can weaken **immunological competence**—the body's ability to defend itself against pathogens.

Organism Resistance   Some organisms, such as the food-borne organism   9
botulism, are particularly virulent, and even tiny amounts may make the most hardy of us ill. Other organisms have mutated and are resistant to the body's defenses as well as to other conventional treatments designed to protect against them. Still other, newer pathogens pose unique challenges for our immune systems—ones that our bodily defenses are ill adapted to fight.

Risk Factors You Can Control

The good news is that we all have some degree of personal control over many risk   10
factors for disease. Too much stress, inadequate nutrition, a low physical fitness level, lack of sleep, misuse or abuse of legal and illegal substances, poor personal hygiene, high-risk behaviors, and other variables significantly increase the risk for a number of diseases. Several factors influence our individual susceptibility to various diseases. Those we have the most control over, via lifestyle decisions and behaviors, are noted on the following list with an asterisk (*).

- Dosage, virulence, and portal of entry of agent
- Age at time of infection
- Preexisting level of immunity*
- Nature and vigor of immune response*
- Genetic factors controlling immune response
- Nutritional status*
- Preexisting diseases*
- Personal habits: smoking, alcohol, exercise, drugs*
- Dual infection or superinfection with other agents
- Psychological factors (e.g., motivation, emotional status, and so on)*

Types of Pathogens and Routes of Transmission

Pathogens enter the body in several ways. They may be transmitted by *direct con-*   11
tact between infected persons, such as during sexual relations, kissing, or touching, or by *indirect contact,* such as by touching an object the infected person has had contact with. The hands are probably the greatest source of infectious disease transmission. You may also **autoinoculate** yourself, or transmit a pathogen from one part of your body to another. For example, you may touch a sore on your lip that is teeming with viral herpes, then transmit the virus to your eye when you scratch your itchy eyelid.

Pathogens are also transmitted by *airborne contact*—you can breathe in air   12
that carries a particular pathogen—or by *food-borne infection* if you eat something contaminated by microorganisms. Recent episodes of food poisoning from *Salmonella* bacteria found in certain foods and *E. coli* bacteria found in undercooked beef have raised concerns about the safety of the U.S. food supply. As a

---

Immunological competence   Ability of the immune system to defend the body from pathogens.

Botulism   A resistant food-borne organism that is extremely virulent.

Autoinoculation   Transmission of a pathogen from one part of the body to another.

direct result of these concerns, food labels now caution consumers to cook meats thoroughly, wash utensils, and take other food-handling precautions.

13   Your best friend may be the source of *animal-borne pathogens*. Dogs, cats, livestock, and wild animals can spread numerous diseases through their bites or feces or by carrying infected insects into living areas and transmitting diseases either directly or indirectly. Although **interspecies transmission** of diseases (diseases passed from humans to animals and vice versa) is rare, it does occur. *Waterborne diseases* are transmitted directly from drinking water and indirectly from foods washed or sprayed with contaminated water. These pathogens can also invade your body if you wade or swim in contaminated streams, lakes, or reservoirs. Pathogens may also transmit *insect-borne diseases* via mosquitoes, ticks, and other hosts that spread disease through sucking or biting. Mothers may transmit diseases *perinatally* to an infant in the womb or as the baby passes through the vagina during birth.

14   We can categorize pathogens into six major types: bacteria, viruses, fungi, protozoa, parasitic worms, and prions.

Bacteria

15   **Bacteria** are single-celled organisms that are plantlike in nature but lack chlorophyll (the pigment that gives plants their green coloring). There are three major types of bacteria: cocci, bacilli, and spirilla. Bacteria can be viewed under a standard light microscope.

16   Although there are several thousand species of bacteria, only approximately a hundred cause diseases in humans. In many cases, it is not the bacteria themselves that cause disease but rather the poisonous substances, called **toxins,** that they produce. The following are the most common bacterial infections.

17   ***Staphylococcal Infections***   Staphylococci are normally present on our skin at all times and usually cause few problems. But when there is a cut or break in the **epidermis,** or outer layer of the skin, staphylococci may enter and cause a localized infection. If you have ever suffered from acne, boils, styes (infections of the eyelids), or infected wounds, you have probably had a staph infection. Although most such infections are readily defeated by your immune system, resistant forms of staph bacteria are on the rise. These bacteria must be treated with heavy doses of antibiotics and pose serious risks to those infected.

18   At least one staph-caused disorder, **toxic shock syndrome,** is potentially fatal. Although most cases of toxic shock syndrome have occurred in menstruating women, the disease was first reported in 1978 in children and continues to be reported in people recovering from wounds, surgery, or other injury. To reduce the likelihood of toxic shock syndrome, women should take the following precautions: (1) avoid superabsorbent tampons except during the heaviest menstrual flow; (2) change tampons at least every four hours; and (3) use napkins at night instead of tampons.

Interspecies transmission   Transmission of disease from humans to animals or from animals to humans.

Bacteria   Single-celled organisms that may cause disease.

Toxins   Poisonous substances produced by certain microorganisms that cause various diseases.

Staphylococci   Round, gram-positive bacteria, usually found in clusters.

Epidermis   The outermost layer of the skin.

Toxic shock syndrome   A potentially life-threatening bacterial infection that is most common in menstruating women who use tampons.

Streptococcal Infections   At least five types of the **streptococcus** microorganism   19
are known to cause bacterial infections. Group A streptococcus causes the most
common diseases, such as streptococcal pharyngitis (strep throat) and scarlet fever.
Group B streptococcus can cause illness in newborn babies, pregnant women, the
elderly, and adults with other illnesses such as diabetes or liver disease.

Pneumonia   In the early twentieth century, **pneumonia** was one of the leading   20
causes of death in the United States. This lung disease is characterized by chronic
cough, chest pain, chills, high fever, fluid accumulation, and eventual respiratory
failure. One of the most common forms of pneumonia is caused by bacterial infection and responds readily to antibiotic treatment in the early stages. Other forms
are caused by viruses, chemicals, or other substances in the lungs and are more
difficult to treat. Although medical advances have reduced the overall incidence of
pneumonia, it continues to be a major threat in the United States and throughout
the world. Vulnerable populations include the poor, the elderly, and those already
suffering from other illnesses.

Legionnaires' Disease   This bacterial disorder gained widespread publicity in   21
1976, when several Legionnaires at the American Legion convention in Philadel-
phia contracted the disease and died before the invading organism was isolated
and effective treatment devised. Although it is not well known, the waterborne nature of Legionnaires' disease has led to several recent outbreaks in the United
States. The symptoms are similar to those of pneumonia, which sometimes makes
identification difficult. In people whose resistance is lowered, particularly the elderly, delayed identification can have serious consequences.

Tuberculosis   A major killer in the United States during the early twentieth cen-   22
tury, **tuberculosis (TB)** was largely controlled in America by 1950 due to improved
sanitation, isolation of infected persons, and treatment with drugs such as *rifampin*
or *isoniazid*. But though many health professionals assumed that TB had been con-
quered, that appears not to be the case. During the past 20 years, several factors
have led to an epidemic rise in the disease: deteriorating social conditions, including overcrowding and poor sanitation; failure to isolate active cases of TB; a weakening of public health infrastructure, which has led to less funding for screening;
and migration of TB to the United States through international travel. In 2002,
there were more than 15,075 active cases of TB in the United States. More than
one-half of all TB cases in the U.S. in 2002 occurred in foreign-born individuals.
Newer strains of multiple drug-resistant TB make this epidemic potentially more
devastating than previous outbreaks.

Although increases in the incidence of TB in the United States are troubling,   23
U.S. statistics pale by comparison to the staggering TB burden in the global population. Assuming no significant improvements in prevention and control occur between now and 2020, the World Health Organization (WHO) estimates that 1 billion people will acquire new TB infection, 200 million will develop active disease,
and 70 million will die.

Streptococci   Round bacteria, usually found in chain formation.

Pneumonia   Disease of the lungs characterized by chronic cough, chest
pain, chills, high fever, and fluid accumulation; may be caused by bacteria,
viruses, chemicals, or other substances.

Tuberculosis (TB)   A disease caused by bacterial infiltration of the respiratory system.

24   Tuberculosis is caused by bacterial infiltration of the respiratory system that results in a chronic inflammatory reaction in the lungs. Airborne transmission via the respiratory tract is the primary and most efficient mode of transmitting TB. People with active cases can transmit the disease while talking, coughing, sneezing, or singing. Fortunately, TB is fairly difficult to catch, and prolonged exposure, rather than single exposure, is the typical mode of infection. Only about 20 to 30 percent of people exposed to an active case will become infected. Symptoms include persistent coughing, weight loss, fever, and spitting up blood. A simple skin test will indicate infection, and treatments are effective for most nonresistant cases. Many people have a form of latent TB in which the bacteria are present in the body but the person is symptom-free and not infectious. Most of these people never develop active TB, unless their immune system becomes compromised.

25 **Periodontal Diseases**   Diseases of the tissue around the teeth, called **periodontal diseases,** affect three out of four adults over age 35. Improper tooth care, including lack of flossing and poor brushing habits, and the failure to obtain professional dental care lead to increased bacterial growth, caries (tooth decay), and gum infections. If left untreated, permanent tooth loss may result.

> *What do you think?*
> **Why do you think we are experiencing global increases in diseases such as TB? • Should we be concerned about diseases in other countries? • Do we have an obligation to help the world's population in its struggle against these diseases? • What policies, programs, and services might help?**

Viruses

26 **Viruses** are the smallest pathogens, approximately 1/500th the size of bacteria. Because of their tiny size, they are visible only under an electron microscope and were not identified until the twentieth century. More than 150 viruses are known to cause diseases in humans, although their role in various cancers and chronic diseases is still unclear.

27   Essentially, a virus consists of a protein structure that contains either *ribonucleic acid (RNA)* or *deoxyribonucleic acid (DNA)*. Incapable of carrying out the normal cell functions of respiration and metabolism, a virus cannot reproduce on its own and can exist only in a parasitic relationship with the cell it invades.

28   Viral diseases can be difficult to treat because many viruses can withstand heat, formaldehyde, and large doses of radiation with little effect on their structure. Drug treatment for viral infections is also limited. Drugs powerful enough to kill viruses generally kill the host cells too, although some medications block stages in viral reproduction without damaging host cells.

29   When exposed to certain viruses, the body produces a protein substance known as **interferon.** Interferon does not destroy the invading microorganisms but sets up a protective mechanism to aid healthy cells in their struggle against

Periodontal diseases   Diseases of the tissue around the teeth.

Viruses   Minute parasitic microbes that live inside another cell.

Interferon   A protein substance produced by the body that aids the immune system by protecting healthy cells.

the invaders. Although interferon research is promising, it should be noted that not all viruses stimulate interferon production.

The Common Cold   Colds are responsible for more days lost from work and more   30 uncomfortable days spent at work than any other ailment. Caused by any number of viruses (some experts claim there may be more than 200 different viruses responsible for the common cold), colds are **endemic** (always present to some degree) among people throughout the world. In the course of a year, Americans suffer more than 1 billion colds. Otherwise healthy people carry cold viruses in their noses and throats most of the time. These viruses are held in check until the host's resistance is lowered. It is possible to "catch" a cold—from the airborne droplets of another person's sneeze or from skin-to-skin or mucous membrane contact—though recent studies indicate that the hands are the greatest avenue for transmitting colds and other viruses. Although many people believe that a cold results from exposure to cold weather or from getting chilled or overheated, experts believe that such things have little or no effect on cold development. Stress, allergy disorders that affect the nasal passages, and menstrual cycles do, however, appear to increase susceptibility.

The best rule of thumb is to keep your resistance level high. Sound nutrition,   31 adequate rest, stress reduction, and regular exercise appear to be the best bets in helping fight off infection. Avoid people with newly developed colds (colds appear to be most contagious during the first 24 hours of onset). If you contract a cold, bed rest, plenty of fluids, and aspirin to relieve pain and discomfort are the tried-and-true remedies for adults. Children should not take aspirin for colds or the flu because this could lead to *Reye's syndrome,* a potentially fatal disease.

Influenza   In otherwise healthy people, **influenza,** or flu, is usually not serious.   32 Symptoms, including headaches, fatigue, aches and pains, fever, and coldlike ailments, generally pass quickly. However, in combination with other disorders or among the elderly, those with respiratory or heart disease, or children under age five, the flu can be very serious. Contrary to common belief, the flu is primarily a respiratory disease. You cannot have a "stomach flu." Nausea, vomiting, and diarrhea are extremely rare with the flu, except in small children. The period of November through March is the typical flu season.

To date, three major varieties of flu virus have been discovered, with many dif-   33 ferent strains existing within each variety. The "A" form of the virus is generally the most virulent, followed by the "B" and "C" varieties. If you contract one form of flu you may develop immunity to it, but you will not necessarily be immune to other forms of the disease. Little can be done to treat flu patients once the infection has become established. Some vaccines have proved effective against certain strains of flu virus, but they are totally ineffective against others. In spite of minor risks, it is recommended that people over age 65, pregnant women, people with heart or lung disease, and those with certain other illnesses be vaccinated. In fall of 2003, an inhaled vaccine called FluMist was released for use with healthy, nonpregnant adults up to age 49. Because the vaccine contains a weakened version of the live virus, people who receive the vaccine may pose a risk to anyone with a weakened immune system who is around them. More investigation into the risks are needed.

Infectious Mononucleosis   Initial symptoms of *mononucleosis,* or *mono,* include   34 sore throat, fever, headache, nausea, chills, and pervasive weakness/fatigue. As the disease progresses, lymph nodes may enlarge, and jaundice, spleen enlargement, aching joints, and body rashes may occur.

Endemic   Describing a disease that is always present to some degree.

Influenza   A common viral disease of the respiratory tract.

35   Caused by the *Epstein-Barr virus,* mono is readily detected through a *monospot test,* a blood test that measures the percentage of specific forms of white blood cells. Because many viruses are caused by transmission of body fluids, many people once believed that young people contracted mono through kissing (hence its nickname, "the kissing disease"). Although this is still considered a possible cause, mono is not believed to be highly contagious. It does not appear to be easily spread through normal, everyday personal contact.

36   Treatment of mono is often a lengthy process that involves bed rest, balanced nutrition, and medications. Gradually, the body develops immunity to the disease, and the person returns to normal activity.

37   **Hepatitis**   One of the most highly publicized viral diseases is **hepatitis,** a virally caused inflammation of the liver. Hepatitis symptoms include fever, headache, nausea, loss of appetite, skin rashes, pain in the upper right abdomen, dark yellow (with brownish tinge) urine, and jaundice (yellowing of the whites of the eyes and the skin). In some regions of the United States and among certain segments of the population, hepatitis has reached epidemic proportions. Internationally, viral hepatitis is a major contributor to acute and chronic liver disease and accounts for high morbidity and mortality. Currently, there are seven known forms, with the following three indicating the highest rate of incidence (see the Centers for Disease Control and Prevention [CDC] website for further information on the types not discussed here).

- *Hepatitis A (HAV).* HAV is contracted from eating food or drinking water contaminated with human excrement. Each year, more than 150,000 people in the United States are infected, typically through something in the household, sexual contact, day care attendance, or international travel. Fortunately, people with HAV do not become chronic carriers.
- *Hepatitis B (HBV).* This disease, spread primarily through body fluids, particularly during unprotected sex, can lead to chronic liver disease or liver cancer. However, it can also be contracted via sharing needles when injecting drugs, or passed by an infected mother to her baby during birth. One of the fastest growing sexually transmitted infections (STIs) in the United States, with more than 300,000 new cases per year, HBV infection is more prevalent than human immunodeficiency virus (HIV). More than 1.2 million people are chronic carriers. Most people recover within six months, although some become chronic carriers.
- *Hepatitis C (HCV).* HCV infections are on an epidemic rise in many regions of the world, as resistant forms are emerging. Currently, it is estimated that there are 150,000 new cases of HCV in the United States each year, with more than 4 million people infected. More than 85 percent of those infected develop chronic infections; if the infection is left untreated, the person may develop cirrhosis of the liver, liver cancer, or liver failure. Liver failure due to chronic HCV is the leading cause of liver transplants in the United States. Some cases can be traced to blood transfusions or organ transplants.

38   In the United States, hepatitis continues to be a major threat in spite of a safe blood supply and massive efforts at education about hand washing and safer sex. Treatment of all forms of viral hepatitis is somewhat limited.

39   **Measles**   Measles is a viral disorder that often affects young children. Symptoms, which appear about ten days after exposure, include an itchy rash and a high fever.

Hepatitis   A virally caused disease in which the liver becomes inflamed, which produces symptoms such as fever, headache, and jaundice.

Measles   A viral disease that produces symptoms including an itchy rash and a high fever.

German measles (rubella) is a milder viral infection that is believed to be transmitted by inhalation, after which it multiplies in the upper respiratory tract and passes into the bloodstream. It causes a rash, especially on the upper extremities. It is not generally a serious health threat and usually runs its course in three to four days. The major exceptions to this rule are newborns and pregnant women. Rubella can damage a fetus, particularly during the first trimester, by creating a condition known as congenital rubella in which the infant may be born blind, deaf, cognitively impaired, or with heart defects. Immunization has reduced the incidence of both measles and German measles. Infections in children not immunized against measles can lead to fever-induced problems such as rheumatic heart disease, kidney damage, and neurological disorders.

Other Pathogens

Fungi   Hundreds of species of **fungi,** multicellular or unicellular primitive plants, inhabit our environment. Many fungi are useful, providing such foodstuffs as edible mushrooms, and are used to make some cheeses. But some species of fungi can produce infections. *Candidiasis* (a vaginal yeast infection), athlete's foot, ringworm, and jock itch are examples of fungal diseases. Keeping the affected area clean and dry plus treatment with appropriate medications will generally bring prompt relief.   40

Protozoa   Protozoa are microscopic, single-celled organisms that are generally associated with tropical diseases such as African sleeping sickness and malaria. Although these pathogens are prevalent in nonindustrialized countries, they are largely controlled in the United States. The most common protozoal disease in the United States is *trichomoniasis,* which we will discuss later in this chapter's section on STIs. A common waterborne protozoan disease in many regions of the country is *giardiasis.* People who drink or are exposed to the *Giardia* pathogen may suffer intestinal pain and discomfort weeks after infection. Protection of water supplies is the key to prevention.   41

Parasitic Worms   **Parasitic worms** are the largest of the pathogens. Ranging in size from the small pinworms typically found in children to the relatively large tapeworms found in all warm-blooded animals, most parasitic worms are more a nuisance than a threat. Of special note today are the worm infestations associated with eating raw fish in Japanese sushi restaurants. Cooking fish and other foods to temperatures sufficient to kill the worms and their eggs can prevent this.   42

Prions   A **prion,** or unconventional virus, is a self-replicating, protein-based *agent* that can infect humans and other animals. Believed to be the underlying cause of spongiform diseases such as "mad cow disease," this agent systematically destroys brain cells. We will say more about prion-based diseases later in this chapter.   43

German measles (rubella)   A milder form of measles that causes a rash and mild fever in children and may cause damage to a fetus or a newborn baby.

Fungi   A group of plants that lack chlorophyll and do not produce flowers or seeds; several microscopic varieties are pathogenic.

Protozoa   Microscopic, single-celled organisms.

Parasitic worms   The largest of the pathogens, most of which are more a nuisance than a threat.

Prions   A self-replicating protein-based agent that systematically destroys brain cells.

Section Review 1

Directions.

1. On a separate sheet of paper, write a brief summary of the main points of the sections you have just read.

2. Mark each of the following statements True (T), False (F), or Can't Tell (CT). Mark the statement Can't Tell if it cannot be determined to be either true or false based on the material in the passage. Refer to the passage as necessary to verify your answer.

_____ 1. Infectious diseases are relatively recent in human history.

_____ 2. Exposure to an infectious disease does not necessarily result in contraction of the disease.

_____ 3. The hands are probably the greatest source of the transmission of pathogens.

_____ 4. Approximately 1,000 species of bacteria cause human illnesses.

_____ 5. Toxic shock syndrome and strep throat are both caused by bacterial infection.

Directions. Write the letter of the best answer in the space provided.

_____ 1. Which of the following risk factors is most within your control?
    a. environmental pollution
    b. response to stress
    c. aging
    d. food additives

_____ 2. An important concern regarding tuberculosis in the United States today is that
    a. tuberculosis is one of the country's leading fatal diseases.
    b. tuberculosis is highly contagious.
    c. newer stains of TB are drug resistant.
    d. tuberculosis frequently leads to HIV diseases.

_____ 3. Flu is different from the common cold in that
    a. flu symptoms almost always last longer.
    b. there are more flu viruses.
    c. there is no immunity to flu.
    d. flu can pose a serious risk for people in certain categories.

_____ 4. Which of the following diseases is not caused by a virus?
    a. influenza
    b. tuberculosis
    c. chicken pox
    d. hepatitis

_____ 5. We can infer from the passage that protozoal diseases would be least controlled in
    a. India.
    b. the United States.
    c. France.
    d. Sweden.

Your Body's Defenses: Keeping You Well

Although all the pathogens just described pose a threat if they take hold in your body, the chances that they will do so are actually quite small. First, they must overcome a number of effective barriers, many of which were established in your body before you were born.   44

Physical and Chemical Defenses

Perhaps our most critical early defense system is the skin. Layered to provide an intricate web of barriers, the skin allows few pathogens to enter. **Enzymes,** complex proteins manufactured by the body that appear in body secretions such as sweat, provide additional protection; they destroy microorganisms on skin surfaces by producing inhospitable pH levels. Microorganisms that flourish at a selected pH will be weakened or destroyed as these changes occur. A third protection is our frequent slight elevations in body temperature, which create an inhospitable environment for many pathogens. Only when cracks or breaks occur in the skin can pathogens gain easy access to the body.   45

The linings of the body provide yet another protection. Mucous membranes in the respiratory tract and other linings of the body trap and engulf invading organisms. *Cilia,* hairlike projections in the lungs and respiratory tract, sweep invaders toward body openings, where they are expelled. Tears, nasal secretions, earwax, and other secretions found at body entrances contain enzymes designed to destroy or neutralize pathogens. Finally, any organism that manages to breach such initial lines of defense faces a formidable specialized network of defenses thrown up by the immune system.   46

The Immune System: Your Body Fights Back

Immunity is a condition of being able to resist a particular disease by counteracting the substance that produces the disease. Any substance capable of triggering an immune response is called an **antigen.** An antigen can be a virus, a bacterium, a fungus, a parasite, or a tissue or cell from another individual. When invaded by an antigen, the body responds by forming substances called **antibodies** that are matched to the specific antigen much as a key is matched to a lock. Antibodies belong to a mass of large molecules known as *immunoglobulins,* a group of nine chemically distinct protein substances, each of which plays a role in neutralizing, setting up for destruction, or actually destroying antigens.   47

Once an antigen breaches the body's initial defenses, the body begins a process of antigen analysis. It considers the size and shape of the invader, verifies that the antigen is not part of the body itself, and then produces a specific antibody to destroy or weaken the antigen. This process, which is much more complex than described here, is part of a system called *humoral immune responses.* Humoral immunity is the body's major defense against many bacteria and bacterial toxins.   48

Cell-mediated immunity is characterized by the formation of a population of lymphocytes that can attack and destroy the foreign invader. These lymphocytes   49

Enzymes   Organic substances that cause bodily changes and destruction of microorganisms.

Antigen   A substance capable of triggering an immune response.

Antibodies   Substances produced by the body that are individually matched to specific antigens.

constitute the body's main defense against viruses, fungi, parasites, and some bacteria. Key players in this immune response are specialized groups of white blood cells known as *macrophages* (a type of phagocytic, or cell-eating, cell) and *lymphocytes,* other white blood cells in the blood, lymph nodes, bone marrow, and certain glands.

50   Two forms of lymphocytes in particular, the *B-lymphocytes* (B-cells) and *T-lymphocytes* (T-cells), are involved in the immune response. There are different types of B-cells, named according to the area of the body in which they develop. Most are manufactured in the soft tissue of the hollow shafts of the long bones. T-cells, in contrast, develop and multiply in the thymus, a multilobed organ that lies behind the breastbone. T-cells assist the immune system in several ways. *Regulatory T-cells* help direct the activities of the immune system and assist other cells, particularly B-cells, to produce antibodies. Dubbed "helper T's," these cells are essential for activating B-cells, other T-cells, and macrophages. Another form of T-cell, known as the "killer T" or "cytotoxic T," directly attacks infected or malignant cells. Killer T-cells enable the body to rid itself of cells that have been infected by viruses or transformed by cancer; they are also responsible for the rejection of tissue and organ grafts. The third type of T-cell, "suppressor T," turns off or suppresses the activity of B-cells, killer T-cells, and macrophages. Suppressor T-cells circulate in the bloodstream and lymphatic system where they neutralize or destroy antigens, thus enhancing the effects of the immune response and helping to return the activated immune system to normal levels. After a successful attack on a pathogen, some of the attacker T- and B-cells are preserved as *memory T-* and *B-cells* that enable the body to quickly recognize and respond to subsequent attacks by the same kind of organism at a later time. Thus, macrophages, T- and B-cells, and antibodies are the key factors in mounting an immune response.

51   Once a person has survived an infectious disease, he or she becomes immune to that disease, which means that in all probability he or she will not develop it again. Upon subsequent attack by the disease-causing microorganism, their memory T- and B-cells are quickly activated to come to their defense.

52 **Autoimmune Diseases**   Although white blood cells and the antigen–antibody response generally work in our favor by neutralizing or destroying harmful antigens, the body sometimes makes a mistake and targets its own tissue as the enemy, builds up antibodies against that tissue, and attempts to destroy it. This is known as *autoimmune disease* (*auto* means "self"). Common autoimmune disorders are rheumatoid arthritis, systemic lupus erythematosus (SLE), and myasthenia gravis.

53   In some cases, the antigen–antibody response completely fails to function. The result is a form of *immune deficiency syndrome*. Perhaps the most dramatic case of this syndrome was the "bubble boy," a youngster who died in 1984 after living his short life inside a sealed-off environment designed to protect him from all antigens. A much more common immune system disorder is *acquired immune deficiency syndrome (AIDS),* which we will discuss later in this chapter.

Fever

54 If an infection is localized, pus formation, redness, swelling, and irritation often occur. These symptoms indicate that the invading organisms are being fought systematically. Another indication is the development of a fever, or a rise in body temperature above the norm of 98.6°F. Fever is frequently caused by toxins secreted by pathogens that interfere with the control of body temperature. Although this elevated temperature is often harmful to the body, it is also believed to act as a form of protection. Raising body temperature by even one or two degrees provides an environment that destroys some disease-causing organisms. A fever also stimulates the body to produce more white blood cells, which destroy more invaders.

Pain

Although we do not usually think of pain as a defense mechanism, it is a response   55
to injury, and it plays a valuable role in the body's response to invasion. Pain may
be either *direct pain,* caused by the stimulation of nerve endings in an affected
area, or **referred pain,** meaning that it is present in one place although the source
is elsewhere. Most pain responses are accompanied by inflammation. Pain tends
to be the earliest sign that an injury has occurred and often causes the person to
slow down or stop the activity that was aggravating the injury, thereby protecting
against further damage. Because it is often one of the first warnings of disease, persistent pain should not be overlooked or masked with short-term pain relievers.

Vaccines: Bolstering Your Immunity

Recall that once people have been exposed to a specific pathogen, subsequent at-   56
tacks will activate their memory T- and B-cells, thus giving them immunity. This is
the principle on which **vaccination** is based.

A vaccine consists of killed or attenuated (weakened) versions of a disease-   57
causing microorganism, or an antigen that is similar to but less dangerous than
the disease antigen. It is administered to stimulate the person's immune system
to produce antibodies against future attacks—without actually causing the disease.
Vaccines are given orally or by injection, and this form of artificial immunity is
termed **acquired immunity,** in contrast to **natural immunity,** which a mother
passes to her fetus via their shared blood supply.

Depending on the virulence of the organism, vaccines containing live, atten-   58
uated, or dead organisms are given for a variety of diseases. In some instances, if
a person is already weakened by other health problems, vaccination may provoke
an actual mild case of the disease. Figure 7.1 on page 293 shows the recommended schedule for childhood vaccinations.

Emerging and Resurgent Diseases

Although our immune systems are remarkably adept at responding to many chal-   59
lenges, they are threatened by an army of microbes that is so diverse, virulent, and
insidious that the invaders appear to be gaining ground. According to the WHO's
World Health Report issued in 2002, trends such as the aging of the population (the
young and old are particularly vulnerable), the urbanization of developing countries, poverty, environmental pollution, globalization of the food supply, and crum-
bling health care systems bode very badly for the future. As international travel increases (more than 1 million people per day cross international boundaries), with
germs transported from remote regions of developing countries to huge urban centers within a matter of hours, the likelihood of infection by microbes previously unknown on U.S. soil increases.

Referred pain   Pain that is present at one point, but whose source is elsewhere.

Vaccination   Inoculation with killed or weakened pathogens or similar,
less dangerous antigens in order to prevent or lessen the effects of a disease.

Acquired immunity   Immunity developed during life in response to disease, vaccination, or exposure.

Natural immunity   Immunity passed to a fetus by its mother.

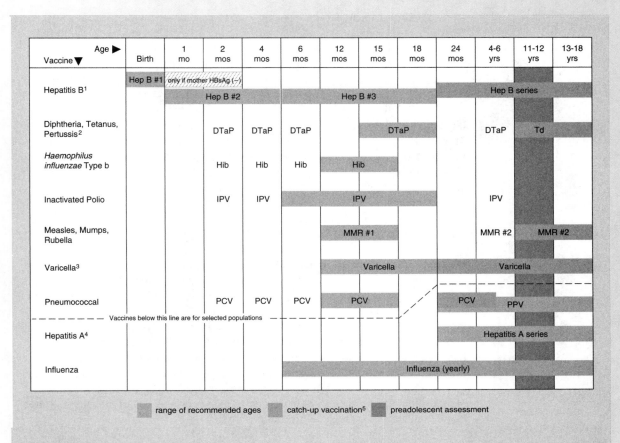

Figure 7.1

Recommended Childhood and Adolescent Immunization Schedule, 2003

1. Mothers who have tested positive for hepatitis B (HBV) should consult their doctors about their infant's vaccinations.

2. Tetanus and diphtheria toxoids (Td) are recommended at age 11–12 years if at least 5 years have elapsed since the last dose of tetanus and diphtheria vaccines. Subsequent routine Td boosters are recommended every 10 years.

3. Varicella is recommended at any visit or after age 12 months for children who lack a reliable history of chicken pox. Susceptible persons over 13 years should receive 2 doses, given at least 4 weeks apart.

4. Hepatitis A (HAV) vaccine is recommended for use in selected states and regions and for certain high-risk groups; consult your physician.

5. "Catch-up vaccination" indicates age groups that warrant special effort to administer any missed vaccines.

Source: Centers for Disease Control and Prevention, "Recommended Childhood and Adolescent Immunization Schedule," *Morbidity and Mortality Report* 52, no. 4 (2003): Q1–Q4.

Tiny Microbes: Lethal Threats

60 Today's arsenal of antibiotics appears to be increasingly ineffective. Penicillin-resistant strains of diseases are on the rise as microbes become able to outlast and outsmart even the best of our antibiotic weapons. Old scourges are back, and new ones are emerging.

61 **"Mad Cow Disease"**   The American beef industry has been the subject of a great amount of media attention, with the first confirmed case of *bovine spongiform encephalitis* (BSE, or "mad cow disease") being detected in December 2003. BSE may be linked to a disease in humans known as *new variant Creutzfeldt-Jakob disease*

(NvCJD). Both disorders are invariably fatal brain diseases with unusually long incubation periods measured in years, and both are caused by unconventional transmittable agents known as *prions.*

BSE is thought to have been transmitted when cows were fed a protein-based substance (slaughterhouse leftovers from sheep and other cows) to help them put on weight and grow faster. Failure to treat this protein by-product sufficiently to kill the BSE organism allowed it to infect the cows. The disease is believed to be transmitted to humans through the meat of these slaughtered cows. The resultant variant of BSE in humans, known as NvCJD disease and characterized by progressively worsening neurological damage and possible death, was noted in ten people in England and linked by some studies to the BSE-diseased cows. It should be noted that this link has not yet been scientifically verified.   62

A related prion-caused disease, *chronic wasting disease,* has been found in deer and is similar to BSE. Studies are under way investigating the implications of this disease for human health.   63

Dengue and Dengue Hemorrhagic Fever   Transmitted by mosquitoes, **dengue** viruses are the most widespread insect-borne viruses in the world. Today, dengue is found on most continents, and more than one-half of all United Nations member states are threatened. Dengue symptoms include flulike nausea, aches, and chronic fatigue and weakness. As urban areas become increasingly infected with mosquitoes, nearly 1.5 billion people, including about 600 million children, are at risk. Each year, it is estimated that more than 100 million people are infected, and more than 8,000 die. A more serious form of the disease, **dengue hemorrhagic fever,** can kill children in 6 to 12 hours, as the virus causes capillaries to leak and spill fluid and blood into surrounding tissue. Dengue is on the rise in the United States, largely because of increased international travel.   64

Ebola Hemorrhagic Fever (Ebola HF)   Another emerging disease, Ebola HF is a severe, often fatal disease in humans and nonhuman primates (monkeys, gorillas, and chimpanzees). Although much about Ebola HF is unknown, researchers believe that the virus is animal-borne and normally occurs in animal hosts that are native to the African continent. The virus is spread via direct contact with blood and/or secretions, and possibly through the air. With an incubation period of 2 to 21 days, the course of the disease is quick and characterized by fever, headache, joint and muscle aches, sore throat, and weakness, followed by diarrhea, vomiting, stomach pain, and internal and external bleeding. Although there have been no known cases of human transmission in the United States, several outbreaks have occurred in various regions of Africa. In 1995, an Ebola HF outbreak in Zaire killed 245 of the 316 people infected, thus forcing strict government-enforced quarantine of the entire region. Subsequent infections in other regions of the world have caused increasing concern. Fortunately, Ebola HF is not as prevalent worldwide as dengue fever.   65

Cryptosporidium   In 1993, the intestinal parasite *Cryptosporidium,* or crypto, infected the municipal water supply of Milwaukee, Wisconsin. The result was the largest waterborne protozoan disease outbreak ever recognized in this country; it caused many deaths and sickened hundreds of thousands of people with acute diarrhea. Exactly how the water supply became infected remains in question; how-   66

Dengue   A disease transmitted by mosquitoes, which causes flulike symptoms.

Dengue hemorrhagic fever   A more serious form of dengue.

ever, the fact that humans, birds, and animals can carry the infective agent and be highly contagious suggests many possible routes. Today crypto is one of the most common waterborne diseases in the United States.

67 ***Escherichia coli O157:H7***   *Escherichia coli O157:H7* is one of more than 170 types of *E. coli* bacteria that can infect humans. Commonly called *E. coli O157:H7*, it produces a lethal toxin and can cause severe illness or death. Eating ground beef that is rare or undercooked is a common way of becoming infected. Drinking unpasteurized milk or juices and drinking or swimming in sewage-contaminated water or public pools can also cause infection via ingestion of feces that contain *E. coli*. In 2003, several children were infected at a fair in Oregon when they petted infected farm animals and did not wash their hands. Recent findings indicate that simple changes in the way cattle are fed prior to slaughter may reduce the growth of *E. coli* in cattle stomachs.

68 ***Cholera***   Cholera, an infectious disease transmitted through fecal contamination of food or water supplies, has been rare in the United States since the early 1900s. Recent epidemic outbreaks in the Western Hemisphere (more than 900,000 cases), however, have started to affect the United States. Efforts to control cholera may be increasingly difficult as international travel and trade increase.

69 ***Hantavirus***   Transmitted via rodent feces, this virus was responsible for many deaths in the southwestern United States in 1994 before experts were able to identify the culprit. Victims were believed to have come into contact with this organism through breathing the virus-laden dust in rodent-infested homes. Within hours, victims showed serious symptoms as their lungs filled with fluid; they subsequently experienced respiratory collapse and died. Today, cases of hantavirus have been noted in more than 20 states, and vaccines are being developed to counteract it.

70 ***Bioterrorism: The New Global Threat***   The idea of using infectious microorganisms as weapons is not new. In fact, in the English wars with Native Americans, blankets impregnated with scabs from patients with smallpox were traded to Native Americans in hopes of causing disease. The threat of deliberate spreading of deadly microorganisms is a topic of much discussion among today's world leaders, particularly after the instances of anthrax delivered via the mail following the September 11, 2001, terrorist attacks.

Section Review 2

Directions.

1. On a separate sheet of paper, write a brief summary of the main points of the sections you have just read.

2. Mark each of the following statements True (T), False (F), or Can't Tell (CT). Mark the statement Can't Tell if it cannot be determined to be either true or false based on the material in the passage. Refer to the passage as necessary to verify your answer.

_____ 1. T-cells are a more important part of the body's defense against bacterial invasion than B-cells.

_____ 2. Fever is a reaction to pathogens that actually destroys some germs.

_____ 3. It is more important to immunize children against rubella than the measles, because rubella is generally a longer-lasting and more serious illness.

_____ 4. Scientists have not yet verified the link between mad cow disease and NvCJD.

_____ 5. Up to now, incidents of hantavirus in the United States have been restricted to
the southwestern states.

Directions.   Write the letter of the best answer in the space provided.

_____ 1. All of the following are part of the body's defense mechanisms *except*
  a. fever.
  b. pain.
  c. enzymes.
  d. antigens.

_____ 2. The cells that restore normalcy to immune system functioning after disease are
  a. suppressor T's.
  b. helper T's.
  c. killer T's.
  d. B-lymphocytes.

_____ 3. All of the following trends were cited as concerns in WHO's 2002 *World Health
Report except*
  a. increasing birthrates.
  b. population aging.
  c. pollution.
  d. weakening health care systems.

_____ 4. The author states that Ebola HF is
  a. a greater worldwide threat than dengue.
  b. always fatal.
  c. native to the African continent.
  d. transmitted primarily by airborne pathogens.

_____ 5. Eating beef that hasn't been fully cooked is a way to become infected with
  a. mad cow disease.
  b. *E-coli* 0157:H7.
  c. cryptosporidium.
  d. hantavirus.

Sexually Transmitted Infections

Sexually transmitted infections (STIs) have been with human beings since earli-   71
est recorded history. Today, there are more than 20 known types of STIs. Once referred to as *venereal diseases* and then as *sexually transmitted diseases,* the current

> **Sexually transmitted infections (STIs)**   Infectious diseases transmitted
> via some form of intimate, usually sexual, contact.

Men and Women

- Sore bumps or blisters near sex organs or mouth
- Burning or pain when urinating
- Swelling or redness in throat
- Fever, chills, aches
- Swelling of lymph nodes near genitals or swelling of genitals
- Feeling the need to urinate frequently

Men Only

- A drip or drainage from penis

Women Only

- Vaginal discharge or odor from the vagina
- Pain in the lower pelvis or deep in the vagina during sex
- Burning or itching around the vagina
- Bleeding from the vagina at times other than the regular menstrual periods

Figure 7.2
Signs or Symptoms of an STI

terminology is more reflective of the number and types of these communicable diseases. More virulent strains and more antibiotic-resistant forms spell trouble for at-risk populations in the days ahead.

72   A report issued by the CDC in 2000 indicated that there were 16.2 million new occurrences of STIs in 1999, an increase of more than 3.5 million since 1988. Although exact numbers are not available for each STI, the number of cases did increase for several diseases in 2001 after years of decline. Syphilis was among those showing the greatest increase. According to Felicia Stewart of the Kaiser Family Health Foundation, "[T]here is no indication that STIs are coming rapidly under control. . . . In fact, people vastly underestimate risks and fail to take precautions. A . . . Kaiser survey found that just 14% of men and 8% of women felt at risk for STIs, even though at least one third will get one."

73   Early symptoms of an STI are often mild (Figure 7.2). Left untreated, some of these infections can have grave consequences, such as sterility, blindness, central nervous system destruction, disfigurement, and even death. Infants born to mothers carrying the organisms for these infections are at risk for a variety of health problems. As with many communicable diseases, much of the pain, suffering, and anguish associated with STIs can be eliminated through education, responsible action, simple preventive strategies, and prompt treatment.

Possible Causes: Why Me?

74 Several reasons have been proposed to explain the present high rates of STIs. The first relates to the moral and social stigma associated with these infections. Shame and embarrassment often keep infected people from seeking treatment. Unfortunately, they usually continue to be sexually active, thereby infecting unsuspecting

partners. People who are uncomfortable discussing sexual issues may also be less likely to use and ask their partners to use condoms to protect against STIs and pregnancy.

Another reason proposed for the STI epidemic is our culture's casual attitude   75
about sex. Bombarded by media hype that glamorizes easy sex, many people take sexual partners without considering the consequences. Others are pressured into sexual relationships they don't really want. Generally, the more sexual partners a person has, the greater the risk for contracting an STI. Evaluate your own attitude about STIs by completing the Assess Yourself box on page 300.

Ignorance—about the infections, their symptoms, and the fact that someone   76
can be asymptomatic (symptom-free) but still infected—is also a factor. A person who is infected but asymptomatic can unknowingly spread an STI to an unsuspecting partner, who may, in turn, ignore or misinterpret any symptoms. By the time either partner seeks medical help, he or she may have infected several others.

Modes of Transmission

STIs are generally spread through some form of intimate sexual contact. Sexual in-   77
tercourse, oral–genital contact, hand–genital contact, and anal intercourse are the most common modes of transmission. More rarely, pathogens for STIs are transmitted from mouth to mouth or through contact with fluids from body sores. Although each STI is a different infection caused by a different pathogen, all STI pathogens prefer dark, moist places, especially the mucous membranes lining the reproductive organs. Most of them are susceptible to light, excess heat, cold, and dryness, and many die quickly on exposure to air. (A toilet seat is not a likely breeding ground for most bacterial or viral STIs!) Although most STIs are passed on by sexual contact, other kinds of close contact, such as sleeping on sheets used by someone who has pubic lice, may also infect you. Like other communicable infections, STIs have both pathogen-specific incubation periods and periods of time during which transmission is most likely, called periods of communicability.

Chlamydia

Chlamydia, a disease that often presents no symptoms, tops the list of the most   78
commonly reported infections in the United States. Chlamydia infects about 800,000 people annually in the United States, the majority of them women. Public health officials believe that the actual number of cases is probably closer to 3 or 4 million because these figures represent only those cases reported. College students account for more than 10 percent of infections, and these numbers seem to be increasing yearly.

The name of the disease is derived from the Greek verb *chlamys,* meaning   79
"to cloak," because, unlike most bacteria, *Chlamydia* bacteria can live and grow only inside other cells. Although many people classify chlamydia as either *nonspecific* or *nongonococcal urethritis (NGU),* a person may have NGU without having the organism for chlamydia.

In males, early symptoms may include painful and difficult urination, fre-   80
quent urination, and a watery, puslike discharge from the penis. Symptoms in females may include a yellowish discharge, spotting between periods, and occasional spotting after intercourse. However, many chlamydia victims display no symptoms and therefore do not seek help until the disease has done secondary damage. Females are especially likely to be asymptomatic; more than 70 percent do not realize they have the disease until secondary damage occurs.

Chlamydia   Bacterially caused STI of the urogenital tract.

81   The secondary damage resulting from chlamydia is serious in both sexes. Men can suffer damage to the prostate gland, seminal vesicles, and bulbourethral glands as well as arthritis-like symptoms and damage to the blood vessels and heart. In women, chlamydia-related infection can injure the cervix or fallopian tubes, which causes sterility, and can damage the inner pelvic structure, which leads to *pelvic inflammatory disease (PID)*. If an infected woman becomes pregnant, she has a high risk for miscarriage and stillbirth. *Chlamydia* may also be responsible for one type of **conjunctivitis,** an eye infection that affects not only adults but also infants, who can contract the disease from an infected mother during delivery. Untreated conjunctivitis can cause blindness. If detected early, chlamydia is easily treatable with antibiotics.

> *What Do You Think?*
> *Why do you think that even though many college students have heard about the risks of STDs and HIV disease, they remain apathetic, fail to use condoms, and in general, act irresponsibly? • What actions do you think could be taken to make you and your friends engage in self-protecting behaviors?*

Pelvic Inflammatory Disease

82 **Pelvic inflammatory disease (PID)** is a term used to describe a number of infections of the uterus, fallopian tubes, and ovaries. Although PID often results from an untreated STI, especially chlamydia or gonorrhea, it is not actually an STI. Several nonsexual factors increase the risk of PID, particularly excessive vaginal douching, cigarette smoking, and substance abuse.

83   In the United States, PID affects 11 percent of women of reproductive age. Approximately 1 million women experience PID each year, and 20 percent require hospitalization for treatment. Symptoms vary but generally include acute inflammation of the pelvic cavity, severe pain in the lower abdomen, menstrual irregularities, fever, nausea, painful intercourse, tubal pregnancies, and severe depression. Major consequences of untreated PID are infertility, ectopic pregnancy, chronic pelvic pain, and recurrent upper genital infections. Risk factors include young age at first sexual intercourse, multiple sex partners, high frequency of sexual intercourse, and change of sexual partners within the past 30 days. Regular gynecological examinations and early treatment for STI symptoms reduce risk.

Gonorrhea

84 One of the most common STIs in the United States, **gonorrhea** is surpassed only by chlamydia in number of cases. The Institute of Medicine estimates that there are more than 800,000 cases per year and that large numbers go unreported.

Conjunctivitis   Serious inflammation of the eye caused by any number of pathogens or irritants; can be caused by STDs such as chlamydia.

Pelvic inflammatory disease (PID)   Term used to describe various infections of the female reproductive tract.

Gonorrhea   Second most common STD in the United States; if untreated, may cause sterility.

ASSESS YOURSELF

Sexually Transmitted Infections: Attitude and Belief Scale

The following quiz will help you evaluate whether your beliefs and attitudes about STIs lead you to take risks that increase your risk of infection.

DIRECTIONS

Indicate that you believe the following items are true or false by circling the T or the F. Then consult the answer key that follows.

1. You can usually tell whether someone is infected with an STI, especially HIV infection.   T   F

2. Chances are that if you haven't caught an STI by now, you probably have a natural immunity and won't get infected in the future.   T   F

3. A person who is successfully treated for an STI needn't worry about getting it again.   T   F

4. So long as you keep yourself fit and healthy, you needn't worry about STIs.   T   F

5. The best way for sexually active people to protect themselves from STIs is to practice safer sex.   T   F

6. The only way to catch an STI is to have sex with someone who has one.   T   F

7. Talking about STIs with a partner is so embarrassing that it's better not to raise the subject and instead hope the other person will.   T   F

8. STIs are mostly a problem for people who have numerous sex partners.   T   F

9. You don't need to worry about contracting an STI as long as you wash yourself thoroughly with soap and hot water immediately after sex.   T   F

10. You don't need to worry about contracting AIDS if no one you know has ever come down with it.   T   F

11. When it comes to STIs, it's all in the cards. Either you're lucky or you're not.   T   F

12. The time to worry about STIs is when you come down with one.   T   F

13. As long as you avoid risky sexual practices, such as anal intercourse, you're pretty safe from STIs.   T   F

14. The time to talk about safer sex is before any sexual contact occurs.   T   F

15. A person needn't be concerned about an STI if the symptoms clear up on their own in a few weeks.   T   F

INTERPRETING YOUR SCORE

First, add up the number of items you got right. The higher your score, the lower your risk. The lower your score, the greater your risk. A score of 13 correct or better may indicate that your attitudes toward STIs would probably decrease your risk of contracting them. Yet, even one wrong response on this test may in-

ASSESS YOURSELF (continued)

crease your risk of contracting an STI. You should also recognize that attitudes have little effect on behavior unless they are carried into actions. Knowledge alone isn't sufficient to protect yourself from STIs. You need to ask yourself how you are going to put knowledge into action by changing your behavior to reduce your chances of contracting an STI.

ANSWER KEY

1. False. While some STIs have telltale signs, such as the appearance of sores or blisters on the genitals or disagreeable genital odors, others do not. Several STIs, such as chlamydia, gonorrhea (especially in women), internal genital warts, and even HIV infection in its early stages, cause few if any obvious signs or symptoms. You often cannot tell whether your partner is infected with an STI. Many of the nicest-looking and best-groomed people carry STIs, often unknowingly. The only way to know whether a person is infected with HIV is by means of an HIV-antibody test.

2. False. If you practice unprotected sex and have not contracted an STI to this point, count your blessings. The thing about good luck is that it eventually runs out.

3. False. Sorry. Successful treatment does not render immunity against reinfection. You still need to take precautions to avoid reinfection, even if you have had an STI in the past and were successfully treated. If you answered true to this item, you're not alone. About one in five college students polled in a recent survey of more than 5,500 college students across Canada believed that a person who gets an STI cannot get it again.

4. False. Even people in prime physical condition can be felled by the tiniest of microbes that cause STIs. Physical fitness is no protection against these microscopic invaders.

5. True. If you are sexually active, practicing safer sex is the best protection against contracting an STI.

6. False. STIs can also be transmitted through non-sexual means, such as by sharing contaminated needles or, in some cases, through contact with disease-causing organisms on towels and bedsheets or even toilet seats.

7. False. Because of the social stigma attached to STIs, it's understandable that you may feel embarrassed about raising the subject with your partner.

But don't let embarrassment prevent you from taking steps to protect your own and your partner's welfare.

8. False. It stands to reason that people who are sexually active with numerous partners stand a greater chance that one of their sexual partners will carry an STI. Nevertheless, all it takes is one infected partner to pass along an STI to you, even if he or she is the only partner you've had, or even if the two of you had sex only once. STIs are a potential problem for anyone who is sexually active.

9. False. While washing your genitals immediately after sex may have some limited protective value, it is no substitute for practicing safer sex.

10. False. You can never know whether you may be the first among your friends and acquaintances to become infected. Moreover, symptoms of HIV infection may not appear for years after initial infection with the virus, so you may have sexual contacts with people who are infected but don't know it and who are capable of passing along the virus to you. You, in turn, may then pass it along to others, whether or not you are aware of any symptoms.

11. False. Nonsense. While luck may play a part in determining whether you have a sexual contact with an infected partner, you can significantly reduce your risk of contracting an STI.

12. False. The time to start thinking about STIs (thinking helps, but worrying only makes you more anxious than you need be) is now, not after you have contracted an infection. Some STIs, like herpes and AIDS, cannot be cured. The only real protection you have against them is prevention.

13. False. Any sexual contact between the genitals, or between the genitals and the anus, or between the mouth and genitals, is risky if one of the partners is infected with an STI.

14. True. Unfortunately, too many couples wait until they have commenced sexual relations to have "a talk."

15. False. Several STIs, notably syphilis, HIV infection, and herpes, may produce initial symptoms that clear up in a few weeks. But while the early symptoms may subside, the infection is still at work within the body and requires medical attention. Also, as noted previously, the infected person is capable of passing along the infection to others, regardless of whether noticeable symptoms were ever present.

Source: Jeffrey S. Nevid with Fern Gotfried, *Choices: Sex in the Age of STDs* (Boston: Allyn & Bacon, 1995), 10–13. © Copyright 1995 by Allyn and Bacon. Reprinted by permission.

Health economists estimate that the annual cost of gonorrhea and its complications is more than $1.1 billion. Caused by the bacterial pathogen *Neisseria gonorrhoeae,* this infection primarily infects the linings of the urethra, genital tract, pharynx, and rectum. It may spread to the eyes or other body regions via the hands or body fluids, typically during vaginal, oral, or anal sex. Most victims are males between the ages of 20 and 24; sexually active females between the ages of 15 and 19 are also at high risk.

In males, a typical symptom is a white milky discharge from the penis accompanied by painful, burning urination two to nine days after contact. This is usually enough to send most men to the physician for treatment. However, about 20 percent of all males with gonorrhea are asymptomatic. 85

In females, the situation is just the opposite: only 20 percent experience any discharge, and few develop a burning sensation upon urinating until much later in the course of the infection (if ever). The organism can remain in the woman's vagina, cervix, uterus, or fallopian tubes for long periods with no apparent symptoms other than an occasional slight fever. Thus, a woman can be unaware that she has been infected and is infecting her sexual partners. 86

If the infection is detected early, antibiotic treatment is generally effective within a short period of time. If the infection goes undetected in a woman, it can spread throughout the genital–urinary tract to the fallopian tubes and ovaries, thus causing sterility or, at the very least, severe inflammation and PID. The bacteria can also spread up the reproductive tract or, more rarely, can spread through the blood and infect the joints, heart valves, or brain. If an infected woman becomes pregnant, the infection can cause conjunctivitis in her infant. To prevent this, physicians routinely administer silver nitrate or penicillin preparations to the eyes of newborn babies. 87

Untreated gonorrhea may spread to the prostate, testicles, urinary tract, kidney, and bladder. Blockage of the vasa deferentia due to scar tissue may cause sterility. In some cases, the penis develops a painful curvature during erection. 88

Syphilis

Syphilis is also caused by a bacterial organism, the *spirochete* known as *Treponema pallidum.* Because it is extremely delicate and dies readily upon exposure to air, dryness, or cold, the organism is generally transferred only through direct sexual contact. Typically, this means contact between sexual organs during intercourse, but in rare instances, the organism enters the body through a break in the skin, through deep kissing, or through some other transmission of body fluids. 89

Syphilis is called the "great imitator" because its symptoms resemble those of several other infections. Left untreated, syphilis generally progresses through distinct stages. It should be noted, however, that some people experience no symptoms at all. 90

Primary Syphilis   The first stage of syphilis, particularly for males, is often characterized by the development of a **chancre** (pronounced "shank-er"), a sore at the site of initial infection. This dime-sized chancre is painless, but it oozes with bacteria, ready to infect an unsuspecting partner. Usually the chancre appears three to four weeks after contact. 91

Syphilis   One of the most widespread STDs; characterized by distinct phases and potentially serious results.

Chancre   Sore often found at the site of syphilis infection.

92   In males, the site of the chancre tends to be the penis or scrotum because this is the site where the organism first enters the body. But if the infection was contracted through oral sex, the sore can appear in the mouth, throat, or other "first contact" area. In females, the site of infection is often internal, on the vaginal wall or high on the cervix. Because the chancre is not readily apparent, the likelihood of detection is not great. In both males and females, the chancre will completely disappear in three to six weeks.

93   **Secondary Syphilis**   From a month to a year after the chancre disappears, secondary symptoms may appear, including a rash or white patches on the skin or on the mucous membranes of the mouth, throat, or genitals. Hair loss may occur, lymph nodes may enlarge, and the victim may develop a slight fever or a headache. In rare cases, sores develop around the mouth or genitals. As during the active chancre phase, these sores contain infectious bacteria, and contact with them can spread the infection. In a few cases, there may be arthritic pain in the joints. Because symptoms vary so much and appear so much later than the sexual contact that caused them, the victim seldom connects the two. The infection thus often goes undetected even at this second stage. Symptoms may persist for a few weeks or months and then disappear, thus leaving the victim thinking that all is well.

94   **Latent Syphilis**   After the secondary stage, the syphilis spirochetes begin to invade body organs. Symptoms, including infectious lesions, may reappear periodically for two to four years after the secondary period. After this period, the infection is rarely transmitted to others, except during pregnancy, when it can be passed to the fetus. The child will then be born with *congenital syphilis,* which can cause death or severe birth defects such as blindness, deafness, or disfigurement. Because in most cases the fetus does not become infected until after the first trimester, treatment of the mother during this period will usually prevent infection of the fetus.

95   In some instances, a child born to an infected mother will show no apparent signs of the infection at birth but within several weeks will develop body rashes, a runny nose, and symptoms of paralysis. Congenital syphilis is usually detected before it progresses much further. But sometimes the child's immune system will ward off the invading organism, and further symptoms may not surface until the teenage years. Fortunately, most states protect against congenital syphilis by requiring prospective marriage partners to be tested for syphilis prior to obtaining a marriage license.

96   If untreated, latent syphilis will progress and infect more and more organs.

97   **Late Syphilis**   Years after syphilis has entered the body, its effects become all too evident. Late-stage syphilis indications include heart damage, central nervous system damage, blindness, deafness, paralysis, premature senility, and, ultimately, insanity.

98   **Treatment for Syphilis**   Because the organism is bacterial, it is treated with antibiotics. The major obstacle to treatment is misdiagnosis of this "imitator" infection.

Pubic Lice

99   **Pubic lice,** often called "crabs," are small parasites that are usually transmitted during sexual contact. More annoying than dangerous, they move easily from

---

Pubic lice   Parasites that can inhabit various body areas, especially the genitals; also called "crabs."

partner to partner during sex. They have an affinity for pubic hair and attach them-selves to the base of these hairs, where they deposit their eggs (nits). One to two weeks later, these nits develop into adults that lay eggs and migrate to other body parts, thus perpetuating the cycle.

Treatment includes washing clothing, furniture, and linens that may harbor   100 the eggs. It usually takes two to three weeks to kill all larval forms. Although sex-ual contact is the most common mode of transmission, you can "catch" pubic lice from lying on sheets that an infected person has slept on. Sleeping in hotel and dormitory rooms in which sheets are not washed regularly, or sitting on toilet seats where the nits or larvae have been dropped and lie in wait for a new carrier, will put you at risk.

Genital HPV

Genital warts (also known as venereal warts or condylomas) are caused by a small   101 group of viruses known as **human papillomaviruses (HPVs).** A person becomes in-fected when an HPV penetrates the skin and mucous membranes of the genitals or anus through sexual contact. HPV is among the most common forms of STI. The virus appears to be relatively easy to catch. The typical incubation period is from six to eight weeks after contact. Many people have no symptoms, particularly if the warts are located inside the reproductive tract. Others may develop a series of itchy bumps on the genitals that range in size from small pinheads to large cauli-flower-like growths. On dry skin (such as the shaft of the penis), the warts are com-monly small, hard, and yellowish-gray, resembling warts that appear on other parts of the body. Genital warts are of two different types: (1) *full-blown genital warts* that are noticeable as tiny bumps or growths, and (2) the much more prevalent *flat warts* that are not usually visible to the naked eye.

Risks and Treatments of Genital Warts   Many genital warts eventually disappear   102 on their own. Others grow and generate unsightly flaps of irregular flesh on the ex-ternal genitalia. If they grow large enough to obstruct urinary flow or become irri-tated by clothing or sexual intercourse, they can cause significant problems.

The greatest threat from genital warts lies in the apparent relationship be-   103 tween them and a tendency for *dysplasia,* or changes in cells that may lead to a precancerous condition. It is known that within five years after infection, 30 per-cent of all HPV cases progress to the precancerous stage. If precancerous cases are left untreated, 70 percent of them will result in actual cancer. New research also implicates HPV as a possible risk factor for coronary artery disease, possibly be-cause it causes an inflammatory response in artery walls. In addition, venereal warts pose a threat to a pregnant woman's fetus if it is exposed to the virus during birth. Cesarean deliveries may be considered in serious cases.

Genital warts can be treated with topical medications or removed by being   104 frozen with liquid nitrogen. Large warts may require surgical removal.

Candidiasis (Moniliasis)

Unlike many STIs, which are caused by pathogens that come from outside the   105 body, the yeastlike fungus caused by the *Candida albicans* organism normally in-

---

Genital warts   Warts that appear in the genital area or the anus; caused by the human papillomaviruses (HPVs).

Human papillomaviruses (HPV)   A small group of viruses that cause genital warts.

habits the vaginal tract in most women. Only under certain conditions, in which the normal chemical balance of the vagina is disturbed, will these organisms multiply and cause problems.

106   The likelihood of **candidiasis** (also known as moniliasis or a *yeast infection*) increases if a woman has diabetes; if her immune system is overtaxed or malfunctioning; if she is taking birth control pills, other hormones, or broad-spectrum antibiotics; or if she uses douches or spermicides. All of these factors decrease the acidity of the vagina and create favorable conditions for a yeastlike infection.

107   Symptoms of candidiasis include severe itching and burning of the vagina and vulva, swelling of the vulva, and a white, cheesy vaginal discharge. These symptoms are collectively called **vaginitis,** or inflammation of the vagina. When this microbe infects the mouth, whitish patches form, and the condition is referred to as *thrush*. This monilial infection also occurs in males and is easily transmitted between sexual partners.

108   Candidiasis strikes at least half a million American women a year. Antifungal drugs applied on the surface or by suppository usually cure it in just a few days. For approximately one out of ten women, however, nothing seems to work, and the infection returns again and again. Symptoms can be aggravated by contact of the vagina with soaps, douches, perfumed toilet paper, chlorinated water, and spermicides. Tight-fitting jeans and pantyhose can provide the combination of moisture and irritant the organism thrives on.

Trichomoniasis

109   Unlike many STIs, **trichomoniasis** is caused by a protozoan. Although as many as half of the men and women in the United States may carry this organism, most remain free of symptoms until their bodily defenses are weakened. Both men and women may transmit the infection, but women are the more likely candidates for infection. Symptoms include a foamy, yellowish, unpleasant-smelling discharge accompanied by a burning sensation, itching, and painful urination. These symptoms are most likely to occur during or shortly after menstruation, but they can appear at any time or be absent altogether. Although usually transmitted by sexual contact, the "trich" organism can also be spread by toilet seats, wet towels, or other items that have discharged fluids on them. You can also contract trichomoniasis by sitting naked on the locker room bench at your local gym. Treatment includes oral metronidazole, usually given to both sexual partners to avoid the possible "ping-pong" effect of repeated cross-infection so typical of STIs.

General Urinary Tract Infections

110   Although *general urinary tract infections (UTIs)* can be caused by various factors, some forms are sexually transmitted. Anytime invading organisms enter the genital area, they can travel up the urethra and enter the bladder. Similarly, organisms normally living in the rectum, urethra, or bladder may travel to the sexual organs and eventually be transmitted to another person.

111   You can also get a UTI through autoinoculation, often during the simple task of wiping yourself after defecating. Wiping from the anus forward can transmit

Candidiasis   Yeastlike fungal disease often transmitted sexually.

Vaginitis   Set of symptoms characterized by vaginal itching, swelling, and burning.

Trichomoniasis   Protozoan infection characterized by foamy, yellowish discharge and unpleasant odor.

organisms found in feces to the vaginal opening or the urethra. Contact between the hands and the urethra and between the urethra and other objects are also common means of autoinoculation. Women, with their shorter urethras, are more likely to contract UTIs. Hand washing with soap and water prior to sexual intimacy, foreplay, and so on, is recommended. Treatment depends on the nature and type of pathogen.

Herpes

Herpes is a general term for a family of infections characterized by sores or eruptions on the skin. Herpes infections range from mildly uncomfortable to extremely serious. **Genital herpes** is an infection caused by the herpes simplex virus (HSV).   112

There are two types of HSV. Historically, the herpes simplex type 2 virus was considered the primary culprit in genital herpes, and herpes simplex virus type 1 was thought to affect the area of the lips and other body areas. We now know that both type 1 and type 2 can infect any area of the body and produce lesions (sores) in and around the vaginal area, on the penis, around the anal opening, on the buttocks or thighs, and occasionally on other parts of the body. HSV remains in certain nerve cells for life and can flare up, or cause symptoms, when the body's ability to maintain itself is weakened.

The *prodromal* (precursor) phase of the infection is characterized by a burning sensation and redness at the site of infection. During this time, prescription medicines will often keep the disease from spreading. However, this phase of the disease is quickly followed by the second phase, in which a blister filled with a clear fluid containing the virus forms. If you pick at this blister or otherwise touch the site and spread this fluid with fingers, lipstick, lip balm, or other products, you can autoinoculate other body parts. Particularly dangerous is the possibility of spreading the infection to your eyes, for a herpes lesion on the eye can cause blindness.   113

Over a period of days, the unsightly blister will dry up and disappear, and the virus will travel to the base of an affected nerve supplying the area and become dormant. Only when the victim becomes overly stressed, when diet and sleep are inadequate, when the immune system is overworked, or when excessive exposure to sunlight or other stressors occurs will the virus become reactivated (at the same site every time) and begin the blistering cycle all over again. These sores cast off (shed) viruses that can be highly infectious. However, it is important to note that a herpes site can shed the virus even when no overt sore is present, particularly during the prodromal stages (the interval between the earliest symptoms and blistering). People may get genital herpes by having sexual contact with others who don't know they are infected or who are having outbreaks of herpes without any sores. A person with genital herpes can also infect a sexual partner during oral sex. The virus is spread only rarely, if at all, by touching objects such as a toilet seat or hot tub seat.   114

Genital herpes is especially serious in pregnant women because the baby could be infected as it passes through the vagina during birth. Many physicians recommend cesarean deliveries for infected women. Additionally, women who have a history of genital herpes appear to have a greater risk of cervical cancer.   115

Although there is no cure for herpes at present, certain drugs can reduce symptoms. Unfortunately, they seem to work only if the infection is confirmed during the first few hours after contact. As you may guess, this is rather rare. The effectiveness of other treatments, such as L-lysine, is largely unsubstantiated. Newer over-the-counter medications seem to be moderately effective in reducing the severity of symptoms. Although lip balms and cold-sore medications may pro-   116

> **Genital herpes**   STI caused by the herpes simplex virus.

vide temporary relief, remember that rubbing anything on a herpes blister can spread herpes-laden fluids to other body parts.

117 ***Preventing Herpes***   You can take precautions to reduce your risk of herpes.

- Avoid any form of kissing if you notice a sore or blister on your partner's mouth. Kiss no one, not even a peck on the cheek, if you know that you have a herpes lesion. Allow time after the sores go away before you start kissing again.
- Be extremely cautious if you have casual sexual affairs. Not every partner will feel obligated to tell you that he or she has a problem. It's up to you to protect yourself.
- Wash your hands immediately with soap and water after any form of sexual contact.
- If you have questionable sores or lesions, seek medical help at once. Do not be afraid to name your contacts.
- If you have herpes, be responsible in your sexual contacts with others. If you have any suspicious lesions that might put your partner at risk, say so. Find an appropriate time and place, and hold a candid discussion.
- Reduce your risk of herpes outbreaks by avoiding excessive stress, sunlight, or whatever else appears to trigger an episode.

Section Review 3

Directions.

1. On a separate sheet of paper, write a brief summary of the main points of the sections you have just read.

2. Mark each of the following statements True (T), False (F), or Can't Tell (CT). Mark the statement Can't Tell if it cannot be determined to be either true or false based on the material in the passage. Refer to the passage as necessary to verify your answer.

_____ 1. Syphilis is the most common STD in the United States among white heterosexuals.

_____ 2. Men are more likely to notice symptoms of gonorrhea than women.

_____ 3. The cause of genital warts is currently unknown.

_____ 4. Candidiasis is more common among women in their twenties than women in their thirties.

_____ 5. A woman who has genital herpes is usually advised to have a cesarean delivery to avoid infecting the baby.

Cumulative Review 1 (pages 280–307)

Directions. Write the letter of the best answer in the space provided.

_____ 1. The body's first line of defense against pathogens is
   a. the skin.
   b. mucous membranes.
   c. humoral immunity.
   d. lymphocytes.

_____ 2. Which of the following is not mentioned as a reason for the high rate of STIs?

a. casual sexual relationships

b. embarrassment

c. high divorce rates

d. failure to recognize symptoms

_____ 3. The pathogens that cause STIs prefer environments that are

a. dark and dry.

b. dark and moist.

c. cold and moist.

d. hot and dry.

_____ 4. Chlamydia may cause *all* of the following *except*

a. heart damage.

b. deafness.

c. miscarriage.

d. conjunctivitis.

_____ 5. Which of the following is associated with late-stage syphilis?

a. the formation of a chancre

b. hair loss

c. arthritic pain

d. insanity

Directions. Answer each question in complete sentences, without copying word-for-word from the passage.

1. What causes the common cold? What is the best treatment for the common cold?

_____

_____

_____

2. What is *immune deficiency syndrome?*

_____

_____

_____

3. What is PID? How is PID different from STIs?

_____

_____

_____

4. How are pubic lice transmitted?

_____

_____

_____

5. Briefly explain the primary stages of the herpes cycle.

_____

_____

_____

Vocabulary Exercise 1

Directions. Choose the meaning for the underlined word that best fits the context. You may consult the dictionary as needed.

_____ 1. . . . our immune systems are remarkably
            <u>adept</u> at protecting us. [Paragraph 2]
            a. experienced
            b. skillful
            c. weak
            d. organized

_____ 2. . . . a weakening of public health
            <u>infrastructure</u> . . . [Paragraph 22]
            a. the basic resources needed for mainte-
                nance and growth
            b. system of services
            c. a profession and its members
            d. knowledge and its application

_____ 3. Tuberculosis is caused by bacterial <u>infiltration</u>
            of the respiratory system . . . [Paragraph 24]
            a. destruction
            b. invasion
            c. control
            d. elimination

_____ 4. Incapable of carrying out the normal cell
            functions of respiration and <u>metabolism</u> . . .
            [Paragraph 27]
            a. digestion
            b. division
            c. conversion of energy and material
            d. sensitivity to external stimuli

_____ 5. Although these pathogens are <u>prevalent</u> in
            nonindustrialized countries . . . [Paragraph 41]
            a. native
            b. rare
            c. widespread
            d. causing problems

_____ 6. . . . which create an <u>inhospitable</u> environment
            for many pathogens. [Paragraph 45]
            a. unwelcome; unfavorable
            b. receptive
            c. unfamiliar
            d. inaccessible; unable to be entered

_____ 7. . . . any organism . . . faces a <u>formidable</u> spe-
            cialized network of defenses . . . [Paragraph 46]
            a. weakened
            b. complex
            c. difficult to understand
            d. powerful

_____ 8. Fever is frequently caused by toxins <u>secreted</u>
            by pathogens . . . [Paragraph 54]
            a. hidden
            b. protected
            c. produced
            d. destroyed

_____ 9. . . . an army of microbes that is so diverse, virulent, and <u>insidious</u> . . . **[Paragraph 59]**
   a. varied
   b. treacherous
   c. powerful
   d. plentiful; numerous

_____ 10. The first relates to the moral and social
<u>stigma</u> associated with these infections.
[Paragraph 74]
   a. obligation
   b. concern
   c. shame
   d. problem

HIV/AIDS

Acquired immune deficiency syndrome (AIDS) is a significant global health   118
threat. Since 1981, when AIDS was first recognized, more than 60 million people
in the world have become infected with **human immunodeficiency virus (HIV),**
the virus that causes AIDS. Today, more than 42 million people are estimated to be
living with HIV or AIDS, and an estimated 5 million new cases were diagnosed
worldwide in 2002. Women are becoming increasingly affected by the virus and
account for approximately 50 percent of cases. In the United States, as of 2002,
more than 886,575 men, women, and children with AIDS have been reported to
the CDC, and at least 501,669 have died. The CDC estimates that at least 40,000
new infections occur each year in the United States.

A Shifting Epidemic

Under old definitions, people with HIV were diagnosed as having AIDS only when   119
they developed blood infections, the cancer known as Kaposi's sarcoma, or any of
21 other indicator diseases, most of which were common in males. The CDC has
expanded the indicator list to include pulmonary tuberculosis, recurrent pneumonia, and invasive cervical cancer. Perhaps the most significant new indicator is a
drop in the level of the body's master immune cells, called CD4s, to 200 per cubic
millimeter (one-fifth the level in a healthy person).

AIDS cases have been reported state by state throughout the United States   120
since the early 1980s as a means of tracking the disease. While the numbers of
actual reported cases have always been suspect, improved reporting and surveillance methods have helped increase accuracy. Today, the CDC recommends that
all states report HIV infections as well as AIDS. Because of medical advances in
treatment and increasing numbers of HIV-infected persons who do not progress to
AIDS, it is believed that AIDS incidence statistics may not provide a true picture of
the epidemic, the long-term costs of treating HIV-infected individuals, and other
key information. HIV incidence data also provide a better picture of infection
trends. Currently, most states mandate that those who test positive for the HIV
antibody be reported.

Acquired immune deficiency syndrome (AIDS)   Extremely virulent
sexually transmitted disease that renders the immune system inoperative.

Human immunodeficiency virus (HIV)   The slow-acting virus that
causes AIDS.

What do you think?

Do you favor mandatory reporting of HIV and AIDS cases? • If you knew that your name and vital statistics would be "on file" if you tested positive for HIV, would you be less likely to take the HIV test? • On the other hand, do people who carry this contagious fatal disease have a responsibility to inform the general public and the health professionals who will provide their care? Explain your answer.

Women and AIDS

121 HIV is an equal-opportunity pathogen that can attack anyone who engages in high-risk behaviors. This is true regardless of race, gender, sexual orientation, or socio-economic status. Consider the following facts:

- Women are 4 to 10 times more likely than men to contract HIV through unprotected sexual intercourse with an infected partner.
- By 2002, women accounted for more than 50 percent of all AIDS cases in the United States.
- HIV/AIDS due to heterosexual sexual transmission is increasing faster in rural America than in any other part of the country. Women most at risk are ethnic minorities and the economically disadvantaged. Among sexually active heterosexual teenagers, college students, and health care workers, nearly 60 percent of HIV cases are women.
- Most women with AIDS were infected through heterosexual exposure to HIV, followed by injection drug use (sharing needles).
- Women of color are disproportionately affected by HIV; African American and Hispanic women together account for 76 percent of AIDS cases among women in the United States, though they comprise less than 25 percent of all U.S. women.
- Of all AIDS cases among women, 61 percent were reported from five states: New York (26 percent), Florida (13 percent), New Jersey (10 percent), California (7 percent), and Texas (5 percent).
- AIDS is the leading cause of death among African American women age 25 to 44, and the fourth leading cause of death among all American women in this age group.
- AIDS is one of the top ten causes of death for people age 15 to 64 in the United States.

Compounding the problems are serious deficiencies in our health and social service systems, including inadequate treatment for women addicts and lack of access to child care, health care, and social services for families headed by single women. Women with HIV/AIDS are of special interest because they are the major source of infection in infants. Virtually all new HIV infections among children in the United States are attributable to perinatal transmission of HIV.

122   Although contracting HIV is a serious problem for both males and females, women often have an even more difficult time protecting themselves from infection and taking care of themselves once they become ill. Irrefutable evidence indicates that HIV/AIDS disproportionately affects women. This discrepancy can be traced to biological and socioeconomic factors.

123   Biological factors include:

- HIV can enter through mucous membrane surfaces of the genital tract; the vagina has a greater exposed mucous membrane than does the urethra of the penis.
- The vaginal area is more likely to incur micro-tears during sexual intercourse, which facilitates entry of HIV.

- During intercourse, a woman is exposed to more semen than is the male to vaginal fluids.
- Semen is more likely to enter the vagina with force, whereas vaginal fluids do not enter the penis with force.
- Women who have STIs are more likely to be asymptomatic and therefore unaware they have an STI; STIs increase the risk of HIV transmission.

Socioeconomic factors include: 124

- There are more HIV-infected men than HIV-infected women in the United States; thus, it is more likely for a woman to have an HIV-infected male partner.
- Women have been underrepresented in clinical trials for HIV treatment and prevention.
- Many cultural norms place women in subordination to men, especially in developing nations. This reduces women's decision-making power and ability to negotiate safer sex.
- Women are more vulnerable to sexual abuse from their male partners.
- Women are more likely to be economically dependent on men.
- Women may be less likely to seek medical treatment because of lack of money, caregiving burdens, and transportation problems.
- In the United States, HIV-positive women are more likely than HIV-positive men to be younger and less educated.

How HIV Is Transmitted

HIV typically enters one person's body when another person's infected body fluids   125
(semen, vaginal secretions, blood, etc.) gain entry through a breach in body defenses. Mucous membranes of the genital organs and the anus provide the easiest route of entry. If there is a break in the mucous membranes (as can occur during sexual intercourse, particularly anal intercourse), the virus enters and begins to multiply. After initial infection, HIV multiplies rapidly, invading the bloodstream and cerebrospinal fluid. It progressively destroys helper T-lymphocytes, thus weakening the body's resistance to disease. The virus also changes the genetic structure of the cells it attacks. In response to this invasion, the body quickly begins to produce antibodies.

Despite some myths, HIV is not a highly contagious virus. Studies of people   126
living in households with a person with HIV/AIDS have turned up no documented cases of HIV infection due to casual contact. Other investigations provide overwhelming evidence that insect bites do not transmit HIV.

Engaging in High-Risk Behaviors   AIDS is not a disease of gay people or minor-   127
ity groups. If you engage in high-risk behaviors, you increase your risk for the disease. If you do not practice these behaviors, your risk is minimal. Anyone who engages in unprotected sex is at risk, especially sex with a partner who has engaged in other high-risk behaviors. Sex with multiple partners is the greatest threat.

Exchange of Body Fluids   The greatest risk factor is the exchange of HIV-infected   128
body fluids during vaginal and anal intercourse. Substantial research evidence indicates that blood, semen, and vaginal secretions are the major fluids of concern. Most health officials state that saliva is not a high-risk body fluid unless blood is present. But the fact that the virus has been found in isolated samples of saliva does provide a good rationale for using caution when engaging in deep, wet kissing.

Initially, public health officials also included breast milk in the list of high-   129
risk fluids because a few infants apparently contracted HIV while breast-feeding. Subsequent research has indicated that HIV transmission could have been caused by bleeding nipples as well as by actual consumption of breast milk and other fluids. Infection through contact with feces and urine is believed to be highly unlikely though technically possible.

130 ***Receiving a Blood Transfusion Prior to 1985***   A small group of people became infected with HIV after receiving blood transfusions. In 1985, the Red Cross and other blood donation programs implemented a stringent testing program for all donated blood. Today, because of these massive screening efforts, the risk of receiving HIV-infected blood is almost nonexistent.

131 ***Injecting Drugs***   A significant percentage of AIDS cases in the United States are believed to result from sharing or using HIV-contaminated needles and syringes. Though users of illegal drugs are commonly considered the only members of this category, others may also share needles—for example, people with diabetes who inject insulin or athletes who inject steroids. People who share needles and also engage in sexual activities with members of high-risk groups, such as those who exchange sex for drugs, increase their risks dramatically.

132 ***Mother-to-Infant Transmission (Perinatal)***   Approximately one in three of the children who has contracted AIDS received the virus from an infected mother while in the womb or while passing through the vaginal tract during delivery.

Symptoms of HIV Disease

133 A person may go for months or years after infection by HIV before any significant symptoms appear. The incubation time varies greatly from person to person. Children have shorter incubation periods than do adults. Newborns and infants are particularly vulnerable to AIDS because human beings do not become fully immunocompetent (that is, their immune system is not fully developed) until they are 6 to 15 months old. New information suggests that some very young children show the "adult" progression of AIDS.

134 For adults who receive no medical treatment, it takes an average of 8 to 10 years for the virus to cause the slow, degenerative changes in the immune system that are characteristic of AIDS. During this time, the person may experience a large number of opportunistic infections (infections that gain a foothold when the immune system is not functioning effectively). Colds, sore throats, fever, tiredness, nausea, night sweats, and other generally non-life-threatening conditions commonly appear, and are described as pre-AIDS symptoms.

Testing for HIV Antibodies

135 Once antibodies have formed in reaction to HIV, a blood test known as the **ELISA** test may detect their presence. If sufficient antibodies are present, the ELISA test will be positive. When a person who previously tested *negative* (no HIV antibodies present) has a subsequent test that is *positive,* seroconversion is said to have occurred. In such a situation, the person would typically take another ELISA test, followed by a more expensive, precise test known as the **Western blot,** to confirm the presence of HIV antibodies.

136 It should be noted that these tests are not AIDS tests per se. Rather, they detect antibodies for the disease that would indicate the presence of HIV in the person's body. Whether the person will develop AIDS depends to some extent on the strength of the immune system. However, the vast majority of all infected people develop some form of the disease.

ELISA   Blood test that detects presence of antibodies to HIV virus.

Western blot   A test more accurate than the ELISA to confirm presence of HIV antibodies.

As testing for HIV antibodies has been perfected, scientists have explored   137
various ways of making it easier for individuals to be tested. Health officials distinguish between *reported* and *actual* cases of HIV infection because it is believed
that many HIV-positive people avoid being tested. One reason may be fear of
knowing the truth. Another is the fear of discrimination from employers, insurance companies, and medical staff if a positive test becomes known to others.
However, early detection and reporting are important, because immediate treatment for someone in the early stages of HIV disease is critical.

New Hope and Treatments

New drugs have slowed the progression from HIV to AIDS and have prolonged   138
life expectancies for many AIDS patients. While these new therapies offered the
promise of life for many, they may have inadvertently led to increases in risky behaviors. This may have led to a noteworthy rise in cases by 2 percent in 2002. Although the death rate from AIDS has declined each year since 1995, many fear
that we are taking steps backward. Advocates for AIDS patients believe the medications still cost too much money and cause too many side effects. Multidrug treatment for AIDS for one person now exceeds $20,000 per year.

Current treatments combine selected drugs, especially protease inhibitors   139
and reverse transcriptase inhibitors. Protease inhibitors (for example, Amprenavir,
Ritonavir, and Saquinavir) resemble pieces of the protein chain that the HIV protease normally cuts. They block the HIV protease enzyme from cutting the protein
chains needed to produce new viruses. Older AIDS drugs work by preventing the
virus from infecting new cells.

Although protease inhibitors show promise, they have proved difficult to   140
manufacture, and some have failed while others have been successful. Side effects
vary, and getting the right dose is critical for effectiveness. All of the protease
drugs seem to work best in combination with other therapies. These combination
treatments are still quite experimental, and no combination has proved to be absolute for all people as yet. Also, as with other antiviral treatments, resistance to
the drugs can develop. Individuals who already show resistance to AZT may not
be able to use a protease-AZT combination. This can pose a problem for many
people who have been taking the common drugs and then find their options for
combination therapy limited.

Although these drugs provide new hope and longer survival for people living   141
with HIV, we are still a long way from a cure. In addition, the number of people
becoming HIV-infected each year has not declined, which means that we are still
a long way from beating this disease.

Preventing HIV Infection

Although scientists have been searching for an HIV vaccine since 1983, they have   142
had no success so far. The only way to prevent HIV infection is to avoid risky behaviors. HIV infection and AIDS are not uncontrollable conditions. You can reduce
your risk by the choices you make in sexual behaviors and by taking responsibility
for your health and the health of your loved ones. The Skills for Behavior Change
box on page 315 presents ways to reduce your risk for contracting HIV.

Noninfectious Diseases

Typically, when we think of major noninfectious ailments, we think of "killer"   143
diseases such as cancer and heart disease. Clearly, these diseases make up the
major portion of life-threatening diseases—accounting for nearly two-thirds of all
deaths. Yet, although these diseases capture much media attention, other chronic

SKILLS FOR BEHAVIOR CHANGE

Staying Safe in an Unsafe Sexual World

HIV transmission depends on specific behaviors; this is true of other STIs as well. The following will help you protect yourself and reduce your risk.

- Avoid casual sexual partners. Ideally, have sex only if you are in a long-term, mutually monogamous relationship with someone who is equally committed to the relationship and whose HIV status is negative.
- Avoid unprotected sexual activity involving the exchange of blood, semen, or vaginal secretions with people whose present or past behaviors put them at risk for infection. Do not be afraid to ask intimate questions about your partner's sexual past. Remember, whenever you choose to have sexual relations, you expose yourself to your partner's history. Postpone sexual involvement until you are assured that he or she is not infected.
- All sexually active adults who are not in a lifelong monogamous relationship should practice safer sex by using latex condoms. Remember, however, that condoms still do not provide 100% safety.
- Never share injecting needles with anyone for any reason.
- Never share any devices through which the exchange of blood could occur, including needles, razors, tattoo instruments, body-piercing instruments, and any other sharp objects.
- Avoid injury to body tissue during sexual activity. HIV can enter the bloodstream through microscopic tears in anal or vaginal tissues.
- Avoid unprotected oral sex or any sexual activity in which semen, blood, or vaginal secretions could penetrate mucous membranes through breaks in the membrane. Always use a condom or a dental dam during oral sex.
- Avoid using drugs that may dull your senses and affect your ability to make decisions about responsible precautions with potential sex partners.

- Wash your hands before and after sexual encounters. Urinate after sexual relations and, if possible, wash your genitals.
- Although total abstinence is the only absolute means of preventing the sexual transmission of HIV, abstinence can be a difficult choice to make. If you have any doubt about the potential risks of having sex, consider other means of intimacy, at least until you can assure your safety. Try massage, dry kissing, hugging, holding and touching, and masturbation (alone or with a partner).
- Be sure medical professionals take appropriate precautions to prevent potential transmission, including washing their hands and wearing gloves and masks. All equipment used for treatment should be properly sterilized.
- If you are worried about your own HIV status, have yourself tested. Don't risk infecting others inadvertently.
- If you are a woman and HIV-positive, you should take the steps necessary to ensure that you do not become pregnant.
- If you suspect that you may be infected or if you test positive for HIV antibodies, do not donate blood, semen, or body organs.

At no time in your life is it more important to communicate openly than when you are considering an intimate relationship. Ask questions, so you can then make an informed decision about whether to get involved. Remember that you can't tell if someone has an STI. Anyone who has ever had sex with anyone else or has injected drugs is at risk, and they may not even know it. The following will help you to communicate about potential risks.

- Remember that you have a responsibility to your partner to disclose your own status. You also have a responsibility to yourself to stay healthy. Ask about your partner's HIV status. Suggest going through the testing together as a means of sharing something important.
- Be direct, honest, and determined in talking about sex before you become involved. Do not act silly

or evasive. Get to the point, ask clear questions, and do not be put off in receiving a response. A person who does not care enough to talk about sex probably does not care enough to take responsibility for his or her actions.
- Discuss the issues without sounding defensive or accusatory. Develop a personal comfort level with the subject prior to raising the issue with your partner. Be prepared with complete information, and articulate your feelings clearly. Reassure your partner that your reasons for desiring abstinence or safer sex arise from respect and not distrust. Sharing feelings is easier in a calm, suspicion-free environment in which both people feel comfortable.
- Encourage your partner to be honest and to share feelings. This will not happen overnight. If you have never had a serious conversation with this person before you get into an intimate situation, you cannot expect honesty and openness when the lights go out.
- Analyze your own beliefs and values ahead of time. Know where you will draw the line on certain actions, and be very clear with your partner about what you expect. If you believe that using a condom is necessary, make sure you communicate this.
- Decide what you will do if your partner does not agree with you. Anticipate potential objections or excuses, and prepare your responses accordingly.
- Ask about your partner's history. Although it may seem as though you are prying into another person's business, your own health future depends upon knowing basic information about your partner's past sexual practices and use of injectable drugs.
- Discuss the significance of monogamy in your partner's relationships. Ask, "How important is a committed relationship to you?" Decide early how important this relationship is to you and how much you are willing to work at arriving at an acceptable compromise on lifestyle.

conditions can also cause pain, suffering, and disability. Fortunately, most of them can be prevented or their symptoms relieved.

Generally, noninfectious diseases are not transmitted by a pathogen or by any   144
form of personal contact. Lifestyle and personal health habits are often implicated as underlying causes. Healthy changes in lifestyle and public health efforts aimed at research, prevention, and control can minimize the effects of these diseases.

Chronic Lung Disease

Chronic lung diseases pose a serious and significant threat to Americans today. Col-   145
lectively, they have become the fourth leading cause of death, with most sufferers liv-ing with a condition known as chronic **dyspnea,** or chronic breathlessness. Depend-ing on the situation, dyspnea may limit the ability to climb stairs, walk unassisted, or even sleep. Chronic lung disease can result in major disability and lack of function as the lungs fill with mucous, become susceptible to bacterial or viral infections, or cause acute stress on the heart as they struggle to get valuable oxygen. Chronic cough, ex-cessive phlegm, wheezing, and coughing up blood are frequent symptoms. Over time, many of these underlying conditions lead to hospitalization and possible death.

Among the more deadly chronic lung diseases are the **chronic obstructive**   146
pulmonary diseases (COPDs): asthma, emphysema, and chronic bronchitis. Other chronic lung diseases also cause significant health risks, the most common of which are allergy-induced problems and hay fever. Each of these may exacer-bate or contribute to the development of COPD.

Allergy-Induced Respiratory Problems

An **allergy** occurs as a part of the body's attempt to defend itself against a specific   147
antigen or *allergen* by producing specific *antibodies*. When foreign pathogens such as bacteria or viruses invade the body, the body responds by producing antibodies to destroy these invading antigens. Under normal conditions, the production of an-tibodies is a positive element in the body's defense system. However, for unknown reasons, in some people the body overreacts by developing an overly elaborate protective mechanism against relatively harmless substances. The resultant *hyper-sensitivity reaction* to specific allergens or antigens in the environment is fairly common, as anyone who has awakened with a runny nose or itchy eyes will tes-tify. Most commonly, these hypersensitivity, or allergic, responses occur as a reac-tion to environmental antigens such as molds, animal dander (hair and dead skin), pollen, ragweed, or dust. Once excessive antibodies to these antigens are pro-duced, they trigger the release of **histamines,** chemical substances that dilate blood vessels, increase mucous secretions, cause tissues to swell, and produce other allergy-like symptoms, particularly in the respiratory system (Figure 7.3).

Although many people think of allergies as childhood diseases, in reality al-   148
lergies tend to become progressively worse with time and with increased expo-

---

Dyspnea   Chronic breathlessness.

Chronic obstructive pulmonary diseases (COPDs)   A collection of chronic lung diseases including asthma, emphysema, and chronic bronchitis.

Allergy   Hypersensitive reaction to a specific antigen or allergen in the en-vironment in which the body produces excessive antibodies to that antigen or allergen.

Histamines   Chemical substances that dilate blood vessels, increase mu-cous secretions, and produce other symptoms of allergies.

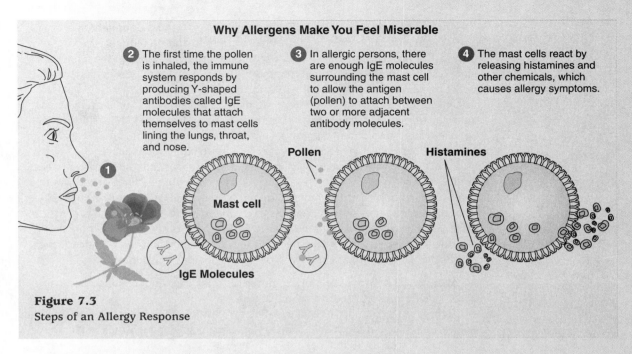

Why Allergens Make You Feel Miserable

② The first time the pollen is inhaled, the immune system responds by producing Y-shaped antibodies called IgE molecules that attach themselves to mast cells lining the lungs, throat, and nose.

③ In allergic persons, there are enough IgE molecules surrounding the mast cell to allow the antigen (pollen) to attach between two or more adjacent antibody molecules.

④ The mast cells react by releasing histamines and other chemicals, which causes allergy symptoms.

Pollen

Histamines

Mast cell

IgE Molecules

Figure 7.3
Steps of an Allergy Response

sure to allergens. In these circumstances, allergic responses become chronic in nature, and treatment becomes difficult. Many people take allergy shots to reduce the severity of their symptoms, with some success. In most cases, once the offending antigen has disappeared, allergy-prone people suffer few symptoms. Although allergies can cause numerous problems, one of the most significant effects is on the immune system.

Hay Fever

149   Perhaps the best example of a chronic respiratory disease is **hay fever.** Usually considered a seasonally related disease (most prevalent when ragweed and flowers are blooming), hay fever is common throughout the world. Hay fever attacks, which are characterized by sneezing and itchy, watery eyes and nose, make countless people miserable. The disorder appears to run in families, and research indicates that lifestyle is not as great a factor in developing hay fever as it is in other chronic diseases. Instead, an overzealous immune system and exposure to environmental allergens including pet dander, dust, pollen from various plants, and other substances appear to be the critical factors that determine vulnerability. For those people who are unable to get away from the cause of their hay fever response, medical assistance in the form of injections or antihistamines may provide the only relief.

Asthma

150   Unfortunately, for many persons who suffer from allergies such as hay fever, their condition often becomes complicated by the development of one of the major COPDs: asthma, emphysema, or bronchitis. **Asthma** is a long-term, chronic inflammatory disorder that blocks air flow in and out of the lungs. Asthma causes tiny airways in the lung to overreact with spasms in response to certain triggers.

Hay fever   A chronic respiratory disorder that is most prevalent when ragweed and flowers bloom.

Asthma   A chronic respiratory disease characterized by attacks of wheezing, shortness of breath, and coughing spasms.

Symptoms include wheezing, difficulty breathing, shortness of breath, and coughing spasms. Although most asthma attacks are mild and non-life-threatening, they
can trigger bronchospasms (contractions of the bronchial tubes in the lungs) that
are so severe that without rapid treatment, death may occur. Between attacks,
most people have few symptoms.

A number of things can trigger an asthma attack, including air pollutants;   151
particulate matter, such as wood dust; indoor air pollutants, such as sidestream
smoke from tobacco; and allergens, such as dust mites, cockroach saliva, and pet
dander. Stress is also believed to trigger attacks in some individuals.

Asthma can occur at any age, but it is most likely in children between infancy   152
and age 5 and in adults before age 40. In childhood, asthma strikes more boys than
girls; in adulthood, it strikes more women than men. Also, the asthma rate is 50 percent higher among African Americans than whites, and four times as many African
Americans die of asthma than do whites. Midwesterners appear to be more prone to
asthma than people from other areas of the country. In recent years, concern over
the rise in incidence of asthma has grown considerably. Consider these points:

- Asthma has become the most common chronic disease of childhood and accounts for one-fourth of all school absences.
- Asthma is the number one cause of hospitalization and absenteeism.
- Asthma affects more than 17 million Americans, including 5 million children;
  13 percent of all students age 5 to 19 have it.
- The number of asthma sufferers has increased by more than 65 percent since
  the 1980s; one in ten new asthma cases is diagnosed in people over age 65.
- The death toll from asthma has nearly doubled since 1980 to more than 5,000
  persons per year.

People with asthma have one of two distinctly different types. The most common
type, known as *extrinsic* (or *slow onset*) *asthma,* is most commonly associated
with allergic triggers. This form tends to run in families and begins to develop in
childhood. Often, by adulthood, a person has few episodes, or the disorder completely goes away. *Intrinsic asthma* also may have allergic triggers, but the main
difference is that any unpleasant event or stimulant may trigger an attack. A common form of extrinsic asthma is *exercise-induced asthma (EIA),* which may or may
not have an allergic connection. Some athletes have no allergies yet live with
asthma. Cold, dry air is believed to exacerbate EIA; thus, keeping the lungs moist
and warming up prior to working out may reduce risk. The warm, moist air
around a swimming pool is one of the best environments for people with asthma.

Relaxation techniques appear to help some asthma sufferers. Drugs may be   153
necessary for serious cases. Determining whether a specific allergen provokes
asthma attacks, taking steps to reduce exposure, avoiding triggers such as certain
types of exercise or stress, and finding the most effective medications are big
steps in asthma prevention and control. Numerous new drugs are available that
cause fewer side effects than do older medications. Finding a doctor who special-
izes in asthma treatment and stays up-to-date on possible options is critical.

Emphysema

Emphysema involves the gradual destruction of the **alveoli** (tiny air sacs) of the lungs.   154
As the alveoli are destroyed, the affected person finds it more and more difficult to ex-

---

Emphysema   A respiratory disease in which the alveoli become distended
or ruptured and are no longer functional.

Alveoli   Tiny air sacs of the lungs.

hale. The victim typically struggles to take in a fresh supply of air before the air held in the lungs has been expended. The chest cavity gradually begins to expand, thus producing the barrel-shaped chest characteristic of the chronic emphysema victim.

155   The cause of emphysema is uncertain. There is, however, a strong relationship between emphysema and long-term cigarette smoking and exposure to air pollution. Victims of emphysema often suffer discomfort over a period of many years. In fact, studies have shown that lung function decline may begin well before age 50 and the early morning "smoker's cough" may signal that damage has already begun. What most of us take for granted—the easy, rhythmic flow of air in and out of the lungs—becomes a continuous struggle for people with emphysema. Inadequate oxygen supply, combined with the stress of overexertion on the heart, eventually takes its toll on the cardiovascular system and leads to premature death.

Bronchitis

156   **Bronchitis** refers to an inflammation of the lining of the bronchial tubes. These tubes, the *bronchi*, connect the windpipe with the lungs. When the bronchi become inflamed or infected, less air is able to flow from the lungs, and heavy mucous begins to form. *Acute bronchitis* is the most common of the bronchial diseases and results in millions of visits to the doctor every year at a cost of more than $300 million per year. More than 95 percent of these acute cases are caused by viruses; however, they are often misdiagnosed and treated with antibiotics, even though little evidence supports this treatment. Typically, misdiagnosis occurs when a cluster of symptoms is labeled as bronchitis, despite the fact that there is no true laboratory diagnosis. *Chronic bronchitis,* in contrast, is defined by the presence of a productive (mucous-laden) cough most days of the month, more than three months a year, for two successive years without underlying disease to explain the cough. Typically, cigarette smoking causes chronic bronchitis, and once bronchitis begins, secondary bacterial or viral infections often make the condition worse. Air pollution and industrial dusts and fumes are also risk factors.

Sleep Apnea

157   **Sleep apnea,** although not as life threatening as asthma and other COPDs, affects about 5 percent of the general population. This condition is characterized by periodic episodes when breathing stops completely for ten seconds or longer. Each time it occurs, the sleeper awakens and breathing resumes, but the pattern causes a restless night's sleep. Over time, sleep apnea can lead to high blood pressure and subsequent risk of cardiovascular disease. Reducing alcohol use, changing sleeping position and schedules, and other medical interventions are common treatments.

What Do You Think?
Which of the respiratory diseases described in this section do you or your family have problems with? • How many of your college friends have these COPDs? • What difficulties do they have in controlling their diseases? • Why do you think the incidence of COPDs, as a group, is increasing? • What actions can you or your community take to reduce risks and problems from these diseases?

Bronchitis   An inflammation of the lining of the bronchial tubes.

Sleep apnea   Disorder in which a person has numerous episodes of breathing stoppage during a night's sleep.

Section Review 4

Directions.

1. On a separate sheet of paper, write a brief summary of the main points of the sections you have just read.

2. Mark each of the following statements True (T), False (F), or Can't Tell (CT). Mark the statement Can't Tell if it cannot be determined to be either true or false based on the material in the passage. Refer to the passage as necessary to verify your answer.

_____ 1. A person with sleep apnea may actually stop breathing for several seconds while asleep.

_____ 2. AIDS cannot be transmitted through kissing.

_____ 3. Avoiding the use of drugs that dull your senses is one way to reduce your risk for HIV disease.

_____ 4. Allergies are usually worse in children than in adults.

_____ 5. The incidence of chronic bronchitis in the United States has decreased during the last several years, largely because fewer people are now smoking.

Directions.   Write the letter of the best answer in the space provided.

_____ 1. Regarding the transmission of AIDS, the authors suggest that
a. fewer people are contracting AIDS each year.
b. gay individuals are most at risk.
c. AIDS is transmitted almost exclusively through sexual contact.
d. AIDS is often inadvertently transmitted through blood transfusions.

_____ 2. When testing for the presence of HIV with the ELISA test
a. a positive test would be followed by a confirming test.
b. a positive test is a clear indication that AIDS has developed.
c. seroconversion may result from too frequent testing.
d. the Western blot is usually administered to confirm negative results.

_____ 3. Which of the following *is* an infectious disease?
a. AIDS
b. cancer
c. asthma
d. emphysema

_____ 4. Allergic symptoms are caused by
a. exposure to pollen.
b. destruction of respiratory cells by pathogens.
c. the formation of IgE antibodies that trigger the release of histamines.
d. the failure of the immune system to respond to pathogens.

_____ 5. Asthma is best described as
   a. an infectious disease resulting from an increased susceptibility of the lungs to invasive antigens.
   b. a childhood illness affecting boys and girls approximately equally.
   c. a chronic disease whose primary symptoms are sneezing and coughing.
   d. a respiratory illness whose attacks are sometimes severe.

Neurological Disorders

Headaches

158 Almost all of us have experienced at least one major headache. In fact, more than 80 percent of women and 65 percent of men experience headaches on a regular basis. Common types of headaches and their treatments are described below.

159 ***Tension Headache***   Tension headaches, also referred to as muscular contraction headaches, are generally caused by muscle contractions or tension in the neck or head. This tension may be caused by actual strain placed on neck or head muscles due to overuse, static positions held for long periods of time, or tension triggered by stress. Recent research indicates that tension headaches may be a product of a more "generic mechanism" in which chemicals deep inside the brain may cause the muscular tension, pain, and suffering often associated with an attack. Possible triggers include red wine, lack of sleep, fasting, menstruation, or other factors, and the same symptoms (sensitivity to light and sound, nausea, and/or throbbing pain) may characterize different types of headaches. Relaxation, hot-water treatment, and massage have surfaced as the new holistic treatments, while aspirin, Tylenol, Aleve, and Advil remain the old standby forms of pain relief. Although such painkillers may bring temporary relief of symptoms, it is believed that, over time, the drugs may dull the brain's own pain-killing weapons and result in more rather than fewer headaches.

160 ***Migraine Headache***   **Migraine** is not just a name for an unusually bad headache; it is a specific diagnosis, involving pain that begins on one side of the head, often accompanied by nausea and sensitivity to light and sounds. Many migraine sufferers experience the sensation of an "aura" in their visual field, typically some form of disturbance such as flashing lights or blind spots, along with numbness or weakness on one side of the body or slurred speech, all signals of an ensuing bad headache. Most people report pain behind or around one eye and always on the same side of the head—a pain that can last for hours or days and then disappear. A migraine can strike at any time, although the hormonal changes around menstruation and ovulation often seem to set off migraines in women, who are three times more likely to get them than men.

161   Patients report that migraines can be triggered by emotional stress, weather, certain foods, lack of sleep, and a litany of other causes. When tested under laboratory settings, however, much of this evidence is inconclusive. What is known is that migraines occur when blood vessels dilate in the membrane that surrounds the brain. Historically, treatments have centered on reversing or preventing this dilation, with the most common treatment derived from the rye fungus *ergot*. Today, many fast-acting ergot compounds are available by nasal spray, thus vastly

> **Migraine**   A condition characterized by localized headaches that possibly result from alternating dilation and constriction of blood vessels.

increasing the speed of relief. However, ergot drugs have many side effects, the least of which may be that they are habit forming, which causes users to wake up with "rebound" headaches each morning after use.

Critics of the blood vessel dilation theory question why only blood vessels of   162
the head dilate in these situations. Furthermore, why aren't people who exercise or take hot baths more prone to migraine attacks? They suggest that migraines originate in the cortex of the brain, where certain pain sensors are stimulated.

When true migraines occur, relaxation is only minimally effective. Often,   163
strong pain-relieving drugs prescribed by a physician are necessary. Imitrex, a drug tailor-made for migraines, works for about 80 percent of those who try it. Recently, treatment with lidocaine has also shown promising results, and newer drugs called triptans, such as Zomig, Amerge, and Maxalt, are now available.

Secondary Headaches   Secondary headaches arise as a result of some other un-   164
derlying condition. Hypertension, blocked sinuses, allergies, low blood sugar, diseases of the spine, the common cold, poorly fitted dentures, problems with eyesight, and other problems can trigger this condition. Relaxation and pain relievers such as aspirin are of little help in treating secondary headaches. Rather, medications or other therapies designed to relieve the underlying organic cause of the headache must be included in the treatment regimen.

Seizure Disorders

The word **epilepsy** is derived from the Greek *epilepsia,* meaning "seizure." Approxi-   165
mately 1 percent of all Americans suffer from some form of seizure-related disorder. These disorders are generally caused by abnormal electrical activity in the brain and are characterized by loss of control of muscular activity and unconsciousness. Symptoms vary widely from person to person. Common forms of epilepsy include the following.

- *Grand mal, or major motor seizure.* These seizures are often preceded by a shrill cry or a seizure aura (body sensations such as ringing in the ears or a specific smell or taste). Convulsions and loss of consciousness generally occur and may last from 30 seconds to several minutes or more. Keeping track of the length of time elapsed is one aspect of first aid.
- *Petit mal, or minor seizure.* These seizures involve no convulsions. Rather, a minor loss of consciousness that may go unnoticed occurs. Minor twitching of muscles may take place, usually for a shorter time than for grand mal convulsions.
- *Psychomotor seizure.* These seizures involve both mental processes and muscular activity. Symptoms may include mental confusion and a listless state characterized by activities such as lip smacking, chewing, and repetitive movements.
- *Jacksonian seizure.* This is a progressive seizure that often begins in one part of the body, such as the fingers, and moves to other parts, such as the hand or arm. Usually only one side of the body is affected.

In most cases, people afflicted with seizure disorders can lead normal, seizure-free lives when under medical supervision. Public ignorance about these disorders is one of the most serious obstacles confronting them. Improvements in medication and surgical intervention to reduce some causes of seizures are among the most promising treatments today.

Epilepsy   A neurological disorder caused by abnormal electrical brain activity; can be accompanied by altered consciousness or convulsions.

> **What Do You Think?**
> *Do you suffer from recurrent headaches or other neurological problems?*
> • *What might cause your problems?* • *What actions could you take to re-*
> *duce your risks and symptoms?*

Other Neurological Disorders

166   Parkinson's disease and multiple sclerosis are two other conditions related to the nervous system. Parkinson's has come to public attention due to actor Michael J. Fox's announcement that he suffers from it. **Parkinson's disease** is a chronic, slowly progressive condition that typically strikes after age 50. The symptom most commonly associated with the disease is a tremor. These tremors can become so severe that simple daily tasks can become difficult or impossible. The most common theories for the causes of the disease are familial disposition, acceleration of age-related changes, and exposure to environmental toxins. Although the disease is progressive and incurable, drug therapies can keep the symptoms under control, possibly for years.

167   **Multiple sclerosis (MS)** is a degenerative disease in which myelin, a material composed of fats that serves as an insulator and conduit for transmission of nerve impulses, breaks down and causes nerve malfunction. MS typically appears between ages 15 and 50 and is characterized by periods of relapse, when symptoms flare up, and remissions, when symptoms are not present. Symptoms can range in severity from fatigue and episodic numbness to severe weakness. Most MS patients have few flare-ups and can lead fairly normal lives. Theories for the cause of MS are inconclusive.

Gender-Related Disorders

Menstrual Problems

168   **Premenstrual syndrome (PMS)** comprises the mood changes and physical symptoms that occur in some women a week to ten days preceding the menstrual period. Symptoms include depression, tension, irritability, headaches, tender breasts, bloated abdomen, backache, abdominal cramps, acne, fluid retention, diarrhea, and fatigue. About 80 percent of all women have some negative symptoms associated with their menstrual cycle; about 3 to 5 percent have more severe symptoms, which are known collectively as **premenstrual dysphoric disorder (PMDD).** Unlike PMS, PMDD symptoms are severe and difficult to manage. They include severe mood disturbances in addition to the physical symptoms associated with PMS.

169   Strategies for managing PMS include decreasing caffeine and salt intake, increasing intake of complex carbohydrates, practicing stress reduction techniques,

Parkinson's disease   A chronic, progressive neurological condition that causes tremors and other symptoms.

Multiple sclerosis (MS)   A degenerative neurological disease in which myelin, an insulator of nerves, breaks down.

Premenstrual syndrome (PMS)   The mood changes and physical symptoms that occur in many women prior to menstruation.

Premenstrual dysphoric disorder (PMDD)   A group of symptoms similar to but more severe than PMS; often involves mood disturbances.

and getting exercise. These strategies can also help PMDD. The use of SSRI antidepressants has shown significant promise in the treatment of the mood disturbances associated with PMDD.

Dysmenorrhea, a condition that causes pain in the lower abdomen just before or after menstruation, and toxic shock syndrome (discussed elsewhere in this chapter) are other problems associated with menstruation.   170

Endometriosis

Whether the incidence of **endometriosis** is on the rise in the United States or whether the disorder is simply attracting more attention is difficult to determine. Victims of endometriosis tend to be women between the ages of 20 and 40. Symptoms include severe cramping during and between menstrual cycles, irregular periods, unusually heavy or light menstrual flow, abdominal bloating, fatigue, painful bowel movements with periods, painful intercourse, constipation, diarrhea, menstrual pain, infertility, and low back pain.   171

Endometriosis is characterized by the abnormal growth and development of endometrial tissue (the tissue lining the uterus) in regions of the body other than the uterus. Among the most widely accepted theories concerning its causes are the transmission of endometrial tissue to other body regions during surgery or birth; backward flow of menstrual fluid through the fallopian tubes during menstruation; and abnormal cell migration through the movement of body fluids. Women with cycles shorter than 27 days and those with flows lasting over a week are at increased risk. The more aerobic exercise a woman engages in and the earlier she starts it, the less likely she is to develop endometriosis.   172

Treatment ranges from bed rest and stress reduction to **hysterectomy** (the removal of the uterus) and/or the removal of one or both ovaries and fallopian tubes. Recently, physicians have been criticized by some segments of the public for being too quick to select hysterectomy as the treatment of choice. More conservative treatments that involve dilation and curettage, surgically scraping endometrial tissue off the fallopian tubes and other reproductive organs, and combinations of hormone therapy have become more acceptable. Hormonal treatments include gonadotropin-releasing hormone (GnRH) analogs, various synthetic progesterone-like drugs (Provera), and oral contraceptives.   173

Digestion-Related Disorders

Diabetes

Diabetes is a serious, widespread, and costly chronic disease, affecting not just the more than 18 million Americans who must live with it, but their families and communities. Between 1990 and 2000, diagnosed diabetes increased 49 percent among U.S. adults, which gives it the dubious distinction of being the fastest-growing chronic disease in American history. A recent CDC study indicated that diabetes seems to be increasing even more dramatically among younger adults—up by almost 70 percent among those in their thirties. More than 2,200 people are diagnosed with diabetes each day in America, and more than 200,000 die each year of related complications, thus making diabetes the sixth leading cause of death in America today.   174

Endometriosis   Abnormal development of endometrial tissue outside the uterus; results in serious side effects.

Hysterectomy   Surgical removal of the uterus.

175   What causes this serious disease? In healthy people, the *pancreas,* a powerful enzyme-producing organ, secretes the hormone **insulin** in sufficient quantities to allow the body to use or store glucose (blood sugar). When the pancreas fails to produce enough insulin to regulate sugar metabolism or when the body fails to use insulin effectively, a disease known as **diabetes mellitus** occurs. Diabetics exhibit **hyperglycemia,** or elevated blood sugar levels, and high glucose levels in their urine. Other symptoms include excessive thirst, frequent urination, hunger, tendency to tire easily, wounds that heal slowly, numbness or tingling in the extremities, changes in vision, skin eruptions, and, in women, a tendency toward vaginal yeast infections.

176   The most serious form, known as type 1 (insulin-dependent) diabetes, is an autoimmune disease in which the immune system destroys the insulin-making beta cells. Type 1 diabetics typically must depend on insulin injections or oral medications for the rest of their lives because insulin is not present in their bodies. Type 2 (non-insulin-dependent) diabetes, in which insulin production is deficient or the body resists or is unable to utilize available insulin, tends to develop in later life. People with type 2 diabetes can often control their symptoms with a healthy diet, weight control, and regular exercise. They may be able to avoid oral medications or insulin indefinitely. A third type of diabetes, *gestational diabetes,* can develop in a woman during pregnancy. The condition usually disappears after childbirth, but it does leave the woman at greater risk of developing type 2 diabetes at some point.

177 ***Understanding Risk Factors***   Diabetes tends to run in families. Being overweight, coupled with inactivity, dramatically increases the risk of type 2 diabetes. Older persons and mothers of babies weighing more than 9 pounds also run an increased risk. Approximately 80 percent of all type 2 patients are overweight at the time of diagnosis. Weight loss and exercise are important factors in lowering blood sugar and improving the efficiency of cellular use of insulin. Both can help to prevent overwork of the pancreas and the development of diabetes. In fact, recent findings show that modest, consistent physical activity and a healthy diet can cut a person's risk of developing type 2 diabetes by nearly 60 percent. African Americans, Hispanics, and Native Americans have the highest rates of type 2 diabetes in the world—much higher than that of Caucasians. The reasons for this increased risk are not clear.

178 ***Controlling Diabetes***   Most physicians attempt to control diabetes with a variety of insulin-related drugs. Most of these drugs are taken orally, although self-administered hypodermic injections are prescribed when other treatments are inadequate. Recent breakthroughs in individual monitoring and implantable insulin monitors and insulin infusion pumps that regulate insulin intake "on demand" have provided many diabetics with the opportunity to lead normal lives. Newer forms of insulin that last longer in the body and have fewer side effects are now available. An insulin inhaler is being tested and may soon be available.

Lactose Intolerance

179 As many as 50 million Americans are unable to eat dairy products such as milk, cheese, ice cream, and other foods that the rest of us take for granted. These people

Insulin   A hormone produced by the pancreas; required by the body for the metabolism of carbohydrates.

Diabetes mellitus   A disease in which the pancreas fails to produce enough insulin or the body fails to use insulin effectively.

Hyperglycemia   Elevated blood sugar levels.

suffer from **lactose intolerance,** which means that they have lost the ability to produce the digestive enzyme *lactase*, which is necessary for the body to convert milk sugar (lactose) into glucose. That glass of milk becomes a source of stomach cramping, diarrhea, nausea, gas, and related symptoms. Once diagnosed, however, lactose intolerance can be treated by introducing low-lactose or lactose-free foods into the diet. Through trial and error, people usually find that they can tolerate one type of low-lactose food better than others. As an alternative to eating foods without lactose, some purchase special products that contain the missing lactase and thus eat dairy foods without serious side effects. Most large grocery chains, food cooperatives, and drug stores have these products available in liquid or tablet form. It should be noted, however, that these products do not work for everyone. Someone who is lactose intolerant may need to experiment before settling into a diet that works.

Colitis and Irritable Bowel Syndrome

Ulcerative colitis is a disease of the large intestine in which the mucous membranes   180
of the intestinal walls become inflamed. Victims with severe cases may have as many as 20 bouts of bloody diarrhea a day. Colitis can also produce severe stomach cramps, weight loss, nausea, sweating, and fever. Although some experts believe that colitis occurs more frequently in people with high stress levels, this theory is controversial. Hypersensitivity reactions, particularly to milk and certain foods, have also been considered as a cause. It is difficult to determine the cause of colitis because the disease goes into unexplained remission and then recurs without apparent reason. This pattern often continues over periods of years and may be related to the later development of colorectal cancer. Since the cause of colitis remains unknown, treatment focuses on relieving the symptoms. Increasing fiber intake and taking anti-inflammatory drugs, steroids, and other medications designed to reduce inflammation and soothe irritated intestinal walls can relieve symptoms.

Many people develop a related condition known as **irritable bowel syn-**   181
drome (IBS), characterized by nausea, pain, gas, diarrhea attacks, or cramps that occur after eating certain foods or when a person is under unusual stress. IBS symptoms commonly begin in early adulthood. Symptoms may vary from week to week and can fade for long periods of time, only to return. The cause is unknown, but researchers suspect that people with IBS have digestive systems that are overly sensitive to food and drink, stress, and certain hormonal changes. They may also be more sensitive to pain signals from the stomach. Stress management, relaxation techniques, regular activity, and diet can bring IBS under control in the vast majority of cases. Problems with diarrhea can be reduced by cutting down on fat and avoiding caffeine and excessive amounts of sorbitol, a sweetener found in dietetic foods and chewing gum.

Peptic Ulcers

An ulcer is a lesion or wound that forms in body tissue as a result of some irritant. A   182
peptic ulcer is a chronic ulcer that occurs in the lining of the stomach or the section

---

Lactose intolerance   The inability to produce lactase, an enzyme needed to convert milk sugar into glucose.

Ulcerative colitis   An inflammatory disorder that affects the mucous membranes of the large intestine, producing bloody diarrhea.

Irritable bowel syndrome (IBS)   Nausea, pain, gas, or diarrhea caused by certain foods or stress.

Peptic ulcer   Damage to the stomach or intestinal lining, usually caused by digestive juices.

of the small intestine known as the *duodenum*. The lining of these organs becomes irritated, the protective covering of mucous is reduced, and the gastric acid begins to digest the dying tissue, just as it would a piece of food. Typically, this irritation causes pain that disappears when the person eats, but it returns about an hour later.

183   Research indicates that most peptic ulcers result from infection by a common bacterium, *Helicobacter pylori*. The disorder, which affects more than 4 million Americans every year, generally responds to antibiotics. Peptic ulcers caused by excess stomach acid or overuse of stomach-irritating drugs such as aspirin and ibuprofen can be treated with acid-reducing medications.

What Do You Think?
What role can a healthy diet play in reducing risks for and symptoms of the diseases discussed here? • Are you or any of your family members at risk for these problems? • What actions can you take today that will cut your risk?

Musculoskeletal Diseases

Arthritis

184 Called the "nation's primary crippler," **arthritis** strikes one in seven Americans, or more than 38 million people. Symptoms range from the occasional tendinitis of the weekend athlete to the severe pain of rheumatoid arthritis. There are more than 100 types of arthritis diagnosed today. Together, they cost the U.S. economy over $65 billion per year in lost wages and productivity and untold amounts in hospital and nursing home services, prescriptions, and over-the-counter pain relief.

185   **Osteoarthritis,** also known as degenerative joint disease, is a progressive deterioration of bones and joints that has been associated with the wear-and-tear theory of aging. More recent research indicates that as joints are used, they release enzymes that digest cartilage while other cells in the cartilage try to repair the damage. When the enzymatic breakdown overpowers cellular repair, the cartilage is destroyed, thus causing bones to rub against each other. Weather extremes, excessive strain, and injury often lead to osteoarthritis flare-ups, but a specific precipitating event does not seem to be necessary. Obesity, joint trauma, and repetitive joint usage all contribute to increased risk, and thus are important targets for prevention.

186   Of the 20.7 million Americans with osteoarthritis, the majority of them are women. Although age and injury are undoubtedly factors, heredity, abnormal use of the joint, diet, abnormalities in joint structure, and impaired blood supply to the joint may also contribute. Joint replacement and bone fusion are common surgical repair techniques. For most people, anti-inflammatory drugs and pain relievers such as aspirin and cortisone-related agents ease discomfort. Heat, mild exercise, and massage may also relieve the pain.

187   **Rheumatoid arthritis** is an autoimmune disease involving chronic inflammation that can appear at any age, but most commonly between ages 20 and 45. Rheumatoid arthritis is three times more common among women than among

---

Arthritis   Painful inflammatory disease of the joints.

Osteoarthritis   A progressive deterioration of bones and joints that has been associated with the "wear and tear" theory of aging.

Rheumatoid arthritis   A serious inflammatory joint disease.

men during early adulthood but equally common among men and women in the over-70 age group. Symptoms include stiffness, pain, and swelling of multiple joints, often including the joints of the hands and wrists; they can be gradually progressive or sporadic, with occasional unexplained remissions.

Treatment for rheumatoid arthritis is similar to that for osteoarthritis. Emphasis is placed on pain relief and attempts to improve the functional mobility of the patient. Sometimes immunosuppressant drugs can reduce the inflammatory response.   188

Fibromyalgia

Fibromyalgia is a chronic, painful, rheumatoid-like disorder that affects as many as 5 to 6 percent of the general population. Persons with fibromyalgia experience an array of symptoms, including headaches, dizziness, numbness and tingling, itching, fluid retention, chronic joint pain, abdominal or pelvic pain, and even occasional diarrhea. Suspected causes include sleep disturbances, stress, emotional distress, viruses, and autoimmune disorders; however, none has been proved in clinical trials. Because of fibromyalgia's multiple symptoms, it is usually diagnosed only after myriad tests have ruled out other disorders. The American College of Rheumatology identifies these major diagnostic criteria: 189

- History of widespread pain of at least three months' duration in the axial skeleton as well as in all four quadrants of the body
- Pain in at least 11 of 18 paired tender points on digital palpation of about 4 kilograms of pressure

Fibromyalgia primarily affects women in their 30s and 40s. It can be extremely debilitating, causing feelings of unrelieved pain, bloating or swelling, and fatigue. Many people with fibromyalgia also become depressed and report chronic fatigue-like symptoms. Treatment varies based on the severity of symptoms. Typically, adequate rest, stress management, relaxation techniques, dietary supplements and selected herbal remedies, and pain medications are prescribed.

Systemic Lupus Erythematosus

Systemic lupus erythematosus (SLE), or **lupus,** is an autoimmune disease in which antibodies destroy or injure organs such as the kidneys, brain, and heart. The symptoms vary from mild to severe and may disappear for periods of time. A butterfly-shaped rash covering the bridge of the nose and both cheeks is common. Nearly all SLE sufferers have aching joints and muscles, and 60 percent of them develop redness and swelling that move from joint to joint. The disease affects 1 in 700 Caucasians but 1 in 250 African Americans; 90 percent of all victims are females. Extensive research has not yet found a cure for this sometimes fatal disease.   190

Low Back Pain

Approximately 80 percent of all Americans will experience low back pain (LBP) at some point. Some LBP episodes result from muscular damage and may be short-lived and acute. Other episodes may involve dislocations, fractures, or other problems with spinal vertebrae or discs, thus resulting in chronic pain or requiring   191

Fibromyalgia   A chronic rheumatoid-like disorder that can be highly painful and difficult to diagnose.

Lupus   A disease in which the immune system attacks the body and produces antibodies that destroy or injure organs such as the kidneys, brain, and heart.

surgery. Low back pain is epidemic throughout the world. It is the major cause of disability for people age 20 to 45 in the United States, who suffer more frequently and severely from this problem than older people do. Low back pain causes more lost work time in the United States than any other illness except upper respiratory infections. In fact, costs associated with back injury exceeded those associated with all other industrial injuries combined.

192   Almost 90 percent of all back problems occur in the lumbar spine region (lower back). You can avoid many problems by consciously maintaining good posture. Other preventive hints include:

- Purchase a firm mattress, and avoid sleeping on your stomach.
- Avoid high-heeled shoes, which often tilt the pelvis forward.
- Control your weight.
- Lift objects with your legs, not your back.
- Buy a good chair for doing your work, preferably one with lumbar support.
- Move your car seat forward so your knees are elevated slightly.
- Warm up before exercising.
- Engage in regular exercise, particularly exercises that strengthen the abdominal muscles and stretch the back muscles.

Other Maladies

193   During the past 20 years, several afflictions have surfaced that seem to be products of our time. Some of these health problems relate to specific groups of people; some are due to technological advances; and others have not been explained (Table 7.1).

Chronic Fatigue Syndrome

194   Fatigue is a subjective condition in which people feel tired before they begin activities, lack the energy to accomplish tasks that require sustained effort and attention, or become abnormally exhausted after normal activities. In the late 1980s, several U.S. clinics noted a characteristic set of symptoms including chronic fatigue, headaches, fever, sore throat, enlarged lymph nodes, depression, poor memory, general weakness, nausea, and symptoms remarkably similar to mononucleosis.

Table 7.1
Other Modern Afflictions

DISEASE	DESCRIPTION	TREATMENT
Cystic fibrosis	Inherited disease occurring in 1 out of every 1,600 births. Characterized by pooling of large amounts of mucus in lungs, digestive disturbances, and excessive sodium excretion. Results in premature death.	Most treatments are geared toward relief of symptoms. Antibiotics are administered for infection. Recent strides in genetic research suggest better treatments and potential cure in the near future.
Sickle-cell anemia	Inherited disease affecting 8–10% of all African Americans. Disease affects hemoglobin, forming sickle-shaped red blood cells that interfere with oxygenation. Results in severe pain, anemia, and premature death.	Reduce stress, and attend to minor infections immediately. Seek genetic counseling.
Cerebral palsy	Disorder characterized by the loss of voluntary control over motor functioning. Believed to be caused by a lack of oxygen to the brain at birth, brain disorders or an accident before or after birth, poisoning, or brain infections.	Follow preventive actions to reduce accident risks; improved neonatal and birthing techniques show promise.
Graves' disease	A thyroid disorder characterized by swelling of the eyes, staring gaze, and retraction of the eyelid. Can result in loss of sight. The cause in unknown, and the disease can occur at any age.	Medication may help control symptoms. Radioactive iodine supplements also may be administered.

Despite extensive testing, no viral cause has been found. In the absence of a   195
known pathogen, many researchers believe that the illness, commonly referred to
as *chronic fatigue syndrome (CFS)*, may have strong psychosocial roots. Our heightened awareness of health makes some of us scrutinize our bodies so carefully that
the slightest deviation becomes amplified. In addition, people who suffer from depression seem to be good candidates for CFS. Experts worry, however, that too
many people approach CFS as something that is "in the person's head" and that
such an attitude may prevent scientists from doing the serious research needed to
find a cure.

The diagnosis of CFS depends on two major criteria and eight or more mi-   196
nor criteria. The major criteria are debilitating fatigue that persists for at least six
months and the absence of other illnesses that could cause the symptoms. Minor
criteria include headaches, fever, sore throat, painful lymph nodes, weakness, fatigue after exercise, sleep problems, and rapid onset of these symptoms. Treatment focuses on improved nutrition, rest, counseling for depression, judicious exercise, and development of a strong support network.

Repetitive Stress Injuries

The Bureau of Labor Statistics estimates that 25 percent of all injuries in the labor   197
force that result in lost work time are due to a **repetitive stress injury (RSI).** These
are injuries to nerves, soft tissue, or joints that result from the physical stress of repeated motions. They are estimated to cost employers more than $22 billion a
year in workers' compensation and an additional $85 billion in related costs, such
as absenteeism.

One of the most common RSIs is **carpal tunnel syndrome.** Hours spent typ-   198
ing at the computer, flipping groceries through computerized scanners, or other
jobs made simpler by technology can irritate the median nerve in the wrist, thus
causing numbness, tingling, and pain in the fingers and hands. Although carpal
tunnel syndrome risk can be reduced by proper placement of the keyboard,
mouse, wrist pads, and other techniques, RSIs are often overlooked until significant damage has been done. Better education and ergonomic workplace designs
can eliminate many injuries of this nature.

Repetitive stress injury (RSI)   An injury to nerves, soft tissue, or joints
due to the physical stress of repeated motions.

Carpal tunnel syndrome   A common occupational injury in which the
median nerve in the wrist becomes irritated, thus causing numbness, tingling, and pain in the fingers and hands.

Section Review 5

Directions.

1. On a separate sheet of paper, write a brief summary of the main points of the sections you have just read.

2. Mark each of the following statements True (T), False (F), or Can't Tell (CT). Mark the
statement Can't Tell if it cannot be determined to be either true or false based on
the material in the passage. Refer to the passage as necessary to verify your answer.

_____ 1. All serious headaches share the same basic causes.

_____ 2. Endometriosis is characterized as a condition in which the tissue within the uterus becomes inflamed or infected.

_____ 3. The cause of colitis is unknown.

_____ 4. Osteoarthritis is twice as common as rheumatoid arthritis.

_____ 5. Approximately one out of every 20 African Americans suffers from sickle-cell anemia.

Summary

- The major uncontrollable risk factors for contracting infectious diseases are heredity, age, environmental conditions, and organism resistance. The major controllable risk factors are stress, nutrition, fitness level, sleep, hygiene, avoidance of high-risk behaviors, and drug use.
- The major pathogens are bacteria, viruses, fungi, protozoa, prions, and parasitic worms. Bacterial infections include staphylococcal infections, streptococcal infections, pneumonia, Legionnaire's disease, tuberculosis, and periodontal diseases. Major viruses include the common cold, influenza, mononucleosis, hepatitis, and measles.
- Your body uses a number of defense systems to keep pathogens from invading. The skin is the body's major protection, helped by enzymes. The immune system creates antibodies to destroy antigens. In addition, fever and pain play a role in defending the body. Vaccines bolster the body's immune system against specific diseases.
- Emerging and resurgent diseases pose significant threats for future generations. Many factors contribute to these risks. Possible solutions focus on a public health approach to prevention.
- Sexually transmitted infections (STIs) are spread through intercourse, oral sex, anal sex, hand–genital contact, and sometimes through mouth-to-mouth contact. Major STIs include chlamydia, pelvic inflammatory disease (PID), gonorrhea, syphilis, pubic lice, genital warts, candidiasis, trichomoniasis, and herpes. Sexual transmission may also be involved in some general urinary tract infections.
- Acquired immune deficiency syndrome (AIDS) is caused by the human immunodeficiency virus (HIV). HIV is not confined to certain high-risk groups. Globally, HIV/AIDS has become a major threat to the world's population. Anyone can get HIV by engaging in high-risk sexual activities that include exchange of body fluids, by having received a blood transfusion before 1985, and by injecting drugs (or having sex with someone who does). Women appear to be particularly susceptible to infection. You can cut your risk for AIDS by deciding not to engage in risky sexual activities.
- Chronic lung diseases include allergies, hay fever, asthma, emphysema, and chronic bronchitis. Allergies are part of the body's natural defense system. Chronic obstructive pulmonary diseases are the fifth leading cause of death in the United States.
- Neurological conditions include headaches, seizure disorders, Parkinson's disease, and multiple sclerosis. Headaches may be caused by a variety of factors, the most common of which are tension, dilation and/or rapid contraction of blood vessels in the brain, chemical influences on muscles and vessels that cause inflammation and pain, and underlying physiological and psychological disorders.
- Premenstrual syndrome (PMS) and premenstrual dysphoric disorder (PMDD) are conditions related to the menstrual cycle. Endometriosis is the buildup of endometrial tissue in regions of the body other than the uterus.
- Diabetes occurs when the pancreas fails to produce enough insulin to regulate sugar metabolism. Other conditions, such as colitis, irritable bowel syndrome (IBS), and peptic ulcers, are the direct result of functional problems in various digestion-related organs or systems.
- Musculoskeletal diseases such as arthritis, lower back pain, repetitive stress injuries, and other problems cause significant pain and disability in millions of people. Chronic fatigue syndrome (CFS) and repetitive stress injuries (RSIs, such as carpal tunnel syndrome) have emerged in the past decade as major chronic maladies. CFS is associated with depression. Repetitive stress injuries are preventable by proper equipment placement and usage.

Questions for Discussion and Reflection

1. What are the major controllable risk factors for contracting infectious diseases? Using this knowledge, how would you change your current lifestyle to prevent such infection?
2. What is a pathogen? What are the similarities and differences between pathogens and antigens? Discuss uncontrollable and controllable risk factors that can threaten your health.
3. What are the six types of pathogens? What are the various means by which they can be transmitted? How have social conditions among the poor and homeless increased the risks for certain diseases, such as tuberculosis, influenza, and hepatitis? Why are these conditions a challenge to the efforts of public health officials?
4. Identify possible reasons for the spread of emerging and resurgent diseases. Indicate public policies and programs that might reduce this trend.
5. Identify five STIs. What are their symptoms? How do they develop? What are their potential long-term effects?
6. Should Americans be concerned about soaring HIV/AIDS rates elsewhere in the world? Explain your answer.
7. What are some of the major noninfectious chronic diseases affecting Americans today? Do you think there is a pattern in the types of diseases that we get? What are the common risk factors?
8. List common respiratory diseases affecting Americans. Which of these diseases has a genetic basis? An environmental basis? An individual basis? What, if anything, is being done to prevent, treat, and control each of these conditions?
9. Describe the symptoms and treatment of diabetes. What is the difference between type 1 diabetes and type 2 diabetes?
10. What are the major disorders of the musculoskeletal system? Why do you think there aren't any cures? Describe the difference between osteoarthritis and rheumatoid arthritis.

Accessing Your Health on the Internet

Visit the following Internet sites to explore further topics and issues related to personal health. To visit these organizations' websites, go to the Companion Website for *Health: The Basics, Sixth Edition* at www.aw-bc.com/donatelle, click on the book image, and select "Accessing Your Health on the Internet" from the navigation menu on the left.

1. *American Academy of Allergy, Asthma, and Immunology.* Provides an overview of asthma and allergies. Offers interactive quizzes to test your knowledge and an "ask an expert" section.
2. *American Diabetes Association.* Excellent resource for diabetes information.
3. *Centers for Disease Control and Prevention (CDC).* Home page for the government agency dedicated to disease intervention and prevention, with links to all the latest data and publications put out by the CDC, including the *Morbidity and Mortality Weekly Report, HIV/AIDS Surveillance Report,* and the *Journal of Emerging Infectious Diseases,* and access to the CDC research database, Wonder.
4. *National Center for Chronic Disease Prevention and Health Promotion.* Provides access to a wide range of information from this CDC-affiliated organization dedicated to chronic diseases and health promotion.
5. *World Health Organization (WHO).* Provides access to the latest information on world health issues, including infectious disease, put out by WHO. Provides direct access to publications and fact sheets, with keywords to help users find topics of interest.

Further Reading

Champeau, D., and R. Donatelle. *AIDS and STIS: A Global Perspective.* Englewood Cliffs, NJ: Prentice Hall, 2002.

An overview of issues, trends, and ethics surrounding the global pandemic of HIV/AIDS and STIs.

Chin, J., ed. *Control of Communicable Diseases Manual,* 17th ed. Washington, DC: American Public Health Association, 2003.

Outstanding pocket reference for information on infectious diseases. Updated every three to five years to cover emerging diseases.

National Center for Health Statistics. *Monthly Vital Statistics Report and Advance Data from Vital and Health Statistics.* Hyattsville, MD: Public Health Service.

Detailed government reports, usually published monthly, concerning mortality and morbidity data for the United States. Includes changes occurring in the rates of particular diseases and in health practices so patterns and trends can be analyzed.

Cumulative Review 2 [Pages 310–331]

Directions. Write the letter of the best answer in the space provided.

_____ 1. Regarding AIDS treatment, the authors suggest that
    a. a cure for AIDS is unlikely to be found.
    b. current treatments accomplish little.
    c. current treatments have enabled AIDS sufferers to live longer.
    d. few AIDS patients can tolerate the severe side effects of most AIDS drugs.

_____ 2. The authors imply that epileptic seizures
    a. can be cured with proper medication.
    b. can be controlled with proper medication.
    c. cannot be effectively treated through medication.
    d. increase in severity as the individual ages.

_____ 3. Which of the following statements regarding women and AIDS is *not* true?
    a. Women are at greater risk than men to contract AIDS from unprotected sex.
    b. Poor women are at greater risk than wealthy women.
    c. Most women with AIDS were infected through homosexual contact.
    d. Approximately three-fourths of all American women with AIDS are African American or Hispanic.

_____ 4. IBS is usually managed by all of the following *except*
    a. medication.
    b. diet.
    c. exercise.
    d. relaxation techniques for the management of stress.

_____ 5. Regarding low back pain, the authors suggest that
    a. surgery is the most effective treatment.
    b. medications are not helpful.
    c. good posture can help avoid problems.
    d. exercise should be avoided.

Directions. Answer each question in complete sentences, without copying word-for-word from the passage.

1. Who is most at risk for AIDS? What are the best ways to avoid HIV infection?

_____

_____

_____

2. Explain the difference between type 1 diabetes and type 2 diabetes.

_____

_____

_____

3. Explain the difference between osteoarthritis and rheumatoid arthritis.

_____

_____

_____

4. What is fibromyalgia? How is it treated?

_____

_____

_____

5. Who is most likely to suffer from carpal tunnel syndrome? Why?

_____

_____

_____

Vocabulary Exercise 2

Directions. Choose the meaning for the underlined word that best fits the context. You may consult the dictionary as needed.

_____ 1. . . . to include pulmonary tuberculosis, <u>recurrent</u> pneumonia . . . [Paragraph 119]
   a. fatal
   b. reoccurring
   c. infectious
   d. widespread; common

_____ 2. . . . most states <u>mandate</u> that those who test positive for the HIV antibody be reported. [Paragraph 120]
   a. inquire
   b. punish
   c. require
   d. treat

_____ 3. <u>Irrefutable</u> evidence indicates that HIV/AIDS disproportionately affects women. [Paragraph 122]
   a. can't be disproved
   b. can't be proven
   c. a large quantity
   d. unreliable

_____ 4. Each of these may <u>exacerbate</u> or contribute to the development of COPD. [Paragraph 146]
   a. make worse
   b. lead to
   c. cause
   d. control

_____ 5. ...due to overuse, <u>static</u> positions held for long periods of time... [Paragraph 159]
  a. unusual
  b. uncomfortable
  c. strained
  d. stationary

_____ 6. ...certain foods, lack of sleep, and a <u>litany</u> of other causes. [Paragraph 161]
  a. long list
  b. concentration
  c. form of prayer
  d. written accumulation

_____ 7. ...migraines occur when blood vessels <u>dilate</u> in the membrane that surrounds the brain. [Paragraph 161]
  a. shrink
  b. widen
  c. tighten
  d. leak

_____ 8. ...a specific <u>precipitating</u> event does not seem to be necessary. [Paragraph 185]
  a. causing
  b. rapid
  c. extraordinary
  d. accidental

_____ 9. ...it is usually diagnosed only after <u>myriad</u> tests have ruled out other disorders. [Paragraph 189]
  a. special
  b. diagnostic
  c. laboratory
  d. numerous

_____ 10. The major criteria are <u>debilitating</u> fatigue that persists... [Paragraph 196]
  a. extreme
  b. chronic
  c. weakening
  d. long-lasting

Critical Response Questions

1. How do heredity and lifestyle contribute to good health? In your opinion, which contributes more?

2. What role should the government play in preventing the spread of STIs and other infectious diseases?

3. How might you change your lifestyle to improve your health now and in the future?

4. What areas of medical research are most important to pursue now? What should be the primary goals of medical research during the next five years?

5. Should high schools and colleges require students to learn about STIs? Why or why not?

6. Explain the arguments for and against universal health care (medical insurance for all citizens). What is your opinion on this issue?

7. Will there ever be a cure for the common cold? Explain your answer.

CHAPTER

Political Science

CIVIL RIGHTS

Directions.

1. Begin by surveying the chapter to look for answers to the following questions.

   - What is the chapter about?
   - What subtopics will be discussed?
   - What will you learn from reading and studying the chapter?
   - How interesting does the chapter look?
   - How difficult does the chapter look?
   - How familiar to you is the chapter material? That is, how much previous knowledge of the subject do you have?

   When you have completed your survey, write a summary on a separate sheet of paper of what you've learned about the chapter from the survey. Your summary should include answers to the previous questions, as well as any other information and comments you wish to add.

2. While reading the chapter, look for organizational patterns. Recognizing the patterns should help you better grasp the relationship of ideas within each paragraph and section and distinguish main ideas more easily.

   Also, form questions from the headings and subheadings (generally, write one question per heading or subheading). Write your questions on a sheet of paper and, after completing each section, mentally review the main points of the section, mark the text, and write the answer(s) to your question(s), as well as any other information that seems important to you.

SAMPLE TEXTBOOK CHAPTER

From *American Government: Continuity and Change,* 2006 Edition, by Karen O'Connor and Larry J. Sabato. New York: Pearson, 2006.

1   **THERE IS NO QUESTION that in the 1980s, crime in the United States, and in particular New York City, was out of control and Americans demanded that their governments do something about it. Governments at all levels responded with more police and more prisons. But, now that crime is on the wane and no longer even on Americans' list of top ten concerns, ordinary cit-**

izens are asking the question that troubled John Locke and Thomas Hobbes over three centuries ago: how much liberty should you give up to the government in return for safety? Case after case makes it clear that people of color, whether native or foreign born, are subject to civil rights deprivations at far higher rates than other identifiable groups. On February 4, 1999, for example, Amadou Diallo, a 22-year-old unarmed African immigrant, stood in the vestibule of his apartment building in the Bronx, New York. Four white plainclothes police officers, who were patrolling the neighborhood in an unmarked car, opened fire on him, eventually firing 41 shots. He died at the scene. There were no witnesses. The four officers, who eventually were charged with second-degree murder, were members of New York City's Street Crimes Unit. This unit was created in the early 1990s by then-Mayor Rudy Giuliani to help lower the crime rate. Known to have targeted blacks, members of the unit admitted to stopping and searching as many as 225,000 citizens since its establishment.

2   Members of New York City's frightened minority community, African Americans and new immigrants alike, along with liberal activists and everyday citizens, turned their anger on city police and the mayor, who they believed had used overly aggressive, and often racially biased, techniques to reduce crime. In the months after the shooting, citizens from all walks of life, from future Democratic presidential candidate Al Sharpton and actress Susan Sarandon to street cleaners, protested at City Hall, and even marched from the federal courthouse over the Brooklyn Bridge and into Manhattan in a procession reminiscent of many 1960s civil rights marches. Over 1,500 protesters were arrested at one demonstration, the largest New York City had seen in twenty-five years. Eventually, all four police officers charged with Diallo's killing were acquitted at trial.

3   THE DECLARATION OF INDEPENDENCE, written in 1776, boldly proclaims: "We hold these truths to be self-evident, that all men are created equal, that they are endowed by their Creator with certain unalienable rights." The Constitution, written eleven years later, is silent on the concept of equality. Only through constitutional amendment and Supreme Court definition and redefinition of the rights contained in the Constitution have Americans come close to attaining equal rights. Even so, as our opening vignette highlights, some citizens have yet to experience full equality and the full enjoyment of civil rights many Americans take for granted.

4   The term **civil rights** refers to the government-protected rights of individuals against arbitrary or discriminatory treatment by governments or individuals based on categories such as race, sex, national origin, age, religion, or sexual orientation. The Framers considered some civil rights issues. But, as James Madison reflected in *Federalist No. 42*, one entire class of citizens—slaves—were treated in the new Constitution more as property than as people. Delegates to the Constitutional Convention put political expediency before the immorality of slavery and basic civil rights. Moreover, the Constitution considered white women full citizens for purposes of determining state population, but voting qualifications were left to the states, and none allowed women to vote at the time the Constitution was ratified.

5   Since the Constitution was written, concepts of civil rights have changed dramatically. The addition of the Fourteenth Amendment, one of three Civil War Amendments ratified from 1865 to 1870, introduced the notion of equality into the Constitution by specifying that states could not deny "any person within its

civil rights
Refers to the government-protected rights of individuals against arbitrary or discriminatory treatment by governments or individuals based on categories such as race, sex, national origin, age, religion, or sexual orientation.

jurisdiction equal protection of the laws." Throughout history, the Fourteenth Amendment's equal protection guarantees have been the linchpin of efforts to expand upon the original intent of the amendment to allow its provisions to protect a variety of other groups from discrimination.

The Fourteenth Amendment has generated more litigation to determine and specify its meaning than any other provision of the Constitution. Within a few years of its ratification, women—and later, African Americans and other minorities and disadvantaged groups—took to the courts to seek expanded civil rights in all walks of life. But, the struggle to augment rights was not limited to the courts. Public protest, civil disobedience, legislative lobbying, and appeals to public opinion all have been part of the arsenal of those seeking equality. The Diallo case incorporates all of those actions. Ordinary citizens and celebrities took to the streets, legislators held hearings, police officers were put on trial, and the media reported it all.

Since passage of the Civil War Amendments (1865–1870), there has been a fairly consistent pattern of the expansion of civil rights to more and more groups. In this chapter, we will explore how notions of equality and civil rights have changed in this country as well as current debates over the scope and methods as it seeks to ensure equal rights for all its citizens. To do so, we will discuss slavery, its abolition, and the achievement of voting rights for African Americans and women by examining the evolution of African American rights and women's rights in tandem. To appreciate how each group has drawn ideas, support, and success from the other, throughout this chapter we will consider their parallel developments as well as those of other historically disadvantaged political groups, including Hispanics (now the largest minority group in the United States), Native Americans, the gay and lesbian community, and those with disabilities.

- First, we will discuss *slavery, abolition, and winning the right to vote,* from *1800 to 1890.*

- Second, we will examine African Americans' and women's next *push for equality* from *1890 to 1954,* using two of the Supreme Court's most famous decisions, *Plessy* v. *Ferguson* (1896) and *Brown* v. *Board of Education* (1954), as bookends for our discussion.

- Third, we will analyze *the civil rights movement* and the Civil Rights Act of 1964 and its effects, including its facilitation.

- Fourth, we will discuss the development of a new *women's rights movement* and its push for an equal rights amendment to the U.S. Constitution.

- Fifth, we will present the efforts of *other groups,* including Hispanic Americans, Native Americans, gays and lesbians, and Americans with disabilities, to *mobilize for rights* using methods often modeled after the actions of African Americans and women.

- Finally, we will explore *other continuing controversies in civil rights,* including affirmative action.

SLAVERY, ABOLITION, AND WINNING THE RIGHT TO VOTE, 1800–1890

TODAY, WE TAKE THE RIGHTS OF WOMEN and blacks to vote for granted. Since 1980, women have outvoted men at the polls in presidential elections; in the 1990s, in fact, African Americans and women became the core of the Democratic Party. But, it wasn't always this way. The period from 1800 to 1890 was one of tremendous change and upheaval in America. Despite the Civil War and the freeing of the slaves, the promise of equality guaranteed to African Americans by the Civil War Amendments failed to become a reality. Women's rights activists also began to make claims for equality, often using the arguments enunciated for the abolition of slavery, but they too fell far short of their goals.

Slavery and Congress

9 Congress banned the slave trade in 1808, after the expiration of the 20-year period specified by the Constitution. In 1820, blacks made up 25 percent of the U.S. population and were in the majority in some southern states. By 1840, that figure had fallen to 20 percent. After the introduction of the cotton gin (a machine invented in 1793 that separated seeds from cotton very quickly), the South became even more dependent on agriculture and cheap slave labor as its economic base. At the same time, technological advances were turning the northern states into an increasingly industrialized region, which deepened the cultural and political differences and animosity between the North and the South.

10 As the nation grew westward in the early 1800s, conflicts between northern and southern states intensified over the admission of new states to the union with free or slave status. The first major crisis occurred in 1820, when Missouri applied for admission to the union as a slave state—that is, one in which slavery would be legal. Missouri's admission would have weighted the Senate in favor of slavery and therefore was opposed by northern senators. To resolve this conflict, Congress passed the Missouri Compromise of 1820. The Compromise prohibited slavery north of the geographical boundary at 36 degrees latitude. This act allowed Missouri to be admitted to the union as a slave state, and to maintain the balance of slave and free states, Maine was carved out of a portion of Massachusetts.

The First Civil Rights Movements: Abolition and Women's Rights

11 The Missouri Compromise solidified the South in its determination to keep slavery legal, but it also fueled the fervor of those who opposed slavery. William Lloyd Garrison, a white New Englander, galvanized the abolitionist movement in the early 1830s. Garrison, a newspaper editor, founded the American Anti-Slavery Society in 1833; by 1838, it had more than 250,000 members. Given the U.S. population today, the National Association for the Advancement of Colored People (NAACP) would need 3.8 million members to have the same kind of overall proportional membership. (In 2004, NAACP membership exceeded 500,000.)

12 Slavery was not the only practice that people began to question in the decades following the Missouri Compromise. In 1840, for example, Garrison and Frederick Douglass, a well-known black abolitionist writer, left the Anti-Slavery Society when it refused to accept their demand that women be allowed to participate equally in all its activities. Custom dictated that women not speak out in public, and most laws made women second-class citizens. In most states, for example, women could not divorce their husbands or keep their own wages and inheritances. And, of course, they could not vote.

13 Elizabeth Cady Stanton and Lucretia Mott, who were to found the first women's rights movement, attended the 1840 meeting of the World Anti-Slavery Society in London with their husbands. After their long journey, they were not allowed to participate in the convention because they were women. As they sat in the balcony, apart from the male delegates, they paused to compare their status to that of the slaves they sought to free. They concluded that women were not much better off than slaves, and they resolved to meet to address these issues. In 1848, they finally sent out a call for the first women's rights convention. Three hundred

women and men, including Frederick Douglass, attended the first meeting for
women's rights, which was held in Seneca Falls, New York.

The Seneca Falls Convention in 1848 attracted people from all over New   14
York State and other states as well who believed that men and women should be
able to enjoy all rights of citizenship equally. It passed resolutions calling for the
abolition of legal, economic, and social discrimination against women. All of the
resolutions reflected the attendees' dissatisfaction with contemporary moral
codes, divorce and criminal laws, and the limited opportunities for women in education, the church, medicine, law, and politics. Ironically, only the call for woman
suffrage failed to win unanimous approval. Most who attended the Seneca Falls
meeting continued to press for women's rights along with the abolition of slavery.

The 1850s: The Calm Before the Storm

By 1850, much was changing in America: the Gold Rush had spurred westward   15
migration, cities grew as people were lured from their farms, railroads and the
telegraph increased mobility and communication, and immigrants flooded into
the United States. The woman's movement gained momentum, and slavery continued to tear the nation apart. Harriet Beecher Stowe's *Uncle Tom's Cabin*, a novel
that depicted the evils of slavery, further inflamed the country. *Uncle Tom's Cabin*
sold more than 300,000 copies in 1852. Equivalent sales today would top 4 million copies.

The tremendous national reaction to Stowe's work, which later prompted   16
President Abraham Lincoln to call Stowe "the little woman who started the big
war," had not yet faded when a new controversy over the Missouri Compromise
of 1820 became the lightning rod for the first major civil rights case to be addressed by the U.S. Supreme Court. In *Dred Scott* v. *Sandford* (1857), the Court
bluntly had ruled that the Missouri Compromise, which prohibited slavery north
of a set geographical boundary, was unconstitutional. Furthermore, the Court
went on to add that slaves were not U.S. citizens, and as a consequence, slaves
could not bring suits in federal court.

The Civil War and Its Aftermath: Civil Rights Laws and Constitutional Amendments

The Civil War had many causes, but slavery was clearly a key issue. During the   17
war (1861–1865), abolitionists continued to press for an end to slavery. They were
rewarded when President Abraham Lincoln issued the Emancipation Proclamation, which provided that all slaves in states still in active rebellion against the
United States would be freed automatically on January 1, 1863. Designed as a
measure to gain favor for the war in the North, the Emancipation Proclamation
did not free all slaves—it freed only those who lived in the Confederacy, which
was made up of states that had seceded from the union. Complete abolition of
slavery did not occur until congressional passage and ultimate ratification of the
Thirteenth Amendment in 1865.

Thirteenth Amendment
One of the three Civil War
Amendments; specifically
bans slavery in the United
States.

Black Codes
Laws denying most legal
rights to newly freed slaves;
passed by southern states
following the Civil War.

The Civil War Amendments.   The **Thirteenth Amendment** was the first   18
of the three Civil War Amendments. It banned all forms of "slavery [and] invol-
untary servitude." Although southern states were required to ratify the Thirteenth Amendment as a condition of their readmission to the Union after the
war, most of the former Confederate states quickly passed laws that were designed to restrict opportunities for newly freed slaves. These **Black Codes** prohibited African Americans from voting, sitting on juries, or even appearing in
public places. Although Black Codes differed from state to state, all empowered

local law-enforcement officials to arrest unemployed blacks, fine them for vagrancy, and hire them out to employers to satisfy their fines. Some state codes went so far as to require African Americans to work on plantations or to be domestics. The Black Codes laid the groundwork for Jim Crow laws, which later would institute segregation in all walks of life in the South.

19   An outraged Congress enacted the Civil Rights Act of 1866 to invalidate some state Black Codes. President Andrew Johnson vetoed the legislation, but—for the first time in history—Congress overrode a presidential veto. The Civil Rights Act formally made African Americans citizens of the United States and gave the Congress and the federal courts the power to intervene when states attempted to restrict the citizenship rights of male African Americans in matters such as voting. Congress reasoned that African Americans were unlikely to fare well if they had to file discrimination complaints in state courts, where most judges were elected. Passage of a federal law allowed African Americans to challenge discriminatory state practices in the federal courts, where judges were appointed for life by the president.

20   Because controversy remained over the constitutionality of the act (since the Constitution gives states the right to determine qualifications of voters), the **Fourteenth Amendment** was proposed simultaneously with the Civil Rights Act to guarantee, among other things, citizenship to all freed slaves. Other key provisions of the Fourteenth Amendment barred states from abridging "the privileges or immunities of citizenship" or depriving "any person of life, liberty, or property without due process of law," or "deny any person within its jurisdiction the equal protection of the laws."

Fourteenth Amendment
One of the three Civil War Amendments; guarantees equal protection and due process of law to all U.S. citizens.

21   Unlike the Thirteenth Amendment, which had near-unanimous support in the North, the Fourteenth Amendment was opposed by many women because it failed to guarantee suffrage for women. During the Civil War, women's rights activists put aside their claims for expanded rights for women, most notably the right to vote, and threw their energies into the war effort. They were convinced that once slaves were freed and given the right to vote, women similarly would be rewarded with the franchise. They were wrong.

22   In early 1869, after ratification of the Fourteenth Amendment (which specifically added the word "male" to the Constitution for the first time), women's rights activists met in Washington, D.C., to argue against passage of any new amendment that would extend suffrage to black males and not to women. The convention resolved that "a man's government is worse than a white man's government, because, in proportion as you increase the tyrants, you make the condition of the disenfranchised class more hopeless and degraded."

23   In spite of these arguments, the **Fifteenth Amendment** was passed by Congress in early 1869. It guaranteed the "right of citizens" to vote regardless of their "race, color or previous condition of servitude." Gender was not mentioned.

Fifteenth Amendment
One of the three Civil War Amendments; specifically enfranchised newly freed male slaves.

24   Women's rights activists were shocked. Abolitionists' continued support of the Fifteenth Amendment, which was ratified by the states in 1870, prompted many women's rights supporters to leave the abolition movement and to work solely for the cause of women's rights. Twice burned, Susan B. Anthony and Elizabeth Cady Stanton decided to form their own group, the National Woman Suffrage Association (NWSA), to achieve that goal. (Another, more conservative group, the American Woman Suffrage Association, also was formed.) In spite of the NWSA's opposition, however, the Fifteenth Amendment was ratified by the states in 1870.

Civil Rights, Congress, and the Supreme Court

25   Continued southern resistance to African American equality led Congress to pass the Civil Rights Act of 1875, designed to grant equal access to public accommodations such as theaters, restaurants, and transportation. The act also prohibited

the exclusion of African Americans from jury service. By 1877, however, national interest in the legal condition of African Americans waned. Most white Southerners and even some Northerners never had believed in true equality for "freedmen," as former slaves were called. Any rights that freedmen received had been contingent on federal enforcement. Federal occupation of the South ended in 1877. National troops were no longer available to guard polling places and to prevent whites from excluding black voters, and southern states quickly moved to limit African Americans' access to the ballot. Other forms of discrimination also were allowed by judicial decisions upholding **Jim Crow laws,** which required segregation in public schools and facilities including railroads, restaurants, and theaters. Some Jim Crow laws, specifically known as miscegenation laws, barred interracial marriage.

All these laws, at first glance, appeared to conflict with the Civil Rights Act 26 of 1875. In 1883, however, a series of cases decided by the Supreme Court severely damaged the vitality of the 1875 act. The **Civil Rights Cases (1883)** were five separate cases involving the convictions of private individuals found to have violated the Civil Rights Act by refusing to extend accommodations to African Americans in theaters, a hotel, and a railroad. In deciding these cases, the Supreme Court ruled that Congress could prohibit only state or governmental action and not private acts of discrimination. The Court thus seriously limited the scope of the Civil Rights Act by concluding that Congress had no authority to prohibit private discrimination in public accommodations.

The Court's opinion in the Civil Rights Cases provided a moral reinforce- 27 ment for the Jim Crow system. Southern states viewed the Court's ruling as an invitation to gut the reach and intent of the Thirteenth, Fourteenth, and Fifteenth Amendments.

In devising ways to make certain that African Americans did not vote, 28 Southerners had to avoid the intent of the Fifteenth Amendment. This amendment did not guarantee suffrage; it simply said that states could not deny anyone the right to vote on account of race or color. To exclude African Americans in a seemingly racially neutral way, southern states used three devices before the 1890s: (1) poll taxes (small taxes on the right to vote that often came due when poor African American sharecroppers had the least amount of money on hand); (2) some form of property-owning qualifications; and, (3) "literacy" or "understanding" tests, which allowed local voter registration officials to administer difficult reading-comprehension tests to potential voters whom they did not know.

These voting restrictions had an immediate impact. By the late 1890s, black 29 voting fell by 62 percent from the Reconstruction period, while white voting fell by only 26 percent. To make certain that these laws did not further reduce the numbers of poor or uneducated white voters, many southern states added a **grandfather clause** to their voting qualification provisions, granting voting privileges to those who failed to pass a wealth or literacy test only if their grandfathers had voted before Reconstruction. Grandfather clauses effectively denied the descendents of slaves the right to vote.

While African Americans continued to face wide-ranging racism on all 30 fronts, women also confronted discrimination. During this period, married women, by law, could not be recognized as legal entities. Women often were treated in the same category as juveniles and imbeciles, and in many states they were not entitled to wages, inheritances, or custody of their children.

Jim Crow laws

Laws enacted by southern states that discriminated against blacks by creating "whites only" schools, theaters, hotels, and other public accommodations.

Civil Rights Cases (1883)

Name attached to five cases brought under the Civil Rights Act of 1875. In 1883, the Supreme Court decided that discrimination in a variety of public accommodations, including theaters, hotels, and railroads, could not be prohibited by the act because it was private, not state, discrimination.

grandfather clause

Voting qualification provision in many southern states that allowed only those whose grandfathers had voted before Reconstruction to vote unless they passed a wealth or literacy test.

Section Review 1

Directions.

1. On a separate sheet of paper, write a brief summary of the main points of the sections you have just read.

2. Mark each of the following statements True (T), False (F), or Can't Tell (CT). Mark the statement Can't Tell if it cannot be determined to be either true or false based on the material in the passage. Refer to the passage as necessary to verify your answer.

_____ 1. The police officers who shot Amadou Diallo were charged with second-degree murder but were found not guilty at their trial.

_____ 2. The original U.S. Constitution guarantees equal rights for all American citizens.

_____ 3. Most American women in the 1850s wanted the right to vote.

_____ 4. Abolitionists and women's rights activists were united in their support of the Thirteenth, Fourteenth, and Fifteenth Amendments.

_____ 5. Poll taxes and literacy tests were used by southern states to prevent African Americans from voting.

Directions. Write the letter of the best answer in the space provided.

_____ 1. The term *civil rights* refers to
   a. protections provided by the Constitution.
   b. rights listed in the Declaration of Independence.
   c. government efforts to protect citizens from discrimination.
   d. fundamental rights that no government can alter.

_____ 2. When the Constitution was ratified
   a. women were defined as citizens with the same rights as men.
   b. women were not allowed to own property.
   c. no states allowed women to vote.
   d. women had voting rights in only one state.

_____ 3. The abolitionist movement was aided by
   a. the Supreme Court decision in *Dred Scott v. Sandford.*
   b. Stowe's novel *Uncle Tom's Cabin.*
   c. the discovery of gold in California.
   d. the growth of railroads.

_____ 4. The Fifteenth Amendment to the Constitution guaranteed
   a. voting rights for all Americans.
   b. voting rights for women.
   c. voting rights for black Americans.
   d. due process of law for all American citizens.

_____ 5. In the 1880s, the U.S. Supreme Court
     a. undermined congressional efforts to expand civil rights.
     b. supported congressional efforts to expand civil rights.
     c. determined that Congress had no authority to pass civil rights legislation.
     d. convicted five private individuals for acts of public discrimination.

THE PUSH FOR EQUALITY, 1890–1954

THE PROGRESSIVE ERA (1890–1920) WAS CHARACTERIZED by a concerted effort to reform political, economic, and social affairs. Evils such as child labor, the concentration of economic power in the hands of a few industrialists, limited suffrage, political corruption, business monopolies, and prejudice against African Americans all were targets of progressive reform efforts. Distress over the legal inferiority of African Americans was aggravated by the U.S. Supreme Court's decision in ***Plessy v. Ferguson (1896),*** a case that some commentators point to as the Court's darkest hour.   31

In 1892, a group of African Americans in Louisiana decided to test the constitutionality of a Louisiana law mandating racial segregation on all public trains. They convinced Homer Plessy, a man of seven-eighths Caucasian and one-eighth African descent, to board a train in New Orleans and proceed to the "whites only" car. He was arrested when he refused to take a seat in the car reserved for African Americans as required by state law. Plessy challenged the law, arguing that the Fourteenth Amendment prohibited racial segregation.   32

The Supreme Court disagreed. After analyzing the history of African Americans in the United States, the majority concluded that the Louisiana law was constitutional. The justices based their decision on their belief that separate facilities for blacks and whites provided equal protection of the laws. After all, they reasoned, African Americans were not prevented from riding the train; the Louisiana statute required only that the races travel separately. Justice John Marshall Harlan was the lone dissenter. He argued that "the Constitution is colorblind" and that it was senseless to hold constitutional a law "which, practically, puts the badge of servitude and degradation upon a large class of our fellow citizens."   33

Not surprisingly, the separate-but-equal doctrine enunciated in *Plessy* v. *Ferguson* soon came to mean only separate, as new legal avenues to discriminate against African Americans were enacted into law throughout the South. The Jim Crow system soon expanded and became a way of life and a rigid social code in the American South. Journalist Juan Williams notes in *Eyes on the Prize:*   34

> There were Jim Crow schools, Jim Crow restaurants, Jim Crow water fountains, and Jim Crow customs—blacks were expected to tip their hats when they walked past whites, but whites did not have to remove their hats even when they entered a black family's home. Whites were to be called "sir" and "ma'am" by blacks, who in turn were called by their first names by whites. People with white skin were to be given a wide berth on the sidewalk; blacks were expected to step aside meekly.

By 1900, equality for African Americans was far from the promise first offered by the Civil War Amendments. Again and again, the Supreme Court nullified the intent of the amendments and sanctioned racial segregation while the states avidly followed its lead.   35

The Founding of the National Association for the Advancement of Colored People

In 1909, a handful of individuals active in a variety of progressive causes, including woman suffrage and the fight for better working conditions for women and children, met to discuss the idea of a group devoted to the problems of the Negro.   36

Plessy v. *Ferguson* (1896)
Plessy challenged a Louisiana statute requiring that railroads provide separate accommodations for blacks and whites. The Court found that separate-but-equal accommodations did not violate the equal protection clause of the Fourteenth Amendment.

Major race riots recently had occurred in several American cities, and progressive reformers were concerned about these outbreaks of violence and the possibility of others. Oswald Garrison Villard, the influential publisher of the *New York Evening Post*—and the grandson of William Lloyd Garrison—called a conference to discuss the problem. This group soon evolved into the National Association for the Advancement of Colored People (NAACP). Along with Villard, its first leaders included W. E. B. DuBois, a founder of the Niagara Movement, a group of educated African Americans who took their name from their first meeting place in Niagara Falls, Ontario, Canada.

Key Women's Groups

37 The struggle for women's rights was revitalized in 1890 when the National and American Woman Suffrage Associations merged. The new organization, the National American Woman Suffrage Association (NAWSA), was headed by Susan B. Anthony. Unlike NWSA, which had sought a wide variety of expanded rights for women, this new association was devoted largely to securing woman suffrage. Its task was greatly facilitated by the proliferation of women's groups that emerged during the Progressive era. In addition to the rapidly growing temperance movement—the move to ban the sale of alcohol, which many women blamed for a variety of social ills—women's groups were created to seek protective legislation in the form of maximum hour or minimum wage laws for women and to work for improved sanitation, public morals, education, and the like. Other organizations that were part of what was called the "club movement" were created to provide increased cultural and literary experiences for middle-class women. With increased industrialization, for the first time some women found that they had the opportunity to pursue activities other than those centered on the home.

38   One of the most active groups lobbying on behalf of women during this period was the National Consumers' League (NCL), which successfully lobbied for Oregon legislation limiting women to eight hours of work a day. Curt Muller was then charged and convicted of employing women more than eight hours a day in his small laundry. When he appealed his conviction to the U.S. Supreme Court, the NCL sought permission from the state to conduct the defense of the statute.

39   At the urging of NCL attorney and future U.S. Supreme Court Justice Louis Brandeis, NCL members amassed an impressive array of sociological and medical data that were incorporated into what became known as the Brandeis brief. This contained only three pages of legal argument. More than one hundred pages were devoted to nonlegal, sociological data that were used to convince the Court that Oregon's statute was constitutional. In agreeing with the NCL in *Muller* v. *Oregon* (1908), the Court relied heavily on these data to document women's unique status as mothers to justify their different legal treatment.

40   Women seeking the vote used reasoning reflecting the Court's opinion in *Muller*. Discarding earlier notions of full equality, NAWSA based its claim to the right to vote largely on the fact that women, as mothers, should be enfranchised. Furthermore, although many members of the suffrage movement were NAACP members, the new women's movement—called the **suffrage movement** because of its focus on the vote alone and not on broader issues of women's rights—took on racist overtones. Suffragists argued that if undereducated African Americans could vote, why couldn't women? Some NAWSA members even argued that "the enfranchisement of women would ensure immediate and durable white supremacy."

suffrage movement
The drive for voting rights for women that took place in the United States from 1890 to 1920.

41   Diverse attitudes clearly were present in the growing suffrage movement, which often tried to be all things to all people. Its roots in the Progressive movement gave it an exceptionally broad base that transformed NAWSA from a small organization of just over ten thousand members in the early 1890s to a true social movement of more than 2 million members in 1917. By 1920, a coalition of women's groups, led by NAWSA and the newer, more radical National Woman's

Nineteenth Amendment
Amendment to the Constitution that guaranteed women the right to vote.

Party, was able to secure ratification of the **Nineteenth Amendment** to the Constitution. It guaranteed all women the right to vote—fifty years after African American males were enfranchised by the Fifteenth Amendment.

After passage of the suffrage amendment in 1920, the fragile alliance of diverse women's groups that had come together to fight for the vote quickly disintegrated. Women returned to their home groups, such as the NCL or the Women's Christian Temperance Union, to pursue their individualized goals. In fact, after the tumult of the suffrage movement, widespread organized activity on behalf of women's rights did not reemerge until the 1960s. In the meantime, however, the NAACP continued to fight racism and racial segregation. In fact, its activities and those of others in the civil rights movement would later give impetus to a new women's movement.   42

Litigating for Equality

During the 1930s, leaders of the NAACP began to sense that the time was right to launch a full-scale challenge in the federal courts to the constitutionality of *Plessy*'s separate-but-equal doctrine. Clearly, the separate-but-equal doctrine and the proliferation of Jim Crow laws were a bar to any hope of full equality for African Americans. Traditional legislative channels were unlikely to work, given blacks' limited or nonexistent political power. Thus, the federal courts and a long-range litigation strategy were the NAACP's only hopes. The NAACP mapped out a long-range strategy that would first target segregation in professional and graduate education.   43

Test Cases.   The NAACP opted first to challenge the constitutionality of Jim Crow law schools. In 1935, all southern states maintained fully segregated elementary and secondary schools. Colleges and universities also were segregated, but most states did not provide for postgraduate education for African Americans. NAACP lawyers chose to target law schools because they were institutions that judges could well understand, and integration there would prove less threatening to most whites.   44

Lloyd Gaines, a graduate of Missouri's all-black Lincoln University, sought admission to the all-white University of Missouri Law School in 1936. He was immediately rejected. In the separate-but-equal spirit, the state offered to build a law school at Lincoln (although no funds were allocated for the project) or, if he didn't want to wait, to pay his tuition at an out-of-state law school. Gaines rejected the offer, sued, lost in the lower courts, and appealed to the U.S. Supreme Court.   45

Gaines's case was filed at an auspicious time. A constitutional revolution of sorts occurred in Supreme Court decision making in 1937. Before this time, the Court was most receptive to and interested in the protection of economic liberties. In 1937, however, the Court reversed itself in a series of cases and began to place individual freedoms and personal liberties on a more protected footing. Thus, in 1938, Gaines's lawyers pleaded his appeal to a far more sympathetic Supreme Court. NAACP attorneys argued that the creation of a separate law school of a lesser caliber than that of the University of Missouri would not and could not afford Gaines an equal education. The justices agreed and ruled that Missouri had failed to meet the separate-but-equal requirements of *Plessy*. The Court ordered Missouri either to admit Gaines to the school or to set up a law school for him.   46

Recognizing the importance of the Court's ruling, in 1939 the NAACP created a separate, tax-exempt legal defense fund to devise a strategy that would build on the Missouri case and bring about equal educational opportunities for all African American children. The first head of the NAACP Legal Defense and Educational Fund, commonly referred to as the LDF, was Thurgood Marshall, who later be-   47 came the first African American to serve on the U.S. Supreme Court. Sensing that the Court would be more amenable to the NAACP's broader goals if it were first forced to address a variety of less threatening claims to educational opportunity, Marshall and the LDF brought a series of carefully crafted test cases to the Court.

48   The first case involved H. M. Sweatt, a 46-year-old African American mail carrier, who applied for admission to the all-white University of Texas Law School in 1946. Rejected on racial grounds, Sweatt sued. The judge gave the state six months to establish a law school or to admit Sweatt to the university. The university then rented a few rooms in downtown Houston and hired two local African American attorneys to be part-time faculty members. (At that time, there was only one full-time African American law school professor in the United States.) The state legislature saw the handwriting on the wall and authorized $3 million for the creation of the Texas State University for Negroes. One hundred thousand dollars of that money was to be for a new law school in Austin across the street from the state capitol building. It consisted of three small basement rooms, a library of more than ten thousand books, access to the state law library, and three part-time first-year instructors as the faculty. Sweatt declined the opportunity to obtain an education there and instead chose to continue his legal challenge.

49   While working on the Texas case, the LDF also decided to pursue a case involving George McLaurin, a retired university professor who had been denied admission to the doctoral education program at the University of Oklahoma. Marshall reasoned that McLaurin, at age 68, would be immune from the charges that African Americans wanted integration in order to intermarry with whites. After a lower court ordered McLaurin's admission, the university reserved a dingy alcove in the cafeteria for him to eat in during off-hours, and he was given his own table in the library behind a shelf of newspapers. In what surely "was Oklahoma's most inventive contribution to legalized bigotry since the adoption of the 'grandfather clause,'" McLaurin was forced to sit outside classrooms while lectures and seminars were conducted inside.

50   The Supreme Court handled these two cases together. The eleven southern states filed an *amicus curiae* (friend of the court) brief, in which they argued that *Plessy* should govern both cases. The LDF received assistance, however, from an unexpected source—the U.S. government. In a dramatic departure from the past, the administration of President Harry S Truman filed a friend-of-the-court brief urging the Court to overrule *Plessy*. Earlier, Truman had issued an executive order desegregating the military.

51   Since the late 1870s, the U.S. government never had sided against the southern states in a civil rights matter and never had submitted an *amicus* brief supporting the rights of African American citizens. President Truman believed that because many African Americans had fought and died for their country in World War II, this kind of executive action was proper. The Court traditionally gives great weight to briefs from the U.S. government. The Court, however, did not overrule *Plessy*, but the justices found that the measures taken by the states in each case failed to live up to the strictures of the separate-but-equal doctrine. The Court unanimously ruled that the remedies to each situation were inadequate to afford a sound education. In the *Sweatt* case, for example, the Court declared that the "qualities which are incapable of objective measurement but which make for greatness in a law school . . . includ[ing] the reputation of the faculty, experience of the administration, position and influence of the alumni, standing in the community, traditions and prestige" made it impossible for the state to provide an equal education in a segregated setting.

52   In 1950, after these decisions were handed down, the LDF concluded that the time had come to launch a full-scale attack on the separate-but-equal doctrine. The decisions of the Court were encouraging, and the position of the U.S. government and the population in general appeared to be more receptive to an outright overruling of *Plessy*.

Brown v. Board of
Education (1954)
U.S. Supreme Court deci-
sion holding that school
segregation is inherently
unconstitutional because it
violates the Fourteenth
Amendment's guarantee of
equal protection; marked
the end of legal segregation
in the United States.

equal protection clause
Section of the Fourteenth
Amendment that guaran-
tees that all citizens receive
"equal protection of the
laws."

Brown v. Board of Education

Brown v. Board of Education (1954) actually   53
was four cases brought from different areas of the South and border states involving public elementary or high school systems that mandated separate schools
for blacks and whites. In *Brown*, LDF lawyers, again led by Thurgood Marshall,
argued that *Plessy*'s separate-but-equal doctrine was unconstitutional under the
equal protection clause of the Fourteenth Amendment, and that if the Court
was still reluctant to overrule *Plessy*, the only way to equalize the schools was to
integrate them. A major component of the LDF's strategy was to prove that the
intellectual, psychological, and financial damage that befell African Americans
as a result of segregation precluded any court from finding that equality was
served by the separate-but-equal policy.

In *Brown*, the LDF presented the Supreme Court with evidence of the   54
harmful consequences of state-imposed racial discrimination. To buttress its
claims, the LDF introduced the now-famous doll study, conducted by Kenneth
Clark, a prominent African American sociologist who had long studied the negative effects of segregation on African American children. His research revealed
that black children not only preferred white dolls when shown black dolls and
white dolls, but that most liked the white doll better, many adding that the black
doll looked "bad." This information was used to illustrate the negative impact of
racial segregation and bias on an African American child's self-image.

The LDF's legal briefs were supported by important *amicus curiae* briefs sub-   55
mitted by the U.S. government, major civil rights groups, labor unions, and religious groups decrying racial segregation. On May 17, 1954, Chief Justice Earl
Warren delivered the fourth opinion of the day, *Brown v. Board of Education*.
Writing for the Court, Warren stated:

> To separate [some school children] from others . . . solely because of their race
> generates a feeling of inferiority as to their status in the community that may
> affect their hearts and minds in a way very unlikely ever to be undone. We
> conclude, unanimously, that in the field of public education the doctrine of
> "separate but equal" has no place.

There can be no doubt that *Brown* was the most important civil rights case   56
decided in the twentieth century. It immediately evoked an uproar that shook the
nation. Some segregationists called the day the decision was handed down Black
Monday. The governor of South Carolina denounced the decision, saying, "Ending segregation would mark the beginning of the end of civilization in the South
as we know it." The LDF lawyers who had argued these cases and those cases
leading to *Brown*, however, were jubilant.

Remarkable changes had occurred in the civil rights of Americans since   57
1890. Women had won the right to vote, and after a long and arduous trail of litigation in the federal courts, the Supreme Court had finally overturned its most
racist decision of the era, *Plessy v. Ferguson*. The Court boldly proclaimed that
separate but equal (at least in education) would no longer pass constitutional
muster. The question then became how *Brown* would be interpreted and implemented. Could it be used to invalidate other Jim Crow laws and practices? Would
African Americans ever be truly equal under the law?

Section Review 2

Directions.

1. On a separate sheet of paper, write a brief summary of the main points of the sections you have just read.

2. Mark each of the following statements True (T), False (F), or Can't Tell (CT). Mark the statement Can't Tell if it cannot be determined to be either true or false based on the material in the passage. Refer to the passage as necessary to verify your answer.

_____ 1. The Supreme Court's ruling in *Plessy* v. *Ferguson* supported the policy of separate-but-equal.

_____ 2. NAWSA grew larger and stronger after achieving voting rights for women.

_____ 3. The NAACP used federal court cases to win civil rights for African Americans.

_____ 4. The Supreme Court's ruling in *Brown* v. *Board of Education* overturned the separate-but-equal policy.

_____ 5. Thurgood Marshall was one of the Supreme Court justices who voted to end school desegregation in 1954.

Cumulative Review 1 (Pages 336–348)

Directions. Write the letter of the best answer in the space provided.

_____ 1. An important achievement of the National Consumers' League was
   a. the passage of a consumers' bill of rights.
   b. the guarantee of voting rights for Oregon women.
   c. the establishment of an 8-hour workday for Oregon women.
   d. the establishment of an 8-hour workday for American women.

_____ 2. One result of the Missouri Compromise was
   a. the admission of Missouri into the Union as a free state.
   b. the admission of Missouri into the Union as a slave state.
   c. the creation of an imbalance between the number of slave states and free states.
   d. a weakening of the abolitionist movement.

_____ 3. The Supreme Court's rulings in the Civil Rights Cases of 1883
   a. enhanced the effects of the Thirteenth, Fourteenth, and Fifteenth Amendments.
   b. expanded voting opportunities for African Americans.
   c. restricted the ability of state governments to discriminate.
   d. encouraged southern whites to continue segregation efforts.

_____ 4. The passage suggests that during the Progressive Era, women's groups
  a. grew in number and scope.
  b. were ineffective because they lacked leadership.
  c. were ineffective because they could not agree on goals.
  d. opposed the efforts of the NAACP.

_____ 5. We can infer from the passage that the *Gaines* case
  a. was the most important civil rights case heard by the Supreme Court.
  b. might have had a different result if filed during a different time period.
  c. overturned the Court's separate-but-equal doctrine.
  d. launched Thurgood Marshall's career as a civil rights lawyer.

Directions.   Answer each question in complete sentences, without copying word-for-word from the passage.

1. When and where was the first women's rights convention held? How did it come about?

_____

_____

_____

2. What were the primary purposes of the Civil War amendments?

_____

_____

_____

3. What is a grandfather clause? How did southern states use such clauses to continue voter discrimination?

_____

_____

_____

4. Explain why *Plessy v. Ferguson* is considered by some to be the Supreme Court's "darkest hour."

_____

_____

_____

5. What was Thurgood Marshall's contribution to the civil rights movement?

_____

_____

_____

Vocabulary Exercise 1

Directions. Choose the meaning for the underlined word that best fits the context. You may consult the dictionary as needed.

_____ 1. . . . now that crime is on the wane . . .
[Paragraph 1]
a. increase
b. a period of change
c. decline
d. public attention

_____ 2. . . . reminiscent of many 1960s civil rights marches. [Paragraph 2]
a. concerned with
b. reminding (of a past experience)
c. colorful
d. causing or seeking change

_____ 3. Delegates . . . put political expediency before the immorality of slavery . . . . [Paragraph 4]
a. convenience
b. disagreement
c. agreement
d. resolve

_____ 4. . . . it also fueled the fervor of those who opposed slavery. [Paragraph 11]
a. concern
b. anger
c. passion
d. power

_____ 5. . . . and ultimate ratification of the Thirteenth Amendment in 1865. [Paragraph 17]
a. unavoidable
b. uncertain
c. successful
d. final

_____ 6. . . . puts the badge of servitude and degradation . . . . [Paragraph 33]
a. slavery
b. discrimination
c. debasement
d. discontent

_____ 7. . . . while the states avidly followed its lead. [Paragraph 35]
a. carefully
b. hesitantly
c. with resistance, criticism, or opposition
d. enthusiastically

_____ 8. . . . the proliferation of women's groups . . . . [Paragraph 37]
a. obstruction
b. rapid growth
c. forceful advocacy
d. success

_____ 9. Gaines's case was filed at an auspicious time. [Paragraph 46]
a. favorable
b. uncertain
c. fateful
d. likely

_____ 10. . . . precluded any court from finding . . . . [Paragraph 53]
a. encouraged
b. discouraged
c. prevented
d. opposed

THE CIVIL RIGHTS MOVEMENT

OUR NOTION OF CIVIL RIGHTS HAS CHANGED profoundly since the *Brown* deci-   58
sion in 1954. *Brown* served as a catalyst for change, sparking the development of
the modern civil rights movement. Women's work in that movement and the student protest movement that arose in reaction to the U.S. government's involvement in Vietnam gave women the experience needed to form their own organizations to press for full equality. As African Americans and women became more and
more successful, they served as models for other groups who sought equality—
Hispanic Americans, Native Americans, homosexuals, the disabled, and others.

School Desegregation After *Brown*

One year after *Brown,* in a case referred to as *Brown* v. *Board of Education II* (1955),   59
the Court ruled that racially segregated systems must be dismantled "with all deliberate speed." To facilitate implementation, the Court placed enforcement of
Brown in the hands of appointed federal district court judges, who were considered more immune to local political pressures than were elected state court judges.

    The NAACP and its LDF continued to resort to the courts to see that   60
Brown was implemented, while the South entered into a near conspiracy to avoid
the mandates of *Brown II.* In Arkansas, for example, Governor Orval Faubus,
who was facing a reelection bid, announced that he would not "be a party to any
attempt to force acceptance of change to which people are overwhelmingly opposed." The day before school was to begin, he announced that National Guards-
men would surround Little Rock's Central High School to prevent African
American students from entering. While the federal courts in Arkansas continued to order the admission of African American children, the governor remained
adamant. Finally, President Dwight D. Eisenhower sent federal troops to Little
Rock to protect the rights of the nine students attending Central High.

    In reaction to the governor's outrageous conduct, the Court broke with tra-   61
dition and issued a unanimous decision in *Cooper* v. *Aaron* (1958), which was filed
by the Little Rock School Board asking the federal district court for a two-and-
one-half-year delay in implementation of its desegregation plans. Each justice
signed the opinion individually, underscoring his individual support for the notion that "no state legislator or executive or judicial officer can war against the
Constitution without violating his undertaking to support it." The state's actions
thus were ruled unconstitutional and its "evasive schemes" illegal.

A New Move for African American Rights

In 1955, soon after *Brown II,* the civil rights movement took another step for-   62
ward—this time in Montgomery, Alabama. Rosa Parks, the local NAACP's
Youth Council adviser, decided to challenge the constitutionality of the segregated bus system. First, Parks and other NAACP officials began to raise money
for litigation and made speeches around town to garner public support. Then, on
December 1, 1955, Rosa Parks made history when she refused to leave her seat
on a bus to move to the back to make room for a white male passenger. She was
arrested for violating an Alabama law banning integration of public facilities, including buses. After she was freed on bond, Parks and the NAACP decided to
enlist city clergy to help her cause. At the same time, they distributed 35,000
handbills calling for African Americans to boycott the Montgomery bus system
on the day of Parks's trial. Black ministers used Sunday services to urge their
members to support the boycott. On Monday morning, African Americans
walked, carpooled, or used black-owned taxicabs. That night, local ministers decided that the boycott should be continued. A new, 26-year-old minister, Martin

Luther King Jr., was selected to lead the newly formed Montgomery Improvement Association.

63   As the boycott dragged on, Montgomery officials and local business owners began to harass the city's African American citizens. The residents held out, despite suffering personal hardship for their actions, ranging from harassment to bankruptcy to job loss. In 1956, a federal court ruled that the segregated bus system violated the equal protection clause of the Fourteenth Amendment. After a year of walking, black Montgomery residents ended their protest when city buses were ordered to integrate. The first effort at nonviolent protest had been successful. Organized boycotts and other forms of nonviolent protest, including sit-ins at segregated restaurants and bus stations, were to follow.

Formation of New Groups

64   The recognition and respect that Martin Luther King Jr. earned within the African American community helped him to launch the Southern Christian Leadership Conference (SCLC) in 1957, soon after the end of the Montgomery bus boycott. Unlike the NAACP, which had northern origins and had come to rely largely on litigation as a means of achieving expanded equality, the SCLC had a southern base and was rooted more closely in black religious culture. The SCLC's philosophy reflected King's growing belief in the importance of nonviolent protest and civil disobedience.

65   On February 1, 1960, students at the all-black North Carolina Agricultural and Technical College participated in the first sit-in. Black students marched to a local lunch counter, sat down, and ordered cups of coffee. They were refused service and sat at the counter until police arrived. When the students refused to leave, they were arrested and jailed. Soon thereafter, African American college students around the South did the same. Their actions were the subject of extensive national media attention.

66   Over spring break 1960, with the assistance of an $800 grant from the SCLC, 200 student delegates—black and white—met at Shaw University in North Carolina to consider recent sit-in actions and to plan for the future. Later that year, the Student Nonviolent Coordinating Committee (SNCC) was formed.

67   Whereas the SCLC generally worked with church leaders in a community, SNCC was much more of a grassroots organization. Always perceived as more radical than the SCLC, SNCC tended to focus its organizing activities on the young, both black and white.

68   In addition to joining the sit-in bandwagon, SNCC also came to lead what were called freedom rides, designed to focus attention on segregated public accommodations. Bands of college students and other civil rights activists traveled by bus throughout the South in an effort to force bus stations to desegregate. Often these protesters were met by angry mobs of segregationists and brutal violence, as local police chose not to defend protesters' basic constitutional rights to free speech and peaceful assembly. African Americans were not the only ones to participate in freedom rides; increasingly, white college students from the North began to play an important role in SNCC.

69   While SNCC continued to sponsor sit-ins and freedom rides, in 1963, Martin Luther King Jr. launched a series of massive nonviolent demonstrations in Birmingham, Alabama, long considered a major stronghold of segregation. Thousands of blacks and whites marched to Birmingham in a show of solidarity. Peaceful marchers were met there by the Birmingham police commissioner, who ordered his officers to use dogs, clubs, and fire hoses on the marchers. Americans across the nation were horrified as they witnessed on television the brutality and abuse heaped on the protesters. As the marchers hoped, these shocking scenes helped convince President John F. Kennedy to propose important civil rights legislation.

The Civil Rights Act of 1964

Both the SCLC and SNCC sought full implementation of Supreme Court deci-   70
sions dealing with race and an end to racial segregation and discrimination. The
cumulative effect of collective actions including sit-ins, boycotts, marches, and
freedom rides—as well as the tragic bombings and deaths inflicted in retalia-
tion—led Congress to pass the first major piece of civil rights legislation since the
post–Civil War era, the Civil Rights Act of 1964. Several events led to the consideration of this legislation.

In 1963, President John F. Kennedy requested that Congress pass a law ban-   71
ning discrimination in public accommodations. Seizing the moment, Martin
Luther King Jr. called for a monumental march on Washington, D.C., to demonstrate widespread support for far-ranging anti-discrimination legislation. It was
clear that national laws outlawing discrimination were the only answer: southern
legislators would never vote to repeal Jim Crow laws. The March on Washington
for Jobs and Freedom was held in August 1963, only a few months after the
Birmingham demonstrations. More than 250,000 people heard King deliver his
famous "I Have a Dream" speech from the Lincoln Memorial. Before Congress
had the opportunity to vote on any legislation, however, John F. Kennedy was as-
sassinated on November 22, 1963, in Dallas, Texas.

When Vice President Lyndon B. Johnson, a southern-born former Senate   72
majority leader, succeeded Kennedy as president, he put civil rights reform at the
top of his legislative priority list, and civil rights activists gained a critical ally.
Thus, through the 1960s, the movement subtly changed in focus from peaceful
protest and litigation to legislative lobbying. Its focus broadened from integration
of school and public facilities and voting rights to issues of housing, jobs, and
equal opportunity.

The push for civil rights legislation in the halls of Congress was helped by   73
changes in public opinion. Between 1959 and 1965, southern attitudes toward integrated schools changed enormously. The proportion of Southerners who said that
they would not mind their child's attendance at a racially balanced school doubled.

In spite of strong presidential support and the sway of public opinion, the Civil   74
Rights Act of 1964 did not sail through Congress. Southern senators, led by South
Carolina's Strom Thurmond, a Democrat who later switched to the Republican
Party, conducted the longest filibuster in the history of the Senate. For eight weeks,
Thurmond led the effort to hold up voting on the civil rights bill until cloture was
invoked and the filibuster ended. Once passed, the **Civil Rights Act of 1964:**

- outlawed arbitrary discrimination in voter registration and expedited voting
  rights lawsuits.
- barred discrimination in public accommodations engaged in interstate
  commerce.
- authorized the Department of Justice to initiate lawsuits to desegregate public facilities and schools.
- provided for the withholding of federal funds from discriminatory state and
  local programs.
- prohibited discrimination in employment on grounds of race, color, religion,
  national origin, or sex.
- created the Equal Employment Opportunity Commission (EEOC) to monitor and enforce the bans on employment discrimination.

As challenges were made to the Civil Rights Act of 1964, other changes con-   75
tinued to sweep the United States. African Americans in the North, who believed
that their brothers and sisters in the South were making progress against discrimination, found themselves frustrated. Northern blacks were experiencing high un-

Civil Rights Act of 1964
Legislation passed by Congress to outlaw segregation
in public facilities and racial
discrimination in employ-
ment, education, and vot-
ing; created the Equal Employment Opportunity
Commission.

employment, poverty, discrimination, and little political clout. Some, including Black Muslim leader Malcolm X, even argued that, to survive, African Americans must separate themselves from white culture in every way. These increased tensions resulted in riots in many major cities from 1964 to 1968, when many African Americans in the North took to the streets, burning and looting to vent their rage. The assassination of Martin Luther King Jr. in 1968 triggered a new epidemic of race riots.

The Impact of the Civil Rights Act of 1964

76 Many Southerners were adamant in their belief that the Civil Rights Act of 1964 was unconstitutional because it went beyond the scope of Congress's authority to legislate under the Constitution, and lawsuits were quickly brought to challenge the act. The Supreme Court upheld its constitutionality when it found that Congress was within the legitimate scope of its commerce power as outlined in Article I.

77 **Education.**   One of the key provisions of the Civil Rights Act of 1964 authorized the Department of Justice to bring actions against school districts that failed to comply with *Brown* v. *Board of Education.* By 1964, a full decade after *Brown,* fewer than 1 percent of African American children in the South attended integrated schools.

78   In *Swann* v. *Charlotte-Mecklenburg School District* (1971), the Supreme Court ruled that all vestiges of state-imposed segregation, called **de jure discrimination,** or discrimination by law, must be eliminated at once. The Court also ruled that lower federal courts had the authority to fashion a wide variety of remedies including busing, racial quotas, and the pairing of schools to end dual, segregated school systems.

de jure discrimination
Racial segregation that is a direct result of law or official policy.

79   In *Swann,* the Court was careful to distinguish *de jure* from **de facto discrimination,** which is unintentional discrimination, often attributable to housing patterns or private acts. The Court noted that its approval of busing was a remedy for intentional, government-imposed or sanctioned discrimination only.

de facto discrimination
Racial discrimination that results from practice (such as housing patterns or other social factors) rather than the law.

80   Over the years, forced, judicially imposed busing found less and less favor with the Supreme Court, even in situations where *de jure* discrimination had existed. In 1992, the Supreme Court ruled that in a situation where all-black schools still existed despite a 1969 court order to dismantle the *de jure* system, so long as the segregation was not a result of the school board's actions, the school district's actions could be removed from court supervision. In 1995, the Court ruled 5–4 that city school boards can use plans to attract white suburban students to mostly minority urban schools only if both city and suburban schools still show the effects of segregation, thus reversing a lower court desegregation order. Today, the trend is toward dismantling court-ordered desegregation plans, although school districts still are under orders not to discriminate. Still, especially in the North, school segregation has increased steadily over the past 15 years.

81 **Employment.**   Title VII of the Civil Rights Act of 1964 prohibits employers from discriminating against employees for a variety of reasons, including race, sex, age, and national origin. (In 1978, the act was amended to prohibit discrimination based on pregnancy.) In 1971, in one of the first major cases decided under the act, the Supreme Court ruled that employers could be found liable for discrimination if the effect of their employment practices was to exclude African Americans from certain positions. African American employees were allowed to use statistical evidence to show that they had been excluded from all but one department of the Duke Power Company, because it required employees to have a high school education or pass a special test to be eligible for promotion.

The Supreme Court ruled that although the tests did not appear to discrimi- 82
nate against African Americans, their effects—that there were no African American employees in any other departments—were sufficient to shift to the employer
the burden of proving that no discrimination occurred. Thus, the Duke Power
Company would have to prove that the tests were a business necessity that had a
"demonstrable relationship to successful performance" of a particular job.

The notion of "business necessity," as set out in the Civil Rights Act of 1964 83
and interpreted by the federal courts, was especially important for women.
Women long had been kept out of many occupations on the strength of the belief
that customers preferred to deal with male personnel. Conversely, males were
barred from flight-attendant positions because the airlines believed that passen-
gers preferred to be served by young, attractive women. Similarly, many large factories, manufacturing establishments, and police and fire departments refused to
hire women by subjecting them to arbitrary height and weight requirements,
which also disproportionately affected Hispanics. Like the tests declared illegal
by the Court, these requirements often could not be shown to be related to job
performance and were eventually ruled illegal by the federal courts.

THE WOMEN'S RIGHTS MOVEMENT

JUST AS IN THE ABOLITION MOVEMENT IN THE 1800S, women from all walks of 84
life also participated in the civil rights movement. Women were important members of new groups such as SNCC and the SCLC as well as more traditional
groups such as the NAACP, yet they often found themselves treated as second-
class citizens. At one point during an SNCC national meeting, its chair openly
proclaimed: "The only position for women in the SNCC is prone." Statements
and attitudes like these led some women to found early women's liberation groups
that were generally quite radical but small in membership.

Litigation for Equal Rights

As discussed earlier, initial efforts to convince the Supreme Court to declare 85
women enfranchised under the equal protection clause of the Fourteenth Amendment were uniformly unsuccessful. The paternalistic attitudes of the Supreme
Court, and perhaps society as well, continued well into the 1970s. As late as 1961,
Florida required women who wished to serve on juries to travel to the county
courthouse and register for that duty. In contrast, all men who were registered
voters automatically were eligible to serve. When Gwendolyn Hoyt was convicted
of bludgeoning her adulterous husband to death with a baseball bat, she appealed
her conviction, claiming that the exclusion of women from her jury prejudiced her
case. She believed that female jurors—her peers—would have been more sympathetic to her and the emotional turmoil that led to her attack on her husband and
her claim of temporary insanity. She therefore argued that her trial by an all-male
jury violated her rights as guaranteed by the Fourteenth Amendment.

In rejecting her contention, Justice John Harlan (the grandson of the lone dis- 86
senting justice in *Plessy*) wrote in *Hoyt* v. *Florida* (1961): "Despite the enlightened
emancipation of women from the restrictions and protections of bygone years, and
their entry into many parts of community life formerly considered to be reserved
to men, a woman is still regarded as the center of home and family life."

These kinds of attitudes and decisions (*Hoyt* was unanimously reversed in 87
1975) were not sufficient to forge a new movement for women's rights. Shortly
after *Hoyt*, however, three events occurred to move women to action. In 1961,
soon after his election, President John F. Kennedy created the President's Commission on the Status of Women. The commission's report, *American Women*,

released in 1963, documented pervasive discrimination against women in all walks of life. In addition, the civil rights movement and the publication of Betty Friedan's *The Feminine Mystique* (1963), which led some women to question their lives and status in society, added to their dawning recognition that something was wrong. Soon after, the Civil Rights Act of 1964 prohibited discrimination based not only on race but also on sex. Ironically, that provision had been added to Title VII of the Civil Rights Act by southern Democrats. These senators saw a prohibition against gender discrimination in employment as a joke, and viewed its addition as a means to discredit the entire act and ensure its defeat. Thus, it was added at the last minute and female members of Congress seized the opportunity to garner support for the measure.

88   In 1966, after the **Equal Employment Opportunity Commission** failed to enforce the law as it applied to sex discrimination, female activists formed the National Organization for Women (NOW). From its inception, NOW was modeled closely on the NAACP. Women in NOW were similar to the founders of the NAACP; they wanted to work within the system to prevent discrimination. Initially, most of this activity was geared toward achievement of equality either by passage of an equal rights amendment to the Constitution, or by judicial decision.

Equal Employment Opportunity Commission
Federal agency created to enforce the Civil Rights Act of 1964, which forbids discrimination on the basis of race, creed, national origin, religion, or sex in hiring, promotion, or firing.

89   Not all women agreed with the notion of full equality for women. Members of the National Consumers' League, for example, feared that an equal rights amendment would invalidate protective legislation of the kind specifically ruled constitutional in *Muller* v. *Oregon* (1908). Nevertheless, from 1923 to 1972, a proposal for an equal rights amendment was made in every session of every Congress. Every president since Harry S Truman backed it, and by 1972 public opinion favored its ratification.

90   Finally, in 1972, in response to pressure from NOW, the National Women's Political Caucus, and a wide variety of other feminist groups, Congress voted in favor of the **Equal Rights Amendment (ERA)** by overwhelming majorities (84–8 in the Senate; 354–24 in the House). The amendment provided that:

Equal Rights Amendment (ERA)
Proposed amendment that would bar discrimination against women by federal or state governments.

Equality of rights under the law shall not be denied or abridged by the United States or by any state on account of sex.
The Congress shall have the power to enforce, by appropriate legislation, the provisions of this article.

91   Within a year, twenty-two states ratified the amendment, most by overwhelming margins. But, the tide soon turned. In *Roe* v. *Wade* (1973), the Supreme Court decided that women had a constitutionally protected right to privacy that included the right to terminate a pregnancy. Almost overnight, *Roe* gave the ERA's opponents political fuel. Although privacy rights and the ERA have nothing to do with each other, opponents effectively persuaded many people in states that had yet to ratify the amendment that the two were linked. They also claimed that the ERA and feminists were anti-family and that the ERA would force women out of their homes and into the workforce because husbands would no longer be responsible for their wives' support.

92   These arguments and the amendment's potential to make women eligible for the military draft brought the ratification effort to a near standstill. In 1974 and 1975, the amendment only squeaked through the Montana and North Dakota legislatures, and two states—Nebraska and Tennessee—voted to rescind their earlier ratifications. By 1978, one year before the deadline for ratification was to expire, thirty-five states had voted for the amendment—three short of the three-fourths necessary for ratification. Efforts in key states such as Illinois and Florida failed as opposition to the ERA intensified. Faced with the prospect of defeat, ERA supporters heavily lobbied Congress to extend the deadline for ratification. Congress extended the ratification period by three years, but to no avail. No additional states ratified the amendment and three more rescinded their votes.

What began as a simple correction to the Constitution turned into a highly 93
controversial proposed change. Even though large numbers of the public favored
the ERA, opponents needed to stall ratification in only thirteen states while supporters had to convince legislators in thirty-eight. The success that women's rights
activists were having in the courts was hurting the effort. When women first
sought the ERA in the late 1960s, the Supreme Court had yet to rule that women
were protected by the Fourteenth Amendment's equal protection clause from any
kind of discrimination, thus clearly showing the need for an amendment. But, as
the Court widened its interpretation of the Constitution to protect women from
some sorts of discrimination, in the eyes of many, the need for a new amendment
became less urgent. The proposed amendment died without being ratified on
June 30, 1982.

While several women's groups worked toward passage of the ERA, NOW 94
and several other groups, including the American Civil Liberties Union (ACLU),
formed litigating arms to pressure the courts. But, women faced an immediate
roadblock in the Supreme Court's interpretation of the equal protection clause of
the Fourteenth Amendment.

The Equal Protection Clause and Constitutional Standards of Review

The Fourteenth Amendment protects all U.S. citizens from state action that vi- 95
olates equal protection of the laws. Most laws, however, are subject to what is
called the *rational basis* or *minimum rationality test*. This lowest level of scrutiny
means that governments must allege a rational foundation for any distinctions
they make. Early on, however, the Supreme Court decided that certain freedoms were entitled to a heightened standard of review. As early as 1937, the
Supreme Court recognized that certain freedoms were so fundamental that a
very heavy burden would be placed on any government that sought to restrict
those rights. When fundamental freedoms such as those guaranteed by the First
Amendment or **suspect classifications** such as race are involved, the Court uses
a heightened standard of review called **strict scrutiny** to determine the constitutional validity of the challenged practices, as detailed in Table 8.1. Beginning
with *Korematsu* v. *U.S.* (1944), which involved a constitutional challenge to the
internment of Japanese Americans as security risks during World War II, Justice Hugo Black noted that "all legal restrictions which curtail the civic rights of
a single racial group are immediately suspect," and should be given "the most
rigid scrutiny." In *Brown* v. *Board of Education* (1954), the Supreme Court again
used the strict scrutiny standard to evaluate the constitutionality of race-based
distinctions. In legal terms, this means that if a statute or governmental practice
makes a classification based on race, the statute is presumed to be unconstitutional unless the state can provide "compelling affirmative justifications": that
is, unless the state can prove the law in question is necessary to accomplish a
permissible goal and that it is the least restrictive means through which that
goal can be accomplished. (In *Korematsu*, the Court concluded that the national
risks posed by Japanese Americans were sufficient enough to justify their internment.)

During the 1960s and into the 1970s, the Court routinely struck down as 96
unconstitutional practices and statutes that discriminated on the basis of race.
"Whites-only" public parks and recreational facilities, tax-exempt status for private schools that discriminated, and statutes prohibiting racial intermarriage were
declared unconstitutional. In contrast, the Court refused even to consider the fact
that the equal protection clause might apply to discrimination against women. Finally, in a case argued in 1971 by Ruth Bader Ginsburg (now an associate justice
of the Supreme Court) as director of the Women's Rights Project of the ACLU,

suspect classification
Category or class, such as
race, that triggers the highest standard of scrutiny
from the Supreme Court.

strict scrutiny
A heightened standard of
review used by the Supreme
Court to determine the
constitutional validity of a
challenged practice.

TABLE 8.1   The Equal Protection Clause and Standards of Review Used by the Supreme Court to Determine Whether It Has Been Violated

Type of Classification (What kind of statutory classification is at issue?)	Standard of Review (What standard of review will be used?)	Test (What does the Court ask?)	Example (How does the Court apply the test?)
Fundamental freedoms (including religion, assembly, press, privacy). Suspect classifications (including race, alienage, and national origin)	Strict scrutiny or heightened standard	Is classification necessary to the accomplishment of a permissible state goal? Is it the least restrictive way to reach that goal?	*Brown* v. *Board of Education* (1954): Racial segregation not necessary to accomplish the state goal of educating its students.
Gender	Intermediate standard	Does the classification serve an important governmental objective, and is it substantially related to those ends?	*Craig* v. *Boren* (1976): Keeping drunk drivers off the roads may be an important governmental objective, but allowing 18- to 21-year-old women to drink alcoholic beverages while prohibiting men of the same age from drinking is not substantially related to that goal.
Others (including age, wealth, and mental retardation)	Minimum rationality standard	Is there any rational foundation for the discrimination?	*City of Cleburne* v. *Cleburne Living Center* (1985): Zoning restrictions against group homes for the retarded have rational basis.

the Supreme Court ruled that an Idaho law granting a male parent automatic preference over a female parent as the administrator of their deceased child's estate violated the equal protection clause of the Fourteenth Amendment. *Reed* v. *Reed* (1971), the Idaho case, turned the tide in terms of constitutional litigation. Although the Court did not rule that gender was a suspect classification, it concluded that the equal protection clause of the Fourteenth Amendment prohibited unreasonable classifications based on gender.

97   In 1976, the Court ruled that gender-discrimination complaints would be judged by a new, judicially created intermediate standard of review a step below strict scrutiny. In *Craig* v. *Boren* (1976), the Court carved out a new test to be used in examining claims of gender discrimination: "to withstand constitutional challenge, . . . classifications by gender must serve important governmental objectives and must be substantially related to achievement of those objectives." According to the Court, an intermediate standard of review was created within what previously was a two-tier distinction—strict scrutiny and rational basis.

98   Men, too, can use the Fourteenth Amendment to fight gender-based discrimination. Since 1976, the Court has applied the intermediate standard of constitutional review to most claims that it has heard involving gender. Thus, the following kinds of practices have been found to violate the Fourteenth Amendment:

- Single-sex public nursing schools.
- Laws that consider males adults at age 21 but females at age 18.
- Laws that allow women but not men to receive alimony.
- State prosecutors' use of peremptory challenges to reject men or women to create more sympathetic juries.
- Virginia's maintenance of an all-male military college, the Virginia Military Institute.
- Different requirements for a child's acquisition of citizenship based on whether the citizen parent is a mother or a father.

In contrast, the Court has upheld the following governmental practices and laws:

- Draft registration provisions for males only.
- State statutory rape laws that apply only to female victims.

99   The level of review used by the Court is crucial. Clearly, a statute excluding African Americans from draft registration would be unconstitutional. But, because gender is not subject to the same higher standard of review that is used in racial-discrimination cases, the exclusion of women from the requirements of the Military Selective Service Act was ruled permissible because the government policy was considered to serve "important governmental objectives."

100   This history has perhaps clarified why women's rights activists continue to argue that until the passage of an equal rights amendment, women will never enjoy the same rights as men. An amendment would automatically raise the level of scrutiny that the Court applies to gender-based claims, although there are clear indications that the women justices on the Court are inclined toward requiring states to show "exceedingly persuasive justifications" for their actions.

101   In 1963, Congress passed the Equal Pay Act that requires employers to pay women and men equal pay for equal work. Women have won important victories under the act, but a large wage gap between women and men continues to exist. In spite of the fact that the Equal Pay Act is 40 years old, women in 2002 earned 77 percent of what men earned. In fact, a study done by the AFL-CIO shows that this discrimination will cost a 21-year-old female college graduate more than one million dollars over her career.

Statutory Remedies for Gender Discrimination

102   In part because of the limits of the intermediate standard of review and the fact that the equal protection clause applies only to *governmental* discrimination, women's rights activists began to bombard the courts with gender-discrimination cases. Other cases have been filed under Title VII of the Civil Rights Act, which prohibits discrimination by private (and, after 1972, public) employers. Key victories under Title VII include:

- Consideration of sexual harassment as gender discrimination.
- Inclusion of law firms, which many argued were private partnerships, in the coverage of the act.
- A broad definition of what can be considered sexual harassment, which includes same-sex harassment.
- Allowance of voluntary affirmative action programs to redress historical discrimination against women.

Title IX

Provision of the Educational Amendments of 1972 that bars educational institutions receiving federal funds from discriminating against female students.

103   Other victories have come under **Title IX** of the Education Amendments of 1972, which bars educational institutions receiving federal funds from discriminating against female students. Holding school boards or districts responsible for sexual harassment of students by teachers, for example, was ruled actionable under Title IX by the U.S. Supreme Court.

104   Title IX, which parallels Title VII, greatly expanded the opportunities for women in elementary, secondary, and postsecondary institutions. It bars educational institutions receiving federal funds from discriminating against female students. Since women's groups, like the NAACP before them, saw eradication of educational discrimination as key to improving other facets of women's lives, they lobbied for it heavily. Most of today's college students did not go through school being excluded from home economics or shop classes because of their gender.

Nor, probably, did many attend schools that had no team sports for females. Yet, this was commonly the case in the United States prior to passage of Title IX. Still, sport facilities, access to premium playing times, and equipment quality remain unequal in many high schools and colleges.

Section Review 3

Directions.

1. On a separate sheet of paper, write a brief summary of the main points of the sections you have just read.

2. Mark each of the following statements True (T), False (F), or Can't Tell (CT). Mark the statement Can't Tell if it cannot be determined to be either true or false based on the material in the passage. Refer to the passage as necessary to verify your answer.

_____ 1. Arkansas' Governor Faubus opposed the integration of Arkansas schools.

_____ 2. The SCLC, under the leadership of Dr. Martin Luther King Jr. used strategies similar to those used by the NAACP to win civil rights in the South for African Americans.

_____ 3. The Civil Rights Act of 1964 was delayed in Congress by a filibuster of southern senators.

_____ 4. By the mid-1960s, most American men believed that women should have equal rights.

_____ 5. A public school that would only admit female students would probably violate the Fourteenth Amendment.

Directions. Write the letter of the best answer in the space provided.

_____ 1. The civil rights organization that relied primarily on litigation to achieve racial equality was
   a. the SCLC.
   b. the NAACP.
   c. SNCC.
   d. NOW.

_____ 2. Compared to the SCLC, SNCC was
   a. more radical.
   b. less radical.
   c. more successful.
   d. restricted to college students.

_____ 3. The Equal Rights Amendment (ERA)
   a. was added to the U.S. Constitution in 1972.
   b. was added to the U.S. Constitution in 1979.
   c. was never added to the U.S. Constitution.
   d. did not win ratification in any southern states.

_____ 4. The intermediate standard of review
   a. identified gender as a suspect classification.
   b. has not been applied to gender-related claims.
   c. created a different standard of review for gender-related cases than for race-related cases.
   d. allows states to determine when discrimination is necessary.

_____ 5. Before passage of Title IX of the Education Amendments of 1972
   a. women were not admitted into most American colleges.
   b. all classes were open to students of both genders.
   c. many schools did not have women's sports teams.
   d. no colleges had women's sports teams.

OTHER GROUPS MOBILIZE FOR RIGHTS

AFRICAN AMERICANS AND WOMEN ARE NOT the only groups that have suffered   105
unequal treatment under the law. Denial of civil rights has led many other disadvantaged groups to mobilize. Their efforts have many parallels to the efforts made by African Americans and women. In the wake of the successes of those two groups, and sometimes even before, other traditionally disenfranchised groups organized to gain full equality. Many of them also recognized that litigation and the use of test-case strategies would be key to further civil rights gains. Others have opted for more direct, traditional action. Hispanics were the next group to follow blacks and women in their quest to end discrimination, especially through the courts.

Hispanic Americans

Hispanic Americans now are the largest minority group in the United States. Un-   106
til the 1920s, most Hispanics lived in the southwestern United States. In the decades that followed, large numbers of immigrants from Mexico and Puerto Rico came to the United States. These new Mexicans, who quickly became a source of cheap labor, also tended to settle in the Southwest, where they most frequently were employed as migratory farm workers. In contrast, Puerto Ricans mainly moved to New York City. Both groups tended to live in their own neighborhoods, where life was centered around the Roman Catholic Church and the customs of their homeland. Both groups, however, largely lived in poverty.

By the mid-1970s, as the Mexican American and Puerto Rican American   107
populations continued to grow through immigration and childbirth, immigrants from Cuba and several other island and Latin American nations came to the United States seeking a better life. Their problems, however, were often confounded by their need to learn a new language. This language barrier has continued to depress voter registration and voter turnout while contributing to the continued poverty and discrimination suffered by Hispanics.

The earliest push for greater Hispanic rights occurred in the mid-1960s, well   108
before the next major influx of Hispanics to the United States. This new movement included many tactics drawn from the African American civil rights movement, including sit-ins, boycotts, marches, and other activities designed to attract publicity to their cause. Like blacks, women, and Native Americans, Hispanic Americans have some radical militant groups, but the movement has been dominated by more conventional organizations. For example, in 1965, Cesar Chavez organized migrant workers into the United Farm Workers Union and led them in their strike against growers in California. This strike was eventually coupled with

a national boycott of several farm products. Other, more conventional groups have tried to use other unions and even the Roman Catholic Church as mechanisms to mobilize Hispanics for greater rights.

109   Hispanics also have relied heavily on litigation. Key groups are the Mexican American Legal Defense and Educational Fund (MALDEF) and the Puerto Rican Legal Defense and Educational Fund. MALDEF was founded in 1968 after members of the League of United Latin American Citizens (LULAC), the nation's largest and oldest Hispanic organization, met with NAACP LDF leaders and, with their assistance, secured a $2.2-million start-up grant from the Ford Foundation. It was created to bring test cases to force school districts to allocate more funds to schools with predominantly low-income minority populations, to implement bilingual education programs, to force employers to hire Hispanics, and to challenge election rules and apportionment plans that undercount or dilute Hispanic voting power.

110   MALDEF lawyers quickly moved to bring major test cases to the U.S. Supreme Court, both to enhance the visibility of their cause and to win cases. MALDEF has been successful in its efforts to expand voting rights and opportunities to Hispanic Americans. In 1973, for example, it won a major victory when the Supreme Court ruled that multimember electoral districts (in which more than one person represents a single district) in Texas discriminated against African Americans and Hispanic Americans. In multimember systems, legislatures generally add members to larger districts instead of drawing smaller districts in which a minority candidate could get a majority of the votes necessary to win.

111   While enjoying greater access to elective office, Hispanics still suffer discrimination. Language barriers and substandard educational opportunities continue to plague their progress. In 1973, the U.S. Supreme Court refused to find that a Texas law under which the state appropriated a set dollar amount to each school district per pupil, while allowing wealthier districts to enrich educational programs from other funds, violated the equal protection clause of the Fourteenth Amendment. The lower courts had found that wealth was a suspect classification entitled to strict scrutiny. Using that test, the lower courts had found the Texas plan discriminatory. In contrast, a divided Supreme Court concluded that education was not a fundamental freedom, and that a charge of discrimination based on wealth would be examined only under a minimal standard of review (the rational basis test).

112   Throughout the 1970s and 1980s, inter-school-district inequalities persisted, and they frequently had their greatest impact on poor Hispanic children. Recognizing that the increasingly conservative federal courts offered no recourse, in 1984, MALDEF filed suit in state court alleging that the Texas school finance policy violated the Texas constitution. In 1989, it won a case in which a state district judge elected by the voters of only a single county declared the state's entire method of financing public schools to be unconstitutional under the state constitution. In 2004, it entered into a settlement with the state of California in a case brought four years earlier to address, in MALDEF's words, "the shocking inequities facing public school children across the state." Its leaders objected to shorter school calendars for schools where enrollment was predominantly Hispanic and other poor students.

113   MALDEF continues to litigate in a wide range of areas of concern to Hispanics. High on its agenda today are affirmative action, the admission of Hispanic students to state colleges and universities, health care for undocumented immigrants, and challenging unfair redistricting practices that make it more difficult to elect Hispanic legislators. It litigates to replace at-large electoral systems with single-district elections to ensure the election of more Hispanics, as well as challenging many state redistricting plans to ensure that Hispanics are adequately represented. Its highly successful Census 2000 educational outreach campaign, moreover, sought to decrease undercounting of Hispanics.

MALDEF also continues to be at the fore of legislative lobbying for ex-   114
panded rights. Since 2002, it has worked to oppose restrictions concerning dri-
ver's license requirements for undocumented immigrants, to gain greater rights
for Hispanic workers, and to ensure that redistricting plans do not silence Hispanic voters. It won a victory on this issue in California in 2004. MALDEF also
focuses on the rights of Hispanic workers and the effects of legislative redistricting on the voting strength of Hispanics.

Native Americans

Native Americans are the first true Americans, and their status under U.S. law is   115
unique. Under the U.S. Constitution, Indian tribes are considered distinct governments, a situation that has affected Native Americans' treatment by the
Supreme Court in contrast to other groups of ethnic minorities. *Minority* is a
term that accurately describes American Indians. It is estimated that there were
as many as 10 million Indians in the New World at the time Europeans arrived in
the 1400s, with 3 to 4 million living in what is today the United States. By 1900,
the number of Indians in the continental United States had plummeted to less
than 2 million. Today, there are 2.7 million.

Many commentators would agree that for years Congress and the courts ma-   116
nipulated Indian law to promote the westward expansion of the United States.
The Northwest Ordinance of 1787, passed by the Continental Congress, specified that "good faith should always be observed toward the Indians; their lands
and property shall never be taken from them without their consent, and their
property rights, and liberty, they shall never be invaded or disturbed, unless in just
and lawful wars authorized by Congress." These strictures were not followed. Instead, over the years, "American Indian policy has been described as 'genocide-at-
law' promoting both land acquisition and cultural extermination." During the
eighteenth and nineteenth centuries, the U.S. government isolated Indians on
reservations as it confiscated their lands and denied them basic political rights.
Indian reservations were administered by the federal government, and Native
Americans often lived in squalid conditions.

With passage of the Dawes Act in 1887, however, the government switched   117
policies to promote assimilation over separation. Each Indian family was given
land within the reservation; the rest was sold to whites, thus reducing Indian
lands from about 140 million acres to about 47 million. Moreover, to encourage
Native Americans to assimilate, Indian children were sent to boarding schools off
the reservation, and native languages and rituals were banned. Native Americans
didn't become U.S. citizens, nor were they given the right to vote, until 1924.

At least in part because tribes were small and scattered (and the number of   118
Indians declining), Native Americans formed no protest movement in reaction to
these drastic policy changes. It was not until the 1960s, at the same time women
were beginning to mobilize for greater civil rights, that Indians, too, began to mobilize to act. In the late 1960s, Indians, many trained by the American Indian
Law Center at the University of New Mexico, began to file hundreds of test cases
in the federal courts involving tribal fishing rights, tribal land claims, and the tax-
ation of tribal profits. The Native American Rights Fund (NARF), founded that
same year, became the NAACP LDF of the Indian rights movement.

Like the civil rights and women's rights movements, the movement for Na-   119
tive American rights had a radical as well as a more traditional branch. In 1973,
for example, national attention was drawn to the plight of Indians when members
of the radical American Indian movement took over Wounded Knee, South
Dakota, the site of the massacre of 150 Indians by the U.S. Army in 1890. Just
two years before the protest, the treatment of Indians had been highlighted in the
best-selling *Bury My Heart at Wounded Knee,* which in many ways served to mo-

bilize public opinion against the oppression of Native Americans in the same way *Uncle Tom's Cabin* had against slavery.

120   Native Americans have won some very important victories concerning hunting, fishing, and land rights. Native American tribes all over America have sued to reclaim lands they say were stolen from them by the United States, often more than two hundred years ago. Today, these land rights allow Native Americans to play host to a number of casinos across the country.

121   One of the largest Indian land claims was filed in 1972 on behalf of the Passamaquoddy and the Penobscot tribes, which were seeking return of 12.5 million acres in Maine—about two-thirds of the entire state—and $25 billion in damages. The suit was filed by the Native American Rights Fund and the Indian Service Unit of a legal services office that was funded by the now defunct U.S. Office of Economic Opportunity. It took intervention from the White House for the parties to reach a settlement in 1980, giving each tribe over $40 million.

122   Native Americans also are litigating to gain access to their sacred places. All over the nation, they have filed lawsuits to stop the building of roads and new construction on ancient burial grounds or other sacred spots. "We are in a battle for the survival of our very way of life," said one tribal leader. "The land is gone. All we've got left is our religion."

123   Native Americans have not fared particularly well in areas such as religious freedom, especially where tribal practices come into conflict with state law. The Supreme Court has used the rational basis test to rule that a state could infringe on religious exercise (use of peyote as a sacrament in religious ceremonies) by a neutral law, and has limited Indian access to religious sites during timber harvesting. Congress attempted to restore some of those rights through passage of the Religious Freedom Restoration Act. The law, however, was later ruled unconstitutional by the Supreme Court.

124   Native Americans continue to fight the negative stereotypes that plague their progress. Indians contend, for example, that the popular names of thousands of high school, college, and professional sports teams are degrading. This charge has caused some school districts and universities to change the names of their sports teams. Professional teams such as the Atlanta Braves, Cleveland Indians, and Washington Redskins also are under attack. Even the U.S. Commission on Civil Rights has weighed in on the matter, requesting an end to Indian names, mascots, and logos.

125   While efforts to pressure teams to change their names wage on, Indian tribes have found themselves locked in a controversy with the Department of the Interior over its handling of Indian trust funds, which are to be paid out to Indians for the use of their lands. In 1996, several Indian tribes filed suit to force the federal government to account for the billions of dollars it has collected over the years for its leasing of Indian land, which it took from the Indians and held in trust since the late nineteenth century, and to force reform of the system. As the result of years of mismanagement, the trust, administered by the Department of the Interior, has no records of monies taken in or how they were disbursed. The ongoing class action lawsuit includes 500,000 Indians, who claim that they are owed more than $10 billion. The trial judge found massive mismanagement of the funds, which generate up to $500 million a year, and at one time threatened to hold Secretary of the Interior Gail Norton in contempt. After this case was largely deadlocked for five years, in early 2004, a mediator was appointed to help bring greater resolution to the conflict.

Gays and Lesbians

126   Until very recently, gays and lesbians have had an even harder time than other groups in achieving full rights. However, gays and lesbians have, on average, far higher household incomes and educational levels than these other groups, and

they are beginning to convert these advantages into political clout at the ballot box and through changes in public opinion. Like African Americans and women early in their quests for greater civil rights, gays and lesbians initially did not fare well in the Supreme Court. In the late 1970s, the Lambda Legal Defense and Education Fund, the Lesbian Rights Project, and Gay and Lesbian Advocates and Defenders were founded by gay and lesbian activists dedicated to ending legal restrictions on the civil rights of homosexuals. Although these groups have won important legal victories concerning HIV/AIDS discrimination, insurance policy survivor benefits, and even some employment issues, they generally were not as successful as other historically disadvantaged groups.

In 1993, for example, President Bill Clinton tried to get an absolute ban on discrimination against homosexuals in the armed services, who were subject to immediate discharge if their sexual orientation was discovered. Military leaders and then-Senator Sam Nunn (D–GA), as chair of the Senate Armed Services Committee, led the effort against Clinton's proposal. Eventually, Clinton and Senate leaders compromised on what was called the "Don't Ask, Don't Tell" policy. It stipulated that gays and lesbians would no longer be asked if they were homosexual, but they were barred from revealing their sexual orientation (under threat of discharge from the service). 127

However, the public's views toward homosexuality were clearly beginning to change, as signaled by the Court's 1996 decision in *Romer* v. *Evans*. In this case, the Court ruled that an amendment to the Colorado constitution that denied homosexuals the right to seek protection from discrimination was unconstitutional under the equal protection clause of the Fourteenth Amendment. 128

In 2000, Vermont became the first state to recognize civil unions, marking another landmark in the struggle for equal rights for homosexuals. However, it was the Supreme Court's decision in *Lawrence* v. *Texas* (2003) that really put homosexual rights on the public agenda. In this case, the Court reversed an earlier ruling by finding a Texas statute that banned sodomy to be unconstitutional. Writing for the majority, Justice Anthony Kennedy stated, "[homosexuals'] right to liberty under the due process clause gives them the full right to engage in their conduct without intervention of the government." 129

Following the Court's ruling in *Lawrence,* many Americans were quick to call for additional rights for homosexuals. Many corporations also responded to this amplified call for equal rights. For example, Wal-Mart announced it would ban job discrimination based on sexual orientation. In addition, editorial pages across the country praised the Court's ruling, arguing that the national view toward homosexuality had changed. In November 2003, the Massachusetts Supreme Court further agreed when it ruled that denying homosexuals the right to civil marriage was unconstitutional. The U.S. Supreme Court later refused to hear an appeal of this case. 130

Still, in 2004, many conservative groups and Republican politicians made same-sex marriage an issue. Referendums or amendments prohibiting same-sex marriage were placed on 11 state ballots and all were passed overwhelmingly by voters. 131

Disabled Americans

Disabled Americans also have lobbied hard for anti-discrimination legislation as well as equal protection under the Constitution. In the aftermath of World War II, many veterans returned to a nation unequipped to handle their disabilities. The Korean and Vietnam Wars made the problems of disabled veterans all the more clear. These disabled veterans saw the successes of African Americans, women, and other minorities, and they too began to lobby for greater protection against discrimination. In 1990, in coalition with other disabled people, veterans finally were able to convince Congress to pass the Americans with Disabilities Act (ADA). 132

The statute defines a disabled person as someone with a physical or mental impairment that limits one or more "life activities," or who has a record of such impairment. It thus extends the protections of the Civil Rights Act of 1964 to all of those with physical or mental disabilities. It guarantees access to public facilities, employment, and communication services. It also requires employers to acquire or modify work equipment, adjust work schedules, and make existing facilities accessible. Thus, for example, buildings must be accessible to those in wheelchairs, and telecommunications devices must be provided for deaf employees.

133   In 1999, the U.S. Supreme Court issued a series of four decisions redefining and significantly limiting the scope of the ADA. The cumulative impact of these decisions was to limit dramatically the number of people who can claim coverage under the act. Moreover, these cases "could profoundly affect individuals with a range of impairments—from diabetes and hypertension to severe nearsightedness and hearing loss—who are able to function in society with the help of medicines or aids but whose impairments may still make employers consider them ineligible for certain jobs." Thus, pilots who need glasses to correct their vision cannot claim discrimination when employers fail to hire them because of their correctable vision. In 2004, however, the Court ruled 5–4 that disabled persons could sue states that failed to make reasonable accommodations to assure that courthouses are handicapped accessible.

134   Simply changing the law, although often an important first step in achieving civil rights, is not the end of the process. Attitudes must also change. As history has shown, that can be a very long process and will be longer given the Court's decisions.

CONTINUING CONTROVERSIES IN CIVIL RIGHTS

135   SINCE PASSAGE OF MAJOR CIVIL RIGHTS LEGISLATION in the 1960s and the Supreme Court's continued interest in upholding the civil rights of many groups, African Americans, women, Hispanics, Native Americans, gays and lesbians, and the disabled have come much closer to the attainment of equal rights. Yet, all of these groups still remain far from enjoying full equality under the Constitution in all walks of life. Private discrimination that cannot be legislated against is one major continuing source of discrimination. Gender equality, for example, has increased but a 2003 poll shows that 12 percent of Americans still would not vote for a woman for president. More strikingly, in response to suggestions that an amendment be added to the Constitution to ban same-sex marriages, 55 percent of those polled in July 2004 favored this type of legislation.

136   Today, while most Americans agree that discrimination is wrong, most whites believe that affirmative action programs, which were designed in the late 1960s and early 1970s to remedy vestiges of discrimination against African Americans in particular, are no longer needed. White men are particularly opposed to principles of affirmative action, believing that qualified minorities should not receive preference over equally qualified white men.

Affirmative Action

137   How did affirmative action come to be such a controversial issue? More than 50 years after *Brown* v. *Board of Education* (1954), the civil rights debate centers on the question of equality of opportunity versus equality of results. Most civil rights and women's rights organizations argue that the lingering and pervasive burdens of racism and sexism can be overcome only by taking race or gender into account in fashioning remedies for discrimination. They argue that the Constitution is not

and should not be blind to color or sex. Therefore, busing should be used to integrate schools, and women should be given child-care assistance to allow them to compete equally in the marketplace.

The counterargument holds that if it was once wrong to use labels to discriminate against a group, it should be wrong to use those same labels to help a group. Laws should be neutral, or color-blind. According to this view, quotas and other forms of **affirmative action,** policies designed to give special attention or compensatory treatment to members of a previously disadvantaged group, should be illegal. As early as 1871, Frederick Douglass ridiculed the idea of racial quotas, arguing that they would promote "an image of blacks as privileged wards of the state." They were "absurd as a matter of practice" because some could use them to argue that blacks "should constitute one-eighth of the poets, statesmen, scholars, authors and philosophers."   138

The debate over affirmative action and equality of opportunity became particularly intense during the presidential administration of Ronald Reagan, in the wake of two court cases that were generally decided in favor of affirmative action shortly before Reagan's election. In 1978, the Supreme Court for the first time fully addressed the issue of affirmative action. Alan Bakke, a 31-year-old paramedic, sought admission to several medical schools and was rejected because of his age. The next year, he applied to the University of California at Davis and was placed on its waiting list. The Davis Medical School maintained two separate admission committees—one for white students and another for minority students. Bakke was not admitted to the school, although his grades and standardized test scores were higher than those of all of the African American students admitted to the school. In *Regents of the University of California* v. *Bakke* (1978), a sharply divided Court concluded that Bakke's rejection had been illegal because the use of strict quotas was inappropriate. The medical school, however, was free to "take race into account."   139

Bakke was quickly followed by a 1979 case in which the Court ruled that a factory and a union could voluntarily adopt a quota system in selecting black workers over more senior white workers for a training program. These kinds of programs outraged blue-collar Americans who traditionally had voted for the Democratic Party. In 1980, they abandoned the party in droves to support Ronald Reagan, an ardent foe of affirmative action.   140

For a while, in spite of the addition of Reagan-appointed Justice Sandra Day O'Connor to the Court, the Court continued to uphold affirmative action plans, especially when there was clear-cut evidence of prior discrimination. In 1987, for example, the Court for the first time ruled that a public employer could use a voluntary plan to promote women even if there was no judicial finding or prior discrimination.   141

In all these affirmative action cases, the Reagan administration strongly urged the Court to invalidate the plans in question, but to no avail. With changes on the Court, however, including the 1986 elevation to chief justice of William H. Rehnquist, a strong opponent of affirmative action, the continued efforts of the Reagan administration finally began to pay off as the Court heard a new series of cases signaling an end to the advances in civil rights law. In a three-month period in 1989, the Supreme Court handed down five civil rights decisions limiting affirmative action programs and making it harder to prove employment discrimination.   142

The Legislative Response.   In February 1990, congressional and civil rights leaders unveiled legislation designed to overrule the Court's rulings, which, according to the bill's sponsor, "were an abrupt and unfortunate departure from its historic vigilance in protecting the rights of minorities." The bill passed both houses of Congress but was vetoed by President Reagan's successor, George   143

affirmative action
Policies designed to give special attention or compensatory treatment to members of a previously disadvantaged group.

Bush, and Congress failed to override the veto. In late 1991, however, Congress and the White House reached a compromise on a weaker version of the civil rights bill, which was passed by overwhelming majorities in both houses of Congress. The Civil Rights Act of 1991 overruled the five Supreme Court rulings noted above, but it specifically prohibited the use of quotas.

144   The Supreme Court, however, has not stayed silent on the issue. In 1995, the Court ruled that Congress, like the states, must show that affirmative action programs meet the strict scrutiny test outlined in Table 8.1. In 1996, the U.S. Court of Appeals for the Fifth Circuit also ruled that the University of Texas Law School's affirmative action admissions program was unconstitutional, throwing the college and university admissions programs in Texas, Oklahoma, and Mississippi into turmoil. Later that year, the U.S. Supreme Court refused to hear the case, thereby allowing the Court of Appeals decision to stand.

145   By 2002, the U.S. Supreme Court once again found the affirmative action issue ripe for review. In *Grutter* v. *Bollinger* (2003), the Court voted to uphold the constitutionality of the University of Michigan's law school admissions policy, which gave preference to minority applicants. However, in a companion case, the Court struck down Michigan's undergraduate point system, which gave minority applicants 20 automatic points simply because they were minorities.

146   Taken together, these cases set the stage for a new era in affirmative action in the United States. Although the use of strict quotas and automatic points is not constitutional, the Court clearly believes that there is a place for some preferential treatment, at least until greater racial and ethnic parity is achieved. However, as Justice Sandra Day O'Connor noted in *Grutter*, "a program must remain flexible enough to ensure that each applicant is evaluated as an individual and not in a way that makes an applicant's race or ethnicity the defining feature of his or her application."

Other Continuing Controversies in Civil Rights

147   Race is not the only issue that continues to breed civil rights controversies. Recent developments with two corporations illustrate the reality that discrimination persists in the United States.

148   Beginning in the mid-1990s, many gay rights activists charged that the Cracker Barrel restaurant chain discriminated against homosexuals by requiring that employees exhibit "heterosexual values" on the job. Following allegations that employees were fired because they were gay and a series of boycotts by gay rights activists, Cracker Barrel adopted a new anti-discrimination policy that included protections for sexual orientation.

149   More recently, the nation's largest employer, Wal-Mart, has been embroiled in a series of discrimination suits. First, six California women filed a claim against the chain, charging that they were the victims of gender discrimination. These women asserted that they were paid lower wages and offered fewer opportunities for advancement than their male colleagues. In June 2004, a federal judge broadened their suit to include 1.6 million women in a class action lawsuit.

150   In addition, nine illegal immigrants who worked as janitors at Wal-Marts in New Jersey are suing the company for discriminating against them by paying them lower wages and giving them fewer benefits based solely on their ethnic origin. Another group of Wal-Mart employees from 21 states are also suing the corporation, claiming that executives knowingly conspired to hire illegal immigrants and, in doing so, violated the workers' civil rights by refusing to pay Social Security and other wage compensation benefits. These suits are representative of a growing trend in discrimination suits filed by immigrants who believe they have been persecuted or disadvantaged following changes in security and immigration law after 9/11.

Section Review 4

Directions.

1. On a separate sheet of paper, write a brief summary of the main points of the sections you have just read.

2. Mark each of the following statements True (T), False (F), or Can't Tell (CT). Mark the statement Can't Tell if it cannot be determined to be either true or false based on the material in the passage. Refer to the passage as necessary to verify your answer.

_____ 1. Native Americans have been highly successful in protecting their religious practices from state and local laws.

_____ 2. MALDEF is an organization that has played an important role in the fight for equal rights for homosexuals.

_____ 3. In overturning Colorado's 1992 state constitutional amendment, the U.S. Supreme Court applied the Fourteenth Amendment to homosexuals.

_____ 4. In *Bakke,* the Supreme Court ruled against the use of affirmative action quotas.

_____ 5. Most Americans oppose affirmative action.

SUMMARY

WHILE THE FRAMERS AND OTHER AMERICANS basked in the glory of the newly adopted Constitution and Bill of Rights, their protections did not extend to all Americans. In this chapter, we have shown how rights have been expanded to ever-increasing segments of the population. To that end, we have made the following points:

1. **Slavery, Abolition, and Winning the Right to Vote, 1800–1890**
   When the Framers tried to compromise on the issue of slavery, they only postponed dealing with a volatile question that was later to rip the nation apart. Ultimately, the Civil War was fought to end slavery. Among its results were the triumph of the abolitionist position and adoption of the Thirteenth, Fourteenth, and Fifteenth Amendments. During this period, women also sought expanded rights, especially the right to vote, but to no avail.

2. **The Push for Equality, 1890–1954**
   Although the Civil War Amendments were added to the Constitution, the Supreme Court limited their application. As Jim Crow laws were passed throughout the South, the NAACP was founded in the early 1900s to press for equal rights for African Americans. Women's groups also were active during this period, successfully lobbying for passage of the Nineteenth Amendment, which assured them the right to vote. Women's groups such as the National Consumers' League (NCL), for example, began to view litigation as a means to its ends, as it was forced to go to court to argue for the constitutionality of legislation protecting women workers.

3. **The Civil Rights Movement**
   In 1954, the U.S. Supreme Court ruled in *Brown* v. *Board of Education* that state-segregated school systems were unconstitutional. This victory empowered African Americans as they sought an end to other forms of pervasive discrimination. Bus boycotts, sit-ins, freedom rides, pressure for voting rights, and massive nonviolent demonstrations became common tactics. This activity culminated in the passage of the Civil Rights Act of 1964, which gave African Americans another weapon in their legal arsenal.

4. **The Women's Rights Movement**
   After passage of the Civil Rights Act, a new women's rights movement arose. Several women's rights groups were created, and while some sought a constitutional amendment, others attempted to litigate under the equal protection clause. Over the years, the Supreme Court developed different tests to determine the constitutionality of various forms of discrimination. In general, strict scrutiny, the most stringent standard,

was applied to race-based claims. An intermediate standard of review was developed to assess the constitutionality of gender-discrimination claims.

5. **Other Groups Mobilize for Rights**
Building on the successes of African Americans and women, other groups, including Hispanic Americans, Native Americans, gays and lesbians, and the disabled, organized to litigate for expanded civil rights as well as to lobby for antidiscrimination laws.

6. **Continuing Controversies in Civil Rights**
None of the groups discussed in this chapter has yet reached full equality. One policy, affirmative action, which was designed to remedy education and employment discrimination, continues to be very controversial. And, gays, lesbians, women, and immigrants continue to use the courts to seek remedies for costly employment discrimination.

KEY TERMS

affirmative action, p. 368
Black Codes, p. 340
Brown v. *Board of Education* (1954), p. 348
civil rights, p. 337
Civil Rights Act of 1964, p. 354
Civil Rights Cases (1883), p. 342
de facto discrimination, p. 355
de jure discrimination, p. 355
Equal Employment Opportunity Commission, p. 357
equal protection clause, p. 348
Equal Rights Amendment (ERA), p. 357
Fifteenth Amendment, p. 341
Fourteenth Amendment, p. 341
grandfather clause, p. 342
Jim Crow laws, p. 342
Nineteenth Amendment, p. 346
Plessy v. *Ferguson* (1896), p. 344
strict scrutiny, p. 358
suffrage movement, p. 345
suspect classification, p. 358
Thirteenth Amendment, p. 340
Title IX, p. 360

SELECTED READINGS

Bacchi, Carol Lee. *The Politics of Affirmative Action: 'Women,' Equality and Category Politics*. Thousand Oaks, CA: Sage, 1996.
Eastland, Terry. *Ending Affirmative Action: The Case for Colorblind Justice*. New York: Basic Books, 1997.
Freeman, Jo. *The Politics of Women's Liberation*. New York: Backinprint.com, 2000.

Guinier, Lani. *Who's Qualified?* Boston: Beacon Press, 2001.
Kluger, Richard. *Simple Justice*, reprint ed. New York: Vintage, 2004.
Mansbridge, Jane J. *Why We Lost the ERA*. Chicago: University of Chicago Press, 1986.
McClain, Paula D., and Joseph Stewart Jr. *"Can We All Get Along?" Racial and Ethnic Minorities in American Politics*, 3rd ed. Boulder, CO: Westview, 2001.
McGlen, Nancy E., et al. *Women, Politics, and American Society*, 4th ed. New York: Longman, 2004.
Nobles, Melissa. *Shades of Citizenship: Race and the Census in Modern America*. Palo Alto, CA: Stanford University Press, 2000.
Reed, Adolph, Jr. *Without Justice for All: The New Liberalism and Our Retreat from Racial Equity*. Boulder, CO: Westview, 1999.
Rodriguez, Clara E. *Changing Race: Latinos, the Census, and the History of Ethnicity in the United States*. New York: New York University Press, 2000.
Rosales, Francisco A., and Arturo Rosales, eds. *Chicano! The History of the Mexican American Civil Rights Movement*. Houston, TX: Arte Publico, 1996.
Verba, Sidney, and Gary R. Orren. *Equality in America: The View from the Top*. Cambridge, MA: Harvard University Press, 1985.
Williams, Juan. *Eyes on the Prize: America's Civil Rights Years, 1954–1965*. New York: Penguin, 1987.
Wilson, William Julius. *The Bridge over the Racial Divide: Rising Inequality and Coalition Politics*. Berkeley: University of California Press, 1999.

WEB EXPLORATIONS

For more on civil rights generally, see http://www.civilrightsproject.harvard.edu/
For more on abolition, the American Anti-Slavery Society, and its leaders, see http://www.loc.gov/exhibits/african/afam005.html
For more about the history of Jim Crow in the South, see http://www.jimcrowhistory.org/
To read the full text of *Brown* v. *Board of Education* (1954), see http://caselaw.lp.findlaw.com/cgi-bin/getcase.pl?court=US&vol=347&invol=483
For more about the Montgomery bus boycott and Dr. Martin Luther King Jr., see http://www.stanford.edu/group/King/about_king/encyclopedia/bus_boycott.html
For more about NOW and the EEOC, see http://www.now.orghttp://www.eeoc.gov/
For more about the Equal Rights Amendment, see http://www.equalrightsamendment.org/
For more about the ACLU Women's Rights Project, see http://www.aclu.org/WomensRights/WomensRightsMain.cfm
To learn more about MALDEF, see http://www.maldef.org/
For more about the Native American Rights Fund, see http://www.narf.org/
For more about gay and lesbian rights groups, see http://www.glaad.org/
For more about disability advocacy groups, see http://www.aapd-dc.org/

Cumulative Review 2 [Pages 352–371]

Directions. Write the letter of the best answer in the space provided.

_____ 1. The Americans with Disabilities Act
   a. extends civil rights to citizens with disabilities.
   b. ensures employment for Americans with disabilities.
   c. provides counseling for war veterans.
   d. defines disability as a permanent, physical impairment.

_____ 2. Compared to other American minorities, Hispanic American civil rights activists
   a. are similar in that they are affiliated with the church and religion.
   b. are similar in that they are dominated by moderate factions.
   c. are different in that they have been dominated by radical factions.
   d. are different in that they have failed to achieve their goals.

_____ 3. Since *Swann* in 1971, the use of busing to end school desegregation has
   a. gained increasing support in the courts.
   b. been outlawed by the U.S. Congress.
   c. eliminated *de facto* segregation in most states.
   d. had decreasing support in the Supreme Court.

_____ 4. In recent years, Wal-Mart has been sued for all of the following complaints *except*
   a. gender discrimination.
   b. paying lower wages to illegal immigrants.
   c. hiring illegal immigrants.
   d. firing gay employees.

_____ 5. Regarding affirmative action, President George Bush
   a. supported Congress's 1990 legislation.
   b. vetoed Congress's 1990 legislation but supported compromise legislation in 1991.
   c. vetoed all Congressional affirmative action legislation.
   d. only supported affirmative action legislation that was quota based.

Directions. Answer each question in complete sentences, without copying word-for-word from the passage.

   1. Explain how Rosa Parks contributed to the American civil rights movement.

   _____

   _____

   _____

2. What were the main provisions of the Civil Rights Act of 1964?

_____

_____

_____

3. How is the status of Native Americans different under U.S. law from that of other minorities?

_____

_____

_____

4. Which three events of the 1960s led to the formation of a new women's rights movement?

_____

_____

_____

5. Explain the Supreme Court's ruling in *Lawrence v. Texas*. How did this ruling affect the rights of homosexuals?

_____

_____

_____

Vocabulary Exercise 2

Directions. Choose the meaning for the underlined word that best fits the context.

_____ 1. *Brown* served as a <u>catalyst</u> for change . . . .
[Paragraph 58]
  a. stimulus
  b. advocate
  c. opponent
  d. demand

_____ 2. . . . the governor remained <u>adamant</u>.
[Paragraph 60]
  a. disagreeable
  b. flexible
  c. furious
  d. obstinate

_____ 3. . . . the Supreme Court ruled that all <u>vestiges</u> of state-imposed segregation . . .
[Paragraph 78]
   a. causes
   b. institutions
   c. traces
   d. examples

_____ 4. The <u>paternalistic</u> attitudes of the Supreme Court . . . [Paragraph 85]
   a. unfriendly
   b. overprotective
   c. equal
   d. unfair

_____ 5. From its <u>inception</u> . . . [Paragraph 88]
   a. idea
   b. stage of development
   c. beginning
   d. philosophy

_____ 6. This lowest level of <u>scrutiny</u> . . . [Paragraph 95]
   a. examination
   b. concern
   c. judgment
   d. ruling or decision

_____ 7. . . . <u>eradication</u> of educational discrimination . . . [Paragraph 104]
   a. criticism
   b. examination
   c. removal
   d. making more radical

_____ 8. . . . to <u>allocate</u> more funds to schools . . .
[Paragraph 109]
   a. review
   b. prevent from reaching
   c. assign
   d. move from one place to another

_____ 9. Following <u>allegations</u> that employees were fired because they were gay . . .
[Paragraph 148]
   a. rumors
   b. assertions; charges
   c. arrests
   d. court verdicts or decisions

_____ 10. . . . dealing with a <u>volatile</u> question . . .
[Summary, point 1]
   a. difficult
   b. unpopular
   c. significant
   d. controversial

Critical Response Questions

1. Why was the NAACP successful in defeating the separate-but-equal education policies of southern schools?

2. Explain the roles of the three branches of government (executive, legislative, judicial) in the establishment of civil rights for American minorities.

3. Do you support or oppose affirmative action? Explain your opinion.

4. Which strategies used by civil rights activists have been most effective? Why?

5. Is more legislation needed to ensure civil rights for all Americans? Justify your answer.

6. In your opinion, should homosexuals be allowed the same marital and parenting rights as heterosexuals? Explain your answer.

7. What inequalities still exist in American society? How might these inequalities be removed?